Governing Rapid Growth in China

After three decades of spectacular economic growth in China, the problem is no longer how to achieve growth, but how to manage its consequences and how to sustain it. The most important consequence, at least as far as Chinese policy makers are concerned, is the rapidly growing inequality: between persons, between rural and urban areas, and between inland and coastal regions. At the same time, the institutions that have to date brought rapid growth are now under stress, and there is a need to reform and innovate on this front in order to sustain rapid growth, and to have growth with equity.

The analytical literature has responded to the emerging policy problems by specifying and quantifying their magnitude, understanding their nature, and proposing policy approaches and solutions. Policy makers have also been looking to analysts for interaction and assistance. This volume brings together a collection of the best available analyses of China's problems in governing rapid growth, focusing on equity and institutions. Contributions include perspectives from leading policy makers who were intimately involved in the reform process, and from leading academics in articles published in top peer-reviewed journals.

Edited by global leading researchers on Chinese development economics and inequality, this book will be of interest to researchers and postgraduate students of development economics, inequality, equity and Chinese growth, as well as to policy analysts and policy makers.

Ravi Kanbur is T. H. Lee Professor of World Affairs, International Professor of Applied Economics and Management, and Professor of Economics at Cornell University, USA.

Xiaobo Zhang is a Senior Research Fellow in the Development Strategy and Governance Division at the International Food Policy Research Institute (IFPRI) and leader of IFPRI's China Program.

Routledge Studies in the Modern World Economy

Governing Rapid Growth in China

Equity and institutions

Edited by
Ravi Kanbur
and Xiaobo Zhang

Routledge
Taylor & Francis Group

LONDON AND NEW YORK

First published 2009 by Routledge
2 Park Square, Milton Park, Abingdon, Oxon, OX14 4RN

Simultaneously published in the USA and Canada
by Routledge
711 Third Avenue, New York, NY 10017 (8th Floor)

Routledge is an imprint of the Taylor & Francis Group,
an informa business

© 2009 selection and editorial matter, Ravi Kanbur and Xiaobo Zhang;
individual chapters, the contributors

Typeset in Times New Roman by
RefineCatch Limited, Bungay, Suffolk

British Library Cataloguing in Publication Data
A catalogue record for this book is available from the British Library

Library of Congress Cataloging in Publication Data
A catalog record for this book has been requested

First issued in paperback in 2013

ISBN13: 978–0–415–74591–8 (pbk)
ISBN13: 978–0–415–77587–8 (hbk)
ISBN13: 978–0–203–88138–5 (ebk)

Contents

Notes on editors

Ravi Kanbur is T. H. Lee Professor of World Affairs, International Professor of Applied Economics and Management, and Professor of Economics at Cornell University. He has a bachelor's degree from Cambridge and a doctorate from Oxford. He has served on the senior staff of the World Bank, including as Principal Adviser to the Chief Economist of the World Bank. The honors he has received include an Honorary Professorship at the University of Warwick, and the Quality of Research Discovery Award of the American Agricultural Economics Association. His vita shows over 160 publications, including in leading economics journals.

Xiaobo Zhang is Senior Research Fellow in the Development Strategy and Governance Division at the International Food Policy Research Institute (IFPRI) and leader of IFPRI's China Program. He holds a B.S. in Mathematics from Nankai University, China; an M.S. in Economics from Tianjin University of Economics and Finance, China; and an M.S. and Ph.D. in Applied Economics and Management from Cornell University. He served as the President of the Chinese Economists Society (CES) from 2005 to 2006.

Acknowledgments

We have received excellent administrative support from Sue Snyder at Cornell University and Rowena L. Natividad from IFPRI, which we gratefully acknowledge. Funding support from the Natural Science Foundation of China (approval number 70828002) to Xiaobo Zhang is also gratefully acknowledged. The Ford Foundation, IFPRI, Temasek Holdings (Private) Limited, Taiwan Semiconductor Manufacturing Company, and the Natural Science Foundation of China sponsored the 2006 Chinese Economists Society Conference, from which we include several keynote speeches in the book. We also thank Shanghai University of Finance and Economics, in particular the School of Economics headed by Professor Guoqiang Tian, for hosting the conference. We are also grateful for the translation of several chapters from Chinese into English by David Kelly.

Ravi Kanbur
Xiaobo Zhang

Permissions

The Publisher would like to thank the following for permission to reprint their material:

2008. *Economics of Transition*, 16(1): 113–139. Reprinted by permission of the publisher, Wiley-Blackwell.

Martin Ravallion and Shaohua Chen, "China's (uneven) progress against poverty", 2007. *Journal of Development Economics*, 82(1): 1–42. Reprinted by permission of the publisher, Elsevier.

List of contributors

Derek Headey Postdoctoral fellow, Development Strategy and Governance Division, International Food Policy Research Institute.

Xiwen Chen Minister of the Office of the Central Leading Group on Rural Work, China.

Jiwei Lou Chairman, China Investment Cooperation, China.

Runsheng Du Former director of Rural Policy of the CCP Committee, and former director of the Rural Department, Research Center for Rural Development (RCRD), State Council, China.

Martin Ravallion Director of Development Research Group of the World Bank, USA.

Shaohua Chen Senior Statistician in the Development Economics Research Group of the World Bank, USA.

Sylvie Démurger CNRS researcher (Chargée de recherche) in economics, University of Lyon 2 – Groupe d'Analyse et de Théorie Economique (GATE), France.

Martin Fournier Professor, University of Lyon 2 – Group d'Analyse et de Théorie Economique (GATE), France.

Li Shi Professor, School of Economics and Business, Beijing Normal University, China.

Wei Zhong Professor, Institute of Economics, Chinese Academy of Social Sciences, China.

Dwayne Benjamin Professor of Economics, University of Toronto, Canada.

Loren Brandt Professor of Economics, University of Toronto, Canada.

John Giles Associate Professor of Economics, Michigan State University; Senior economist in the Development Economics Research Group of the World Bank, USA.

Gregory Chow Professor of Economics and Class of 1913 Professor of Political Economy, Emeritus, at Princeton University.

Assar Lindbeck Professor of International Economics, Institute for International Economic Studies, Stockholm University, Sweden.

Weidong Ji Professor, Graduate School of Law, Kobe University, Japan.

Hongbin Li Professor of Economics, School of Economics and Management, Tsinghua University, China.

Li-An Zhou Associate Professor of Economics, Guanghua School of Management, Peking University, China.

Justin Yifu Lin Chief Economist and Senior Vice President of the World Bank, USA

Fang Cai Director, Institute of Population and Labor Economics, Chinese Academy of Social Sciences, China.

Zhou Li Deputy Director, Rural Development Institute, Chinese Academy of Social Sciences, China.

Hehui Jin Economist, Quantifi Solutions, USA.

Yingyi Qian Professor of Economics, University of California, Berkeley; Dean, School of Economics and Management, Tsinghua University, China.

Barry R. Weingast Senior fellow at the Hoover Institution and the Ward C. Krebs Family Professor in Political Science, Stanford University.

1 China's growth strategies

Derek Headey, Ravi Kanbur, and Xiaobo Zhang

1.1 Introduction

The household responsibility system (HRS), dual-track pricing, township and village enterprises (TVEs), and special economic zones (SEZs) are all household names among development specialists. The two common characteristics of all these reforms are that they took place in post-reform China, and that they were innovative "hybrid" solutions to both the economic and political problems facing Chinese policy makers. Since the late 1970s these reforms have helped China to achieve rapid economic growth and lift hundreds of millions of its people out of poverty, achievements which have generally surprised most observers, including economists, because many of China's development strategies seem to be unorthodox and in defiance of conventional theories of growth and development.

The miraculous growth rate of China's economy has prompted a great deal of study, especially among economists. One strand of the economic literature decomposes China's economic growth into labor, capital, and technology and/or institutional change components. Most of these quantitative studies (Lin 1992; Fan, Zhang, and Zhang 2004) find that institutional change accounts for a significant proportion of the observed economic growth since the reform. In addition, the structural change from low-productivity agriculture to more productive industrial and service sectors also contributed to rapid economic growth. While this body of literature undoubtedly helps to increase an understanding of the major sources of China's growth, it does not address the question of how the institutional changes occurred in the first place.

There is another large body of literature, including many chapters in this volume, examining particular reform measures to justify their logic from an *ex post* point of view. With hindsight, many of the reform measures make good economic sense and fit well into the political economy and governance context; but for any given reforms, there are always alternative paths. It is not clear from the academic literature how the seemingly heterodox strategies arose in the first place. In this volume, in addition to having papers from leading scholars, we also include papers from key policy advisers who were actively involved in the reform process and who have played an instrumental role in some of the key reforms. Their insider view on the internal process of reforms is complementary to the writings of academic "outsiders."

In this opening chapter, we will first review the major views on China's development and reform strategies. Then we discuss why the same forces behind China's rapid growth also create new challenges. In the last section, we make some remarks on the Chinese experience and lessons, and their transferability to other countries.

1.2 A review of China's development strategies

There are numerous studies on this topic. Jefferson (2008) provides an excellent review of China's reform experience and of how the economics literature has tried to explain that experience. One key difference in this chapter is that we try to combine both the insider's and the outsider's views on the reform process. However, in doing so, we constrain ourselves to the major strands of the existing literature rather than trying to provide a comprehensive review.

1.2.1 *Realigning the economy towards China's comparative advantage*

Lin, Cai, and Li (1996, Chapter 13 in this volume) and Lin (2007) argue that China's rapid growth since the reform is mainly due to the rebalancing of China's development strategy away from a central focus on heavy industry and in the direction of more labor-intensive sectors. When the People's Republic of China was first established, China lacked capital and faced international isolation. Influenced by the experience and ideology of the Soviet Union, China placed the development of heavy industry as the top priority if it was to catch up with the developed nations as soon as possible. To achieve this goal, the government suppressed the procurement price for grains, restricted rural migration, and set up some barriers between rural and urban residents. Since this strategy was capital intensive, it violated China's comparative advantage, which was defined by limited capital and abundant labor, and led to nearly three decades of stagnation in per capita income.

Since the economic reforms beginning in the late 1970s, the central government has shifted its development strategies toward more labor-intensive sectors, initially agriculture, and then to increasingly export-oriented rural industries. In the global context, China possesses an obvious comparative advantage in the labor-intensive manufacturing sector. After introducing the open door policy, massive foreign direct investment flowed in and married with China's cheap labor. As a result, both capital and labor resources were more efficiently allocated, which greatly boosted economic efficiency. China's development path therefore re-emphasizes the importance of adhering to comparative advantage in creating labor-intensive, export-oriented economic growth (Krueger 1978, Krueger 1983, Krueger 1984, Little et al. 1970). A variation of this theme is that realignment towards comparative advantage may be necessary for accelerated growth, but is not by itself sufficient. Ravallion and Chen (2007, Chapter 5 of this volume) argue that China's post-1978 economy also benefited from many of the social and infrastructural investments of the pre-1978 period, especially with regard to education, health, and transport infrastructure. Thus, they invoke a fairly standard notion of conditional convergence to explain China's post-1978 catch-up.

However, there are perhaps two problems with the comparative advantage explanation of China's success. First, comparative advantage is nearly always identified *ex post*, or after the event (Wade 1990). Prior to implementing reforms, it may not be so obvious in what products a country will have some specific comparative advantage. Discovering specific comparative advantages may not be achieved under a laissez-faire system because the process of discovering comparatively advantageous activities entails risks and uncertainties, and because the entrepreneurs that carry out these search and discover activities rarely capture all of the rewards to their success (Hausman and Rodrik 2003). Existing research on other East Asia miracles has also argued that the secret of their success was investing in the growth of future areas of comparative advantage (Amsden 1989; Wade 1990). Second, this theory does not explain the process of successful transition in China. Since the late 1970s, policy makers in many other developing countries in Africa and Latin America have attempted to shift their economies away from capital-intensive sectors towards more labor-intensive activities, but many of these countries have experienced sluggish growth at best, stagnation at worst. How did China manage its own process of reform so successfully? We will come to this point when reviewing China's reform process as recounted in this volume by key Chinese policy advisors (Chen, Chapter 2 in this volume; Lou, Chapter 3 in this volume; Du, Chapter 4 in this volume).

1.2.2 Incentives matter

It is sometimes argued that the first and most important principle of economics is that incentives matter (Easterly 2002). A large body of literature has documented that during the planning era China's rural communes or collectives were dogged by weak incentives due to free rider problems, especially in agricultural production (Lin 1990). Farmers did not want to work hard because the fruits of their toil where shared among others, rather than just themselves. Likewise, in the state-owned enterprises (SOEs), shirking was also reported to be a widespread problem (Xu 2003), and many SOEs made significant losses. A major theme of market-oriented reform studies on China is that the post-1978 government gave strong incentives for individuals – including farmers, managers, and local officials – to increase investment and improve productivity. Several major reforms all have the spirit of empowering ordinary people or local governments to make their own economic choices and reap the rewards of those choices.

Take the Household Responsibility System (HRS) – one of the earliest reforms – as an example. The principle of the HRS is that individual households can claim the residual of their own production after fulfilling the grain quota to both the state and collective units. Because peasants could possess all remnants after fulfilling the state quota, their interest in increasing production dramatically increased. The improved incentive system also had the effect of immediately resulting in a much fuller utilization of long-term investments made by the State in agricultural research and development, irrigation, and other infrastructure. In the space of just a few years, agricultural productivity nearly doubled (Fan 1991; Lin 1992); and, as shown by Ravallion and Chen (2007, Chapter 5 in this volume), it was rural reform that triggered China's economic growth and alleviated a record number of people from poverty.

Subsequent SOE reforms followed in the same spirit. Initially, a manager-responsibility-system was introduced to give the SOE managers more discretionary power in making decisions and offering them performance-based pay packages. However, because SOEs had to take care of employees who were not covered by social welfare by providing their own housing, healthcare, and pension, SOEs still struggled to compete with the lower cost town-village and private enterprises. By the middle to late 1990s, most small and medium SOEs were privatized or experiencing large numbers of layoffs.

A variant of the "incentives matter" explanation of China's growth focuses on decentralization within China's government. Most of the literature has paid particular attention to fiscal decentralization as a major drive of China's economic growth (Jin, Qian, and Weingast 2005, Chapter 14 in this volume; Cheung 2008). During central planning, local governments had to turn in most of their local revenues to the central government, and there was no clear rule as to how central finances were to be devolved to lower governments. Since the 1980s China has adopted a series of fiscal reforms aimed at improving the fiscal contract arrangements between different levels of government. After fiscal reforms, local and upper-level governments shared fiscal revenues according to a predetermined formula. Since local governments can keep a significant portion of the increased local revenues, they face stronger incentives to increase local revenue (note the analogy to the HRS).

Of course, fiscal decentralization need not result in faster growth unless local governments have incentives to use increased finances productively, yet governance reforms in China did indeed complement fiscal decentralization with improved incentives. Modern China has always had a centralized merit-based governance structure. In the planning economy era, the evaluation of cadres was based largely on political performance. However, since China's reforms initiated in 1978, political conformity gave way to economic performance and other competence-related indicators as the new criteria for promotion. The promotion of China cadres' is now based largely on yardstick competition in several key economic indicators, including economic and fiscal revenue growth rates, and some central mandates, such as family planning (Li and Zhou 2005, Chapter 12 in this volume). These indicators have been written into local leaders' contracts. This creates tremendous pressure for local government personnel to compete with each other through superior regional performance. Consider the fact that China has over 2,000 counties and that because capital is largely mobile, these counties have to compete for capital in a pro-business environment wherein investors are trying to maximize returns (Cheung 2008). Strong incentives for local governments to achieve rapid economic growth helps to explain why China has grown so quickly in spite of a lack of well-defined property rights protection in the *de facto* legal system (Zhang 2007): competition serves as the disciplinary mechanism by which local governments provide *de jure* protection of investors' property rights. Of course, the existence of strong growth-oriented incentives also explains why protection of the property rights of other groups, such as farmers, has been weak.

To summarize, the Chinese central government has used both fiscal incentives and personnel policies to ensure that local governments use their financial empowerment to increase economic growth. Although there is not much systematic international evidence on the importance of decentralization for economic growth, a research program on decentralization, fiscal systems, and rural development in the mid-1990s across 19 countries (or provinces thereof) found that Jianxi province in China had easily the highest degree of decentralization (Mclean et al. 1998). Other studies have also pointed out that making decentralization and local empowerment schemes work requires the fulfillment of a large number of conditions in addition to fiscal decentralization (Mansuri and Rao 2004; Prud'homme 1995). China has benefited from a number of favorable conditions – ethnic homogeneity, land equality, strong central governance – but China's experience also reiterates the importance of good incentives for local governments, even if the mechanism by which governors are disciplined is not the electorate; so although the principle of incentives is rather universal, the exact forms used to improve incentives in China may not be easily transferable. Moreover, fiscal decentralization can come at a cost, especially insofar as it increases spatial inequality (Kanbur and Zhang 2005, Chapter 6 in this volume; Zhang 2006).

1.2.3 Experimentation and marginal reform as a solution to risk, uncertainty, and opposition

As argued above, good reforms can be very difficult to identify *ex ante*. Even if a good reform measure has been identified, reformers still need a reform strategy capable of overcoming or circumventing political resistance to reform. Indeed, the political challenge of reform can be at least as difficult as the intellectual challenge of identifying the economic direction of reform. Traditional economic models of development generally do not address the political viability of reform (Ahrens 2002). The public choice school – which attempts to apply economic choice-theoretical models to the political arena –

seeks to explain policy decisions in terms of individual incentives and the outcomes of deliberations between political groups, e.g. factions, lobbies, political parties (Rodrik 1996). Such models are generally dissatisfactory in this context because they assume that good policies are known *ex ante* – an assumption we have already questioned – and that the "preferences" (ideologies, beliefs, normative objectives) of individuals and groups are exogenous. This second assumption is also insufficient because as the chapters in this volume by the reform "insiders" demonstrate, successful political reform often requires persuasion, or, more explicitly, changing people's preferences, ideologies, beliefs, and normative objectives.

In that vein, institutional and behavioral economics generally offers a more flexible framework for thinking about the process of reform. According to Denzau and North's (1994) notions of shared mental models, in situations of uncertainty – such as China in 1978 – people act in part upon the basis of myths, dogmas, ideologies, and "half-baked" theories. Moreover, the psychological notion of cognitive dissonance suggests that people do not easily disassociate themselves from their existing mental models, especially without overwhelming evidence to violate the incumbent model.[1] China's insulated, ideology-driven, single-party pre-1978 society meant that the orthodox shared mental model of China's leaders and its people – founded on Maoist and Socialist principles – was a significant barrier to market-oriented reform. Changing this model was therefore both an important precondition of successful reform, and a result of reform. A key insight, then, from the "insider" chapters of this volume is that China's elites chose reform strategies that involved minimized political opposition to reform.

In the political arena, Deng Xiaoping and other market-oriented reformers made use of two strategies aimed at changing the shared mental model of the nation. Influencing the mindset of China's ruling elite was the first obstacle. Deng Xiaoping was relatively unique in that he had lived for a substantial period of time in a western country (France) and had seen the benefits as well as the costs of capitalism, an experience which evidently made his own attitudes relatively pragmatic. In order to change the mindset of other leaders, he encouraged them to take education tours overseas, and he persuaded Singapore's leader, Lee Kuan Yew, to visit China and speak on the issue of reform. Down the line, however, it was also important to address the mindset of the greater population, which had long been taught to venerate Maoist socialism. China's control of the State media, of education, and its tradition of hierarchical governance, meant that the Chinese leadership could very effectively publicize the direction of reform in China. Famous public announcements such as "the Four Modernizations," "socialism with Chinese characteristics," and "seeking truth from facts" all helped to shift people's mindsets, and signal to the broader economy that China was heading in a new direction. While economists largely ignore such hyperbole, the political economy literature regularly emphasizes the importance of credible reform, and more recent research has also emphasized the importance of soft institutional change (in the case of India, for example, see Rodrik and Subramanian 2004).

In the economic arena, Chinese reformers used two related strategies to simultaneously promote economic learning and overcome political resistance to reform: *(1) reforms at the margin* (e.g. dual-track pricing in agriculture and housing); and *(2) more explicit experimentation.*[2] The economic role of these policies is self-discovery in the face of uncertainty. To quote the oft-cited phrase from Ding Xiaoping, the supreme leader in the early reform period, China's reform has been "crossing the river by feeling the stones." The political role is more pragmatic, as noted in the "insider" chapters in this volume that emphasize the important role that experimentation has in overcoming political resistance to reform. However, some economist "outsiders" have also emphasized this role.

1.2.3.1 Reforms at the margin

Studies on the dual-track price reform (Lau, Qian, and Roland 2000) are a noted example. Prior to reform, in the hierarchical property right and entitlement system, urban sectors and, particularly, SOEs came under the control of the central, provincial, and municipal governments and thereby enjoyed privileged access to a variety of scarce materials and capital goods through quotas. There were few quotas, however, for other lower-level state-owned enterprises and even fewer for collectively owned enterprises. The dual pricing system allowed state-owned enterprises to sell unused input quota at market prices to TVEs that were outside the command economy. Such exchanges not only protected the original privileges of higher ranking entitlements, but also presented TVEs with opportunities to access industrial inputs via market channels and to participate in the market economy. In other words, the dual pricing system provided a functional pricing mechanism for rent-sharing through both hierarchical and market systems. Because the dual-price reform initially did not have a negative impact on the SOEs' entitled planned quota, their resistance was muted. Over time, as the private sector grew rapidly and the market price and planned price converged, the dual track was eventually unified into a single track, or market price.

The urban housing reform makes use of the same compensation principle. In the socialist period, *Danwei* (SOEs or government units) were responsible for providing housing to urban residents. Along with economic reform, SOEs were compelled to be more profit driven. Therefore the provision of public housing was slowed down and could not keep up with increasing demand. This forced the government to undertake urban housing reform in the 1990s. The housing reform packages treated the insiders and outsiders differently. Those already living in public housing were allowed to buy their occupied apartments at a discount price. However, employees buying new houses were made to pay market prices with employers contributing some matching funds to a special housing account so as to ease the burden of purchase. Under this policy, the housing market was privatized quickly without causing much resentment. More importantly, the emergence of a semi-private real estate market sent powerful signals to consumers and producers. Since the urban housing reform, China's construction sector has boomed. In just fifteen years, per capita living space in cities has jumped from 8.8 square meters in 1986 to 15.5 square meters in 2001 (China Statistical Yearbooks).

1.2.3.2 Experimentation and learning by doing

Pragmatism, trial and error, evidence-based policy making, and experimentation with small-scale policy reforms that are later scaled up, are all key features of China's reforms. Most successful reforms have experienced pilot experiments and impact evaluations before being scaled up. Learning by experimentation is a key strategy when reformers face huge economic and political uncertainty. When facing choices never seen before, it is extremely risky for agents to make radical choices. For any reform goal, there are potentially many different paths to take (Lou, Chapter 3 in this volume). Due to uncertainty, it is hard to judge which option is more feasible from the *ex ante* point of view. In such circumstances, experimentation can be a useful tool to search for more information and to test and update prior hypotheses. Experiments yield information to help understand what works and what does not. Thus, even failures can be helpful because they can help to eliminate unfavorable options, as shown by Luo (2009). The failure of his laissez-faire price reform experiment in Hebei Province helped him to come up with the idea of dual-track price reform, which is an important example of an experiment where "Washington Consensus" wisdom was contradicted. Moreover, experimentation can help to control the possible disastrous consequence of wrong choices. A wrong choice, at large scale, may be irreversible, and therefore may undermine the credibility and stability of the political leadership, and weaken overall learning capacity.

An important point to note here, in the context of the emergence of randomized microeconomic experiments within development economics (Duflo 2005), is that most of China's experiments were *not* random. Specifically, experiments were often initiated in isolated poor areas. As shown in the chapter by Du (Chapter 4 in this volume), the leaders purposively initiated the household responsibility system as a pilot reform in several remote provinces in order to minimize the potential costs of failure and reduce the political resistances. Similarly, the Wenzhou area, which used to be a remote region in Zhejiang Province but is now one of the most dynamic regions in China, received special permission to be a pilot region for rural industrialization precisely because of its isolation at the time (Zhu 2009). Under the special policy, Wenzhou made bold experiments in reforming TVEs and legalizing private firms. After observing its success, most TVEs and small and medium SOEs were privatized nationwide by the late 1990s. Although such experiments were not so rigorously conducted as to include control groups, the pilots enabled researchers and policy makers to observe what worked and what did not on the ground. Another advantage of China's approach is that it involved an element of experimentation in macroeconomic reform, whereas contemporary randomized experiments are confined to micro-economic experiments (Rodrik 2008). Dual-track prices and special economic zones are two examples.

Such experimentation has been particularly important in overcoming several major obstacles to effective reform in China, related to the country's size, its diversity, and the history and structure of its hierarchical political system. For a large and diverse economy such as China, it is very difficult to derive a single one-size-fits-all blueprint for reform simply by applying textbook economic theories. Instead, trial-and-error processes can help to discover local best practice. Second, the basis for formulating sound market-oriented policies in 1978 was limited. Few bureaucrats had any formal training in orthodox economics, nor even substantial experience of living in market economies. Chinese reforms therefore felt compelled to use experimentation as a collective learning mechanism. Moreover, successful Chinese reformers moved quickly to overcome China's limited research base by employing young recruits to work in think tanks, such as the China Rural Development and Research Center led by Mr Du Runsheng, the author of Chapter 4 in this volume. Such institutions helped in turn to overcome arguably the most binding constraint to effective decision-making in China, information asymmetry. Because China's bureaucrats are rewarded based on perceived merit, bureaucrats always have an incentive to falsify facts, as was the case in the Great Famine in which statistics on experimental yields were grossly falsified. Institutions such as the China Rural Development and Research Center played a key role in reducing these information biases by screening best practices and feeding them back to top policy makers (Keyser 2003).

1.2.4 Pressure as a catalyst for reform

People evaluate the risks and payoffs with regard to the consequence of proposed policy change. However, they often have different (subjective) perceptions of the uncertainty related to change. Exogenous social, economic and political pressures – although adverse in some sense – can help policy makers to induce policy reforms that, in calmer times, would generally be resisted.

The "pressure" which stimulated the earliest reforms of the post-1978 era was the threat of economic crisis. A crisis can have a silver lining in the context of reform in that it may help to update people's perceived risks and payoffs regarding alternative policy options, and thereby realign policy priorities so that new approaches emerge out of previous failures. Therefore, despite the negative effects of any crisis, crises necessitate change and re-examinations of current policies, in a manner analogous to Joseph Schumpeter's notion of creative destruction.

After the Cultural Revolution (1966–1976) China was on the verge of collapse under the planned economy system. More than two-thirds of the people lived on less than $1 per day (US$ in PPP) (Ravallion and Chen 2007, Chapter 5 in this volume). With stagnant agricultural growth and fast population growth, food was in short supply. At the onset of reform, it seemed that China faced extremely high barriers to escaping the low-level equilibrium trap where poverty persisted. However, as shown in Chapter 4 by Du, one of the architects of China's rural reform, crisis may trigger reforms. After the end of the Cultural Revolution, most of the top leaders and the masses realized that the planned system was no longer a viable option, even if there was still uncertainty and debate as to how next to proceed. Under these circumstances, top leaders were more willing to listen to different opinions and allow open policy debate. In other words, the crisis provided would-be reformers with a window of opportunity to push new agendas. Significant reforms do not come automatically and require policy makers to "seize the day" in a timely fashion.

One noted example is the rural reform documented by Du. Chinese farmers, who had suffered terribly under the Great Famine in the late 1950s and early 1960s, still had a vivid memory of the disaster, and knew that collective farming did not work, especially in times of crisis. With another imminent weather shock looming in 1977, the local government in Fengyang County, Anhui Province – the province hardest hit by the famine in the late 1950s[3] – decided to contract the collective land to farmers because they knew that the collective farming system could lead to another famine in the event of severe shocks. Yao (2007) provides an extensive review of land tenure changes in rural China and how the HRS was successfully scaled up (again, largely because farmers elsewhere had similarly critical views of collective farming).

China's joining the World Trade Organization (WTO) is another example of the use of an external pressure to invoke and lock in reform. In the 1990s, banking reform met enormous resistance because State banks did not want to give up their monopoly positions. Many local governments also opposed the reform because they were afraid of losing their ability to direct credit, which made it very difficult for State banks really to operate as commercial banks. Largely as a means of forcing further reforms in the banking and other key sectors, the top leaders made a bold move to enter China into the WTO. Although the WTO gave domestic banks a few years' window of protection, in the end, most of the barriers to entry in the banking sector had to be removed such that State banks were eventually forced to compete on a level playing field. By using external pressure from the WTO accession, the government was able to induce a series of reforms within State banks. Although not complete, most Chinese banks have shed off bad loans, several major state banks have listed their stocks in overseas markets and are subject to the scrutinizing of international financial markets, and local bank branches now find it much easier to refuse loans to local officials. Thus the use of external pressure largely achieved its implicit goals.

1.2.5 *A note on the compatibility of economic and political explanations of the Chinese miracle*

We have discussed four basic types of explanation of China's remarkable economic success: (1) "comparative advantage" (and conditional convergence); (2) "incentives matter" (fiscal decentralization and realignment of incentives towards growth-maximizing activities); (3) experimentation (as an economic and political discovery mechanism); and (4) pressure and crisis as inducers of reform. We conclude this section by noting that all these explanations are highly compatible with each other and complementary, and that together they comprise a compelling and holistic explanation of China's economic miracle.

This holistic explanation of China's success, which incorporates both the outsiders' and insiders' viewpoints, runs as follows. The conventional economic explanation of China's growth – more efficient utilization of China's existing endowments – convincingly accounts for the proximate causes of China's growth, but does not explain the cause of reform or why the process of reform itself was so successful both politically and economically. The successful process of reform is in turn compellingly explained by both the "incentives matter" and "experimentation" arguments. Indeed, both arguments invoke several of the same ingredients of successful reform, such as overcoming information asymmetries by deriving local solutions to local problems, and discovering comparative advantage through trial, error, and observation. Experimentation and marginal reforms, however, also served to overcome political constraints to reform by compensating would-be losers of reform, and convincing potential opponents of the benefits of reform by reducing the uncertainty of outcomes of reform. Finally, the catalyst for reform was an economic and political crisis that jolted Chinese leaders, and to some extent its ordinary people, into re-evaluating their mental models of where the Chinese economy should be heading. This story need not preclude other factors, such as the importance of good leadership (Jones 2005) or good luck, but together these four arguments certainly provide a compelling explanation of three decades of rapid economic growth.

1.3 After three decades of growth: the challenges of the present and the future

After three decades of spectacular economic growth in China, the problem is no longer how to achieve growth but how to manage growth's consequences and how to sustain growth. China's spectacular growth and poverty reduction has been accompanied by rising inequality, environmental degradation, and increasing social tensions. The institutions that have brought rapid growth so far are now under stress, and there is a need to reform and innovate on this front in order to sustain rapid growth, and to obtain growth with equity (Lindbeck 2008, Chapter 10 in this volume; Ji, Chapter 11 in this volume).

Rising inequality is one of China's most serious problems (Demurger et al. 2006, Chapter 7 in this volume; Benjamin, Brandt, and Giles 2005, Chapter 8 in this volume). In particular, the regional dimension of inequality – rural/urban and inland/coastal – dominates in a country as large as China, and especially with its particular history. Regional inequality has become a key issue for China and a number of interventions have been introduced to address the problem. These are discussed in Fan, Kanbur, and Zhang (2009).

As shown by Kanbur and Zhang (2005, Chapter 6 in this volume), the pattern of China's regional inequality closely follows the history of its development strategies in the past half century. The heavy industry-oriented development strategy justified the creation of the household registration system (*hukou*) that was a major contributor to the large rural/urban divide. The open-door policy, which granted preferential treatment to coastal areas, has helped the coast better to exploit its comparative advantage in the international markets, but has left many interior provinces lagging behind. Similarly, the fiscal decentralization policy promoted local government officials to develop their own economies, but differences in initial endowments tends to leave the effective tax rate regressive across Chinese regions (Zhang 2006). Regions with better endowments thereby have more revenues left to invest in public goods and improve the business environment after turning over a portion of their fiscal revenues to the upper-level government and maintaining the daily operation of local government. In contrast, the local governments in poor regions have difficulty in competing with the governments on the coast to attract investment and develop the local nonfarm economy. Their local revenues are sometimes barely sufficient to cover the salaries of civil servants on the public payroll. Consequently, they are more likely to levy heavy taxes on existing enterprises, worsening the business investment environment. In summary, the successful development strategies mentioned in the above section also have some deleterious side effects.

In responding to rising rural/urban disparity and stagnating agricultural growth, China has launched a new rural movement campaign in the past several years (Chen, Chapter 2 in this volume). Agricultural taxation has been abolished; the government has provided direct subsidies for grain production. However, significant challenges remain. Facing rising food and fuel prices, the government has placed a ceiling on the grain procurement price, which may in the long run dampen farmers' incentives to increase grain production.

The interjuridical competition is a key contributing factor to the increasingly serious environmental problems. In order to attract investment, many local governments loosen their environmental regulations to allow polluters to operate as long as they generate lucrative revenues for the local government. In the rapidly industrialized coastal areas, such as Jiangsu Province and Zhejiang Province, the degree of water pollution and industrial waste hazard is alarming. The cost of cleaning up the environment may eat up a large portion of the gains from industrialization.

The investment-driven growth model also induces local officials to collude with investors at the expense of the rights of individuals (Zhang 2007; Chow, Chapter 9 in this volume). In order to attract investment, many local governments provide preferential treatment to investors, such as free land. In the process of procuring farming land for industrial or other commercial use, the compensation to farmers was often far below the market level. Resenting this unfair treatment, many relocated farmers filed petitions to the upper-level government for help, and land disputes have become a breeding ground for social unrest all over China (Yu 2005). How to make local government officials accountable has become an increasingly important issue.

1.4 Concluding remarks

China's experience since 1978 has taught economists many lessons about the process of development, but also about the study of economic development. Our reading of China's history, and of the explanations that economists have proposed to order to explain that history, reiterate the increasingly accepted conclusion that while economic principles may be universal ingredients of successful development strategies, the specific recipes that embody these principles tend to be highly context-specific (Rodrik 2007; Headey 2008). For example, China's strategy contains all the usual elements of successful development – getting incentives right, adhering to comparative advantage, providing secure (but often not private) property rights, investing in human capital, and achieving rapid agricultural growth – but the path which China took from plan to market was almost entirely distinct.

This confirmation of China's adherence to these principles should not be underestimated, but China's unique history, its enormous size, and its distinctive economic system should also remind us that China's specific reform strategies are unlikely to apply to other developing countries, especially small countries and those with very different institutional histories. For example, small countries that rely heavily on external donors for both finance and technical assistance will typically have a limited policy space in which to formulate heterodox policy solutions. Similarly, democracies, even democracies of similar size such as India, have limited ability to experiment in the way that China did; nor do they typically provide such strong incentives for bureaucrats or elected officials to maximize growth.

Given the uniqueness of Chinese history, perhaps the key lessons of China's reform experiences are most valuable for China itself. With rapid economic growth and ballooning revenues, policy makers can easily become complacent and over-confident, ignoring the pragmatic and experimental approaches of yesteryear. Data collected by Heilman (2008) shows that the proportion of policy reforms with experimentation components has declined from around 50 percent in the 1980s, to 40 percent in the 1990s, and down further to just 20 percent since 2001. These statistics are consistent with what is being observed on the ground. The new labor contract law (Cheung 2008), which was passed without little experimentation and limited consultation in 2007, is a noted example. The law generates much controversy in China. For example, the law stipulates that an employer must sign an open-term contract with an employee after finishing two fixed-term contracts. This greatly discourages firms from hiring workers. The reform stories presented in this volume highlight the virtue of pragmatism and experimentation in the reform process. To overcome the emerging challenges, it is important for Chinese policy makers to maintain a pragmatic attitude to reform, and to keep focusing on innovations from the ground. When policy makers become more complacent, they are more likely to make centralized autocratic decisions, neglecting the wisdom of local knowledge and the virtues of experimentation. In essence, China runs the risk of kicking away the ladder by which it has reached its current heights. This is a key lesson for China, from itself.

Notes

1 In psychology, cognitive dissonance is defined as an uncomfortable feeling or stress caused by holding two contradictory ideas simultaneously (e.g. such as "socialism works" and "markets work"). The theory of cognitive dissonance proposes that people have a fundamental cognitive drive to reduce this dissonance by modifying an existing belief, or by rejecting one of the contradictory ideas. From this viewpoint many of Deng's statements can be seen as means of diffusing cognitive dissonance. For example, Deng Xiaoping (quoted in Gittings 2005) emphasized that:

> Planning and market forces are not the essential difference between socialism and capitalism. A planned economy is not the definition of socialism, because there is planning under capitalism; the market economy happens under socialism, too. Planning and market forces are both ways of controlling economic activity.

2 We note that although marginal reforms have some features of experimentation (like experiments, they may be more reversible than wholesale reform, and they also promote learning), they also have some distinguishing features relative to other experimental reforms.
3 According to Yang (1996), the mortality rate in Anhui jumped from 1.19% in the period of 1956–8 to 6.86% in 1960, the highest among all the provinces.

References

Ahrens, Joachim, 2002. *Governance and Economic Development: A Comparative Institutional Approach*, Cheltenham, UK: Edward Elgar.
Amsden, Alice H., 1989. *Asia's Next Giant: South Korea and Late Industrialization*, New York: Oxford University Press.
Benjamin, Dwayne, Loren Brandt, and John Giles, 2005. "The Evolution of Income Inequality in Rural China," *Economic Development and Cultural Change*, 53(4): 769–824, also Chapter 8 in this volume.
Chen, Xiwen, "China is Already Capable of Solving the 'Three Dimensional Rural Problem," Chapter 2 in this volume.
Cheung, Steven N. S., 2008. "The Economic System of China," paper presented at the 2008 Chicago Conference on China's Economic Transformation, July 14–18.

Chow, Gregory, "Rural Poverty in China: Problem and Solution," Chapter 9 in this volume.

Démurger, Sylvie, Martin Fournier, Li Shi, and Wei Zhong, 2006. "Economic Liberalization with Rising Segmentation in China's Urban Labor Market," *Asian Economic Papers*, 5(3): 58–101, Chapter 7 in this volume.

Denzau, A. and Douglass C. North, 1994. "Shared Mental Models: Ideologies and Institutions," *Kyklos*, 47(1): 3–31.

Du, Runsheng, "The Course of China's Rural Reform," Chapter 4 in this volume.

Duflo, Esher, 2005. "Field Experiments in Development Economics," Bureau for Research in Economic Analysis of Development Policy Paper No. 12.

Easterly, William R., 2002. *The Elusive Quest for Growth: Economists' Adventures and Misadventures in the Tropics*, Cambridge: MIT Press.

Fan, Shenggen, 1991. "Effects of Technological Change and Institutional Reform on Production and Growth in Chinese Agriculture," *American Journal of Agricultural Economics*, 73: 266–75.

Fan, Shenggen, Ravi Kanbur, and Xiaobo Zhang, 2009. *Regional Inequality in China: Trends, Explanations and Policy Responses*, Routledge, forthcoming.

Fan, Shenggen, Linxiu Zhang, and Xiaobo Zhang, 2004. "Reform, Investment and Poverty in Rural China," *Economic Development and Cultural Change*, 52(2): 395–422.

Gittings, John, 2005. The Changing Face of China, Oxford: Oxford University Press.

Hausman, Ricardo and Dani Rodrik, 2003. "Economic Development as Self-discovery," *Journal of Development Economics*, 72(2003): 603–33.

Headey, Derek D. 2008. Book Review of "One Economics, Many Recipes: Globalization, Institutions, and Economic Growth" by Dani Rodrik, *Journal of Development Studies*, 44(3): 449–58.

Heilmann, Sebastian. 2008. "Policy Experimentation in China's Economic Rise," *Studies in Comparative International Development*, 43(1): 1–26.

Jefferson, Gary H., 2008. "How Has China's Economic Emergence Contributed to the Field of Economics?" *Comparative Economic Studies*, 50(2): 167–209.

Ji, Weidong. "Redefining Relations between the Rule of Law and the Market: Clues Provided by Four Basic issues in China today," Chapter 11 in this volume.

Jin, Hehui, Yingyi Qian, and Barry Weingast, 2005. "Regional Decentralization and Fiscal Incentives: Federalism, Chinese Style," *Journal of Public Economics*, 89: 1719–42, Chapter 14 in this volume.

Jones, Benjamin, 2005. "Do Leaders Matter? National Leadership and Growth Since World War II," *The Quarterly Journal of Economics*, 120(3): 835–64.

Kanbur, Ravi and Xiaobo Zhang, 2005. "Fifty Years of Regional Inequality in China: A Journey Through Central Planning, Reform and Openness," *Review of Development Economics*, 9(1): 87–106, January 2005, also Chapter 6 in this volume.

Keyser, Catherine, 2003. *Professionalizing Research in Post-Mao China: They System Reform Institute and Policy Making*, New York: M. E. Sharpe.

Krueger, Anne O., 1978. "Alternative Trade Strategies and Employment in LDCs," *American Economic Review*, 68(2): 270–4.

Krueger, Anne O., 1983. *Trade and Employment in Developing Countries*, Chicago: University of Chicago Press.

Krueger, Anne O., 1984. Comparative Advantage and Development Policy Twenty

Years Later, in Moshe Syrquin, Lance Taylor, and Larry E. Westphal (eds), *Economic Structure and Performance*, New York: Academic Press.

Lau, Lawrence, Yingyi Qian, and Gerald Roland, 2000. "Reform without Losers: An Interpretation of China's dual-Track Approach to Transition," *Journal of Political Economy*, 108(1): 120–43.

Li, Hongbin and Li-An Zhou, 2005. "Political Turnover and Economic Performance: The Incentive Role of Personnel Control in China," *Journal of Public Economics*, 89(9–10): 1743–62. Also Chapter 12 in this volume.

Lin, Justin Yifu, 1990. "Collectivization and China's Agricultural Crisis in 1959–1961," *Journal of Political Economy*, 98(6): 1228–52.

Lin, Justin Yifu, 1992. "Rural Reforms and Agricultural Growth in China," *American Economic Review*, 82(1): 34–51.

Lin, Justin Yifu, 2007. "Development and Transition: Idea, Strategy and Viability," The Marshall Lectures for 2007–2008, October 31 and November 1, Cambridge University.

Lin, Justin Yifu, Fang Cai, and Zhou Li, 1996. "The Lessons of China's Transition to a Market Economy," *Cato Journal*, 16 (2), Chapter 13 in this volume.

Lindbeck, Assar, "Economic-Social Interaction during China's Transition," Chapter 10 in this volume.

Little, Ian M. D., Tibor Scitovsky, and Maurice Scott, 1970. *Industry and Trade in Some Developing Countries: A Comparative Study*, New York, London: Oxford University Press and The OECD.

Lou, Jiwei. "Twenty Years Review and Deliberation: The Choice of Priorities in Reform," Chapter 3 in this volume.

Luo, Xiaopeng, 2009. "Collective Learning and Choice of Reform Path," in *Learning from China: How Does China Learn?* edited by Xiaobo Zhang, Arjan de Haan, and Shenggen Fan, World Scientific Series on Economic Development and Growth.

Mansuri, Ghazala and Vijayendra Rao. 2004, "Community-Based and -Driven Development: A Critical Review," *The World Bank Research Observer*, 19(1): 1–39, 2004.

Mclean, Keith, Graham Kerr, and Melissa Williams, 1998. "Decentralization and Rural Development: Characterizing Efforts of 19 Countries," *World Bank Working Paper*. Washington DC.

Prud'homme, Remy, 1995. The Dangers of Decentralization, *World Bank Research Observer*, 10(2): 201–20.

Ravallion, Martin and Shaohua Chen, 2007. "China's (Uneven) Progress against Poverty," *Journal of Development Economics*, 82(1): 1–42, Chapter 5 in this volume.

Rodrik, Dani and Arvind Subramanian, 2004. "From "Hindu Growth" to Productivity Surge: The Mystery of the Indian Growth Transition," *NBER Working Paper Series*, Cambridge, MA.

Rodrik, Dani, 1996. "Understanding Economic Policy Reform," *Journal of Economic Literature* 34(1): 9–41.

Rodrik, Dani, 2007. *One Economics, Many Recipes: Globalization, Institutions and Economic Growth*, Princeton and Oxford: Princeton University Press.

Rodrik, Dani, 2008. "The New Development Economics: We Shall Experiment, But How Shall We Learn?" paper presented at the Brookings Development Conference, May 29–30, 2008, Boston, MA.

Wade, Robert, 1990. *Governing the Market: Economic Theory and the Role of Government in East Asian Industrialization*, Princeton, NJ: Princeton University Press.

Xu, Lixin Collin, 2003. "Control, Incentives and Competition: The Impact of Reform on Chinese State-owned Enterprises," *Economics of Transition*, 8(1): 151–73.

Yang, Dali L., 1996. *Calamity and Reform in China: State, Rural Society, and Institutional Change since the Great Leap Famine*, Stanford University Press.

Yao, Yang., 2007. "The Chinese Land Tenure System: Practice and Perspectives," 49–70, in Gulati, Ashok and Shenggen Fan, eds. *The Dragon and the Elephant: Agricultural and Rural Reforms in China and India*, Johns Hopkins Press.

Yu, Jianrong., 2005. "A Survey of Farmers' Petition on Land Acquisition (Nongcun Tudi Weiquan Kangzheng de Diaocha," Institute of Rural Development, Chinese Academy of Social Sciences, http://www.tecn.cn/data/detail.php?id=7264.

Zhang, Xiaobo, 2006. "Fiscal Decentralization and Political Centralization in China: Implications for Growth and Regional Inequality," *Journal of Comparative Economics*, 34(4): 713–26.

Zhang, Xiaobo, 2007. "Asymmetric Property Rights in China's Economic Growth," *William Mitchell Law Review*, 33(2): 101–16.

Zhu, Kangdui, 2009. "The Independent Choice of Local Government in Civil and Market-Oriented Reformation Process: Research of Wenzhou Model of Interaction Between Civilian and Government," in *Learning from China: How Does China Learn?* Xiaobo Zhang, Arjan de Haan, and Shenggen Fan, eds, World Scientific Series on Economic Development and Growth.

Part I
Policy challenges and options

2 China is already capable of solving the "three-dimensional rural problem"*

Xiwen Chen

The 16th session of Fifth Plenary Session of the Central Committee of the CCP concluded on October 11, 2005, passing some advice from the Central Committee about the 11th five-year plan. There was a lot to this advice, one noticeable part calling for socialist rural reconstruction. The notion of socialist rural reconstruction is not new, it should be noted. It has been proposed several times in Central Committee and State Council documents in the course of the past few score years, but this time differed from the past in at least two respects.

In the first place, the temporal background is different. The phase of economic and social development we are now in is different from the 1950s and 1960s – even from the 1980s. China's industrialization and urbanization had at that time just started; everyone, from top to bottom, realized quite clearly that accumulation drawn from agriculture was a *sine qua non* of China's industrial progress. Hence the most commonly raised requirement at that time was that the countryside should withstand sacrifices and endure patiently. The Central Committee and State Council are quite clear that in the socialist rural reconstruction currently called for, a development phase has begun in which industry is promoting agriculture and the city is bringing the countryside along with it.

Second, the socialist rural reconstruction proposed in the 1950s and 60s had two main aims: one was to change the ownership relations of the means of production in the countryside. By the end of mainland China's land reforms of the late 1940s and early 1950, the rural land system had experienced an extremely profound transformation. The private ownership of small plots established by the land reform movement, the collective public ownership system, and the implementation of advanced agricultural producers' cooperatives in the mid-1950s, were the main contents of the rural reconstruction of that time. A further initial aim of rural reconstruction at that time focused on the extreme shortages of agricultural products, and demanded speeded-up development of production, and in particular, increasing grain output. This time, as everybody may see, the socialist rural reconstruction proposed by the 16th Plenary Session of Fifth Party Congress involves many aspects of the rural economy, including social, cultural, political, even party construction, and is not a unitary goal.

I feel that for at least the following reasons the socialist rural reconstruction presently proposed is quite essential for Chinese economic and social development.

2.1 China's urgent need at present to develop modern agriculture

The most basic fact that now makes it necessary for China to develop modern agriculture is that it has the largest population in the world. The figure in late 2005 was 1.3 billion, and growing. In terms of per capita average agricultural resources, however, we are actually one of the neediest countries in the world. Last year our per capita average cultivated area was 1.4 mu, 40 percent of the world average. Our per capita average water resources last year were more than 2200 cubic meters, again only 28 percent of the world average. It is extremely difficult, with so few per capita average agricultural natural resources, to safeguard grain and economic security, not to mention wealth, for 1.3 billion people. In this process the development of modern agriculture must be speeded up, otherwise such rapid economic development, as well as ever higher social demands, will be very difficult to support.

In recent years, everybody senses that agriculture is facing a series of stern challenges. A massive slide took place in China's grain industry in 2003, when the grain yield was only 861.3 billion catties, a return to the levels of 14 or 15 years before. Between late 2003 and early 2004 an obvious rise appeared in the price of grain. This was a reason for inflation in the middle of the reform process. In terms of the supply of agricultural products, China's major inflation was directly related to the shortage of grain. For example, the price index reached 21.7 percent in 1994, the year of the highest price index in China since the reforms, a major reason for which was the grain price rising over 50 percent in that year.

It was in such tough circumstances that three "No. 1 documents" were issued by the Central Committees, which in these years were well-received by the peasants, who also had praise for the detailed agricultural policies. The policies they most supported were, as they put it, the "two reductions and three subsidies" – i.e. reductions in the agricultural and special production taxes, and subsidies for peasants who grow grain, who buy improved varieties, and who purchase agricultural tools and machinery in certain regions. The figures for these subsidies are quite large: in 2004 the policy subsidy amounted to 45.1 billion yuan, increasing to 25.4 billion in 2005 yuan, and again in 2006.

There is, of course, much discussion as to whether these policies can be sustained. There are economists who disapprove of subsidizing agricultural products, but I think different policies may be appropriate in different development phases. In fact, when this policy appeared, it played an unmistakable part in mobilizing the enthusiasm of peasants to plant and restore the production of grain. I stated just now that the cost of the five policies in the No. 1 document for 2004 totalled 45.1 billion yuan; grain yield in that year grew by 77.6 billion catties; this is the fastest annual production increase in China's history. Carrying on with this policy in 2005, the grain yield increased by 29.6 billion catties, and production increased in the two years by 107.2 billion catties altogether, which is again historically quite rare. How will it be later? I think that when policy is made, every country will size up the situation, and make adjustments according to the actual situation.

All things considered, we have no grounds for optimism at present; for while last year's grain yield recovered to 968 billion catties, it is still 56.6 billion catties short of the 1998 level of output, our historical maximum. We have not actually achieved even the levels of seven or eight years ago. Our own demand last year was 999 billion catties, our output was 968 billion catties, there was a gap between production and demand, and we had to increase imports or draw upon our reserves. From this angle, getting agriculture onto a sustainable and stable growth path is extremely important to China's economic development.

We now face a host of challenges, first that of agricultural resources: there is already such a shortage of land and water resources, but the cultivated area is also constantly being reduced, the situation with pollution of water resources is increasingly serious. As for land, last year the cultivated area was 1.83 billion mu, compared with 1.95 in 1996, a reduction of 120 million mu. The area of arable land surpasses 100 million mu in only 6 of China's 31 province-size units. Hence by 2003 our per capita average area of arable was 1.43 mu, falling in 2004 to 1.41, and in 2005 to 1.40 mu. Industrialization and urbanization have not stopped; hence, no matter how you much you re-establish controls over and protect arable land, it will go on declining. At present, the central authorities have implemented the strictest system for protecting arable land, over 4 million mu may be approved per annum, of which 3 million mu is arable. Moreover, currently it cannot be guaranteed that land that has not been approved for transfer has not been occupied. Hence the erosion of arable land deserves close attention.

As to the issue of water resources, China has a per capita average of 2200 cubic meters. This absolute quantity sounds acceptable, because some colleagues compare this per capita average amount of water resources with Israel's, whose per person average is only 400 cubic meters. One must understand, however, that China is a very big country with differences in the distribution of water resources in space and time. Is our northern political centre and economical core area of Beijing and Tianjin, the actual water resources capacity is at Israel's level. Beijing's per capita average water resources are a little over 400 cubic meters, as are Tianjin's. At the same time, the pattern in Chinese history since at least the Sui and Tang dynasties of shipping southern grain to the north had by the century's end completely changed to one of shipping northern grain to the south. Why was this? Economic development is fast in the south, industrialization and urbanization are advancing more rapidly, and more cultivated land is being occupied; while less grain is being produced due to the economy being more developed, more employment is provided. Therefore, nationally the employed population is everywhere increasing. With reduced production and more mouths to feed, China naturally has insufficient grain of its own, so it needs northern grain to be supplied to the south or has to be imported.

The greatest problem now is that while the north doubtless has great potential for grain, given declining water resources, how long can the north keep providing grain? I am from Shanghai, so I well know how people of the Tai Lake basin and Yangtze River delta are fond of eating rice, but my fellow villagers are less and less inclined to the rice produced locally. Even people from Anhui and Jiangxi are turning to Heilongjiang rice. Hence the area under paddy rice in the northeast has mushroomed in recent years, and grain output has rapidly increased. The problem, though, is that the northeast too is an area lacking in water. Such resource challenges, I feel, thus really require us to speed up the modernization of agriculture.

There is little ground for optimism when it comes to modernizing agriculture. Take infrastructure: China's agriculture is widely called irrigation agriculture. In fact we can actually irrigate only about 700 million mu of arable land. We have also passed through several such changes, first from dry farmland to paddy fields, then to improvement of varieties, and then to mechanization. We should say the most intuitive problem for agriculture is certainly that of water. If this issue is not solved, many places which today have agriculture may not have it tomorrow, but at present the construction of agricultural infrastructure, in particular for irrigation and water conservation have not been set up. Irrigation and water conservation are classified as minor amenities, and the central authorities spare them little attention, but because agriculture makes a modest contribution to GDP growth, local authorities are unwilling to invest much money in it. If this question is not solved, then in as many as eight to ten years or as few as three to five, as a result of issues of inadequate infrastructure and water resources, China's agriculture may have another major crisis.

2.2 Responding to the need to expand internal demand

According to figures provided by the State Statistical bureau, the rural population stood at 745 million last year, accounting for 57 percent of our total national population. This figure was calculated according to the inhabited area, but if computed according to household registration, the agricultural population last year was 949 million. Subtracting the first figure from the second, one finds that at present over 200 million people hold rural *hukous*, but do not reside there – they have gone to the cities. We must be clear, they may have gone to the cities without merging into urban society, they remain in a marginalized status. This problem will have to be addressed in the next round of economic and social development.

I want to explain a point in this process: there are probably 950 million peasants now living in localities at county level and below, the portion of total retail volume of consumables sold at county level and below last year was only 32.9 percent of the entire society's; in other words, the share of consumables purchased by those making up the overwhelming majority of Chinese was quite low.

Why does China, a massively populous country, have such a high degree of foreign trade dependency? Last year GDP was over US$2.2 trillion, but total foreign trade amounted to over US$1.4 trillion, the degree of foreign trade dependency reaching 63.3 percent. Admittedly, China's huge productivity has, following the reform and open policy, needed to find markets, but a major factor is that low income earners are a majority in the country, lacking in purchasing power. In the present stage, everybody has felt that along with our enlarging share in foreign trade markets, various frictions, contradictions, and conflicts have been increasing as well. In order to find a relatively smooth market road for China's economy to continue safely, high priority must certainly be placed on increasing rural incomes; otherwise, a massive population will have negligible purchasing power. Such a big market represented by our population will forever be a big potential but not actual market. From this point of view, advancing new rural reconstruction, prospering the rural economy, and increasing peasant incomes is much more important than "building new housing."

2.3 The need to curb the constantly expanding rural/urban disparity

The urban/rural disparity may be discussed from two angles: first, the quite obvious disparity in residents' incomes. Last year was in Chinese history, an epoch-making one for these incomes, because peasants' incomes topped 3,000 yuan for the first time, while city peoples' incomes topped 10,000 yuan for the first time. Last year, peasants' per capita average income was 3,255 yuan, but only ten provinces surpassed this mean value, while some 21 provinces, cities and autonomous regions averaged less than 3,255 yuan. Highest is Shanghai, the Shanghai peasants' average per person income is 8,277 yuan; lowest is Guizhou Province which averaged only 1,840 yuan. Last year, urban disposable income was 10,493 yuan. A disparity might be seen in the middle of all this .

What should be taken seriously, is that this disparity is larger than it was before the reform and open policy, when everybody was poor and really it was not as big as at present. The income disparity of urban and rural residents in 1978 was 2.57:1; in the initial reform and open policy period, due to the rural bias of policy, the growth of peasants' incomes was quite rapid, so in the mid-1980s the income disparity of urban and rural residents was reduced to 1.86:1. In 2002 it began for the first time to break through to 3:1, and now has basically stabilized at about 3.2:1. In 2003 it stood at 3.23:1, in 2004 at 3.21:1, and in 2005 at 3.22:1. In these years the strength of our policy of supporting agriculture was unprecedented. Despite such forcefulness, the urban/rural disparity has not been reduced, and we have had to realize the difficulty of solving this problem.

This is the overt aspect. The urban/rural disparity in regard to public services offered by the government is even larger than in the case of incomes. Up to the present, the share of our public financial expenditure occupied by expenditure on education and medicine for peasants is probably around 1:4, and certainly lower if calculated on a per capita average. If you were to go to some remote villages, on very many walls would be seen past slogans which remain. If written on a school, it will say "village school managed by peasants"; if written next to a road, it will say "village road repaired by peasants". This reflects the fact that we have had the government public service and infrastructure basically not provided to the countryside for over a decade.

I want to say two matters about the disparities in education and public health. One is compulsory education, where we have made major policy adjustments during these years; a great deal of money was given, but it would be unacceptable if the institutions were not changed. The final result must be displayed in terms of whether humans have equitable access to education, including access to higher education. Before the Cultural Revolution, sons of peasant families at Beijing and Qinghua University averaged some 70 percent of the total number of students; how many would they be now? Jiaotong University in Shanghai is probably 30 percent, and most likely both Beijing and Tsinghua Universities are at this level. As the peasants themselves say, we are not unaware that failure to stay at school can cause a lifetime of suffering, but I am very clear about the present condition: as soon as I go to school, I will immediately be poor. When the money has been paid in full, the family loses everything immediately.

There has already been a major improvement in the medical aspect, and the Centre has put out a great deal of money, all levels of governments participated in the new cooperative medical treatment subsidy of $US40 for peasants, of which they need to put up only $US10; but in overall terms, rural medical services and public health still fall far behind the city, and are not coordinated with overall economic and social development. How many peasants are dying of sickness in a hospital? How many rural women giving birth to a child are able to do so in a hospital?

The backwardness of rural social enterprises is restricting the enhancement of the peasants' quality, more importantly restricting the progress of society as a whole. Speeding up the construction of the rural infrastructure and the development of rural social enterprises is thus an extremely important component of our current construction of a harmonious society.

Compared to the past, the country's financial resources and overall economic strength provide definite conditions for enabling more support in solving the sannong question; in particular, China's economic growth in the 10th Five Year Plan period was much quicker. To give just a few figures,

China's GDP was 8.95 trillion yuan in 2000, last year it was 18.2 trillion renminbi (RMB); financial revenue was RMB 1.34 trillion in 2000, and RMB 3.16 trillion last year; residents' deposits were RMB 6.4 trillion in 2000, and RMB 14.1 trillion last year; society's fixed asset investment totalled RNB 3.3 trillion in 2000, and RNB 8.8 trillion last year. Clearly, China's economic development has seen great growth compared to five years ago. I think the reason that the Centre has proposed new rural reconstruction at this time, was that China as a whole has moved into the development phase of industry-promoting agriculture, and the city driving the country; therefore, state financial resources and the entire range of social funds should be more biased to the countryside, enabling agriculture and the countryside to have more rapid development, and the peasants to have greater wealth. We can now at last truly construct harmony in Chinese society.

Note

* This chapter is based on my keynote address delivered at the annual meetings of Chinese Economist Society, July 1–4, 2006, Shanghai, China.

3   Twenty years' review and deliberation

The choice of priorities in reform *

Jiwei Lou

The current high-speed development of the Chinese economy, and constant raising of the people's standard of living, have already accumulated a great deal of national wealth and fiscal power, and formed a market economy system; but at the same time very many problems are in need of solution, such as disparities of income allocation, regional economic differentials, environmental pollution, etc. The requirement to build a harmonious society conforms extremely well to the reality of contemporary China; the problem is how the issues of disharmony we face are actually to be solved. Many scholars are now reconsidering China's reform path. Some argue that we have taken a wrong road, leading to the present disharmony. This truly is a major issue requiring earnest review and deliberation

3.1 Reform must open its own road

China's reform strategy is not the same as many eastern European transitional states, but I do not think the entire process was deliberately designed. From the entire decision-making process, China's reforms can be seen to have actually been a gradual process of "crossing a river by feeling the stones."

Starting with the rural reforms in 1978, then the urban reform that began to ferment in 1983, the core question was how to reform the economic system as a whole. The Third Plenum of the Twelfth National Party Congress in 1984 proposed to establish a planned commodity economy, whose confirmed operational model was "the state adjusts the market, while the market guides the enterprise." Such a model may be understood as the state adjusting total demand, setting the rules of the game, while resources are allocated by the market; it may also be understood as the state adjusting such market parameters as prices and interest rates, and thereby allocating resources. However it may look at present, I believe that in the historical circumstances of the time this outline was the best, emphasizing both market and government, was the most acceptable to all parties, and left space for experiments with reform.

Since the strategy of reform was "crossing the river by feeling the stones," the main standard of success was whether some systems were created, but how much welfare was delivered to the nation's citizens? The three main measures in rural reform were to implement the household contract system, abolish planned cropping, and greatly raise the price of grain while freeing up other farm prices. These measures introduced the market economy into the rural and agricultural domain, but it was the raising of peasants' incomes that signalled the success of the rural reforms, as agricultural production said farewell to the era of shortages, and market supplies boomed. The fact of the promotion of the welfare of the nation's citizens, paved the way for market-oriented reform.

After the commencement of comprehensive reform in 1984, it was still necessary for reform to make a road for itself. What then was the next step for reform? Should prices or enterprises be reformed first? Over 20 years ago this was profoundly discussed, and many internal debates were carried on. From published articles, we may see that one viewpoint was that price reform should come first, arguing that prices must first be allowed to reflect supply and demand, and further that prices must be freed up, allowing the market to play its role, thus enhancing the efficiency of resources allocation and accumulation of national wealth. Another viewpoint was that enterprise reform should come first, arguing that even though prices provided signals, if the enterprises (primarily state-owned enterprises at that time) did not reform, they would be insensitive to the price signals, and not reflect them, and price guidance would have no effect, hence enterprise reform must be carried out first.

How the order of priority in reform is selected requires us to examine the microeconomic foundation of China's reforms. It was not that we lacked the micro foundations for putting price reform first. Unlike the Soviet Union, China's planned economy was never a highly unified planned economy, but was one of moderate dispersal, multilayered delegation, and layered management. The state-owned enterprises (SOEs) were not all under the direct management of the central authorities, but divided into different levels of management. Moreover, since 1978, reform has also been carried out on a number of aspects of enterprises, for instance the SOEs retaining quite a lot of profit. This may have made China's SOEs sensitive to the price signal in the early reform period, but it also gave them an incentive to pursue profit. Giving priority to price reform, the micro foundation of market allocation of resources can exist (albeit in weak incentive form), and can guarantee to enhance the efficiency of resources allocation. It can further be seen that we should guarantee the interests of individuals, enterprises and the state are all promoted, thus enabling income distribution to be improved, so the price reform should be carried on in coordination with reform of taxation and finance.

If enterprise reform is adopted first, given the irregularity of price signals, the correct allocation of resources cannot be safeguarded, while at the same time other issues may be encountered. In the transition from a planned to a market economy, various institutional transformations including those of social consciousness, human relations, and so on are needed. If ideology is also thought of as an institution, then a genuinely functioning enterprise reform must at that time be an ideological breakthrough; for instance, the state-owned economy must withdraw from some economic domains and so on. However, high-risk reforms with uncertain outcomes cannot be adopted. I felt then that policy makers realized this point, and in 1986 commenced with reforms based primarily on price, taxation and finance. The central committee established a very high-level leading group, and I was at that time one of those in charge of the finance and taxation group within it. In 1987 this group's work stopped for a year, and in 1988 it carried out a new round of price reforms; but there was a problem about how this reform fitted with the other reforms: does price reform necessitate a tight monetary policy? From late 1987 the monetary policy was extremely relaxed; reform under these circumstances would definitely face the danger of inflation. The facts show that in 1988 price reform led immediately to inflation. I argue that there was a certain relationship between the loose monetary policy of the 1988 reforms together with the inflation to which this led, and the subsequent political disturbance.

In 1991 a decline appeared in the entire national economy, with economic growth at about 1 percent, and possibly negative. This has brought an advantage also, which was that prices loosened naturally, and were basically decided by the market. Price reform brought to completion in this way also left behind some flaws. In some very backward yet quite basic institutions such as the taxation system and Centre-regional financial relations, complementary reforms were never effectively carried out. The taxation system was still based on fixed prices; the annual increase of national financial revenue was then only 20 to 30 billion yuan, less than a week's revenue at present. Central finance was quite vacuous; money had to be lent to the regions to maintain their daily expenditure. Preparations for price, taxation, and financial reforms began in 1993. This was a systematic, fundamental reform, the results of which were extremely good. The reason that financial revenues have now grown so quickly, has a great deal to do with the foundations laid by that reform. The managed floating exchange rate system determined at that time has continued unbroken until now, an extremely radical, hugely risky, and highly controversial reform: foreign exchange reserves were at an all-time low of under $US 10 billion, should it be made tradeable in such circumstances? Was it not necessary to have strength before making it tradable? The policy makers accepted such views as, given that the mechanisms and rates of exchange were got right, there would naturally be foreign exchange reserves, and the amount stockpiled prior to reform would not be decisive.

In brief, the formation of the foundation for a market economy in China was hard-won, has created China's present prosperity, and is the institutional and material base whose weak links (will be) strengthened from now on. We may also see in retrospect that far from always being "self-aware," China's reforms are a process of constant learning and difficult exploration. More importantly, the extremely quick economic development that reform has brought caused the continuing enhancement of the citizens' welfare of and people's actual interests; reform became a force for development, and paved its own way.

3.2 China is walking the path of marketization

As mentioned above, the strategy of China's reforms is to "cross the river by feeling the stones", the reforms pave their own way, but looked at from the outside, China's reform path is not that clear. For example, western scholars describe China's reform path in terms of something called the "Beijing consensus," which in fact only describes a phenomenon, indicating that China is maintaining its own independent policy, while at the same time realizing high-speed economic growth and social progress. It is not a constructive analytical frame. Even though the "Washington consensus" comes in for a lot of criticism, it is a usable analytical frame indicating that establishing a market economy had to have to have three aspects: macroscopic economic stability, marketization, and access to the outside world. The concept of marketization is not too consistent, but basically it comprises three points: freedom of entry, enterprise reform, and prices that reflect supply-and-demand relations.

Analyzed objectively, China in fact realizes all three of the Washington consensus requirements. China's macroscopic economy has been continuously quite stable, and financial policy is also very prudent; economic prosperity benefits to a great extent from policy-making freedom, namely individual policy-making freedom, with prices basically decided through the market. The proportion occupied by state economy in the national economy, only about 30 percent, is not high; moreover, much of this consists of listed companies, which are unlike the state-owned enterprises of the era of the traditional planned economy. The Chinese economy is also extremely open, having consistently taken the path of opening to the outside world.

Not long ago I published an article in the journal *Bijiao* (Comparison) comparing the development and reforms of China and Russia, in which I stated that in classical or neoclassical economic terms, the three requirements of the "Washington consensus" are correct—there are indeed three basic essential factors of a market economy. We know of course that some international economists are at present unwilling to discuss the "Washington consensus" any more, arguing that it is not a well-founded concept and has led to calamitous consequences in the Eastern European transitional states.

My analysis is, if the "Washington consensus" is taken as a reform strategy, it seems to have grave faults; the issue lies in treating the goal as a process, and not considering the assumptions it requires. These assumptions are familiar to all, e.g. of infinite access to information, no necessary cost, monotonic production functions, etc., but in fact states with planned economies basically do not conform to these hypotheses. Next, it defines institutions too narrowly, never seeing that apart from the mode of resource allocation being an institution, there are very many institutions that determine resources allocation, including ideology, as previously mentioned. A simple example is the tax system: in the planned economy era the maintenance of state revenue depended mainly on enterprises handing over profits to the state. This was later transformed into handing over taxes and profits; "tax" refers to value added value tax and excise tax; "profit" refers to income tax. In fact, SOEs did not hand over profits. Now less and less is said about taxes and profits, but from this expression, traces may be seen of the tradition. This shows that in the transition of a nation from completely controlled allocation of resources, to a system whose basis is market allocation of resources and whose economic decision-making is individual, if the original system of state revenue collection is not changed, it will financially collapse; but again, for instance, contracts were in the past unnecessary for economic operations; under [central] planning, instructions to underlings were issued by decree, not contracted, whereas a market economy needs a contract system for its operations. In brief, making a transition from a system of state control of information collection and management under the mode of state allocation of resources to system decision-making and the institutions of market allocation of resources, requires the construction of mechanisms and institutions. In this aspect China has taken exactly the right path, and we emphasize this. The "Washington consensus" treats the result as the process, namely the three aspects reforms just mentioned have to be carried out at the same time; it neglects the environment they need to play their role, as well as a mode of information transmission, the cost, and time of transforming the function model, thus initiating calamitous consequences of reform.

Compared to the transitional states of eastern Europe, China's reforms are quite successful. This path was not deliberately designed: in fact some aspects of the early period of the reforms were passive rather than active. Many of the theories and analytic methods of modern economics were only gradually introduced into China later in the 1990s. Fortunately, some theoretical basis for many of our procedures may be found in modern economics; we may say we judged the situation realistically, and proactively sought where results-driven to walk the right road. For nearly half a century, economics has had major developments from the framework described in the early Washington consensus to modern macroeconomics and microeconomics, and China has consciously and subconsciously applied these developments; theories of informational, institutional, and development economics could all be practiced in China. The formulas that western economists bring to instruct transitional states do not actually use the achievements of recent developments in economics, but instead the most traditional, ancient things. While some recent achievements of the development of modern economics often analyse mature markets supposedly more suited to classical economic assumptions, and are used least of all in economical transitional states, precisely where they would have the most utility, the theories guiding transitional economies are oversimplified, and have too much ideological colouring. As I said at Edinburgh University, this can only be seen as tragic for economists.

3.3 Advance reform in a wider scope

Many of the problems appearing in China's current economic and social development are related to the path it has taken. We must speedily realize pricing freedom in things such as interest rates, exchange rates and commodities, and freedom of market entry. The lag in some reforms is considerable and, apart from problems of efficiency of resource allocation, there may also be many to do with income distribution. It is now necessary to make up for missed lessons.

The proposed new requirement for a socialist harmonious society places major pressure on financial departments. In overall terms, economic and social development in China are unbalanced: economic development is quite rapid, but the provision of public goods is quite weak; this is a lesson we must make up for. At this time, we must see if this is something to be done by finance or by the state. We need to divide the roles clearly, and demarcate the boundaries of market and government. Also, in the domains of primary distribution and redistribution, finance plays a role mainly in redistribution, whereas in the sphere of primary distribution it can only act as a supplement. Redistribution mainly solves starting point equity in income distribution; for example, the expenses of compulsory education in the countryside are borne by the state. Fairness of primary distribution is mainly decided by procedural fairness, meaning whether everyone has an equal opportunity to enter the market, and whether competition is equal. Procedural fairness will depend to a great extent on reforms in a variety of domains that should be should positively promoted by finance.

Building a socialist harmonious society requires sorting out the functional divisions of the various levels of government, then promoting balanced development, and enhancing the consistency and efficacy of policy. Finance is closely related to this field. In international terms, the Chinese government is the most decentralized, is the state with the greatest division of powers. In nearly all matters apart from foreign relations and national defence, we cannot distinguish which are functions of the Centre and which are regional; basically, all are cooperative between all levels of government.

In terms of proportions of public servants, Central officials account for over 30 percent of public servants in European countries, whereas in the more highly decentralized US they account for 16–17 percent, while Central authorities in China number little more than 30,000 people. Together with probably another 500,000 people in implementing agencies, Central public servants make up less than 7 percent, 10 percent less than in the USA and the smallest central government in the world. Comparing proportional expenditures, central expenditure accounts for 50–60 percent of national expenditures in the European countries. In England they account for 90 percent, in the USA nearly 50 percent, while in China they only account for 24 percent. In terms of these two proportional relationships, China is highly decentralized, with a large amount of government affairs handed over for completion by local authorities. We are also unusually centralized—the central authorities can define policy for the most basic unit government in all affairs. Some matters embodying the national interest have to be dealt with by the regions, which often take no interest, with the result that they cannot be dealt with properly, while the regions have insufficient resources for the things they are interested in doing. This kind of phenomenon is extremely common, leading to low levels of policy consistency and efficacy. The demarcation of government function and reform of operational mechanisms entail both financial and political reform, and are the foundation of political reform at higher levels. As may be seen from recently issued state documents, we do have very good guiding principles for reform. The question is, how to put them into operation.

Reviewing the course of reform, the basis on which we are building a socialist harmonious society can be seen more clearly; it can be more readily grasped that mere economic reform really is insufficient, and we have to consider reform issues in a wider scope. Today, I raise these issues for everyone's reference, and I hope everybody will apply theory coupled to China's realities, to carry out thorough research and to draw some valuable conclusions.

Note

* This chapter is based on my keynote address given at the annual meetings of Chinese Economist Society, July 1–4, 2006, Shanghai, China.

4 The course of China's rural reform

Runsheng Du

4.1 Reform was facilitated by crisis

For more than 20 years after the victory of the Chinese Revolution, radicalism was in the ascendant and private ownership of land was illegal. The peasantry became estranged from the land, so that when the Cultural Revolution ended, China's economy had been placed in difficulties and an agricultural crisis was induced. The population had grown, and food was in short supply. Per capita grain production never averaged much above 300 kilograms. Of the 800 million peasants, 250 million were impoverished. The nation as a whole could not achieve self-sufficiency in grain and required massive imports.

A turning point took place in 1978 with the Third Plenum of the 11th Central Committee of the CCP, which re-established the emancipation of the mind, the intellectual approach of seeking truth from facts, and the materialist philosophy proposition that practice is the sole standard of truth. It acknowledged that socialism means development of the productive forces, moving together toward wealth. The policy of making class struggle the key link was abolished, and the focus of Party work shifted to modernization. All of these changes liberated people from the previous ideological and institutional environment, providing the possibility of founding a new environment and new institutions.

Over the 30 years following the founding of the nation, an unfair pattern of holding resources had arisen, fostering the rise of vested interests. These interests tended to be conservative, holding back reform in the name of socialist ownership. The system itself suffered from inertia. Institutional economics speaks of institutional "path dependencies." The Chinese system had been following its accustomed path for a long time, and these conservative interests wanted to keep following it. They feared that order would fall into chaos if they left the old track, and the equation of socialism with the system of public ownership, which had been in existence for so long, was decisive. Then, peasants in Yongjia County in the region of Wenzhou, Zhejiang, and in Fengyang County, Anhui, seeking to end their food shortages, implemented a policy of contracting collective land to families. Because it violated what Mao Zedong had advocated, contracted production operated by peasant households had been a forbidden practice.

When I first proposed the household responsibility system (HRS), I was criticized as follows: Chairman Mao had been dead only a few years. Supporting the HRS, a system he opposed, meant forsaking his principles. This was the severe environment that reform faced at first. Our support of the HRS, of institutional innovation, and of transformation of the agents of the rural microeconomy would inevitably involve adjusting a number of interests. To avoid risk, it was necessary to carry out trials first. Also, the HRS could not move ahead on its own. It had to do so in connection with other institutions and be realized in the course of reforming the institutional environment as a whole; but this institutional reform is not something that could be accomplished in one fell swoop. To carry out reform, a strategy of gradual advance was unavoidable.

4.2 The cause of reform must strive to reduce resistance

All land and labor resources in China were held by hundreds of thousands of people's communes. On its appearance, the HRS policy shook the people's communes to the core. This assault on communal ownership was sure to encounter enormous resistance. The greater the impact, the greater this resistance would be. Hence, to promote the HRS and ward off its early demise, resistance to it had to be reduced as much as possible and facilitation boosted.

Three measures to reduce resistance were conceived: first, the reform would not initially call for abandoning the people's communes, but rather would implement a production responsibility system within them. This approach enabled many who would have opposed the change to accept it.

Second, the responsibility system could take a number of forms, among which the populace could choose. One did not impose one's own subjective preference on the populace but respected its choice. Later, it seemed that the masses were bent on choosing the household contract form. A popular saying to explain the system was "Household contract – keep straight on and don't turn back, hand over enough to the state, keep enough in the collective; whatever is left over is your own." The ideas were easy to understand, and the interest allocations were clear. The idea of letting the populace choose for itself also paid off in terms of checking the feasibility of reformers' initial positions.

Thirdly, the reform began in a limited region, where it received popular support, and then widened step by step. In the spring of 1979, the newly established National Agricultural Commission convened a conference with the seven major agricultural provinces in Beijing's Chongwenmen Hotel to discuss the responsibility system issue. Anhui was already experimenting with the HRS, but five of the seven provinces at the meeting disagreed with Anhui's approach. When CCP General Secretary Hua Guofeng held a

Politburo meeting to hear the report, he spoke of how Hunan villagers exchanged labor to help each other every sowing season or harvest, and he supported persisting with the collective approach; but he expressed approval for solitary households in mountainous areas, for whom collective activities were difficult, to adopt the HRS. The Central Committee relayed the "Summary of Discussions on Rural Work Questions" from the National Agricultural Commission's Party group, which continued to stipulate that "there will be no HRS" and "there will be no dividing the land to go it alone." Although people in areas with solitary households were not given explicit permission in the document to carry out the HRS, it was not forbidden either; they would not be subject to criticism and struggle or be corrected coercively. Once transmitted, the authorization of this document by Hua Guofeng opened a small window for the HRS.[1]

In 1980 the window grew wider. At that time, those regions with severe rural poverty became a heavy burden on the state. More provinces were moving from grain self-sufficiency to grain deficits, and fewer provinces had grain surpluses. The state held a long-term planning conference, and Yao Yilin, then director of the State Planning Commission, raised with me the question of how to reduce the problem of food shortages in impoverished regions. I suggested trying the HRS. If the peasants could solve the food problem themselves, they would no longer depend on purchased grain. Once land was contracted to a farmer, he could depend on his own land for food. Yao Yilin thought this made sense and reported as much to Deng Xiaoping, who agreed and declared, "Hardship regions are allowed to carry out the HRS. If it turns out to be mistaken and they come back in, it's nothing special. Rich regions that have enough to eat do not need to start right away."

In 1980, after the central leadership was reorganized on a collective basis, the top central leaders, including Deng Xiaoping and Hu Yaobang, consistently supported allowing different areas to adopt different forms of the agricultural production responsibility system. It was then proposed to divide them into three types of area: impoverished areas would carry out the HRS; advanced ones would adopt specialized contracts with wages linked to output; and intermediate regions could freely choose. In the autumn of 1980, the top leadership held a conference of Party Committee first secretaries of major provinces and cities to discuss the responsibility system, producing the "No. 75 Document," namely "Some Problems in Further Strengthening and Improving the Agricultural Production Responsibility System."[2] The tests had proved instantly effective. By the second year the impoverished areas had food to eat, and other areas too saw increased production. These facts convinced most people and opened the way for rural reform.

4.3 The Central Committee's five "No. 1 Documents"

In late 1981 the Central Committee held a national conference on rural work. Soon after the meeting, the Central Committee's No. 1 Document for 1982 (namely, the conference summary) was drafted and officially affirmed that management of the land by peasant households under the contract system would replace unified collective management by the people's communes. HRS, after 30 years of being proscribed, henceforth became central government policy. Reactions from the populace and cadres were excellent. Party Secretary Hu Yaobang said that the rural work document should again be placed "No. 1" the next year. For the next five years, the Central Committee's No. 1 Documents were all devoted to agricultural issues.[3] Topics for investigation were arranged early in the year, the findings were summarized in the autumn, and the document was drafted in the winter and sent out early the next year.

The first No. 1 Document, issued in 1982, pointed out that HRS was a legitimate policy reform and that this practice, along with other reforms, had been warmly welcomed by the populace and taken up nationally. This reform was the self-perfection of the socialist system; it was different from the private farming of the past and was not something to oppose, like capitalism. Public ownership of land and other means of production would be unchanging for a long time to come, as would the responsibility system. At the time peasants in many regions were worried, given that rural policy had been very changeable in the past (the Guangdong peasants were afraid of "relaxation in the first year, tightening up in the second, eating the words in the third"). They were also concerned that it was a temporary, "expedient" measure. Hence the phrase "unchanging for a long time" had the greatest impact on people's minds, and it was said that the No. 1 Document gave the peasants a "sedative."

Another main point of the document was its respect for people's choices: the populace was allowed to choose freely to suit different areas and conditions. Why was it not imposed as a unified solution? As recognized by institutional economics, forming a stable system must be a process in which the populace chooses for itself. This process includes different sides in mutual dialogue that leads to coordination and integration, according to the requirements of the interests and political pursuits of each side. Given that the Party wanted to give the populace a free choice, we did not need to turn this practice into a law of the state for the time being. We had to treat the law as the outcome of a social choice and eventually provide legal guarantees in the form of law. We needed to allocate one or two years to promote this change in society, and later it would become a national law. Such a process would help the country to absorb the advantages of both public ownership and individual management. The document also proposed sorting out the field of distribution, bringing unified purchasing and marketing within the reform agenda, and carrying on the reform of the price system at a steady pace. It also re-endorsed the development of diversified management of the rural economy and enterprises run by commune and production brigades. It proposed the new concept of specialized households, encouraging individuals and the private sector to engage in specialization and growth, and setting up a professional division of labor. For more than 20 years long-distance trading had been forbidden, as had privately operated or contractual procurement, in essence restricting the circulation of resources. The first No. 1 Document was rich in content, but more importantly, it abolished the forbidden area of HRS in the name of the Central Committee. When delivered to the Central Committee leaders for examination and approval, Deng Xiaoping said after reading it, "I completely agree." Chen Yun told his secretary to make a phone call, saying, "I've read this document. It's fine and will be supported by the cadres and people."

After its release, HRS spread nationwide, liberating both land and labor. In 1978, China's grain yield was approximately 300 billion kilograms. Over more than 20 years of collectivization, the state purchased between 30 and 35 billion kilograms of grain annually. The latitude for state procurement was so small that even if the state increased procurement by only 10 percent, peasants were not able to meet their grain rations. With system reform, grain output increased to 400 billion kilograms by 1984. At the same time, the value of gross agricultural output grew by 68 percent and the peasants' average income per person grew 166 percent. This achievement, which attracted worldwide attention, convinced cadres who held opposing views and unified the way people thought.

Closely following this reform, the comparative advantage of plentiful labor was enhanced by allowing the countryside to establish industry and commerce. The sudden appearance of new rural enterprises, together with foreign and private firms, formed a large non-state economic bloc, rectifying the overly simplified economic form that was a weakness of the public ownership system, and opening huge new sources for growth in peasant incomes. These changes inspired confidence and impelled economic reform throughout the nation.

The 12th National Party Congress was held in September 1982. In his Work Report, Hu Yaobang stated on behalf of the Central Committee that the various forms of the production responsibility system established in recent years in the countryside had liberated the productive forces and needed to be maintained for a long time. They could only gradually be improved on the basis of people's practical experience; in no way should they be rashly changed against the wishes of the people, nor should they be reversed, he said. Reporting to the Fifth National People's Congress on behalf of the State Council, Premier Zhao Ziyang reaffirmed that the output-linked contract system "effectively displays the superiority of the socialist economic system in rural China in the present stage."

In the same year, to consolidate and expand on the achievements of rural reform, in a speech written for the 12th National Party Congress on "Historic Shift in Rural Work," I gave an account of how household output contracting and household work contracting could embody the unification of public and private benefits and of near-term development and the distant goal of modernization. I said that the peasants required the present policies to be stabilized so that they could do well for several years and that I hoped the Party and the government could accept this request. It would help the peasants to escape the difficulties of their self-sufficient economy, by allowing them to produce commodities, to increase their cash income, and to seek their own all-round development.

I gave another speech entitled "Policy Must Continue to Bring Things to Life." While visiting Fujian, I had toured a chicken hatchery where 14 people had each invested 2,000 yuan. The workshop was 100 square meters and hatched 1.2 million chickens annually. Nearby there was a state farm, also with a chicken hatchery, where they had invested several hundred thousand yuan, but hatched only 500,000 chickens per year. I used what I had seen to show that at China's stage of economic development, keeping up economic growth and achieving overall benefits would be very difficult if investment depended only on government (central, or town and village) and if making a living depended on compensation according to work alone in this kind of simplified economic structure.

I argued for a basic structure of coexistence of a variety of economic forms, with public ownership in charge. I also argued for permitting distribution according to the factors of production invested, in addition to distributing income to citizens according to their work; that is, people should receive dividends according to the capital, land, and technology invested, in order to encourage them to increase savings and investment to make up for the shortage of state investment. I raised these issues in view of some disagreements from below about, for example, whether to allow private purchase of tractors and cars, operation of long-distance transport, and formation of partnerships to build fishponds with dividends paid according to stock held.

Here is an anecdote: a leading cadre in Hubei once drove after a private tractor driven by a peasant. When he caught up with him, he blamed the peasant, saying, "If I hadn't been chasing you in a car, you might have gotten away." The peasant replied, "Right! You know a car is faster than a tractor, I know a tractor is faster than an ox cart – so how come you can buy a car, but I can't buy a tractor?" The leading cadre couldn't answer. Party and government cadres claimed that tractors were producer goods, so they could only be publicly owned and could not be bought privately. Hence the No. 1 Document for 1983 (namely "Some Issues in Current Rural Economic Policy") proposed a further goal to strive for: the "Two Shifts and Three Bits." The two shifts were to shift agriculture from economic whole or part self-sufficiency to comparatively large-scale commodity production and to shift from traditional to modern agriculture. All levels of leading cadres in the Party and various government departments were supposed to make every effort to achieve three "bits": a bit more liberation of ideas, a bit bolder reform, and a bit more realistic attitude, to help speed up the two shifts.

In 1983 the pace of rural reform accelerated, and the changes it caused in economic life became more obvious. Household contracting spread to virtually all villages, and rural workers were liberated from their state of being left unused, as the approaches to commodity production were actively expanded. The marketed proportion of agriculture grew from the 51.5 percent of previous years to 59.9 percent. Output value reached 275.3 billion yuan, an increase of 129.9 billion yuan, or 90 percent, over 1978 levels.

In 1984 we proposed freeing up channels for trade so that competition could boost development. Whereas the first two No. 1 Documents had tried to solve problems of the micromanagement of agriculture and rural industry and commerce, in this case the target was fostering market mechanisms.

Developing commodity production requires free trade and fluid factors of production such as capital, land, and labor, and these ideas came into conflict with government policy. In the preceding 20 years a system of unified and fixed state purchases had been carried out in the countryside. Besides mandatory state purchase of three items (grain, cotton, and oil), this system also applied to another 132 items, including live pigs, eggs, sugar, silk thread, silkworm cocoons, yellow bluish dogbane, flue-cured tobacco, and aquatic products, which were purchased by assignment (that is, purchased amounts were subject to quotas, but at a relatively fair market price). It included virtually all agricultural supplementary and local products. For many items purchased by assignment, the quantity purchased accounted for more than 90 percent of the ultimate output. In fact, rural product transactions were monopolized by the public sector. The mobility of capital, land, and labor was institutionally limited by public ownership of the means of production and by the organization of people's communes, as well as by the enforced separation of city and countryside.

Following a thorough investigation, the Central Committee Rural Policy Research Department, which I directed, put together a written suggestion proposing a Central Secretariat conference to discuss this problem. Besides describing the situation, we stated that to help rural people develop commodity production and climb out of poverty, the rural economy urgently required relaxation of government monopolies, controls, and other regulations that had formed over many years and that were preventing peasants from entering the market. Specifically, we suggested the following:

1   The period of land contracts should be extended to 15 years, during which paid transfer of land use rights should be permitted.
2   The free flow of rural private funds should be allowed, combining the cooperative joint stock system with the buying of stock to earn dividends.
3   The peasants should be allowed to go to the cities to seek work, do business, and run enterprises and to be responsible for procuring their own grain ration at market prices.
4   Private individuals should be allowed to run enterprises and hire staff and management.
5   State-operated businesses and state-operated supply and marketing cooperatives should gradually open up to market transactions, withdraw

from their market monopolies, change their form of service, and return supply and marketing cooperatives to private operation.

Most of the leading comrades in attendance expressed support. Of the proposals, items (1), (2), and (3) passed without objection. Item 5 called for a reform of trade, marketing and sales, and financial agencies to occur all in one step with a reconsideration of the state monopoly on purchase and sale of grain. In the first step toward item 5, nearly all mandatory purchases were abolished, with only the grain, cotton, and oil monopolies retained. On the question of employees in item 4, Hu Qiaomu raised the issue of how to deal with party members who were also employers. After discussion, there was still no consensus, and a conclusion proved hard to reach. It was agreed by all that issues that were unclear could be laid aside for later review and handling. This was also a new policy. In the past, firms of eight or fewer employees were ruled not to be capitalist, whereas trials were implemented for firms of more than eight persons. After the meeting Deng Xiaoping was asked for instructions, and he said, "Don't be eager to set limits. Look at it again after three years." All of these principles were to form the contents of the No. 1 Document for 1984.

In 1985 the tasks were to adjust production structure and abolish unified purchasing and marketing. With simultaneous reform of the rural economy's microeconomic management agencies and macroeconomic market environment, China had seen fast growth of agricultural production in 1984. Regarding food grain, that topmost of top priorities, the situation changed from "when you hold grain, your heart feels no pain" to "grain supplies higher, but hard to find buyers." Following an observation trip to the country with Hu Yaobang, I concluded that the cheapness of grain was hurting the peasantry. On the basis of the existing structure of agricultural production, it was impossible to carry out the task of doubling their income, and a new production structure needed to be built. The main issue was that reform of the agricultural procurement system lagged behind the new requirements for rural economic development, causing various provinces to want to guarantee the area sown to grain and obstructing peasants' arrangements for cultivation to meet the needs of the market. For example, even Hainan proposed being self-sufficient in grain, when in fact planting tropical cash crops, which could be exchanged for imported grain through foreign trade, would have been more worthwhile and more popular with the peasants. Increasing production of some goods for foreign exchange in China's southern region and bringing in grain from outside the region would help the North raise its grain yield and increase its income. Then the two regions could both make the most of local conditions.

Everyone was clear on this principle. The problem was that the monopoly procurement institutions in agriculture had been around for a long time. Inertia was strong, and change was difficult. Fortunately, just then the decision on economic reform emerging from the Third Plenary Session of the

12th Central Committee was favorable toward reconstructing the urban and rural relationship, and reform of the system of unified procurement and adjustments to the industrial structure were made central agenda items of the rural reforms in 1985.

In support of these reforms, we proposed a range of tasks such as developing forestry, enhancing transport, supporting rural enterprises, encouraging technological progress, promoting free movement of talented people, enlivening financial markets, perfecting the rural cooperative system, strengthening the building of small cities, and developing the foreign trade-oriented economy. The No. 1 Document for 1985 was entitled "On 10 Policies to Further Enliven the Rural Economy."

In 1986 we increased investment in agriculture and adjusted the urban–rural relationship and the industrial–agricultural relationship. In 1985 the uniform grain procurement system had been changed to contract purchasing. Beyond the contract, purchases negotiated with the government changed to market purchases. Of 132 agricultural products that had been subject to state procurement, only silk thread, medical materials, and tobacco stayed that way, whereas transactions and price setting for the rest were through the market. This reform was originally a thorough one with straightforward goals. Problems arose, however, from raising the grain purchase price without correspondingly raising the price at which it would be sold to city people. Thus, the more grain production increased, the greater the financial subsidy, and massive increases of grain bought at higher prices created a burden too heavy for the state finances to bear. Given the state's inertia in maintaining the distribution of interests – and thus in maintaining the superior status of urban non-agricultural groups – the state sought to lighten its financial burden by reducing the preferential trade terms for the peasants. The concrete measure was a ruling in 1985 to cancel the policy of paying 50 percent more for the grain procured beyond the contract amount and instead to purchase all grain at an increased average price. Although in static terms "three in the morning and four in the evening" is no different from "four in the morning and three in the evening," dynamically this change greatly weakened the role of the procurement policy in stimulating increased grain production. The comparative advantage of sowing farmland with grain dropped, making the peasants who had already shed their collective fetters unwilling to plant more crops. Peasants in Hebei said planting a mou (Chinese unit of land) of wheat was inferior to driving a small flock: the "two types of households" (specialized and primary households in agriculture production) were no match for the burdens caused by the "three households" (referring to three government agencies: industry and commerce administration, taxation, and public security). Many peasants began to diversify their farming activities, start businesses, or leave for the city to work.

The injury to the peasants' interests was reflected immediately in reduced supplies of grain and other agricultural products, producing fluctuations in agricultural, and especially grain, production from then on for years. There were different views at that time about whether this situation was a result of reforms not going far enough or going too far. It was argued that the potential of the HRS had dried up – hence the fluctuation in grain production. Events were to prove this viewpoint wrong.

After developing for several years, supply and demand relations in the national economy changed. Restricted by the Engels coefficient,[4] the growth of residents' expenditures on food was slow, but market exchanges displayed rising costs for agriculture and the margin from trade dropped. In view of this, rural work deployment at the end of 1985 emphasized "putting the status of agriculture in the national economy straight." The top leadership's No. 1 Document for 1986 (namely "On Deployment of Rural Work in 1986") made a commitment to increase investment in agriculture and water facilities and to guarantee a rise in grain production to 450 billion kilograms, starting with the Seventh Five-Year Plan. Part of the income tax turned in by town and village enterprises was assigned for use in supporting agriculture, stabilizing prices of agricultural inputs such as chemical fertilizer, diesel oil, agricultural chemicals, and machinery, and guaranteeing that original subsidies would not vary. These funds have also gone to strengthen technical support of agricultural and rural enterprises and to support grain and export commodities, mainly by introducing new varieties and improving infrastructure. They have also been used to implement the Spark Program, which supports the technological change of rural enterprises by, for instance, designing 100 kinds of complete technical equipment, establishing 500 demonstration enterprises, and promoting them nationally after they yielded practical results, as well as supporting large numbers of technical training and administrative personnel.

In setting out the status and function of agriculture in the national economy, the document stressed agriculture's indispensability as an industry that provides food needed by all human beings. Moreover, in contemporary China, agriculture was the physical foundation that 900 million people depended on for survival and development, and thus was also the economic bastion of the nation's social stability and unity. Yet agriculture was a vulnerable industry, hampered by both natural disasters and market competition. A suitable environment advantageous to its gestation and growth, and systems that guaranteed support, needed to be created for it. These were precisely the topics in need of more work after the problem of micro-level agency had been solved by the rural reforms.

4.4 Political reform admits of no delay

Further reform of Chinese agriculture involves reform of the urban state-owned economy and of the political system. To use a phrase of that time, regarding China's rural reform, all "cheap" methods had been exhausted. If the deep structure was left untouched, no further progress could be made. For just this reason, the historical mission of the series of No. 1 Documents on rural reform was brought to a halt. China's rural reforms were by no means complete but had to seek a path of advancement through the overall reform of the national economy.

Reviewing more than 20 years of rural reform in China, there were no major deviations, only a relapse in understanding initiated by the June 4, 1989, "disturbance." This temporary blockage to understanding was fortunately unable to change the institutional foundation of land management by household contract. All statesmen in power need to treat food security as vital to overall stability. The idea that "first there must be food to eat, next one must build" had become a consensus for a great many leading cadres. In the urban reforms commencing in 1984, market adjustment mechanisms were prepared for introduction. In 1984 the system of price setting by the state changed to a system of price setting by the market. The Central Committee re-examined the decision on this matter at the 1987 Beidaihe meeting, but that year saw poor harvests, price rises, and panic buying in the cities, and people's minds fluctuated. Another factor causing popular dissatisfaction was widespread corruption. Reform of the price mechanism had to be temporarily put aside.

If we had achieved systems of economic and political democracy on time, then when reform led to an essential adjustment of interests, society would have had a stronger mental and physical coping capacity; but in this area knowledge is easy, and practice difficult.

In 1992 Deng Xiaoping traveled to the South and gave a series of speeches that prevented reform relapse and made the reform agenda clearer. The new Central Party Committee General Secretary Jiang Zemin visited Anhui, announcing that the family contract system would not change. The central government made the decision that contracts for land last for 30 years. If needed, this period could be extended further.

There have already been 25 years of rural reform. How will reform deepen, and how will the land system be improved? In particular, how can the family contract system for public land be perfected, maintaining the intimate relationship between peasants and the land, while exploring mutual cooperation and strengthening market competitiveness? These are important questions.

Compared with economic reform, political system reform lags behind. There is a lack of democratic surveillance, which leads to polarization and inequitable distribution. The fruits of reform fall into the hands of the privileged, affecting the income earned by the populace. Moreover, opportunities to own resources are unfairly distributed. The right to control a huge amount of public property is not accompanied by adequate surveillance and democratic participation. In a time of economic transition, there is an inevitable appearance of working for one's own interests under the guise of working for the public, and thus, of the erosion of resources. Political system reform must therefore be initiated, carrying forward democracy, implementing the rule of law, respecting the various rights enjoyed by the people, and guaranteeing that the masses can equitably enjoy the outcomes of economic restructuring.

Decision making regarding important matters touching the interests of the populace should be guaranteed to be public, just, and equitable. Therefore, government function must be regulated by law and a service government must be established.

Notes

1 For more information about this period, see Kathleen Hartford, "Socialist Agriculture Is Dead, Long Live Socialist Agriculture! Organizational Transformations in Rural China," in Elizabeth J. Perry and Christine Wong, eds, *The Political Economy of Reform in Post-Mao China* (Cambridge, MA: Harvard University Press, 1985).
2 See http://news.xinhuanet.com/ziliao/2005–02/04/content_2547020.htm.
3 Whereas these policy documents had in the past been numbered chronologically each year, in 1981 the Central Committee began to use the label "No. 1 Document" to show that a policy was a top priority. After five years, the Committee returned to a chronological numbering system, and the label "No. 1 Document" indicated no special priority.
4 The ratio of food spending to overall household expenses.

Part II
Poverty and inequality

5 China's (uneven) progress against poverty

Martin Ravallion and Shaohua Chen [1]

Abstract

While the incidence of extreme poverty fell dramatically in China over 1980–2001, progress was uneven over time and across provinces. Rural areas accounted for the bulk of the gains to the poor, though migration to urban areas helped. Rural economic growth was far more important to national poverty reduction than urban economic growth; agriculture played a far more important role than the secondary or tertiary sources of GDP. Taxation of farmers and inflation hurt the poor; local government spending helped them in absolute terms; external trade had little short-term impact. Provinces starting with relatively high inequality saw slower progress against poverty, due both to lower growth and a lower growth elasticity of poverty reduction.

5.1 Introduction

This paper aims to document and explain China's record against poverty over the two decades following Deng Xiaoping's initiation of pro-market reforms in 1978. We apply new poverty lines to newly assembled distributional data – much of which has not previously been analyzed – and we address some of the data problems that have clouded past estimates and point to some continuing concerns about the data. We thus aim to offer the longest and most internally consistent series of national poverty and inequality measures, spanning 1980–2001. While data are less complete at the provincial level, we can estimate trends since the mid-1980s.

Armed with these new measures, we address some long-standing questions in development economics, applied to the Chinese setting. How much do poor people share in the gains from economic growth? Does the sectoral and geographic pattern of growth matter? What role is played by urbanization? How did initial distribution influence subsequent rates of growth and poverty reduction? How important are economic policies?

Our principal findings are as follows:

Finding 1: China has made huge overall progress against poverty, but it has been uneven progress. In the 20 years after 1981, the proportion of the population living in poverty fell from 53 to 8 percent. However, there were many setbacks for the poor. Poverty reduction stalled in the late 1980s and early 1990s, recovered pace in the mid-1990s, but stalled again in the late 1990s. Half of the decline in the number of poor came in the first half of the 1980s. Some provinces saw far more rapid progress against poverty than others.

Finding 2: Inequality has been rising, though not continuously and more so in some periods and provinces. In marked contrast to most developing countries, relative inequality is higher in China's rural areas than in urban areas. However, there has been convergence over time with a steeper increase in inequality in urban areas. Relative inequality between urban and rural areas has not shown a trend increase over the period as a whole, once one allows for the higher increase in the urban cost of living. Absolute inequality has increased appreciably. both between and within both urban and rural areas, and absolute inequality is higher in urban areas.

Finding 3: The pattern of growth matters. While migration to urban areas has helped reduce poverty nationally, the bulk of the reduction in poverty came from rural areas. Growth in the primary sector (primarily agriculture) did more to reduce poverty and inequality than either the secondary or tertiary sectors. Starting in 1981, if the same aggregate growth rate had been balanced across sectors, it would have taken 10 years to bring the poverty rate down to 8 percent, rather than 20 years. The geographic composition of growth also mattered. While provinces with higher rural income growth tended to have higher poverty reduction, growth was not higher in the provinces where it would have had the most impact on poverty nationally. The pattern of growth also mattered to the evolution of overall inequality. Rural and (in particular) agricultural growth brought inequality down; urban economic growth was inequality increasing. Rural economic growth reduced inequality in *both* urban and rural areas, as well as between them.

Finding 4: Economy-wide policies have had a mixed record. Agrarian reforms and lower taxes on farmers (notably though public procurement policies) have helped reduce poverty. Controlling inflation has also been pro-poor, both absolutely and relatively. Public spending has reduced poverty, but not inequality, and the gains have tended to come from provincial and local government spending not central spending. The score-card for trade reform is blank; we find no evidence that greater external openness was poverty reducing.

Finding 5: Inequality has emerged as a concern for both growth and poverty reduction. With the same growth rate and no rise in inequality in rural areas, the number of poor in China would have fallen to less than one-quarter of its actual value (a poverty rate in 2001 of 1.5 percent rather than 8 percent). This calculation would be deceptive if the rise in inequality was the "price" of high economic growth, which did help reduce poverty. However, we find no evidence of such an aggregate trade off. The periods of more rapid growth did not bring more rapid increases in inequality. Nor did provinces with more rapid rural income growth experience a steeper increase in inequality. Thus provinces that saw a more rapid rise in inequality saw *less* progress against poverty, not more. Over time, poverty has also become far more responsive to rising inequality. At the outset of China's transition period, levels of poverty were so high that inequality was not a major concern. That has changed. Furthermore, even without a further rise in inequality, the historical evidence suggests that more unequal provinces will face a double handicap in future poverty reduction; they will have lower growth *and* poverty will respond less to that growth.

5.2 Data on income poverty and inequality in China

We draw on the Rural Household Surveys (RHS) and the Urban Household Surveys (UHS) of China's National Bureau of Statistics (NBS).[2] NBS ceased doing surveys during the Cultural Revolution (1966–76) and stated afresh in 1978; the earliest distributional data available to us are for 1980 (for rural areas) and 1981 (urban). While all provinces were included from 1980, 30 percent had sample sizes in the surveys for the early 1980s that NBS considered too small for estimating distributional statistics (though still adequate for the mean). However, this does not appear to be a source of bias; we could not reject the null hypothesis that the first available estimates of our poverty measures were the same for these "small sample" provinces as the rest.[3]

Sample sizes for the early surveys were smaller; 16,000 households were interviewed for the 1980 RHS and about 9,000 for the 1981 UHS. Sample sizes increased rapidly, with 30,000 households in the RHS for 1983. Since 1985, the surveys have had samples of 68,000 in rural areas and 30–40,000 in urban areas. Though smaller, the sample sizes for the early 1980s are still adequate for measuring poverty nationally (they are larger samples than for many national surveys). Also, the Chinese economy was far less diversified in the early 1980s than now, particularly in rural areas where there was very little non-farm activity and less diversity in farm output than now. The more homogeneous rural economy of the early 1980s can be represented with smaller samples. Against this, it can be conjectured that the earliest surveys under-represented remote rural areas that the statistical officers would have had a hard time reaching – probably leading us to underestimate poverty measures for this period.

An unusual feature of these surveys is that their sample frames are based on China's registration system rather than the population census. This means that someone with rural registration who has moved to an urban area (but kept rural registration) is missing from the sample frame. Migrants from rural areas gain from higher earnings (the remittances back home are captured in the RHS), but are probably poorer on average than registered urban residents. Against this likely source of downward bias in poverty estimates from the UHS, the UHS income aggregates do not capture fully the value of the various entitlements and subsidies received exclusively by urban residents, though these have been of declining importance over time.

While NBS has selectively made the micro data (for some provinces and years) available to outside researchers, the complete data are not available to us for any year. Instead we use tabulations of the income distribution following a standardized design in which households are ranked by income per person and all fractiles are population weighted. The majority of these data are unpublished and were provided by NBS.[4] The income aggregates include imputed values for income from own-production, but exclude imputed rents for owner-occupied housing. (Imputation is difficult, given the thinness of housing markets.) The usual limitations of income as a welfare indicator remain. For example, our measures of inequality between urban and rural residents may not adequately reflect other inequalities, such as in access to public services (health, education, water and sanitation – all of which tend to be better provided in urban areas).

There was a change in valuation methods for consumption of own-farm production in the RHS in 1990 when public procurement prices were replaced by local selling prices. (Past estimates have used the "old prices" for the 1980s and the "new prices" for 1990 onwards, ignoring the change.) Until the mid-1990s, public procurement prices for grain were held below market prices. Using these prices to value own consumption overestimates poverty.[5] This practice was largely abandoned from 1990s onwards in favor of using local selling prices for valuation. Using the old valuation method, the imputed value of food consumed from own-farm production accounted for 21.8 percent of aggregate net rural income in 1990; under the new valuation method this rose to 27.4 percent for the same year (RSO 2002); this came almost entirely from a 37.2 percent increase in the imputed value of food consumption in kind for 1990.

While these numbers make clear that there was a substantial change in 1990, not all provinces switched fully to market prices from 1990 onwards. From our discussions with NBS staff is appears that a few provinces (three–five) used a mixture of procurement prices and market prices up to the mid-1990s. Two reasons were given. First, provincial authorities thought that market prices would overvalue consumption from own farm products on the grounds that farmers tend to sell their better quality grain; this is not likely to be a serious source of bias for the poor, given that they tend to consume a large share of their product (Chen and Ravallion, 1996). Second, it was thought that local officials in some poor counties were worried that higher measured incomes would mean fewer public resources from the center; this would entail overestimation of poverty measures in the affected provinces.[6]

With complete access to the micro data we could readily eliminate the inconsistencies in valuation methods over time and across provinces.[7] Without the micro data we have to find an alternative method. To help us correct for the change in valuation methods in 1990, NBS provided tabulations of the distribution in 1990 by both methods, allowing us to estimate what the income distributions for the late 1980s would have looked like if NBS had used the new valuation method. The Appendix describes the correction method in detail. Our corrections entail lower poverty measures in the late 1980s.

In measuring poverty from these surveys, we use two poverty lines. One is the longstanding "official poverty line" for rural areas of 300 Yuan per person per year at 1990 prices. (There is no comparable urban poverty line.) It has been argued by many observers that this line is too low to properly reflect prevailing views about what constitutes "poverty" in China. It can hardly be surprising that in such a rapidly growing economy, perceptions of what income is needed to not be considered poor will rise over time.[8]

In collaboration with the authors, NBS has been developing a new set of poverty lines that appears to better reflect current conditions. Region-specific food bundles are used, with separate food bundles for urban and rural areas, valued at median unit values by province. The food bundles are based on the actual consumption of those between the poorest 15th percentile and the 25th percentile nationally. These bundles are then scaled to reach 2100 calories per person per day, with 75 percent of the calories from foodgrains.[9] Allowance for non-food consumption are based on the nonfood spending of households in a neighborhood of the point at which total spending equals the food poverty line in each province (and separately for urban and rural areas). The methods closely follow Chen and Ravallion (1996).

For measuring poverty nationally we have simply used the means of these regional lines. With a little rounding off, we chose poverty lines of 850 yuan per year for rural areas and 1200 Yuan for urban areas, both in 2002 prices. (Ideally one would build up all national poverty measures by applying the regional poverty lines to the provincial distributions and then aggregating. However, this would entail a substantial loss of information given that we have only 10–12 years of rural data at province level.) We use the 2002 differential between the urban and rural lines to calculate an urban equivalent to the 300 yuan rural line at 1990 prices.

Finally, we convert to prices at each date using the rural and urban consumer price indices (CPI) produced by NBS. For rural areas, there is a concern that the rural prices collected by NBS relate to markets in close proximity to urban centers. (We do not have hard evidence of this but the possibility was noted by provincial NBS offices in our interviews.) We return to this point in the next section.

We also use these urban and rural poverty lines as deflators for urban–rural cost-of-living (COL) adjustments in forming aggregate inequality measures and for measuring inequality between urban and rural areas. Past work in the literature on inequality in China has ignored the COL difference between urban and rural areas, and we will see that this does matter. However, our COL adjustments are not ideal, in that a common deflator is applied to all levels of income.

We provide three poverty measures: The *headcount index* (H) is the percentage of the population living in households with income per person below the poverty line. The *poverty gap index* (PG) gives the mean distance below the poverty line as a proportion of that line (the mean is taken over the whole population, counting the non-poor as having zero gap.) For the *squared poverty gap index* (SPG) the individual poverty gaps are weighted by the gaps themselves, so as to reflect inequality amongst the poor (Foster et al. 1984). For all three, the aggregate measure is the population-weighted mean of the measures across any complete partition of the population into subgroups. Datt and Ravallion (1992) describe our methods for estimating the Lorenz curves and calculating these poverty measures from the grouped data provided by the NBS tabulations.

5.3 Poverty measures for China 1981–2001

The urban population share rose from 19 percent in 1980 to 39 percent in 2002 (Table 5.1).[10] This may be a surprisingly high pace of urbanization, given that there were governmental restrictions on migration (though less so since the mid-1990s).[11] We do not know how much this stemmed from urban

Table 5.1 Summary statistics

	Urban pop. share (%)	Urban–rural COL diff.	Rural	Mean household income per person* Urban	National	Mean (adjusted for COL differential)* Urban	National
1980	19.39	19.35	191.33	n.a.	n.a.	n.a.	n.a.
1981	20.16	19.42	218.19	486.28	272.24	407.20	256.29
1982	21.13	19.50	258.86	514.94	312.97	430.92	295.22
1983	21.62	20.09	292.46	536.94	345.32	447.10	325.89
1984	23.01	20.03	326.35	598.46	388.96	498.59	365.98
1985	23.71	23.20	368.18	604.06	424.11	490.32	397.14
1986	24.52	26.67	377.29	686.49	453.11	541.97	417.67
1987	25.32	29.74	388.74	702.93	468.29	541.78	427.49
1988	25.81	33.30	391.83	686.51	467.89	515.01	423.62
1989	26.21	29.99	363.83	687.38	448.63	528.79	407.07
1990	26.41	25.94	357.20	744.90	459.59	591.48	419.07
1991	26.94	29.38	360.48	798.11	478.38	616.87	429.55
1992	27.46	34.23	381.03	875.78	516.89	652.44	455.56
1993	27.99	37.10	394.00	959.18	552.19	699.61	479.54
1994	28.51	38.90	423.05	1040.88	599.19	749.37	516.08
1995	29.04	38.08	465.25	1091.69	647.17	790.63	559.74
1996	30.48	39.24	526.41	1133.63	711.49	814.17	614.12
1997	31.91	40.05	557.32	1172.58	753.65	837.24	646.64
1998	33.35	40.62	582.30	1240.19	801.71	881.95	682.23
1999	34.78	40.90	604.39	1355.87	865.75	962.27	728.86
2000	36.22	42.17	616.79	1442.99	916.04	1014.95	761.00
2001	37.66	42.03	642.57	1565.20	990.03	1102.00	815.59
2002	39.09	41.18	674.92	1775.41	1105.10.	1257.58	902.67

* Yuan/person/year at 1980 prices.

expansion into rural areas versus actual migration from rural to urban areas.

The cost-of-living differential rises over time, from 19 to 41 percent in 2002. The divergence between urban and rural inflation rates started in the mid-1980s. It could well reflect the impact of urbanization on the prices of commodities that are not traded between sectors, such as housing and services.[12] The (partial) removal of subsidies on urban commodities (including services) could also have shown up in a higher rate of inflation in urban areas. Given that the urban rate of inflation exceeded the rural rate, the aforementioned possibility of an "urban bias" in the rural CPI (section 2) suggests that we may have underestimated the rate of rural poverty reduction since the mid-1980s.

Table 5.1 also gives our estimates of mean income for rural and urban areas. The large disparities in mean incomes between urban and rural areas echo a well-known feature of the Chinese economy, though our COL adjustment narrows the differential considerably.[13] We will return in section 5 to discuss the implications for urban–rural inequality.

Table 5.2 gives our rural poverty measures. Table 5.3 gives our estimates for

Table 5.2 Poverty in rural China, 1980–2001

	Poverty measures (%)					
	Old poverty line			New poverty line*		
	H	*PG*	*SPG*	*H*	*PG*	*SPG*
1980	40.65	10.30	3.67	75.70	26.51	11.95
1981	28.62	6.84	2.35	64.67	19.99	8.44
1982	17.33	3.66	1.10	47.78	12.85	4.95
1983	13.34	2.50	0.65	38.38	9.89	3.63
1984	9.87	1.58	0.35	30.93	7.51	2.58
1985	8.82	1.46	0.34	22.67	5.23	1.71
1986	9.85	1.92	0.52	23.50	5.99	2.16
1987	8.29	1.44	0.35	21.91	5.33	1.83
1988	7.99	1.31	0.35	23.15	5.52	1.89
1989	11.88	2.38	0.66	29.17	7.98	3.05
1990	10.55	1.85	0.44	29.18	7.60	2.76
1991	11.66	2.84	1.17	29.72	8.52	3.43
1992	9.83	2.22	0.86	28.18	7.59	3.03
1993	11.29	2.42	0.71	27.40	7.84	3.13
1994	10.41	2.74	1.00	23.32	7.24	3.19
1995	7.83	2.13	1.01	20.43	5.66	2.16
1996	4.20	1.13	0.58	13.82	3.55	1.50
1997	4.83	0.80	0.18	13.33	3.45	1.23
1998	3.24	0.36	0.05	11.58	2.61	0.81
1999	3.43	0.42	0.07	11.40	2.66	0.85
2000	5.12	0.95	0.24	12.96	3.55	1.33
2001	4.75	0.81	0.19	12.49	3.32	1.21

* Poverty line is 850 yuan per person per year in 2002; rural CPI used to deflate.

Table 5.3 Poverty in urban China, 1981–2002

	Poverty measures (%)					
	Old poverty line			New poverty line*		
	H	PG	SPG	H	PG	SPG
1981	0.82	0.22	0.14	6.01	1.01	0.35
1982	0.15	0.03	0.02	2.16	0.27	0.07
1983	0.12	0.03	0.01	1.56	0.20	0.05
1984	0.29	0.08	0.05	1.27	0.23	0.09
1985	0.23	0.07	0.05	1.08	0.21	0.09
1986	0.22	0.00	0.00	3.23	0.46	0.09
1987	0.78	0.31	0.30	1.62	0.48	0.33
1988	0.77	0.26	0.20	2.07	0.50	0.27
1989	3.66	1.49	0.86	7.05	2.72	1.55
1990	0.75	0.33	0.33	2.58	0.24	0.03
1991	0.00	0.00	0.00	1.66	0.53	0.38
1992	0.00	0.00	0.00	1.13	0.36	0.26
1993	0.50	0.16	0.11	1.01	0.25	0.14
1994	0.47	0.16	0.11	1.19	0.30	0.15
1995	0.31	0.13	0.11	0.85	0.24	0.15
1996	0.18	0.07	0.06	0.61	0.16	0.09
1997	0.20	0.09	0.08	0.70	0.19	0.11
1998	0.00	0.00	0.00	1.16	0.43	0.34
1999	0.00	0.00	0.00	0.57	0.18	0.12
2000	0.20	0.09	0.08	0.63	0.18	0.11
2001	0.00	0.00	0.00	0.50	0.16	0.11
2002	0.00	0.00	0.00	0.54	0.24	0.22

* Poverty line is 1200 yuan per person per year in 2002; urban CPI used to deflate.

urban areas. For all years and all measures, rural poverty incidence exceeds urban poverty, and by a wide margin. Rural poverty measures show a strong downward trend, though with some reversals, notably in the late 1980s, early 1990s and in the last two years of our series. The urban measures also show a trend decline, though with even greater volatility.

Table 5.4 gives the national aggregates and Figure 5.1 plots the national headcount indices for both poverty lines. By the new lines, the headcount index falls from 53 percent in 1981 to 8 percent in 2001. Conservatively assuming the 1981 urban number for 1980, the national index was 62 percent in 1980. There was more progress in some periods than others. There was a dramatic decline in poverty in the first few years of the 1980s. The bulk of this decline came from rural areas. By our new poverty line, the rural poverty rate fell from 65 percent in 1981 (76 percent in 1980) to 23 percent in 1985 (Table 5.2). On weighting by the rural population share, this accounts for 77 percent of the decline in the national poverty rate between 1981 and 2001. By contrast, the late 1980s and early 1990s were a difficult period for China's

Table 5.4 Poverty in China as a whole, 1981–2001

| | Poverty measures (%) | | | | | |
| | Old poverty line | | | New poverty line* | | |
	H	PG	SPG	H	PG	SPG
1981	23.02	5.51	1.90	52.84	16.17	6.81
1982	13.70	2.89	0.87	38.14	10.19	3.92
1983	10.48	1.96	0.52	30.42	7.80	2.85
1984	7.67	1.24	0.28	24.11	5.83	2.01
1985	6.78	1.13	0.27	17.55	4.04	1.33
1986	7.49	1.45	0.40	18.53	4.63	1.65
1987	6.39	1.15	0.33	16.77	4.10	1.45
1988	6.13	1.04	0.31	17.71	4.23	1.47
1989	9.73	2.15	0.71	23.37	6.60	2.65
1990	7.96	1.45	0.41	22.15	5.65	2.04
1991	8.52	2.08	0.85	22.16	6.37	2.61
1992	7.13	1.61	0.63	20.75	5.61	2.27
1993	8.27	1.79	0.54	20.01	5.72	2.29
1994	7.58	2.00	0.74	17.01	5.26	2.32
1995	5.65	1.55	0.75	14.74	4.08	1.58
1996	2.97	0.81	0.42	9.79	2.52	1.07
1997	3.35	0.58	0.15	9.30	2.41	0.87
1998	2.16	0.24	0.04	8.10	1.88	0.65
1999	2.24	0.27	0.05	7.63	1.79	0.60
2000	3.34	0.64	0.18	8.49	2.33	0.89
2001	2.96	0.51	0.12	7.97	2.13	0.80

* Population-weighted means of poverty measures from Tables 5.4 and 5.5.

poor. Progress was restored around the mid-1990s, though the late 1990s saw a marked deceleration, with signs of rising poverty in rural areas.[14]

We can decompose the change in national poverty into a "population shift effect" and a "within sector" effect.[15] Letting P_t denote the poverty measure for date t, while P_t^i is the measure for sector $i = u,r$ (urban, rural), with corresponding population shares n_t^i, we can write an exact decomposition of the change in poverty between $t = 1981$ and $t = 2001$ as:

$$P_{01} - P_{81} = [n_{01}^r (P_{01}^r - P_{81}^r) + n_{01}^u (P_{01}^u - P_{81}^u)] + [(P_{81}^u - P_{81}^r)(n_{01}^u - n_{81}^u)] \qquad (1)$$

$$\underbrace{\qquad\qquad\qquad\qquad}_{\substack{\textit{Within-sector} \\ \textit{effect}}} \qquad \underbrace{\qquad\qquad\qquad}_{\substack{\textit{Population shift} \\ \textit{effect}}}$$

The within-sector effect is the change in poverty weighted by the final year population shares while the population shift effect measures the contribution of urbanization, weighted by the initial urban–rural difference in poverty measures. The "population shift effect" should be interpreted as the *partial* effect of urban–rural migration, in that it does not allow for any

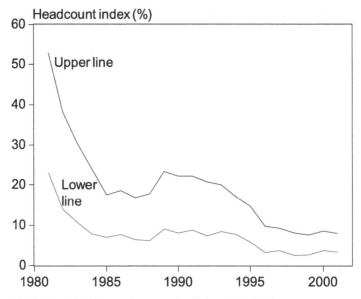

Figure 5.1 National incidence of poverty in China 1981–2001.

effects of migration and remittances on poverty levels within urban and rural areas.[16] For example, urbanization may be an indirect cause of higher rural incomes, but this would not be revealed by the decomposition in (1). Thus it is a descriptive decomposition rather than causal. (Our regression-based decomposition in the next section will be better able to pick up indirect effects.)

Table 5.5 gives the decomposition based on equation (1). We find that 35 percent points of the 45 percent point decline in the national headcount index is accountable to the within-sector term; within this, 33 percent points was due to falling poverty within rural areas while only 2 percent points was due to falling poverty in urban areas. The population shift from rural to urban areas accounted for 10 percent points. The other poverty measures tell a very similar story, though the rural share is slightly higher for SPG than PG, and lowest for H. As can be seen from the lower panel of Table 5.5, the pattern is also similar for the period 1991–2001, the main difference being that the "within-urban" share falls to zero using the old poverty line, with the rural share rising to around 80 percent.

So we find that 75–80 percent of the drop in national poverty incidence is accountable to poverty reduction within the rural sector; most of the rest is attributable to urbanization of the population. Understanding what has driven rural poverty reduction is clearly of first-order importance to understanding the country's overall success against poverty.

Table 5.5 Decomposition of the change in poverty

	Poverty measures (% point change 1981–2001)					
	Old poverty line			New poverty line		
	H	PG	SPG	H	PG	SPG
1981–2001						
Within rural	−14.88	−3.76	−1.35	−32.53	−10.39	−4.51
	(74.2)	(75.2)	(75.7)	(72.5)	(74.0)	(75.0)
Within urban	−0.31	−0.08	−0.05	−2.08	−0.32	−0.09
	(1.5)	(1.7)	(3.0)	(4.6)	(2.3)	(1.5)
Population shift	−4.87	−1.16	−0.39	−10.27	−3.32	−1.42
(rural to urban)	(24.3)	(23.2)	(21.7)	(22.9)	(23.7)	(23.6)
Total change	−20.06	−5.00	−1.78	−44.87	−14.04	−6.01
1991–2001						
Within rural	−4.31	−1.27	−0.61	−10.74	−3.24	−1.38
	(77.5)	(80.9)	(83.7)	(75.7)	(76.4)	(76.2)
Within urban	0.00	0.00	0.00	−0.44	−0.14	−0.10
	(0.00)	(0.00)	(0.0)	(3.1)	(3.3)	(5.5)
Population shift	−1.25	−0.30	−0.13	−3.01	−0.86	−0.33
(rural to urban)	(22.5)	(19.1)	(17.2)	(21.2)	(20.3)	(18.2)
Total change	−5.56	−1.57	−0.73	−14.19	−4.24	−1.81

Note: % of total in parentheses.

5.4 Poverty reduction and economic growth

We begin by examining the relationship between our estimated poverty measures and mean incomes, after which we take a closer look at the role played by the pattern of growth.

The relationship between poverty and growth. Poverty in China fell as mean income rose; the regression coefficient of the log national headcount index on the log national mean is −1.43, with a t-ratio of 15.02. However, this is potentially deceptive, given that both series are nonstationary; the residuals show strong serial dependence (the Durbin–Watson statistics is 0.62). Differencing deals with this problem.[17] Table 5.6 gives regressions of the log difference in each poverty measure against the log difference in mean income per capita. There is a possible upward bias in the OLS estimates stemming from common measurement errors in the dependent and independent variable; when the mean is overestimated the poverty measure will be underestimated. Following Ravallion (2001) we use the GDP growth rate as the instrument for the growth rate in mean income from the surveys, under the assumption that measurement errors in the two data sources are uncorrelated. (China's national accounts have been based largely on administrative data.) Both

Table 5.6 Regressions of the rate of poverty reduction on rate of growth in household mean income from the surveys

	OLS		IVE	
	Headcount index (log difference)			
Constant	0.111	0.037	0.132	0.039
	(3.923)	(3.200)	(2.098)	(3.312)
Mean income	−3.187	−2.660	−3.512	−2.682
(log difference)	(−8.745)	(−15.776)	(−3.886)	(−13.615)
Gini index		3.491		3.488
(log difference)		(10.715)		(10.858)
Gini index (log.diff.)		0.183		0.185
x (year-2000)		(6.445)		(6.183)
AR(1)		−0.701		−0.704
		(−4.200)		(−4.196)
R^2	0.644	0.935	0.637	0.935
DW	2.233	2.680	2.146	2.691
	Poverty gap index (log difference)			
Constant	0.159	0.029	0.179	0.037
	(3.365)	(1.244)	(2.016)	(1.576)
Mean income	−3.922	−2.881	−4.240	−2.995
(log difference)	(7.596)	(−11.865)	(3.538)	(−10.548)
Gini index		5.273		5.254
(log difference)		(7.031)		(7.121)
Gini index x		0.245		0.250
(year-2000)		(4.155)		(4.102)
AR(1)		−0.418		−0.432
		(−1.934)		(−2.120)
R^2	0.561	0.908	0.557	0.907
DW	2.039	2.252	1.990	2.270
	Squared poverty gap index (log difference)			
Constant	0.185	0.007	0.204	0.095
	(2.882)	(0.204)	(1.759)	(1.204)
Mean income	−4.270	−2.737	−4.569	−3.994
(log difference)	(−6.381)	(−6.496)	(−2.946)	(−4.099)
Gini index		6.025		5.781
(log difference)		(4.207)		(3.779)
Gini index x		0.212		0.239
(year-2000)		(2.090)		(2.231)
R^2	0.499	0.873	0.497	0.839
DW	2.070	2.221	2.047	2.175

Note: Poverty measures based on new poverty lines. t-ratios corrected for heteroscedasticity in parentheses. The Instrumental Variables Estimator (IVE) uses the growth rate (log difference) in GDP per capita as the instrument for the growth rate in the survey mean. An interaction effect between time and the change in the log mean was also tested but (highly) insignificant in all cases.

the OLS and IVE results in Table 5.6 confirm studies for other countries indicating that periods of higher economic growth tended to be associated with higher rates of poverty reduction.[18] The implied elasticity of poverty reduction to growth is over three for the headcount index and around four for the poverty gap measures. The IVE elasticity is similar to that for OLS, suggesting that the aforementioned problem of correlated measurement errors is not a serious source of bias.

Notice that the intercepts are positive and significant in Table 5.6. Our OLS results imply that at zero growth, the headcount index would have risen at 11 percent per year (16 percent for PG and 19 percent for SPG). So falling poverty in China has been the net outcome of two strong but opposing forced: rising inequality and positive growth.

Table 5.6 also gives regressions including the change in inequality. It is unsurprising that this has a strong positive effect on poverty. (The regression can be viewed as a log-linear approximation of the underlying mathematical relationship between a poverty measure and the mean and the Lorenz curve on which that measure is based.) What is more interesting is that there is evidence of a strong time trend in the impact of inequality, as indicated by the positive interaction effect between time and the change in inequality. Poverty in China has become more responsive to inequality over this period. Indeed, the size of the interaction effect in Table 5.6 suggests that the elasticity of poverty to inequality was virtually zero around 1980, but the elasticity rose to 3.7 in 2001 for the headcount index and 5–6 for the poverty gap measures.

The pattern of growth. While China's economic growth has clearly played an important role in the country's long-term success against absolute poverty, the data suggest that the sectoral composition of growth has mattered.[19] This can be seen clearly if we decompose the growth rates by income components. Consider first the urban–rural decomposition for the survey mean. The overall mean at date t is $\mu_t = n_t^r \mu_t^r + n_t^u \mu_t^u$ where μ_t^i is the mean for sector $i = r,u$ for rural and urban areas. It is readily verified that the growth rate in the overall mean can be written as:

$$\Delta \ln \mu_t = s_t^r \Delta \ln \mu_t^r + s_t^u \Delta \ln \mu_t^u + [s_t^r - s_t^u (n_t^r / n_t^u)] \Delta \ln n_t^r$$

where $s_t^i = n_t^i \mu_t^i / \mu_t$ (for $i = r,u$) is the income share. We can thus write down the following regression for testing whether the composition of growth matters:

$$\Delta \ln P_t = \eta_0 + \eta^r s_t^r \Delta \ln \mu_t^r + \eta^u s_t^u \Delta \ln \mu_t^u + \eta^n (s_t^r - s_t^u \cdot \frac{n_t^r}{n_t^u}) \Delta \ln n_t^r + \varepsilon_t \quad (2)$$

where ε_t is a white-noise error term. The motivation for writing the regression this way is evident when one notes that if the η^i ($i = r,u,n$) parameters are the same then equation (2) collapses to a simple regression of the rate of poverty reduction on the rate of growth ($\Delta \ln \mu_t$). Thus testing H_0: $\eta^i = \eta$ for all i tells us whether the urban–rural composition of growth matters. Note that this regression decomposition is based on somewhat different assumptions to that used in the analytic decomposition in equation (1) based on the assumption that urbanization follows a Kuznets process. In particular, any systematic within-sector distributional effects of urbanization would now change the measured contribution to poverty.

Table 5.7 gives the results for all three poverty measures. The null hypothesis that $\eta^i = \eta$ for all i is convincingly rejected in all three cases. Furthermore, we cannot reject the null that only the growth rate of rural incomes matters.

A second decomposition is possible for GDP per capita which we can divide into n sources to estimate a test equation of the following form:

$$\Delta \ln P_t = \pi_0 + \sum_{i=1}^{n} \pi_i s_{it} \Delta \ln Y_{it} + \varepsilon_t \tag{3}$$

where Y_{it} is GDP per capita from source i, $s_{it} = Y_{it}/Y_t$ is the source's share, and ε_t is a white-noise error term. In the special case in which $\pi_i = \pi$ for $i = 1, \ldots, n$, equation (3) collapses to a simple regression of the rate of poverty reduction on the rate of GDP growth ($\Delta \ln Y_t$).

With only 21 observations over time there are limits on how far we can decompose GDP. We used a standard classification of its origins, namely "primary" (mainly agriculture), "secondary" (manufacturing and construction) and "tertiary" (services and trade). Figure 5.2 shows how the shares of these sectors evolved over time. The primary sector's share fell from 30 percent in 1980 to 15 percent in 2001, though not montonically. Almost all of this decline was made up for by an increase in the tertiary-sector share; the share of secondary sector has no overall trend, but has been rising in the 1990s. However, it should not be forgotten that these are highly aggregated GDP components; the near stationarity of the secondary sector share over

Table 5.7 Poverty reduction and the rural, urban composition of growth

	Headcount index	Poverty gap index	Squared poverty gap index
Constant	0.033	0.040	0.039
	(0.808)	(0.690)	(0.510)
Growth rate of mean rural income	−2.563	−3.341	−3.722
(share-weighted) (η^r)	(−8.432)	(−7.768)	(−6.637)
Growth rate of mean urban income	0.092	0.519	0.744
(share-weighted) (η^u)	(0.201)	(0.797)	(0.877)
Population shift effect (η^n)	0.735	2.189	3.941
	(0.159)	(0.335)	(0.462)
R^2	0.823	0.796	0.739
D-W	2.671	2.653	2.661

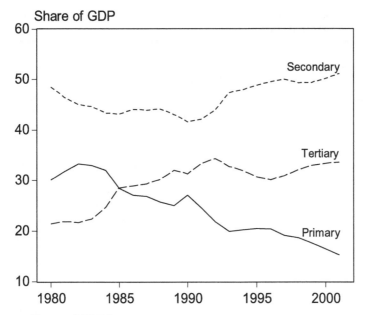

Figure 5.2 Shares of GDP by sector.

the whole period reflects the net effect of both contracting and expanding manufacturing subsectors.

Table 5.8 gives the estimated test equations based on (3) for H and PG, while Table 5.9 gives the results for SPG (for which a slightly different specification is called for, as we will see). We find that the sectoral composition of growth matters to the rate of poverty reduction. The primary sector has far higher impact (by a factor of about four) than either the secondary or tertiary sectors. The impacts of the latter two sectors are similar (and we cannot reject the null that they have the same impact). For SPG we cannot reject the null that only the primary sector matters and Table 5.9 gives the restricted model for this case. Our finding that the sectoral composition of growth matters echoes the findings of Ravallion and Datt (1996) for India, though tertiary sector growth was relatively more important in India than we find for China.

These aggregate results do not tell us about the source of the poverty-reducing impact of primary sector growth. With a relatively equitable distribution of access to agricultural land and higher incidence and depth of poverty in rural areas it is plausible that agricultural growth will bring large gains to the poor. There is evidence for China that this may also involve external effects at the farm–household level. One important source of externalities in rural development is the composition of economic activity locally. In poor areas of southwest China, Ravallion (2005) finds that the composition of local economic activity has non-negligible impacts on consumption growth at the household level. There are significant positive effects

Table 5.8 Poverty reduction and the sectoral composition of growth: Headcount index and poverty gap index

	1	*2*	*3*
	Headcount index (log difference)		
Constant	0.116	0.163	0.155
	(1.059)	(1.656)	(1.761)
Growth rate of GDP per capita	−2.595		
	(−2.162)		
Primary (π_1)		−8.067	−7.852
		(−3.969)	(−4.092)
Secondary (π_2)		−1.751	
		(−1.214)	
Tertiary (π_3)		−3.082	
		(−1.239)	
Secondary+			−2.245
Tertiary			(−2.199)
R^2	0.207	0.431	0.423
D-W	1.553	1.725	1.768
Tests:			
$\pi_1 - \pi_2$		−6.317	−5.607
		(−3.231)	(−3.140)
$\pi_2 - \pi_3$		1.331	
		(0.405)	
	Poverty gap index (log difference)		
Constant	0.160	0.233	0.216
	(1.140)	(1.856)	(1.955)
Growth rate of GDP per capita	−3.133		
	(2.104)		
Primary (π_1)		−11.251	−10.827
		(−3.87)	(−4.07)
Secondary (π_2)		−1.651	
		(−0.90)	
Tertiary (π_3)		−4.271	
		(−1.41)	
Secondary+			−2.623
Tertiary			(−2.06)
R^2	0.173	0.456	0.439
D-W	1.538	1.721	1.772
Tests:			
$\pi_1 - \pi_2$		−9.600	−8.204
		(−3.388)	(−3.29)
$\pi_2 - \pi_3$		2.620	
		(0.644)	

Note: The dependent variable is the first difference over time in the log of the poverty measures based on new poverty lines. t-ratios corrected for heteroscedasticity in parentheses.

Table 5.9 Poverty reduction and the sectoral composition of growth: Squared poverty gap index

	1	2	3	4
Constant	0.184	0.272	0.252	0.033
	(1.059)	(1.852)	(1.900)	(0.463)
Growth rate of GDP per capita	−3.376			
	(1.845)			
Primary (π_1)		−13.257	−12.753	−10.648
		(−3.670)	(−3.762)	(−3.300)
Secondary (π_2)		−1.609		
		(−0.763)		
Tertiary (π_3)		−4.728		
		(−1.486)		
Secondary+			−2.767	
Tertiary			(−1.88)	
R^2	0.151	0.466	0.448	0.344
D-W	1.517	1.754	1.765	1.721
Tests:				
$\pi_1 - \pi_2$			−11.648	−9.986
			(−3.599)	(3.26)
$\pi_2 - \pi_3$			3.119	
			(0.724)	

Note: The dependent variable is the first difference over time in the log of the SPG index; t-ratios corrected for heteroscedasticity in parentheses.

of local economic activity in a given sector on income growth from that sector. And there are a number of significant cross-effects, notably from farming to certain nonfarm activities. The sector that matters most as a generator of positive externalities turns out to be agriculture (Ravallion, 2005).

A natural counterfactual for measuring the contribution of the sectoral composition of growth is the rate of poverty reduction if all three sectors had grown at the same rate. We call this "balanced growth." Then the sector shares of GDP in 1981 would have remained constant over time, with 32 percent of GDP originating in the primary sector. From Table 5.8, the expected rate of change in the headcount index, conditional on the overall GDP growth rate, would then have been $0.155 - 4.039\Delta \ln Y_t$ (where $4.039 = 0.32 \times 7.852 + 0.68 \times 2.245$, based on Table 5.8). For the same GDP growth rate, the mean rate of poverty reduction would then have been 16.3 percent per year, rather than 9.5 percent. Instead of 20 years to bring the headcount index down from 53 percent to 8 percent it would have taken about 10 years.

This calculation would be deceptive if the same overall growth rate would not have been possible with balanced growth. There may well be a trade off, arising from limited substitution possibilities in production and rigidities in some aggregate factor supplies; or the trade-off could stem from aggregate fiscal constraints facing the government in supplying key public infrastructure inputs to private production. It is suggestive in this respect that there is a correlation of −0.414 between the two growth components identified from Table 5.8, $s_{1t}\Delta \ln Y_{1t}$ and $s_{2t}\Delta \ln Y_{2t} + s_{3t}\Delta \ln Y_{3t}$. However, this correlation is only significant at the 6 percent level, and it is clear that there were subperiods (1983–84, 1987–88 and 1994–96) in which both primary sector growth and combined growth in the secondary and tertiary sectors were *both* above average. So these data do not offer strong support for the view that more balanced growth would have meant lower growth.

We have seen that growth accounts for a sizeable share of the variance in rates of poverty reduction. When measured by survey means, growth accounts for about half of the variance; when measured from the national accounts, it accounts for one fifth of the variance. However, the share of variance explained is doubled when we allow for the sectoral composition of growth, with the primary sector emerging as far more important than the secondary or tertiary sectors (though again there may well be heterogeneity within these broad sectors).

5.5 Inequality and growth

The literature has provided numerous partial pictures of inequality in China, focusing on subperiods (such as in Khan and Riskin 1998, who used two surveys spanning 1988–1995; the longest we know of is for 1985–95, in Kanbur and Zhang 1999) and/or selected provinces (such as Tsui 1998) or between urban and rural areas (as studied by Yang 1999). As we will see, these partial pictures can be deceptive. We begin by considering inequality between urban and rural sectors; then within sectors and in the aggregate. Finally we turn to the relationship between inequality and growth.

Inequality between urban and rural areas. Figure 5.3 gives the ratio of the urban mean income to the rural mean. Without our adjustment for the cost-of-living difference, there is a significant positive trend in the ratio of urban to rural mean income. The regression coefficient of the ratio of means on time is 0.047, with a t-ratio of 3.12 (this is corrected for serial correlation in the error term). However, when using the COL-adjusted means the coefficient drops to 0.021 and is not significantly different from zero at the 5 percent level ($t = 1.79$). Notice that there are still some relatively long subperiod trends in which the ratio of the urban to the rural mean was rising, including the period 1986 to 1994. The ratio of means fell sharply in the mid-1990s, though rebounding in the late 1990s.

There is a trend increase in *absolute* inequality between urban and rural areas. This is measured by the difference between the urban and rural means, as in Figure 5.4. The trend in the absolute difference (again calculated as the regression coefficient on time) is 0.044 per year, with a t-ratio of 3.40 (again corrected for serial correlation in the error term). However, here too there were periods that went against the trend, including in the early 1980s and mid-1990s.

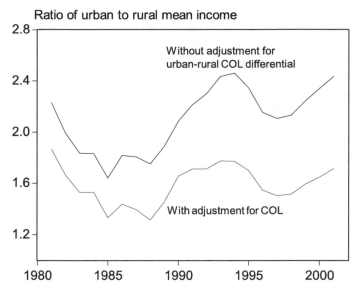

Figure 5.3 Relative inequality between urban and rural China.

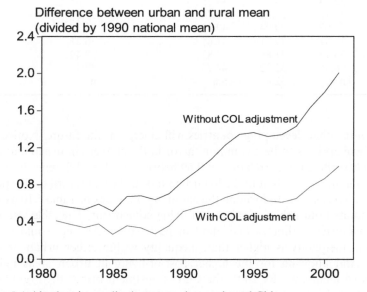

Figure 5.4 Absolute inequality between urban and rural China.

Inequality within urban and rural areas. We find trend increases in inequality within both sectors, though rural inequality fell in the early 1980s and again in the mid-1990s (Table 5.10). In marked contrast to most developing countries, relative income inequality is higher in rural areas, though the rate of increase in inequality is higher in urban areas; it looks likely that the

Table 5.10 Gini indices of income inequality

	Rural	Urban	National	
			Without adjustment for COL difference	*With adjustment for COL difference*
1980	24.99	n.a.	n.a.	n.a.
1981	24.73	18.46	30.95	27.98
1982	24.40	16.27	28.53	25.91
1983	25.73	16.59	28.28	26.02
1984	26.69	17.79	29.11	26.89
1985	26.80	17.06	28.95	26.45
1986	28.48	20.66	32.41	29.20
1987	28.53	20.20	32.38	28.90
1988	29.71	21.08	33.01	29.50
1989	30.96	24.21	35.15	31.78
1990	29.87	23.42	34.85	31.55
1991	31.32	23.21	37.06	33.10
1992	32.03	24.18	39.01	34.24
1993	33.70	27.18	41.95	36.74
1994	34.00	29.22	43.31	37.60
1995	33.98	28.27	41.50	36.53
1996	32.98	28.52	39.75	35.05
1997	33.12	29.35	39.78	35.00
1998	33.07	29.94	40.33	35.37
1999	33.91	29.71	41.61	36.37
2000	35.75	31.86	43.82	38.49
2001	36.48	32.32	44.73	39.45
2002	n.a.	32.65	n.a.	n.a.

pattern in other developing countries will emerge in the future. Notice also that there appears to be a common factor in the changes in urban and rural inequality; there is a correlation of 0.69 between the first difference in the log rural Gini index and that in the log urban index. We will return to this point.

Overall inequality. In forming the national Gini index in Table 5.10 we have incorporated our urban–rural cost of living adjustment. The table also gives the unadjusted estimates (as found in past work). As one would expect, national inequality is higher than inequality within either urban or rural areas. And allowing for the higher cost-of-living in urban areas reduces measured inequality. By 2001, the COL adjustment brings the overall Gini index down by over five percentage points. While a trend increase in national inequality is evident (Figure 5.5), the increase is not found in all subperiods: inequality fell in the early 1980s and the mid-1990s.

The rise in absolute inequality is even more pronounced. Figure 5.6 gives the absolute Gini index, in which income differences are normalized by a fixed mean (for which we use the 1990 national mean). (The absolute Gini is not bounded above by unity.) It is notable that while relative inequality is

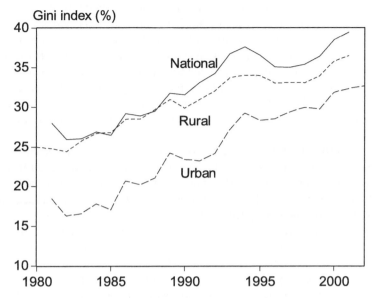

Figure 5.5 Income inequality in rural and urban areas and nationally.

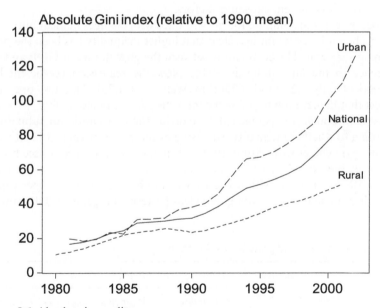

Figure 5.6 Absolute inequality.

higher in rural areas than urban areas, this reverses for absolute inequality, which is higher in urban areas at all dates.

Rising inequality greatly dampened the impact of growth on poverty. On recalculating our rural poverty measures for 2001 using the 2001 rural mean applied to the 1981 Lorenz curve, we find that the incidence of poverty in rural areas (by our upper line) would have fallen to 2.04 percent in 2001, instead of 12.5 percent. The rural PG would have fallen to 0.70 percent (instead of 3.32 percent) while the SPG would have been 0.16 (instead of 1.21). Repeating the same calculations for urban areas, poverty would have virtually vanished. But even with the same urban poverty measures for 2001 (so letting inequality within urban areas rise as it actually did), without the rise in *rural* inequality the national incidence of poverty would have fallen to 1.5 percent.

This begs the question of whether the same growth rate would have been possible without higher inequality. If decontrolling China's economy put upward pressure on inequality then we would be underestimating the level of poverty in 2001 that would have been observed without the rise in inequality, because the lower inequality would have come with a lower mean.

Inequality has certainly risen over time, in line with mean income. The regression coefficient of the Gini index on GDP per capita has a t-ratio of 9.22 (a correlation coefficient of 0.90). But this correlation could well be spurious (in the Granger–Newbold sense); indeed, the Durbin–Watson statistic is 0.45, indicating strong residual autocorrelation. This is not surprising since both inequality and mean income have strong trends, though possibly associated with different causative factors.

A better test is to compare the growth rates with changes in inequality over time.[20] Then it becomes far less clear that higher inequality has been the price of China's growth. The correlation between the growth rate of GDP and log difference in the Gini index is –0.05. Now the regression coefficient has a t-ratio of only 0.22 (and a Durbin–Watson of 1.75). This test does not suggest that higher growth *per se* meant a steeper rise in inequality.

The same conclusion is reached if we divide the series into four subperiods according to whether inequality was rising or falling, as in Table 5.11. If there was an aggregate growth–equity trade-off then we would expect to see higher growth in the period in which inequality was rising. This is not the case; indeed; the two periods with highest growth in household income per capita were when inequality was falling. No clear pattern emerges for GDP growth.

Table 5.11 Inequality and growth by subperiods

	Inequality	*Annualized log difference (%/year)*		
		Gini index	*Mean household income*	*GDP per capita*
1. 1981–85	Falling	−1.12	8.87	8.80
2. 1986–94	Rising	2.81	3.10	7.99
3. 1995–98	Falling	−0.81	5.35	7.75
4. 1999–2001	Rising	2.71	4.47	6.61

These calculations do not reveal any sign of a short-term trade off between growth and equity. Possibly these time periods are too short to capture the effect. Another test is to see whether the provinces that had higher growth rates saw higher increases in inequality; we return to that question in section 5.7.

Inequality and the pattern of growth. What role has the sectoral composition of growth played in the evolution of inequality?[21] Repeating our test based on equation (2) but this time using changes in the log Gini index as the dependent variable we find strong evidence that the evolution of the Gini index is correlated with the urban–rural composition of growth:

$$\Delta \ln G_t = 0.020 - 0.511 \; s_t^r \, \Delta \ln \mu_t^r + 0.466 \; s_t^u \, \Delta \ln \mu_t^u - $$
$$\underset{(1.285)}{} \quad \underset{(-4.399)}{} \quad \underset{(2.651)}{}$$

$$0.366 \, [s_t^r - s_t^u \, (n_t^r \, n_t^u)] \, \Delta \ln n_t^r + \hat{\varepsilon}_t^G \; R^2 = 0.622; \; n = 20 \qquad (4)$$
$$\underset{(-0.208)}{}$$

There is no sign of a population shift effect on aggregate inequality and the rural and urban coefficients add up to about zero. The joint restrictions $\eta^r + \eta^u = 0$ and $\eta^n = 0$ (borrowing the notation of equation 2) pass comfortably, giving the rate of change in inequality as an increasing function of the difference in (share-weighted) growth rates between urban and rural areas:

$$\Delta \ln G_t = 0.015 + 0.499 \, (s_t^u \, \Delta \ln \mu_t^u - s_t^r \, \Delta \ln \mu_t^r) + \hat{\varepsilon}_t^G \; R^2 = 0.619; \; n = 20$$
$$\underset{(2.507)}{} \quad \underset{(5.405)}{}$$
$$(5)$$

Looking instead at the components of GDP by origin, one finds that primary sector growth has been associated with lower inequality overall, while there is no correlation with growth in either the secondary or tertiary sectors (Table 5.12). It is also clear that an important channel through which primary sector growth has been inequality reducing is its effect on the urban–rural income disparity. There is a negative correlation between primary sector growth and the changes in the (log) ratio of urban to rural mean income; the correlation is strongest if one lags primary sector growth by one period, giving the following OLS regression for the log of the ratio of the urban mean ($\overline{Y}_t^u$) to the rural mean ($\overline{Y}_t^r$):

$$\Delta \ln (\overline{Y}_t^u / \overline{Y}_t^r) = 0.044 - 0.969 \, \Delta \ln \, Y_{1t-1} + \hat{\varepsilon}_t^Y \; R^2 = 0.437; \; n = 20 \qquad (6)$$
$$\underset{(2.657)}{} \quad \underset{(-3.802)}{}$$

Table 5.13 gives regressions of the log difference of the Gini index by urban and rural areas on the growth rates (log differences) of both rural and urban mean incomes. We find that higher rural incomes were inequality reducing nationally. This happened in three ways. First, rural economic growth clearly reduced inequality between urban and rural areas; second it reduced inequality within rural areas; thirdly, rural economic growth also reduced inequality within *urban* areas. As in other developing countries, the fortunes of China's

Table 5.12 Inequality and GDP growth by origin

	1	2	3
Constant	−0.072	0.038	0.038
	(0.429)	(1.278)	(3.598)
Growth rate of GDP per capita	0.012		
	(0.544)		
Primary (π_1)		−1.798	−1.755
		(2.244)	(2.819)
Secondary (π_2)		0.170	
		(0.432)	
Tertiary (π_3)		−0.218	
		(−0.272)	
R^2	0.018	0.326	0.316
D-W	2.112	2.112	2.202
$\pi_1 - \pi_2$		−1.968	
		(2.263)	
$\pi_2 - \pi_3$		0.388	
		(0.381)	

Note: The dependent variable is the first difference over time in the log of the Gini.

Table 5.13 Urban and rural inequality and growth in mean urban and rural incomes

	Rural		Urban	
Constant	0.013	0.019	0.006	−0.016
	(0.880)	(2.005)	(0.386)	(−0.853)
Growth rate in mean rural income	−0.476		−1.430	
	(−3.206)		(−5.808)	
Growth rate in mean rural income lagged	0.510		1.014	
	(4.322)		(4.635)	
Double-difference in rural growth rates		−0.504		−1.187
		(−5.878)		(−4.502)
Growth rate in mean urban income	0.075		0.687	0.664
	(0.830)		(3.305)	(2.693)
AR(1)	0.481	0.510		
	(2.208)	(2.554)		
	0.491	0.478	0.690	0.588
D-W			1.741	1.292

urban poor are likely to be linked to rural economic growth through migration, transfers and trade. These linkages can readily entail distributional effects of rural economic growth on urban areas, given that it is more likely to be the urban poor (rather than urban non-poor) who gain from rural economic growth (such as by reduced need for remittances back to rural areas).

However, we also find a strong and roughly offsetting *lagged* growth effect in rural areas, suggesting that it is the positive (negative) shocks to rural incomes that reduce (increase) inequality. This could arise from a short-term effect of rural income changes on migration and remittances. Growth in urban incomes is inequality increasing in the aggregate and within urban areas, but not rural areas. This echoes results of Ravallion and Datt (1996) for India.

What then is driving the co-movement of inequality between urban and rural areas? The answer appears to lie in the role of rural incomes. As we have seen, for both urban and rural areas, the first differences in the log Gini index are negatively correlated with rural income growth. The regression residuals for the changes in rural inequality in Table 5.13 show no significant correlation with those for urban inequality, indicating that rural economic growth is the key common factor.

5.6 Economy-wide policies and poverty

In principle, many policies could matter to the pattern of growth and (hence) rate of poverty reduction. Here we focus on those that have received most attention in the literature, namely agrarian reform, agricultural pricing, macroeconomic stabilization, public spending and openness to external trade.

Agrarian reform. The early 1980s saw high growth in primary sector output and rapid rural poverty reduction in the wake of de-collectivization and the privatization of land-use rights under the "household responsibility system." (Agricultural land had previously been farmed by organized brigades, in which all members shared the output more-or-less equally.) Since this was a one-off event across the whole country, we cannot test its explanatory power. However, the literature has pointed to the importance of these reforms in stimulating rural economic growth at the early stages of China's transition (Fan 1991; Lin 1992; Chow 2002). And (as we have seen) rural economic growth was key to falling poverty in that period. It would not be unreasonable to presume that the agrarian reforms around 1980 accounted for the bulk of rural poverty reduction in the first half of the 1980s, which (as we have also seen) accounted for roughly three-quarters of the total decline in the national poverty rate over 1981–2001.

Agricultural pricing policies. Until recently, the government has operated a domestic foodgrain procurement policy by which farmers are obliged to sell fixed quotas to the government at prices that are typically below the local market price. For some farmers this is an inframarginal tax, given that they produce more foodgrains than their assigned quota; for others it will affect production decisions at the margin. It has clearly been unpopular with farmers (see, for example, Kung's 1995, survey of Chinese farmers' attitudes.)

Reducing this tax by raising procurement prices appears to have stimulated primary sector GDP. We find a strong correlation between the growth rate of primary sector output and the real procurement price of foodgrains (nominal

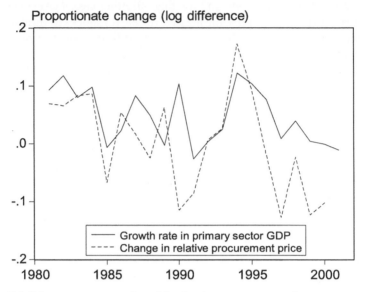

Figure 5.7 Primary sector growth and foodgrain procurement prices.

price deflated by the rural CPI); see Figure 5.7. There is both a current and lagged effect; an OLS regression of the growth rate in primary sector GDP on the current and lagged rates of change in the real procurement price (*PP*) gives:

$$\Delta \ln Y_{1t} = 0.045 + 0.210 \, \Delta \ln PP_t + 0.315 \, \Delta \ln PP_{t-1} + \hat{\varepsilon}_t, \, R^2 = 0.590;$$
$$\phantom{\Delta \ln Y_{1t} = }{\scriptstyle(5.937)}{\scriptstyle(2.152)}{\scriptstyle(3.154)}$$

D–W = 2.60; n = 19 $\hspace{4cm}$ (7)

It is not then surprising that we find a strong negative correlation between the changes in the government's procurement price and changes in inequality; Figure 5.8 plots the two series (lagging the procurement price change by one year); the simple correlation coefficient is –0.609.

Cutting this tax has been an effective short-term policy against poverty.[22] The regression coefficient of $\Delta \ln H_t$ on $\Delta \ln PP_{t-1}$ is –1.060 (t-ratio = –3.043). The channel for this effect was clearly through agricultural incomes. (The regression coefficient changes little if one adds controls for secondary and tertiary sector growth.) The elasticities of national poverty to procurement price changes are even higher for the poverty gap indices; for PG the coefficient is –1.433 (t = –2.929) and for SPG it is –1.708 (t = –3.134).

Macroeconomic stabilization. There were two inflationary periods in China, 1988–89 and 1994–5. Poverty rose in the former period and fell in the latter. However, when one controls for procurement price changes we find an

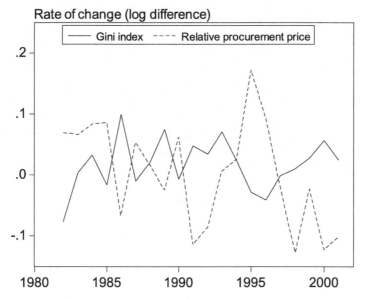

Figure 5.8 Inequality and the procurement price of foodgrains.

adverse effect of lagged changes in the rate of inflation for all three poverty measures; for the headcount index:

$$\Delta \ln H_t = -\, 0.082 - 1.257 \, \Delta \ln PP_{t-1} + 1.249 \, \Delta^2 \ln CPI_{t-1} + \hat{\varepsilon}_t \, R^2$$
$$ {\scriptstyle (-3.058)} \quad {\scriptstyle (-3.688)} \phantom{\Delta \ln PP_{t-1} + } {\scriptstyle (2.493)}$$
$$= 0.491; D - W = 1.86; n = 19 \tag{8}$$

where *CPI* is the rural CPI. (The regression was similar for the other poverty measures.) The strong adverse effect of inflation echoes findings elsewhere.[23] There are also strong (pro-poor) distributional effects of procurement and inflationary shocks as can be seen by the fact that both regressors in (8) remain significant if one controls for the log difference in overall mean income:

$$\Delta \ln H_t = 0.060 - 1.040 \, \Delta \ln PP_{t-1} + 0.882 \, \Delta^2 \ln CPI_{t-1} -$$
$$ {\scriptstyle (3.791)} \quad {\scriptstyle (-8.049)} \phantom{\Delta \ln PP_{t-1} + } {\scriptstyle (4.651)}$$

$$2.335 \, \Delta \ln \bar{Y}_t - 0.739 \, \hat{\varepsilon}_{t-1} + \hat{v}_t \, R^2 = 0.907;$$
$$ {\scriptstyle (-9.843)} \quad {\scriptstyle (-3.775)}$$

$$D - W = 2.28; n = 18 \tag{9}$$

Government spending. Fiscal expansions tended to reduce poverty; when the change in log real public spending is added to equation (8), its coefficient is −0.737 (t = −2.095).[24] However, adding $\Delta \ln \bar{Y}_t$ rendered the public spending variable insignificant (the coefficient dropped to 0.063, t = 0.325). We also tried two decompositions of public spending, namely agriculture and non-agriculture and central and local. We found no evidence that government spending on agriculture had any greater poverty reducing impact than other spending; this was tested by adding the (share-weighted) change in log real public spending on agriculture as an additional regressor. The share of spending on agriculture was generally low (around 6–7 percent until the mid-1990s, falling to 5 percent after that), so it may well be difficult to pick up its impact (even when share-weighted). However, there was a strong indication that spending by provincial and local governments was more effective in reducing poverty than spending by the center.[25] Indeed, we could not reject the null that central government spending had no impact, giving the model:

$$\Delta \ln H_t = 0.003 - 1.601 \, \Delta \ln PP_{t-1} + 1.064 \, \Delta^2 \ln CPI_{t-1} -$$
$$ {\scriptstyle (0.106)} \quad {\scriptstyle (-6.201)} \qquad\qquad {\scriptstyle (2.889)}$$

$$1.319 \, s_t^{GL} \, \Delta \ln GL_t - 0.502 \, \hat{\varepsilon}_{t-1} + \hat{v}_t, \, R^2 = 0.640;$$
$$ {\scriptstyle (-3.988)} \qquad\qquad {\scriptstyle (-1.986)}$$

$$D - W = 1.681; \, n = 19 \tag{10}$$

where s_t^L is the share of local spending in total spending and GL_t is real local spending. (The results were similar without share-weighting; the coefficient on $\Delta \ln GL_t$ was −0.676, t = −2.494.) Changes in log *central* government spending were insignificant when added to this regression (a regression coefficient of −0.100 with a t-ratio of −0.486; other coefficients were affected little).

Here too, there is no sign of a distributional effect of public spending; if we add $s_t^L \, \Delta \ln GL_t$ to equation (9) (controlling for changes in the log mean) then its coefficient drops to −0.305 and is not significantly different from zero (t = −1.271). Public spending has reduced absolute poverty but statistically we can't reject the null that its effect has been roughly distribution-neutral.[26]

External trade. It has been claimed that China's external trade reforms helped reduce poverty (World Bank 2002; Dollar 2004). However, the timing does not suggest that external trade expansion is a plausible candidate for explaining China's progress against poverty. Granted, trade reforms had started in the early 1980s as part of Deng Xiaoping's "Open-Door Policy" – mainly entailing favorable exchange rate and tax treatment for exporters and creation of the first special-economic zone, Shenzhen, near Hong Kong. (Internal trade was also progressively liberalized, though here we only consider external trade.) However, the bulk of the trade reforms did not occur in the early 1980s, when poverty was falling so rapidly, but were later, notably with the extension of the special-economic zone principle to the whole country (from 1986) and from the mid-1990s, in the lead up to China's accession to the World Trade Organization (WTO); Table 5.14 shows that mean tariff rates fell only slightly in the 1980s and non-tariff barriers actually increased. And some of the trade policies of this early period were unlikely to have been good for either equity or efficiency.[27]

Table 5.14 China's external trade openness

	Mean tariff rates (%)				Incidence of non-tariff barriers (%)			
	1980–83	*1984–7*	*1988–90*	*1991–3*	*1980–3*	*1984–7*	*1988–90*	*1991–3*
Primary	22.7	20.6	19.1	17.8	n.a.	19.7	58.9	40.7
Manufactured	36.6	33.2	34.3	37.1	n.a.	16.1	34.4	19.2
All products	31.9	29.2	29.2	30.6	n.a.	17.2	42.6	26.4

Source: Weighted averages from UNCTAD (1994).

Nor does the times series on trade volume (the ratio of exports and imports to GDP) suggest that trade was poverty reducing, at least in the short term; the correlation between changes in trade volume and changes in the log headcount index is 0.00! Nor are changes in trade volume – both current values and lagged up to two-years – significant when added to equations (8), (9), or (10). Trade volume may well be endogenous in this test, though it is not clear that correcting for the bias would imply that it played a more important role against poverty. This would require that trade volume is positively correlated with the omitted variables. However, one would probably be more inclined to argue that trade volume is negatively correlated with the residuals; other (omitted) growth-promoting policies simultaneously increased trade and reduced (absolute) poverty.

Other evidence, using different data and methods, also suggests that trade reform had had relatively little impact on poverty or inequality. Chen and Ravallion (2004b) studied the household level impacts of the tariff changes from 1995 onwards (in the lead up to accession to the WTO). (The induced price and wage changes were estimated by Ianchovichina and Martin 2004, using a CGE model.) There was a positive impact of these trade reforms on mean household income, but virtually no change in aggregate inequality and only slightly lower aggregate poverty. Possibly longer-term impacts will e more positive (such as through growth-promoting access to new technologies and knowledge).

5.7 Poverty at provincial level

So far we have focused solely on the national time series. We now turn to the less complete data available at province level. We focus on rural poverty; urban poverty incidence is so low in a number of provinces that it becomes hard to measure and explain trends.

The series on mean rural incomes from NBS is complete from 1980. However, there are only 11–12 years of provincial distributions available. Table 5.15 gives summary statistics on the "initial" values of the mean, poverty and inequality. For the mean, the first observation is for 1980; for the distributional measures the first available year is 1983 in two-thirds of cases and 1988 for almost all the rest. There are marked differences in starting

Table 5.15 Summary statistics for rural areas by province

Provinces by regional groupings (official codes)		Mean in 1980 (1980 prices)	Distributional data		Value at first year of series				Gini index (%)
			No. years	First year	H (%)	PG (%)	SPG (×100)		
North									
11	Beijing	290.46	10*	1988	0.35	0.14	0.13		24.84
12	Tianjin	277.92	12	1983	3.44	0.65	0.24		23.23
13	Hebei	175.78	12	1983	40.30	10.82	4.22		23.89
14	Shanxi	155.78	12	1983	30.04	7.61	2.75		27.48
15	Inner Mongolia	181.32	12	1983	42.51	10.96	4.07		26.01
Northeast									
21	Liaoning	273.02	11	1988	21.69	6.19	2.48		30.94
22	Jilin	236.30	12	1983	16.79	3.49	1.18		25.90
23	Heilongjian	205.38	11	1988	31.81	9.71	4.24		30.12
East									
31	Shanghai	397.35	12	1983	0.77	0.18	0.09		19.82
32	Jiangsu	217.94	12	1983	19.51	3.90	1.14		20.83
33	Zhejiang	219.18	12	1983	28.04	6.02	1.89		21.33
34	Anhui	184.82	12	1983	25.75	5.13	1.51		19.39
35	Fujian	171.74	11	1988	35.46	7.87	2.49		21.53
36	Jiangxi	180.94	12	1983	30.08	5.39	1.41		17.88
37	Shandong	194.33	12	1983	33.21	6.96	2.03		23.57
Central									
41	Henan	160.78	12	1983	55.58	14.46	5.30		21.47
42	Hubei	169.88	12	1983	24.08	4.45	1.18		20.30
43	Hunan	219.71	12	1983	7.58	0.90	0.19		18.72
44	Guangdong	274.37	11	1988	21.69	4.35	1.29		31.22

45	Guangxi	173.68	12	1983	54.08	14.63	5.53	24.81
46	Hainan	n.a.,	10	1990	50.08	15.52	6.79	28.89
Southwest								
51	Sichuan	187.90	12	1983	40.59	8.32	2.50	19.33
52	Guizhou	161.46	11	1988	34.85	7.83	2.64	23.42
53	Yunnan	150.12	12	1983	34.20	6.84	1.91	22.73
Northwest								
61	Sha'anxi	142.49	12	1983	27.35	5.52	1.63	19.83
62	Gansu	153.33	12	1983	39.34	9.55	3.21	26.18
63	Qinghai	156.10**	11	1988	23.42	6.09	2.38	32.93
64	Ningxia	198.45	12	1983	22.08	5.32	1.81	25.25
65	Xinjiang	232.10	11	1988	22.84	6.23	2.32	33.10

* 1990 missing; ** 1981.

Table 5.16 Trends for rural areas by province

	Mean (1980–2001)	Gini index	Headcount index	Poverty gap index	Squared poverty gap index
Beijing	3.51	3.01	3.46	1.81	0.12
	(3.75)	(3.28)	(0.95)	(0.38)	(0.02)
Tianjin	5.75	1.73	0.94	2.94	0.94
	(4.09)	(4.24)	(0.18)	(0.49)	(0.13)
Hebei	3.36	0.70	−14.11	−14.21	−14.30
	(2.95)	(1.39)	(5.97)	(5.09)	(4.51)
Shanxi	4.16	1.07	−8.26	−7.23	−5.76
	(7.6)	(3.47)	(3.98)	(2.74)	(1.74)
Inner Mongolia	3.94	1.77	−8.03	−6.76	−4.96
	(6.65)	(3.21)	(4.01)	(2.08)	(1.07)
Liaoning	3.34	1.53	−7.19	−4.22	−0.58
	(3.5)	(2.48)	(2.39)	(1.02)	(0.12)
Jilin	4.39	1.28	−5.36	−1.90	1.35
	(−6.05)	(3.00)	(2.19)	(0.56)	(0.29)
Heilongjian	3.24	1.45	−6.78	−4.40	0.86
	(6.24)	(3.86)	(3.96)	(1.89)	(0.22)
Shanghai	5.43	2.07	2.24	3.79	3.04
	(6.44)	(2.27)	(0.38)	(0.46)	(0.36)
Jiangsu	6.01	1.65	−20.02	−18.29	−14.35
	(15.98)	(3.21)	(5.64)	(5.04)	(3.76)
Zhejiang	2.74	1.92	−11.68	−12.61	−13.34
	(2.78)	(4.24)	(9.38)	(6.35)	(4.02)
Anhui	6.66	0.87	−14.36	−14.81	−13.01
	(19.74)	(2.19)	(4.60)	(4.03)	(3.07)
Fujian	4.40	2.35	−22.06	−23.38	−22.87
	(11.29)	(4.03)	(5.13)	(6.25)	(9.81)
Jiangxi	4.48	2.40	−12.29	−9.90	−5.83
	(4.96)	(5.79)	(5.08)	(3.42)	(1.71)
Shandong	5.50	1.25	−12.74	−13.41	−12.32
	(8.17)	(3.75)	(6.38)	(5.66)	(3.45)
Henan	3.09	1.04	−16.10	−18.47	−19.27
	(3.49)	(2.26)	(7.49)	(6.80)	(5.72)
Hubei	2.64	1.87	−13.32	−12.57	−9.76
	(3.71)	(9.67)	(7.36)	(5.84)	(4.60)
Hunan	5.21	1.99	−6.90	−4.01	−0.87
	(12.96)	(9.19)	(3.20)	(1.56)	(0.22)
Guangdong	4.32	−0.36	−28.58	−26.46	−21.74
	(16.28)	(1.00)	(12.29)	(9.51)	(5.88)
Guangxi	5.75	0.45	−11.54	−13.24	−14.41
	(9.42)	(1.13)	(4.82)	(4.14)	(3.86)
Hainan	5.39*	2.12	−10.03	−12.26	−13.47
	(20.46)	(4.75)	(7.60)	(5.88)	(4.75)
Sichuan	3.58	1.76	−11.03	−10.36	−8.17
	(7.08)	(5.81)	(6.51)	(5.23)	(4.02)
Guizhou	2.06	1.05	−6.49	−7.76	−8.35
	(5.38)	(3.47)	(4.98)	(3.66)	(2.85)

Yunnan	1.09	2.55	−0.61	1.39	3.61
	(1.86)	(21.00)	(0.79)	(1.26)	(2.64)
Sha'anxi	2.43	2.41	−3.43	−2.48	−1.32
	(6.56)	(6.47)	(3.74)	(1.85)	(0.74)
Gansu	3.66	1.75	−6.65	−7.35	−7.95
	(5.53)	(5.51)	(4.89)	(3.47)	(2.76)
Qinghai	2.08	1.46	−4.72	−2.98	−1.18
	(3.00)	(1.60)	(2.06)	(0.89)	(0.27)
Ningxia	2.85	2.06	−2.94	−3.27	−3.44
	(2.44)	(4.84)	(1.72)	(1.04)	(0.75)
Xinjiang	0.97	1.39	0.37	1.62	3.21
	(1.66)	(4.72)	(0.25)	(0.68)	(0.97)
Rural China	3.36	1.72	−5.66	−5.39	−5.21
	(4.15)	(12.73)	(−6.10)	(−4.36)	(−3.33)

Note: 22 annual observations 1980–2001 for provincial means except * series which starts in 1990; 10–12 unevenly spaced observations for distributional data. All trends for the mean incorporate an AR(1) error term, while trends for the distributional data are based on OLS regressions.

conditions. Even for inequality, the Gini index around the mid 1980s varied from 18 to 33 percent (Table 5.15).

Table 5.16 gives the trends based on the OLS estimates of $\log X_{it} = \alpha_i^X + \beta_i^X t + v_{it}^X$ for variable X at date t in province i. We assume an AR(1) error term for mean income. However, for the (incomplete, discontinuous) distributional data we have little practical choice but to treat the error term as white noise. Trend growth rates in mean incomes vary from 1 percent per year (in Xinjiang) to almost 7 percent per year (in Anhui). Trends in the Gini index vary from near zero (Guangdong) to 3 percent (Beijing). Guangdong had an astonishing trend rate of decline in H of 29 percent per year. At the other extreme there are six provinces for which the trend was not significantly different from zero, namely Beijing, Tianjin, Shanghai, Yunnan, Ningxia, Xinjiang, though the first three of these started the period with very low poverty rates (Table 5.15).

The literature has pointed to divergence between the coastal and inland provinces.[28] This has been linked to the government's regional policies, which have favored coastal provinces through differential tax treatment and public investment. We confirm expectations that coastal provinces had significantly higher trend rates of poverty reduction.[29] The mean trend rate of decline in the headcount index was 8.43 percent per year for inland provinces (t = 4.14) versus 16.55 percent for the coastal provinces (t = 5.02); the t-statistic for the difference in trends is 2.10.

Poverty and growth at the provincial level. The association between rural income growth and poverty reduction is confirmed in the provincial data. Figure 5.9 plots the trend rate of change in the headcount index against the trend rate of growth in mean rural income across provinces. The figure also identifies the three observations with lowest initial poverty measures, for

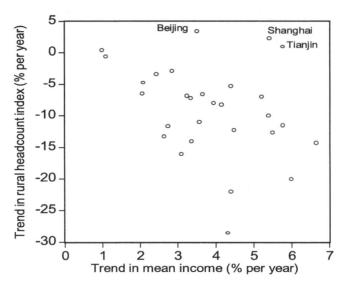

Figure 5.9 Trend rate of change in rural poverty against trend growth rate in mean rural income across 29 provinces.

which there was also an increase (though statistically insignificant) in poverty over time, namely Beijing, Shanghai, and Tianjin.

The regression coefficient of the trend in the headcount index on the trend in rural income is −1.58, which is significant at the 5 percent level (t = −2.05). The 95 percent confidence interval for the impact of a 3 percent growth rate on the headcount index is about (0, 9%). However, if one drops Beijing, Shanghai, and Tianjin then the relationship is steeper and more precisely estimated. The regression coefficient is then −2.43 (t = 4.29). The 95% confidence interval for the poverty impact of a 3% growth rate is then about (4%, 10%).

While higher growth meant a steeper decline in poverty, we see in Figure 5.9 considerable dispersion in the impact of a given rate of growth on poverty. This is also evident if we calculate the "growth elasticity of poverty reduction" as the ratio of the trend in the headcount index to the trend in the mean. This varies from −6.6 to 1.0, with a mean of −2.3.

What explains these diverse impacts of a given rate of growth on poverty? If inequality did not change then the elasticity will depend on the parameters of the initial distribution, roughly interpretable as the mean and "inequality." More generally, with changing distribution, the elasticity will also depend on the trend in inequality. On imposing data consistent parameter restrictions, the following regression is easily interpreted:[30]

$$\beta_i^H / \beta_i^Y = (-\underset{(-4.487)}{5.935} + \underset{(2.560)}{0.0136}\ \bar{y}_{80i}^R)\ (1 - G_{83i}^R) + \underset{(2.392)}{1.365}\ \beta_i^G + \hat{\varepsilon}_t$$

$$R^2 = 0.386;\ n = 29 \tag{11}$$

where $\bar{y}_{80i}^{R}$ is the initial mean for province i less the national mean. At zero trend in inequality and the mean residual, the elasticity is zero at $G_{83}^{R} = 1$ and becomes more negative in provinces with lower initial inequality. At $G_{83}^{R} = 0$, the elasticity at mean income is −6, but goes toward zero as income rises. So a given rate of growth had more poverty-reducing impact in initially less unequal and poorer provinces.

Echoing our results using the national time series data, we find no evidence of a growth–equity trade off in the provincial data. Figure 5.10 plots the trends in the Gini index against the trend in the mean; the correlation coefficient is −0.188. We do not see any sign that higher growth put more upward pressure on inequality. With no evidence of an aggregate trade-off, we are drawn to conclude that rising inequality over time put a brake on the rate of poverty reduction at provincial level. Provinces in which inequality rose less tended to have *higher* rates of poverty reduction (Figure 5.11); the correlation coefficient is 0.517 (t = 3.14).

A simple measure of the cost to the poor of rising inequality can be obtained by projecting the poverty measure in 2001 that one would have expected if the growth process had been distribution neutral, such that all levels of income grew at the same rate. Figure 5.12 compares this simulated poverty measure for rural areas in 2001 with the actual values.[31] The distributional shifts were poverty increasing; indeed, in 23 provinces the poverty rate in 2001 was more than three times higher than one would have expected without the rise in inequality.

One province stands out as an exception to this pattern of rising inequality,

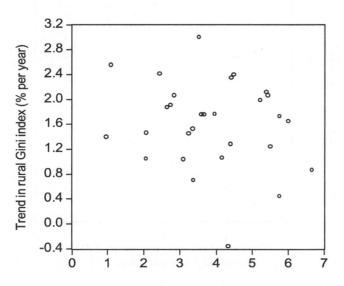

Figure 5.10 Trend in rural Gini index against trend in mean income.

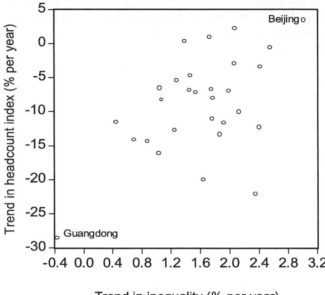

Figure 5.11 Trend in headcount index against trend in Gini index.

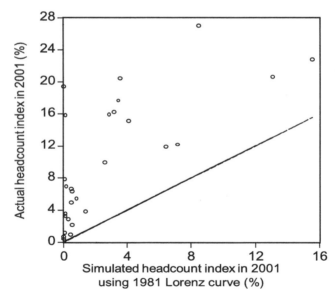

Figure 5.12 Actual poverty in 2001 and simulated level without the rise inequality.

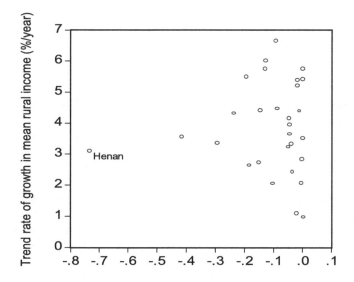

Share weighted total elasticity of the headcount index to growth

Figure 5.13 Growth did not occur where it would have most impact on poverty.

namely Guangdong (the hinterland of Hong Kong). Because inequality showed no upward trend, Guangdong was able to achieve the highest rate of poverty reduction with only a slightly above average rate of growth and despite relatively high initial inequality (Table 5.15).

How pro-poor was the geographic pattern of growth? This can be assessed by seeing whether there was higher growth in the provinces where growth had more impact on poverty nationally. Figure 5.13 gives the scatter plot of growth rates against the total elasticities (ratio of trend in H to trend in mean) weighted by the 1981 shares of total poverty. (The weights assure that this gives the impact on national poverty of growth in a given province.) It is plain that growth has not been any higher in the provinces in which it would have had the most impact on poverty nationally. This also echoes findings for India in the 1990s (Datt and Ravallion 2002).

Explaining the provincial trends. It is instructive to see how much of the interprovincial variance in trend rates of poverty reduction is explicable in terms of two sets of variables: (i) *initial conditions* related to mean incomes and their distribution, and (ii) *location*, notably whether the province is coastal or not (*COAST*). Guangdong is treated as a special case. In accounting for initial distribution, we include both the initial Gini index of rural incomes (G_{83}^R) and the initial ratio of urban mean income to rural mean (*UR*).[32] We postulate that these variables mattered to both the rate of growth and the growth elasticity of poverty reduction. Combining these variables, we obtain the following regression for the trend rate of change in the headcount index:[33]

$$\beta_i^H = -67.877 + 0.141 \; \bar{Y}_{80i} + 0.463 \; G_{83i}^R + 6.797 \; UR_i - 9.291 \; COAST_i -$$
$$ \begin{smallmatrix}(-6.239)\end{smallmatrix} \quad \begin{smallmatrix}(8.090)\end{smallmatrix} \qquad \begin{smallmatrix}(3.313)\end{smallmatrix} \qquad \begin{smallmatrix}(3.201)\end{smallmatrix} \qquad \begin{smallmatrix}(-5.292)\end{smallmatrix}$$

$$25.012 \; GDONG_i + \hat{\varepsilon}_t \qquad R^2 = 0.827; \; n = 28 \tag{12}$$
$$\begin{smallmatrix}(-15.160)\end{smallmatrix}$$

Initially poorer (in terms of mean income) and less unequal provinces (by both measures) had higher subsequent rates of poverty reduction. The effects are large; going from the lowest initial inequality to the highest cuts 7 percent points off the annual rate of poverty reduction. Controlling for the initial mean and distributional variables, being on the coast increased the trend rate of poverty reduction by 9 percent points; being in Guangdong raised it by (a massive) 25 percent points.

There are two ways in which initial inequality mattered. One is through growth; less unequal provinces had higher growth rates, consistent with a body of theory and evidence.[34] This can be seen if we switch to the trend in mean rural income as the dependent variable for equation (11), giving:

$$\beta_i^Y = 14.143 - 0.007 \; \bar{Y}_{80i} - 0.149 \; G_{83i}^R - 1.632 \; UR_i + 0.507 \; COAST_i +$$
$$ \begin{smallmatrix}(3.759)\end{smallmatrix} \quad \begin{smallmatrix}(-1.294)\end{smallmatrix} \qquad \begin{smallmatrix}(-2.526)\end{smallmatrix} \qquad \begin{smallmatrix}(-2.682)\end{smallmatrix} \qquad \begin{smallmatrix}(0.913)\end{smallmatrix}$$

$$1.290 \; GDONG_i + \hat{\varepsilon}_t \qquad R^2 = 0.423; \; n = 28 \tag{13}$$
$$\begin{smallmatrix}(1.875)\end{smallmatrix}$$

Surprisingly, the dummy variables for coastal provinces and Guangdong are insignificant in the growth regression; their effect on poverty appears to be largely distributional.

Second, initial distribution matters independently of growth, as we saw in equation (11). This is consistent with the fact that if one adds the trend rate of growth to equation (12) then both inequality measures remain significant, although the coefficients drop in size (by about one third) and the initial Gini index is only significant at the 10 percent level (the urban rural differential remains significant). Growth has less impact on poverty in more unequal provinces, consistent with cross-country evidence (Ravallion 1997).

5.8 Conclusions

China's success against poverty since the reforms that began in 1978 is undeniable. But a closer inspection of the numbers holds some warnings for the future and some caveats on the implications for fighting poverty in the rest of the developing world.

The specifics of the situation in China at the outset of the reform period should not be forgotten in attempting to draw implications for other developing countries. The Great Leap Forward and the Cultural Revolution had left a legacy of pervasive and severe rural poverty by the mid-1970s. Yet much of the rural population that had been forced into collective farming (with weak incentives for work) could still remember how to farm individually. So there were some relatively easy gains to be had by undoing these failed policies – by decollectivizing agriculture and shifting the responsibility for farming to households. This brought huge gains to the country's (and the world's) poorest. Though we cannot offer a rigorous test against alternative explanations, we would hypothesize that the halving of the national poverty rate in the first few years of the 1980s was largely attributable to picking these "low-lying fruits" of agrarian reform. But this was a one-time reform.

An obvious, though nonetheless important, lesson for other developing countries that is well illustrated by China's experience is the need for governments to do less harm to poor people, by reducing the (explicit and implicit) taxes they face. In China's case, the government has until recently operated an extensive foodgrain procurement system that effectively taxed farmers by setting quotas and fixing procurement prices below market levels. This gave the Chinese government a powerful anti-poverty lever in the short-term, by raising the procurement price – as happened in the mid-1990s, bringing both poverty and inequality down.

When so much of a country's poverty is found in its rural areas, it is not surprising that agricultural growth plays an important role in poverty reduction. China's experience is consistent with the view that agriculture and rural development are crucial to pro-poor growth in most low-income developing countries. However, here too the past efficacy of agricultural growth in reducing poverty in China reflects (at least in part) an unusual historical circumstance, namely the relatively equitable land allocation that could be achieved at the time of breaking up the collectives.

Macroeconomic stability (notably by avoiding inflationary shocks) has also been good for poverty reduction. The adverse impacts on poor people of inflationary shocks probably stemmed from short-term stickiness in some of the key factor and output prices determining their real incomes. Government spending was also poverty reducing, though much more so for spending by provincial and local governments than spending by the central government and public spending as a whole was not inequality reducing. The score card for trade reform is less clear. While the country's success in trade reform may well bring longer term gains to the poor the experience of 1981–2001 does not provide support for the view that China's periods of expanding external trade brought more rapid poverty reduction.

Looking ahead, this study points to some reasons to suspect that it will be more difficult for China to maintain its past rate of progress against poverty without addressing the problem of rising inequality. To the extent that recent history is any guide to the future, we can expect that the historically high levels of inequality found in many provinces today will inhibit future prospects for poverty reduction – just as we have seen how the provinces that started the reform period with (relatively) high inequality had a harder time reducing poverty. At the same time, it appears that aggregate growth is increasingly coming from sources that bring fewer gains to the poorest. Arguably, the low-lying fruits of efficiency-enhancing pro-poor reforms are getting scarce. Inequality is continuing to rise *and* poverty is becoming much more responsive to rising inequality.

5.A Appendix: Adjustments for the change in valuation methods in 1990

The change in valuation methods is clearly not a serious concern for the early 1980s when foodgrain markets had not yet been liberalized (Guo 1992; Chow 2002). Since virtually all foodgrain output was sold to the government, it would have been appropriate to value consumption from own-production at the government's procurement price. However, with the steps toward liberalization of foodgrain markets starting in 1985, a discrepancy emerged between procurement and market prices, with planning prices for foodgrain being substantially lower than market prices in the late 1980s (Chen and Ravallion 1996).

The change in the methods of valuation for income-in-kind in 1990 (whereby planning prices were replaced by local selling prices) creates a problem in constructing a consistent series of poverty measures for China. Table 5.A1 gives our calculations of the key summary statistics by both methods using the *rural* data for 1990 provided by NBS. This entailed about a 10 percent upward revision to NBS estimates of mean rural income and a downward revision to inequality estimates. On both counts, measured poverty fell, as can be seen by comparing the first two rows of numbers in Table 5.A1.

To address this problem in the data for the late 1980s, we calibrated a simple "correction model" to the data for 1990. Note first that the data from the tabulations provided by NBS do not come in equal-sized fractiles. So we must first "harmonize" the data for the old and new prices. To do this we estimated parametric Lorenz curves for each distribution separately and used these to estimate the mean income of all those below each of 100 percentiles of the distribution ranked by income per person. Having lined up the distributions in common factiles, we estimated a flexible parametric model of the log ratio of mean income at new prices to that at the old prices. A cubic

Table 5.A1 Performance of our adjustment method for rural China 1990

	Mean income (Yuan per person)	Gini index (%)	Headcount index (%)	Poverty gap index (%)	Squared poverty gap index (%)
Old valuation method	629.70	31.53	37.63	11.13	4.55
New method: actual	686.30	29.87	29.93	7.85	2.87
New method: Estimated using our correction model	688.05	30.05	29.86	7.86	2.88

function of the percentile gave an excellent fit to the data, in the form of the following regression for the ratio of income valued at the new prices ($Y(new)$) to that at the old prices ($Y(old)$) (t-ratios in parentheses):

$$Y(new) / Y(old) = 1.19272 - 0.20915\,p + 0.23457\,p^2 - 0.12562\,p^3 + \hat{\varepsilon}$$
$$\underset{(5421.5)}{}\quad\underset{(-111.8)}{}\quad\underset{(54.5)}{}\quad\underset{(-44.9)}{}$$
$$R^2 = 0.99959 \tag{A1}$$

where p = cumulative proportion of the population ranked by income per person (i.e. $0<p<1$). On using this regression to estimate the distribution of income in 1990 at the new prices from that based on the old prices we obtained the estimates in the last row of Table 5.A1. It can be seen that the estimates of summary statistics and poverty measures for the new prices accord quite closely to those obtained from the data directly.

We applied this method to estimate a corrected "as if new prices" series for the 1980s. However, since we know that foodgrain prices (as with most other consumer goods) were not freed up until 1985 we only applied this correction method to the "old price" series from 1985 onwards. It is also unlikely that this change happened overnight, so we smooth the transition in data. We do this by replacing the old price series by a weighted mean of the old price series and our estimates of what we would have obtained using new prices. The weight on the estimated new price series rises linearly over time from 0.2 in 1985 to 1.0 in 1989. This is admittedly *ad hoc*, but it seems the most defensible approach with the information available.

Figure 5.A1 shows the effect of our correction method on the time series of

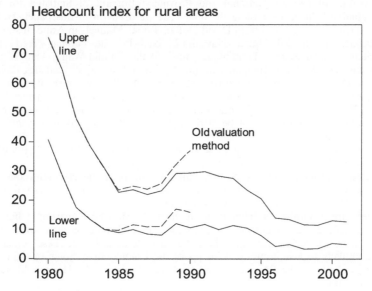

Figure 5.A1 Effect on headcount index of correction for the change in valuation methods.

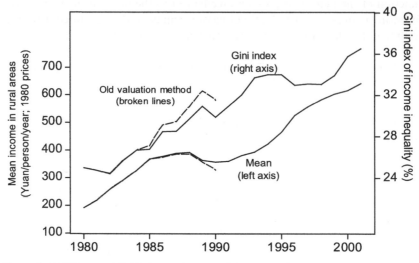

Figure 5.A2 Effect on Gini index and mean of our corrections.

headcount indices of rural poverty. Figure 5.A2 shows the effect on the mean and Gini index.

Notes

1 The authors are grateful to the staff of the Rural and Urban Household Survey Divisions of China's National and Provincial Bureaus of Statistics for their invaluable help in assembling the data base we draw on in this paper. Helpful comments were received from David Dollar, Tamar Manuelyan Atinc, Justin Lin, Michael Lipton, Will Martin, Nathalie Milbach-Bouche, Thomas Piketty, Lant Pritchett, Scott Rozelle, Dominique van de Walle, Shuilin Wang, Alan Winters, seminar/conference participants at the National Bureau of Statistics, Beijing, the McArthur Foundation Network on Inequality, Beijing University, Tsinghua University, the Australian National University, the International Monetary Fund, the World Bank and the journal's anonymous referees. These are the views of the authors and should not be attributed to the World Bank or any affiliated organization.
2 On the history and design of these surveys see Chen and Ravallion (1996) and Bramall (2001).
3 Included provinces had a poverty rate by our main poverty lines that was 1.9 percent points higher, but this is not significantly different from zero (t-ratio = 0.32). This held for all other poverty measures.
4 There are a number of tabulations in the NBS Statistical Yearbook, but they only provide the percentages of households in each income class; without the mean income for each income class and mean household size these tabulations are unlikely to give accurate estimates of the Lorenz curve. Some of these data are available in the Provincial Statistical Yearbooks or the Household Survey Yearbooks.
5 Ravallion and Chen (1999) examine the implications for measuring inequality in China.

6 Yunnan was given as an example by NBS staff, and we verified with Yunnan staff in Kunming that mixture prices had been used up to the mid 1990s. The problem was not confined to poor provinces; for example, Guangxi and Guizhou used market prices only from 1990 onwards.

7 In Chen and Ravallion (1996) we created a consistent series for 1985–90 from the micro data for a few provinces. However, this is not feasible without the complete micro data.

8 Poverty lines across countries tend to be higher the higher the mean income of the country, though with an initially low elasticity at low income (Ravallion 1994).

9 Without the latter condition, the rural food bundles were deemed to be nutritionally inadequate (in terms of protein and other nutrients) while the urban bundles were considered to be preferable. The condition was binding on both urban and rural bundles.

10 The urban population shares are based on the data provided by the census bureau of NBS, including the annual sample surveys used between the decadal censuses. These data are based on addresses rather than registrations so the aforementioned problem of undercounting the urban population based on registrations does not arise.

11 For example, in India (with no such restrictions) the share of the population living in urban areas increased from 23 to 28 percent over the same period.

12 A breakdown of the urban and rural CPI by type of commodity is only available from 1990 onwards. Over this period, the prices of services increased far more than other goods, and far more in urban areas than rural areas. While the overall urban CPI increased by a factor of 2.16 from 1990–2001, as compared to 1.92 for the rural CPI, the services component increased by a factor of 4.83, versus 3.81 in rural areas. Similarly, housing prices increased more steeply in urban areas, and more so than the overall CPI.

13 Since the latter adjustment is based on the poverty lines, it may not be appropriate for the mean (at least toward the end of the period). But it is our best available option.

14 Using different data, Benjamin et al. (2005) also find evidence of a deceleration in the rate of growth in rural incomes in the later part of the 1990s. Indeed, their results indicate a decline in rural incomes, while we still find gains over this period. This could reflect a difference in data sources. Benjamin et al., use survey data for nine provinces collected by Ministry of Agriculture, for which the sample frame is only for agricultural households, while the RHS sample frame is the rural population as whole. The RHS data also indicate stagnation in the growth of rural household income from agriculture; by contrast, rural *non-farm* activities actually did well in this period; income from agriculture accounted for 61 percent of China's rural net income in 1995; this had fallen to 48 percent by 2000 (RSO 2002).

15 This is one of the decompositions for poverty measures proposed by Ravallion and Huppi (1991).

16 This can be interpreted as a "Kuznets process" of migration whereby a representative slice of the rural distribution is transformed into a representative slice of the urban distribution.

17 The correlograms of the first differences of the three log poverty measures shows no significant autocorrelations. While the first difference of the log mean still shows mild positive serial correlation, the residuals of the regression of the log difference of the poverty measure on the on the log difference of the mean shows no sign of serial correlation.

18 Evidence on this point for other countries can be found in Ravallion (2001).

19 The literature has often emphasized the importance of the sectoral composition of growth to poverty reduction; for an overview of the arguments and evidence

see Lipton and Ravallion (1995). The following analysis follows the methods introduced in Ravallion and Datt (1996), which found that the composition of growth mattered to poverty reduction in India.

20 There is no sign of serial correlation in the residuals from the regression of the first difference of log Gini on log GDP. So the (first-order) differenced specification is defensible.

21 The literature on distribution and development has emphasized the importance of the sectoral composition of growth (see, for example, Lipton and Ravallion 1995; Ravallion and Datt 1996; Bourguignon and Morrison 1998).

22 This is only one of many taxes and transfers with bearing on income distribution in China. It would be of interest to see a complete accounting of the incidence of taxes and transfers. This does not appear to exist in the literature at the time of writing.

23 Including Easterly and Fischer (2001) and Dollar and Kraay (2002) both using cross-country data, and Datt and Ravallion (1998) using data for India.

24 On including the current and lagged values separately the homogeneity restriction passed comfortably. The public spending data are from NBS (1996, 2003) and include all types of spending at both central and local levels. The rural CPI was used as the deflator.

25 Local spending accounted for 65.3 percent of the total in 2001; in 1980 it accounted for 45.7 percent.

26 Similarly, if we re-estimate (10) replacing the headcount index by the Gini index, we find that $\Delta \ln GL_t$ is highly insignificant while the other two variables remain significant.

27 For example, a two-tier price system allowed exporters to purchase commodities at a low planning price and then export them at a profit. For this reason, oil was a huge export item until 1986.

28 See Chen and Fleisher (1996), Jian et al. (1996), Sun and Dutta (1997), and Raiser (1998).

29 The costal provinces are Hebei, Liaoning, Shanghai, Jiangsu, Zhejiang, Fujian, Shangdong, and Guangdong; following convention, we do not classify Guangxi as "coastal" though it has a costal area.

30 Starting from an unrestricted regression of β^H / β^M on G_{83}^R, $\bar{y}^R$, G_{83}^R, $\bar{y}^R$ and β^G a joint F-test does not reject the null hypothesis (with prob. = 0.17) that the joint restrictions hold that are needed to obtain (11) as the restricted form.

31 The simulated poverty measure was obtained using the initial Lorenz curve and the 2001 mean.

32 This is defined as the ratio of urban mean in 1985 (the first available data point from the UHS) and the first available rural mean (in two-thirds of the cases 1983).

33 Note that a higher value of the dependent variable means that there was less poverty reduction. We also tried rerunning this regression only using the 20 provinces for which the first year is 1983. The initial Gini index and the urban–rural income differential remained highly significant.

34 For evidence on this point at county level for China see Ravallion (1998) and at village level see Benjamin et al. (2004); on the theory and evidence see Aghion et al. (1999) and Bardhan et al. (1999).

References

Aghion, Philippe, Eve Caroli and Cecilia Garcia-Penalosa, 1999. "Inequality and Economic Growth: The Perspectives of the New Growth Theories", *Journal of Economic Literature* 37(4): 1615–60.

Bardhan, Pranab, Samuel Bowles, and Herbert Gintis, (1999). "Wealth Inequality,

Wealth Constraints and Economic Performance," in A.B. Atkinson and F. Bourguignon (eds) *Handbook of Income Distribution*, vol. I., Amsterdam: North-Holland.

Benjamin, Dwayne, Loren Brandt, and John Giles, 2004. "The Dynamics of Inequality and Growth in Rural China: Does Higher Inequality Impede Growth?" mimeo, University of Toronto.

——. 2005. "The Evolution of Income Inequality in Rural China," *Economic Development and Cultural Change* 53(4): 769–824.

Bourguignon, Francois and C. Morrison, 1998. "Inequality and Development: The Role of Dualism." *Journal of Development Economics* 57 (2), 233–57.

Bramall, Chris. 2001. "The Quality of China's Household Income Survey." *China Quarterly* 167, 689–705.

Chen, Jian and Belton M. Fleisher, 1996. "Regional Income Inequality and Economic Growth in China." *Journal of Comparative Economics*, 22: 141–64.

Chen, Shaohua and Martin Ravallion, 1996. "Data in Transition: Assessing Rural Living Standards in Southern China," *China Economic Review*, 7: 23–56.

——. 2004a. "How Have the World's Poorest Fared Since the Early 1980s?" *World Bank Research Observer*, 19(2): 141–70.

——. 2004b. "Household Welfare Impacts of WTO Accession in China." *World Bank Economic Review*, 18(1): 29–58.

Chow, Gregory C., 2002. *China's Economic Transformation*. Oxford: Blackwell Publishers.

Datt, Gaurav and Martin Ravallion, 1992. "Growth and Redistribution Components of Changes in Poverty Measures: A Decomposition with Applications to Brazil and India in the 1980s." *Journal of Development Economics*, 38: 275–95.

——. 1998. "Farm Productivity and Rural Poverty in India", *Journal of Development Studies* 34: 62–85.

——. 2002. "Has India's Post-Reform Economic Growth Left the Poor Behind," *Journal of Economic Perspectives*, 16(3), 89–108.

Dollar, David, 2004. "Globalization, Poverty, and Inequality since 1980," Policy Research Working Paper 3333, World Bank.

Dollar, David and Aart Kraay, 2002. "Growth *is* Good for the Poor," *Journal of Economic Growth*, 7(3): 195–225.

Easterly, William and Stanley Fischer, 2001. "Inflation and the Poor," *Journal of Money Credit and Banking*, 33(2): 160–78.

Fan, Shenggen, 1991. "Effects of Technological Change and Institutional Reform on Growth in Chinese Agriculture," *American Journal of Agricultural Economics* 73: 266–75.

Foster, James., J. Greer, and E. Thorbecke, 1984. "A Class of Decomposable Poverty Measures", *Econometrica* 52: 761–5.

Guo, Jiann-Jong, 1992. *Price Reform in China, 1979–1986*. New York: St Martin's Press.

Ianchovichina, Elena and Will Martin, 2004. "Impacts of China's Accession to the WTO." *World Bank Economic Review* 18(1): 3–28.

Jian, Tianlun, Jeffrey Sachs and Andrew Warner, 1996. "Trends in Regional Inequality in China." *China Economic Review*, 7(1): 1–21.

Kanbur, Ravi and Xiaobo Zhang, 1999. "Which Regional Inequality? The Evolution of Rural–Urban and Inland–Coastal Inequality in China from 1983 to 1995," *Journal of Comparative Economics* 27: 686–701.

Khan, Azizur and Carl Riskin. 1998. "Income Inequality in China: Composition, Distribution and Growth of Household Income, 1988 to 1995." *The China Quarterly*, 154: 221–53.

Kung, James. 1995. "Equal Entitlement versus Tenure Security under a Regime of Collective Property Rights: Peasants' Preference for Institutions in Post-Reform Chinese Agriculture," *Journal of Comparative Economics* 21: 82–111.

Lin, Justin. 1992. "Rural Reforms and Agricultural Growth in China," *American Economic Review* 82: 34–51.

Lipton, Michael and Martin Ravallion. 1995. "Poverty and Policy", in *Handbook of Development Economics* Volume 3, (edited by Jere Behrman and T.N. Srinivasan) Amsterdam: North Holland.

National Bureau of Statistics. 1996, 2003. *Statistical Yearbook for China*, Beijing: China Statistics Press.

Raiser, Martin. 1998. "Subsidizing Inequality: Economic Reforms, Fiscal Transfers and Convergence Across Chinese Provinces." *Journal of Development Studies*, 34: 1–26.

Ravallion, Martin. 1994. *Poverty Comparisons*. Harwood Academic Press, Chur, Switzerland.

——. 1995. "Growth and Poverty: Evidence for Developing Countries in the 1980s," *Economics Letters*, 48, 411–17.

——. 1997. "Can High Inequality Developing Countries Escape Absolute Poverty?", *Economics Letters*, 56, 51–7.

——. 1998. "Does Aggregation Hide the Harmful Effects of Inequality on Growth?" *Economics Letters*, 61(1), 73–7.

——. 2001. "Growth, Inequality and Poverty: Looking Beyond Averages," *World Development*, 29(11), 1803–15.

——, 2005. "Externalities in Rural Development: Evidence for China," in Ravi Kanbur and Tony Venables (eds) *Spatial Inequality and Development*, Oxford: Oxford University Press.

Ravallion, Martin and Shaohua Chen, 1999. "When Economic Reform is Faster than Statistical Reform: Measuring and Explaining Inequality in Rural China", *Oxford Bulletin of Economics and Statistics*, 61(1), 33–56.

Ravallion, Martin and Gaurav Datt. 1996. "How Important to India's Poor is the Sectoral Composition of Economic Growth?", *World Bank Economic Review*, 10: 1–26.

Ravallion, Martin and Monika Huppi. 1991. "Measuring Changes in Poverty: A Methodological Case Study of Indonesia During an Adjustment Period," *World Bank Economic Review*, 5: 57–82.

Rural Survey Organization, National Bureau of Statistics. 2002. *China: Yearbook of Rural Household Survey*, Beijing: China Statistics Press.

Sun, Haishun and Dilip Dutta. 1997. "China's Economic Growth During 1984–93: A Case of Regional Dualism." *Third World Quarterly*, 18(5): 843–64.

Tsui, Kai-yuen. 1998. "Trends and Inequalities in Rural Welfare in China: Evidence from Rural Households in Guangdong and Sichuan," *Journal of Comparative Economics* 26: 783–804.

United Nations Conference on Trade and Development (UNCTAD). 1994. *Directors of Import Regimes: Part 1: Monitoring Import Regimes*, UNCTAD, Geneva.

World Bank. 1997. *China 2020: Sharing Rising Income*, World Bank, Washington DC.

——. 2000. *World Development Report: Attacking Poverty*, New York: Oxford University Press.

—— . 2002. *Globalization, Growth and Poverty*, World Bank, Washington DC.
—— . 2004. *World Development Indicators*, Washington DC: World Bank.
Yang, Dennis Tao. 1994. "Urban-Biased Policies and Rising Income Inequality in China," *American Economic Review (Papers and Proceedings)*, 89: 306–10.

6 Fifty years of regional inequality in China

A journey through central planning, reform, and openness

Ravi Kanbur and Xiaobo Zhang [*]

Abstract

This paper constructs and analyses a long run time series for regional inequality in China from the Communist Revolution to the present. There have been three peaks of inequality in the last fifty years, coinciding with the Great Famine of the late 1950s, the Cultural Revolution of the late 1960s and 1970s, and finally the period of openness and global integration in the late 1990s. Econometric analysis establishes that regional inequality is explained in the different phases by three key policy variables – the ratio of heavy industry to gross output value, the degree of decentralization, and the degree of openness.

6.1 Introduction

The second half of the twentieth century has seen a tumultuous history unfold in China – the early years of communist rule in the 1950s culminating in the Great Famine, the Cultural Revolution and its aftermath in the late 1960s and the 1970s, the reform of agriculture in the late 1970s and the 1980s, and an explosion of trade and foreign direct investment in the late 1980s and the 1990s. All these events have affected the course of economic growth and income distribution. However, while a large literature has studied growth through these different phases of Chinese history (Lin 1992; Fan, Zhang, and Robinson 2003), few studies have matched the evolution of inequality over the long run with these different periods in Communist Chinese history over its entire course.

This paper presents and analyzes the evolution of Chinese regional inequality since the Communist revolution right up to the present. Most studies on China's inequality (Chen and Ravallion 1996; Aaberge and Li 1997; Tsui 1998; Khan and Riskin 2001) have focused on relatively short periods, mostly during the post-reform years, making use of the new household surveys that became available during this period. Of the studies which come closest to the spirit of our interest in Chinese inequality over the long run, Tsui (1991) stops in 1985 and Lyons (1991) stops in 1987, just as the increase in trade and foreign direct investment was beginning; Yang and Fang

(2000) go up to 1996, but focus only on the rural–urban gap at the national level; and Kanbur and Zhang (1999) disaggregate down to the rural–urban level within provinces to calculate a regional inequality index, and present a decomposition of regional inequality by its rural–urban and inland–coastal components, but their study is only for the post reform years of 1983–1995.

Using a dataset of provincial and national data covering the second half of the twentieth century, we are able to construct a comprehensive time series of regional inequality in China, including its decompositions into rural–urban and inland–coastal components, from 1952 to 2000. We find that changes in regional inequality match the phases of Chinese history remarkably well, as do its rural–urban and inland–coastal components. The peaks of inequality in China have been associated with the Great Famine, the Cultural Revolution, and the current phase of openness and decentralization. We further use econometric analysis to establish that regional inequality is explained to different degrees in different phases by three key policy variables: the share of heavy industry in gross output value, the degree of decentralization, and the degree of openness.

6.2 Constructing a long run time series for regional inequality in China

Ideally, for an analysis of the evolution of inequality over Communist Chinese history we would have available representative national household surveys over the entire period. Unfortunately, while such surveys have been conducted throughout the last fifty years, they are available to researchers only for the post reform period, and in any case sporadically, for restricted years with varying but limited coverage. Thus, for example, Chen and Ravallion (1996) had access to official household survey data but only for four provinces between 1986 and 1990. Aaberge and Li (1997) analyze urban household surveys for Liaoning and Sichuan provinces for the same period, while Tsui (1998) analyzes rural surveys for 1985, 1988, and 1990, but only for Guangdong and Sichuan. Yang (1999) analyzes both rural and urban parts of the household survey for four years between 1986 and 1994, and for Guangdong and Sichuan. This different coverage across studies reflects the differential access to official data. Researchers have also conducted and analyzed independent surveys – for example, Rozelle (1994) did one for Township and Village Enterprises between 1984 to 1989 in Jiangsu province, and Khan and Riskin (2001) conducted household surveys for 1988 and 1995.

The inequality analysis that has been done on household surveys for the late 1980s and 1990s, has been extremely valuable in illuminating specific aspects of the distributional dimensions of Chinese development in the late 1980s and early 1990s. In general these analyses decompose inequality by income sources but few have aligned the patterns of inequality with national development policies. The bottom line is that researchers simply do not have comprehensive access to household surveys which are national and which cover the entire, or even a substantial part of, the half-century sweep of Chinese history that is of interest to us in this paper.

In the face of these data restrictions, we are forced to look for data availability at higher levels of aggregation than at the household level.[1] As it turns out certain types of data are indeed available at the province level, disaggregated by rural and urban areas, stretching back to 1952. This paper constructs a time series of inequality by building up information on real per capita consumption in the rural and urban areas of 28 of China's 30 provinces (unfortunately, data availability is not complete for Tibet and Hainan provinces).[2]

With these subprovincial rural and urban per capita consumption figures, and population weights for these areas, a national distribution of real per capita consumption can be constructed, and its inequality calculated, for each year between 1952 and 2000, thus covering the vast bulk of the period from 1949 to the present. Of course what this means is that overall household level-inequality is being understated, since inequality within the rural and urban areas of each province is being suppressed. Moreover, we cannot say anything about the evolution of household-level inequality *within* these areas. Our measures do provide a lower bound on inequality over this entire period. But the fact remains that our study of inequality is essentially a study of regional inequality.[3]

Using the information available, we calculate the Gini coefficient of inequality using the standard formula. But the bulk of our analysis is done with a second inequality index, a member of the decomposable generalized entropy (GE) class of inequality measures as developed by Shorrocks (1984)[4]:

$$I(y) = \sum_{i=1}^{n} f(y_i) \log\left(\frac{\mu}{y_i}\right) \tag{1}$$

In the above equation, y_i is the ith income measured as Chinese yuan, μ is the total sample mean, $f(y_i)$ is the population share of y_i in the total population and n is total population. A key feature of this measure is that it is additively decomposable. For K exogenously given, mutually exclusive and exhaustive, groups indexed by g:

$$I(y) = \sum_{g}^{K} f_g I_g + I(\mu_1 e_1, \ldots, \mu_K e_K) \tag{2}$$

In equation 2, I_g is inequality in the gth group, μ_g is the mean of the gth group and e_g is a vector of 1's of length n_g, where n_g is the population of the gth group. If n is the total population of all groups, then $f_g = \frac{n_g}{n}$ represents the share of the gth group's population in the total population. The first term on the right hand side of (2) represents the within-group inequality. The second term is the between group, or intergroup, component of total inequality. With our time series of inequality in China over the long term, we are now in a position to investigate dimensions of inequality in the different phases of Chinese development over the past half century.

6.3 Inequality change through the phases of Chinese history: a narrative

Following standard discussions, Communist Chinese history can be divided into several phases: 1949–56 (Revolution and Land Reform), 1957–61 (The Great Leap Forward and the Great Famine), 1962–5 (Post-Famine Recovery), 1966–78 (Cultural Revolution and Transition to Reform), 1979–84 (Rural Reform) and 1985–present (Post Rural Reform, Decentralization and Opening up to Trade and Foreign Direct Investment).

Table 6.1 presents economic indicators for China from 1952 to 2000. It includes three key indicators of economic policy – the share of heavy industry in gross value of total output (a measure of the bias against agriculture and China's comparative advantage), the ratio of trade volume to total GDP (a measure of the degree of openness), and the ratio of local government expenditure to total government expenditure (a measure of decentralization).[5] Figure 6.1 shows the evolution of real per capita GDP through the different phases identified above. Table 6.2 presents long-run inequality series, and Figure 6.2 graphs the evolution of Chinese regional inequality, as measured by the Gini and the GE index, through the six phases of development identified above. The two indices move in close relation to each other, and match the different phases of Chinese development remarkably well.

Over the past fifty years inequality has peaked three times – during the Great Famine, at the end of the Cultural Revolution, and in the current period of global integration. Similarly, there are three major troughs in the overall evolution of inequality – in 1952, right at the beginning of the data series; in 1967, at the end of the recovery from the Great Famine and before the effects of the Cultural Revolution set in; and in 1984, at the end of the rural reform period and the start of the expansion based on global integration. Overall, inequality seems to have been low when policy was encouraging to agriculture and the rural sector generally, and high when this sector was relatively neglected.

These effects can be further investigated by decomposing overall inequality into subcomponents and examining the evolution of these components. The 56 data points in each year from which the overall distribution is constructed, a rural and an urban observation for each of 28 provinces, can be divided into rural and urban observations across the provinces and, using equation (2) the GE index can be decomposed into a "within rural–urban" and a "between rural–urban" component (we will call the latter rural–urban inequality). The overall GE and the between rural–urban component are shown in Table 6.2. The within rural–urban component is the difference between the two.

Table 6.1 China: economic indicators, 1952–2000

Year	GDP (billion)	Import (billion)	Total expenditure (billion)	GOV (billion)	Tariff rate (%)	Trade ratio (%)	Decentralization (%)	Industrialization (%)
1952	67.9	3.8	17.2	81.0	12.8	9.5	25.9	15.3
1953	82.4	4.6	21.9	96.0	11.0	9.8	26.1	17.5
1954	85.9	4.5	24.4	105.0	9.2	9.9	24.7	18.9
1955	91.0	6.1	26.3	110.9	7.6	12.1	23.5	19.7
1956	102.8	5.3	29.9	125.2	10.2	10.6	29.6	21.7
1957	106.8	5.0	29.6	124.1	9.6	9.8	29.0	25.5
1958	130.7	6.2	40.0	164.9	10.4	9.8	55.7	35.2
1959	143.9	7.1	54.3	198.0	9.9	10.4	54.1	43.8
1960	145.7	6.5	64.4	209.4	9.2	8.8	56.7	52.1
1961	122.0	4.3	35.6	162.1	14.5	7.4	55.0	37.7
1962	114.9	3.4	29.5	150.4	14.3	7.0	38.4	32.3
1963	123.3	3.6	33.2	163.5	11.6	6.9	42.1	33.5
1964	145.4	4.2	39.4	188.4	10.4	6.7	42.9	34.4
1965	171.6	5.5	46.0	223.5	10.3	6.9	38.2	30.4
1966	186.8	6.1	53.8	253.4	10.6	6.8	36.9	32.7
1967	177.4	5.3	44.0	230.6	7.3	6.3	38.7	28.1
1968	172.3	5.1	35.8	221.3	12.4	6.3	38.7	26.9
1969	193.8	4.7	52.6	261.3	13.5	5.5	39.3	31.7
1970	225.3	5.6	64.9	313.8	12.5	5.0	41.1	36.4
1971	242.6	5.2	73.2	348.2	9.5	5.0	40.5	39.5
1972	251.8	6.4	76.6	364.0	7.8	5.8	43.7	40.2
1973	272.1	10.4	80.9	396.7	8.7	8.1	44.4	39.9
1974	279.0	15.3	79.0	400.7	9.2	10.5	49.7	38.7
1975	299.7	14.7	82.1	446.7	10.2	9.7	50.1	40.2
1976	274.4	12.9	80.6	453.6	11.6	9.6	53.2	40.3
1977	320.2	13.3	84.4	497.8	19.8	8.5	53.3	41.9
1978	362.4	18.7	112.2	563.4	15.3	9.8	52.6	42.8

Year								
1979	403.8	24.3	128.2	637.9	10.7	11.3	48.9	41.3
1980	451.8	29.9	122.9	707.7	11.2	12.6	45.7	38.5
1981	486.0	36.8	113.8	758.1	14.7	15.1	45.0	34.5
1982	530.2	35.8	123.0	829.4	13.3	14.5	47.0	34.9
1983	595.7	42.2	141.0	921.1	12.8	14.4	46.1	36.1
1984	720.7	62.1	170.1	1083.1	16.6	16.7	47.5	37.0
1985	898.9	125.8	200.4	1333.5	16.3	23.0	60.3	38.6
1986	1020.1	149.8	220.5	1520.7	10.1	25.3	62.1	38.6
1987	1195.5	161.4	226.2	1848.9	8.8	25.8	62.6	38.7
1988	1492.2	205.5	249.1	2408.9	7.5	25.6	66.1	38.4
1989	1691.8	220.0	282.4	2855.2	8.3	24.6	68.5	39.4
1990	1859.8	257.4	308.4	3158.6	6.2	29.9	67.4	38.3
1991	2166.3	339.9	338.7	3478.2	5.5	33.4	67.8	41.5
1992	2665.2	444.3	374.2	4368.4	4.8	34.2	68.7	44.8
1993	3456.1	598.6	464.2	5939.8	4.3	32.6	71.7	49.7
1994	4667.0	996.0	579.3	8592.7	2.7	43.7	69.7	35.5
1995	5749.5	1104.8	682.4	11223.5	2.6	40.9	70.8	33.1
1996	6685.1	1155.7	793.8	12195.3	2.6	36.1	72.9	30.0
1997	7314.3	1180.7	923.4	13749.7	2.7	36.9	72.6	29.2
1998	7801.8	1162.2	1079.8	14320.5	2.7	34.4	71.1	27.0
1999	8206.8	1373.7	1318.8	15063.0	4.1	36.4	68.5	23.6
2000	8940.4	1863.9	1588.7	n.a	4.0	43.9	65.3	n.a.

Note: The effective tariff rate is defined as the ratio of tariff revenue to total imports. Trade ratio is the share of trade (imports plus exports) in total GDP. Decentralization is defined as the share of local governments' expenditure in total government expenditure. The industrialization variable is defined as the ratio of the gross heavy industrial output value relative to the gross agricultural and industrial output value (GOV). GDP, government expenditures, and tariff data for the whole period are from *China Statistical Yearbook* (2001). Prior to 1999, the trade volume, gross agricultural output value, gross industrial output value, and gross heavy industrial output value are available from *Comprehensive Statistical Data and Materials On 50 Years of New China*. Information about the above variables in the years of 1999 and 2000 are from *China Statistical Yearbook* (2000 and 2001).

Table 6.2 Inequalities and decompositions: 1952–2000

Year	Gini (%)	GE (%)	Rural–Urban	Inland–Coast
1952	22.4	9.0	6.9	0.6
1953	24.7	10.7	8.6	0.7
1954	23.2	9.4	7.9	0.6
1955	22.0	8.6	7.3	0.3
1956	22.9	9.4	8.2	0.2
1957	23.8	9.8	8.5	0.1
1958	24.4	10.2	8.8	0.2
1959	29.7	14.3	11.6	0.2
1960	32.2	16.6	13.5	0.3
1961	30.3	14.5	11.2	0.2
1962	28.5	13.1	10.7	0.2
1963	27.6	12.4	9.6	0.2
1964	28.2	12.8	9.5	0.2
1965	26.7	11.8	8.7	0.2
1966	26.6	11.7	9.1	0.2
1967	25.5	10.8	8.5	0.2
1968	26.3	11.3	8.7	0.3
1969	27.1	12.2	9.9	0.3
1970	27.0	12.1	9.8	0.3
1971	26.9	12.1	9.8	0.3
1972	28.1	12.8	9.8	0.3
1973	27.9	12.7	9.9	0.3
1974	28.8	13.5	10.3	0.3
1975	29.5	14.2	11.2	0.5
1976	30.9	15.5	12.1	0.5
1977	30.8	15.4	12.1	0.5
1978	29.3	14.0	11.0	0.4
1979	28.6	13.3	10.1	0.4
1980	28.2	13.1	9.9	0.5
1981	27.0	12.0	9.1	0.6
1982	25.6	10.6	7.2	0.5
1983	25.9	11.1	6.8	0.4
1984	25.6	10.9	6.3	0.4
1985	25.8	11.1	6.6	0.5
1986	26.8	11.9	6.9	0.5
1987	27.0	12.0	6.8	0.6
1988	28.2	13.1	7.7	0.8
1989	29.7	14.4	9.3	1.0
1990	30.1	14.9	9.5	1.0
1991	30.3	14.9	9.9	1.2
1992	31.4	16.0	10.2	1.5
1993	32.2	16.8	10.9	1.7
1994	32.6	17.2	10.8	2.0
1995	33.0	17.7	11.5	2.3
1996	33.4	18.2	11.7	2.6
1997	33.9	18.9	11.7	2.7
1998	34.4	19.6	12.2	2.9
1999	36.3	23.4	12.8	3.2
2000	37.2	24.8	13.9	3.8

Note: Calculated by authors.

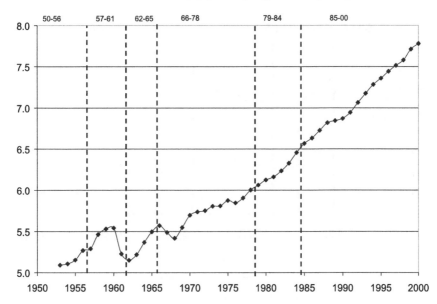

Figure 6.1 Per capita GDP (in logs) in constant 1980 prices.

A key dimension of inequality in China, especially in the post-reform period, is that between inland and coastal provinces (Chen and Fleisher 1996; Zhang and Kanbur 2001). We follow the practice of classifying the provinces of Beijing, Liaoning, Tianjin, Hebei, Shandong, Jiangsu, Shanghai, Zhejang, Fujian, Guangdong, and Guangxi as coastal and the other provinces as inland. We therefore divide our 56 observations into 22 coastal and 34 inland observations and decompose the GE measure accordingly. The "between inland–coastal" component (we will call it inland–coastal inequality thereafter) is reported in Table 6.2.

Figures 6.3–6.5 go a long way in translating the above narrative into impacts on overall inequality and the rural–urban and inland–costal inequalities, and provide some initial hypotheses for econometric testing in the next section. Under the central planning system, the central government had large powers to allocate and utilize financial revenues to achieve the goal of equity despite at the expense of efficiency. With economic reforms, the central government has granted local governments more autonomy in allocating their resources and bearing more responsibilities (Qian and Roland 1998; Zhang and Zhou 1998). While Zhang and Zou (1998) have in particular analyzed the relationship between fiscal decentralization and economic growth for China, few studies have investigated the effect of decentralization on regional inequality. Tsui (1991) detected a positive relationship between decentralization and worsening regional inequality using

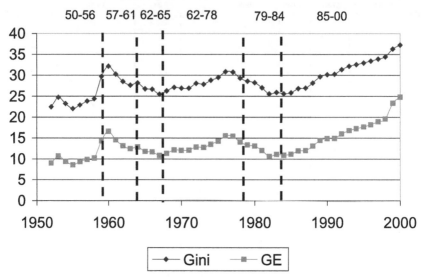

Figure 6.2 The trends of regional inequality.
Note: From Table 6.2.

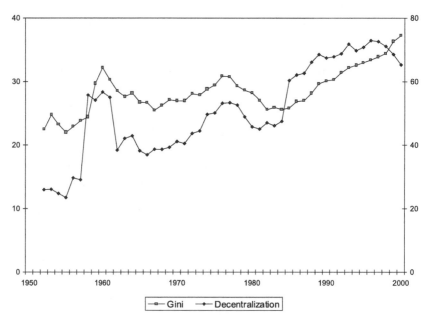

Figure 6.3 Decentralization and overall inequality (Gini coefficient).
Note: The left vertical axis represents Gini coefficient while the right refers to the degree of decentralization.

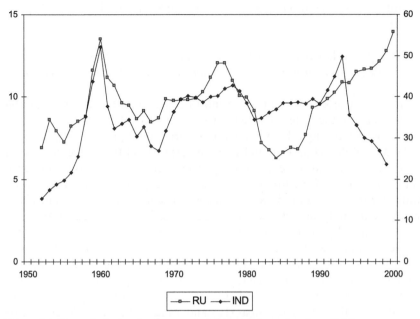

Figure 6.4 Heavy industry development strategy and rural–urban divides.

Note: The left vertical axis represents rural–urban disparity (RU) while the right refers to heavy industry output ratio (IND).

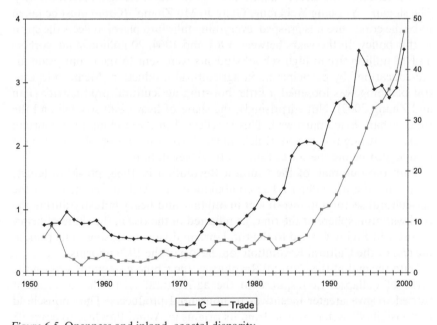

Figure 6.5 Openness and inland–coastal disparity.

Note: The left vertical axis represents inland–coastal disparity (IC) while the right refers to trade ratio (Trade).

a graph analysis based on data series up to 1985. This leads to the following hypothesis:

Hypothesis I. *Greater decentralization increases regional inequality during the economic transition from a planned economy to a market economy.*

In order to accelerate the pace of industrialization after the initial period of land reform, the state extracted massive amounts of resources from agriculture mainly through the suppression of agricultural prices and restrictions on labor mobility (Lin, Cai, and Li 1996). Almost all the scarce investment funds were allocated to heavy industry in neglect of light industry and agriculture. As shown in Figure 6.4, the share of heavy industry in gross output value rose from 0.22 in 1956 to 0.52 in 1960. The main enforcement mechanisms were a trinity of institutions, including the household registration system, the unified procurement and sale of agricultural commodities, and the people's communes. Consequently, the large rural–urban divide became a major feature of China's inequality (Yang 1999; Yang and Fang 2000), and the policies eventually led to the Great Famine. During the Famine, however, most urban residents were protected from starvation at the expense of about 30 million deaths in the rural areas (Lin and Yang 2000). These developments are reflected in the sharp increases, up to 1960, in the rural–urban inequality in Table 6.2 and in Figure 6.4.

In reaction to the Great Famine, agriculture was once again given priority. The slogan, "Yi Liang Wei Gang, Gang Ju Mu Zhang" (Grain must be taken to be the core; once it is grasped, everything falls into place), reflects the spirit of this policy. In the years between 1961 and 1964, 20 million state workers and 17 million urban high school students were sent to the countryside for "re-education" by participating in agricultural production. Meanwhile, central planning was loosened a little, boosting agricultural productivity (Fan and Zhang 2002). Not surprisingly, the share of heavy industry fell and the rural–urban divide narrowed. This is reflected in the declining rural–urban disparity during this period, which pulled down overall inequality to its next trough, just before the start of the Cultural Revolution.

With the outbreak of the Cultural Revolution in 1966, pro-Mao leftists came into the ascendancy. The combination of a lack of incentives in the agricultural sector and investment in military and heavy industry during the cold war atmosphere of the time, as reflected in the rise in the share of heavy industry in Figure 6.4, led to the rural–urban divide increasing to its peak at the end of the Cultural Revolution, on the eve of the 1979 reforms.

With the end of the Cultural Revolution, the Chinese economy was on the verge of collapse. In response to the agricultural crisis, the government started to give greater incentives to household producers. The "household responsibility" system spread from its origins in Anhui Province to cover 98 percent of all villages in China by 1983 (Lin 1992). These and other market-oriented strategies led to a remarkable growth in agricultural output, and the share of heavy industry dropped. The first five years of the post-1979 reforms saw a sharp decline in rural–urban divide. Overall inequality fell as well as shown in Figure 6.3. The above narrative leads to the second hypothesis:

Hypothesis II. *The heavy-industry development strategy, particularly in the prereform period, was a major contributing factor to the large rural–urban divide and to overall inequality.*

The latest phase in Chinese history begins in the mid 1980s. As is well known, this has been a period of accelerating integration into the global economy through greater openness in trade and especially in foreign direct investment. As seen in Figure 6.5, the trade ratio, after showing no trend for 35 years, began a steady increase since the mid 1980s both because of reductions in nominal tariffs and because of increases in import volumes. Between 1984 and 2000, the value of exports grew 11 percent per year. Changes in FDI flows are even more astonishing. We do not of course have long run time series for these, but from an almost isolated economy in the late 1970s, China has become the largest recipient of FDI among developing countries. In order to speed up the integration with the world markets, China has implemented a coastal-biased policy, such as establishing special economic zones in coastal cities and providing favorable tax breaks to coastal provinces. In other words, the opening process has inevitably had regional dimensions.

As is by now well appreciated, and as is shown in Figure 6.1, there has been spectacular growth in the past two decades in large thanks to the reforms and open-door policy. But the gains have not been evenly distributed across regions. Coastal provinces have attracted far more foreign direct investment and generated more trade volume than inland provinces during the liberalization process. In 2000, the three coastal provinces, Guangdong, Jiangsu, and Shanghai, were the top three, while the three inland provinces, Guizhou, Inner Mongolia, and Jilin, were the bottom three in terms of attracting FDI. The above three coastal provinces alone contribute to more than 60 percent of total foreign trade in 2000. The difference in the growth rates between the coastal and inland regions has been as high as three percentage points during the past two decades (Zhang and Zhang 2003).

We can use Guangdong and Sichuan provinces to illustrate how internal geography affects the response to openness. In 1978, the coastal Guangdong Province ranked 14th in labor productivity, which was almost the same as the 15th rank of inland Sichuan province. In a closed economy, Guangdong did not enjoy any obviously better resource endowments than inland provinces. However, after China opened its door to the world, Guangdong has become one of the most favored places for foreign direct investment and international trade which is in large due to its proximity to Hong Kong. Meanwhile, the ranking of labor productivity in Sichuan has declined from 15th in 1978 to 23rd in 2000. Clearly, the relative comparative advantages between the two provinces have changed significantly and are associated with the opening up to the outside and the decentralization which facilitated this response.

The above story of Guangdong and Sichuan is reflected nationwide in the behavior of the inland–coastal component of inequality. The major change in the behavior of this component over the entire fifty-year period comes in the mid-1980s. After relative stability up to this point, inland–coastal inequality began to increase sharply. Although still quite small as a contributor to over-all inequality, its contributions to *changes* in inequality increased dramatic-ally. As shown in Figure 6.5, inland–coastal disparity has closely followed the path of the trade ratio.

When an economy opens up to world markets, theory suggests that there could well be affects on regional inequality, as argued recently by Fujita, Krugman, and Venables (1999). External trade liberalization can change internal comparative advantage and hence location patterns. Coupled with decentralization, opening up to world markets provides local governments an opportunity to better exploit comparative advantage. Trade liberalization could also lead to specialization and industry clustering.

Empirical evidence for the impact of globalization on income distribution in developing countries has been limited, and the findings of existing studies are at best mixed. The existing work for developing countries has been limited to the effects of trade liberalization on wage inequality (Wood 1997; Hanson and Harrison 1999), shedding little light on the effect on regional inequality. Jian, Sachs, and Warner (1996) have argued that China's regional inequality is associated with internal geography. China's rapid change from a closed economy to open economy provides a good testing ground for our third hypothesis:

> Hypothesis III. *Greater openness is associated with greater regional inequality.*

Our narrative of the phases of Chinese development, and of the evolution of inequality and its components, is suggestive of the forces behind the changes in inequality over this half century. We now turn to an econometric analysis of the correlates of inequality, to see if these hypotheses can be confirmed statistically.

6.4 The correlates of regional inequality: an econometric analysis

Our task is to test the association between inequality and its components on the one hand, and heavy industrialization, decentralization, and openness, on the other. Following several analyses on Chinese data (Lin 1992), we use one-period lagged values of the independent variables as regressors to reduce potential endogeneity problems.[6] In the regressions, all the variables are in logarithms. We have compared regressions in levels and log levels and the latter gives better fit based on R^2 and RESET misspecification test. In addition, the heteroscedasticity problem is greatly reduced after taking logarithms.

A central issue in this long run time series is that of structural breaks. It is common in the econometric literature on China (Li 2000) to locate the break at the start of the reforms in the late 1970s. As shown in regression R1 in Tables 6.3–6.4 on overall inequality and rural–urban inequality, the Chow tests indicate a significant break in 1979. The Chow-test p-value is 0.105 in the regression on inland–coastal inequality (R1 in Table 6.5), indicating a marginally significant structural break.

There are two ways to handle this structural break. One way is to estimate the equations separately for the prereform period (1952–1978) and the post-reform period (1979–1999). However, in so doing, some degrees of freedom will be lost. Here, we adopt the second way by estimating the equations for the whole period but allowing coefficients to vary across the two periods. Regressions R2 in Tables 6.3–6.5 provide the estimation results under the varying-coefficient specifications. The Chow-test p-values indicate that structural break has been correctly captured in the new specification.

Because the three inequality series are not stationary, it is important to check whether regressing one on other policy variables produces stationary residuals, which means cointegration among variables. If the residuals are not

Table 6.3 Regressions results: total inequality

Variables	R1	R2	
	Whole period (1952–2000)	*Before reform (1952–1978)*	*Reform (1979–2000)*
Decentralization	0.279**	0.011	0.267**
	(0.072)	(0.068)	(0.056)
Trade ratio	0.295**	0.151**	0.455**
	(0.060)	(0.071)	(0.056)
Heavy industry ratio	0.003	0.488**	−0.161
	(0.111)	(0.113)	(0.128)
Chow test p-value	0.000		0.997
F-test for coefficients (p-value)			0.001
Phillips–Ouliaris test	−3.350		−5.012
KPSS statistic	**0.116**		**0.054**
Adjusted R-square	0.675		0.817

Note: All the variables are in logarithmic forms and independent variables have one-year lag. Figures in parentheses are robust standard errors. * and ** indicate statistical significance at the 10% and 5%, respectively. The null hypothesis of Chow test is that there is no structural break in 1979. The F-test is for testing whether the coefficients are the same across the two periods. Phillips–Ouliaris Z_t test is for testing the null hypothesis of no cointegration. Phillips and Ouliaris (1990) report the critical values for regressions with independent variables only up to 5. The critical values to reject this null hypothesis with three and five independent variable at the 10% significant level are −3.833 and −4.431, respectively. The KPSS statistic is for testing the null hypothesis of cointegration. If the statistic is larger than 0.347, the null will be rejected at the 10% significance level.

Table 6.4 Regressions results: rural–urban inequality

Variables	R1 Whole period (1952–2000)	R2 Before reform (1952–1978)	Reform (1979–2000)
Decentralization	0.256**	−0.018	0.369**
	(0.078)	(0.060)	(0.079)
Trade ratio	0.128**	0.208**	0.406**
	(0.036)	(0.087)	(0.067)
Heavy industry ratio	−0.080	0.458**	0.121
	(0.108)	(0.102)	(0.159)
Chow test p-value	0.000		0.993
F-test for coefficients			0.001
Phillips–Ouliaris test	−2.596		−4.529
KPSS statistic	**0.153**		**0.036**
Adjusted R-square	0.302		0.669

Table 6.5 Regressions results: inland–coastal inequality

Variables	R1 Whole period (1952–2000)	R2 Before reform (1952–1978)	Reform (1979–2000)
Decentralization	0.564**	0.341*	0.440**
	(0.119)	(0.203)	(0.163)
Trade ratio	1.409**	1.070**	1.412**
	(0.072)	(0.280)	(0.133)
Heavy industry ratio	−0.611**	−0.260	−1.100**
	(0.293)	(0.421)	(0.363)
Chow test p-value	0.105		0.242
F-test for coefficients			0.566
Phillips–Ouliaris test	−3.908		−3.895
KPSS statistic	**0.152**		**0.137**
R-square	0.828		0.825

stationary, the regressions with nonstationary data may give spurious results. Here we adopt two cointegration tests. The first one is the Phillips–Ouliaris test (1990, PO for short). The PO test is designed to detect the presence of a unit root in the residuals of regressions among the levels of time series. The null hypothesis is that the residuals have unit roots (no cointegration). The critical values for the PO test can be found in the appendix of Phillips and Ouliaris (1990). In addition to the Phillips–Ouliaris test, we also perform the KPSS test (Kwiatkowski et al. 1992) to check the cointegrated relationship. In contrast to the PO test, the KPSS test is to test the null hypothesis that the regression residuals are stationary (the variables are cointegrated).

Consider Table 6.3 first and start with the results for overall inequality. Regression R2 has better specification than R1 as it does not have structural breaks and passes both cointegration tests. The F-test indicates that the coefficients in the two periods are statistically different. In the prereform period, the heavy industry coefficient is significant and has the highest value (0.488), suggesting that the heavy industry development strategy implemented in the central planning era be a dominant force behind the overall inequality. Turning to the post reform period, the coefficients for decentralization and trade ratio are significantly positive. In particular, trade ratio has the largest impact on overall inequality in this period. The coefficient for decentralization has changed from insignificant to significant, confirming the observation in Figure 6.3 that decentralization has a closer relationship with the overall inequality in the reform period. Despite the importance of heavy industry ratio in the prereform period, it has faded into insignificance in the reform period as China changes its development strategies.

As in Table 6.3, regression R2 with varying coefficients in Table 6.4 has a better specification than regression R1 with constant coefficients. The F-test shows that there exists systematic difference in coefficients across the two periods. The results are similar to Table 6.3. In the prereform period, a greater favoring of heavy industry increases rural–urban spread. The impact of openness on rural–urban divide has almost doubled as China transforms from a closed economy to a more open economy. In the reform period, greater decentralization widens rural–urban disparity.

In Table 6.5 the two specifications on inland–coastal inequality produce similar results. The PO test and KPSS test indicate that the first regression R1 is cointegrated in levels. The coefficients for all the three policy variables are significant with signs in consistent with our hypotheses. In particular, trade ratio has the largest impact on inland–coastal inequality, reflecting the dramatic changes in regional comparative advantage as a result of coastal-biased policy as well as the opening up to the world market. The negative coefficient for the heavy industry ratio tells the same story. In the planned era, most heavy industries were established in the interior regions, thereby reducing the inland–coastal disparity. As China opens up, the coastal region has found itself a pronounced comparative advantage in labor-intensive exporting sectors (usually light industries) in world markets. The faster growth in the coastal region has widened the inland–coastal gap. In the second regression R2, the coefficient for decentralization has increased by nearly 30 percent from the prereform period to the reform period, indicating that greater decentralization has played a larger detrimental effect on inland–coastal inequality.

Overall, these results represent broad support for the hypotheses advanced earlier on heavy industry, decentralization, and openness. Heavy industry increases inequality, especially its rural–urban component, and particularly in the pre-1979 period. Decentralization, when it is significant, increases overall inequality, rural–urban inequality, and inland–coastal inequality.

The trade ratio is associated with greater overall inequality and, in particular, inland–coastal disparity in the reform period.

6.5 Conclusions

The tremendous growth in per capita GDP since the reform period, and its impact on poverty in China, has been much discussed and celebrated (Fan, Zhang, and Zhang 2002). But this has not stopped a concern with growing inequality, for at least two reasons. First, as is well known, the poverty reducing effects of a given growth rate on poverty are lower at higher levels of inequality. Secondly, rising inequality may itself lead to tensions within a country and impede the prospects for future growth through a variety of social, political and economic mechanisms (Kanbur and Lustig 2000).

This study tries to comprehend the driving forces behind the changes in China's regional inequality over half a century. We find that the evolution of inequality matches different political-economic periods in Chinese history. In particular, we find that heavy-industry development strategy plays a key role in forming the enormous rural–urban gap in the prereform period, while openness and decentralization have contributed to the rapid increase in inland–coastal disparity in the reform period of the 1980s and the 1990s.

The empirical finding also has relevance to the ongoing debate on how globalization affects regional inequality in developing countries. Convergence or divergence of a nation's economy is dependent upon not only its domestic policies but also on its openness. With China joining WTO, the economy will become more liberalized, and open, likely resulting in more dramatic shifts in regional comparative advantages. If the government continues to favor the coastal region in its investment strategy, then regional disparity may widen even more. Further liberalizing and investing in the economy in the inland region is thus an important development strategy for the government to both promote economic growth and reduce regional inequality.

Notes

*   The authors would like to thank participants at seminars held in Beijing University, Chinese Academy of Social Sciences, George Washington University, IFPRI, Kansas State University, and at the WIDER conference on Spatial Inequality in Asia.

1 Even when household data are available, regional inequality is still important because it accounts for a significant share of total income inequality in China and its rapid rise may be dangerous to social and political stability, in particular when aligned with political, religious or ethnic tensions.
2 Data for Hainan Province since 1988 are incorporated into Guangdong Province, while data for Chongqing Province since 1997 are included in Sichuan Province.
3 Kanbur and Zhang (1999; 2001) provide detailed discussion about data sources. A number of studies (Lyons 1991; Tsui 1991) have used province level data to study regional inequality in the past, but they did not in general disaggregate by rural and urban areas within provinces. In the recent literature, Yang and Fang (2000) use the

same data sources as we have used, but focus solely on the average rural urban gap at the national level, and do not go into inequalities across provinces.
4 This is the so called "Theil's second measure." Results for the Theil index of inequality, also a member of this family, are similar.
5 See the footnote in Table 6.1 for data sources and definitions for the three indicators.
6 Given data restrictions it is impossible to find suitable alternative instruments covering the entire 50-year period under consideration.

References

Aaberge, Rolf and Xuezeng Li. 1997. "The Trend in Urban Income Inequality in Two Chinese Provinces, 1986–90," *Review of Income and Wealth*, 43: 335–55.

Chen, Jian and Belton M. Fleisher. 1996. "Regional Income Inequality and Economic Growth in China," *Journal of Comparative Economics*, 22: 141–64.

Chen, Shaohua and Martin Ravallion. 1996. "Data in Transition: Assessing Rural Living Standards in Southern China," *China Economic Review*, 7: 23–56.

Fan, Shenggen and Xiaobo Zhang. 2002. "Production and Productivity Growth in Chinese Agriculture: New National and Regional Measures," *Economic Development and Cultural Change*, 50: 819–38.

Fan, Shenggen, Xiaobo Zhang, and Sherman Robinson. 2003. "Structural Change and Economic Growth in China," *Review of Development Economics*, 7: 360–77.

Fan, Shenggen, Linxiu Zhang, and Xiaobo Zhang. 2002. *Growth and Poverty in Rural China: The Role of Public Investment*, IFPRI Policy Report No. 125.

Fujita, Masahisa, Paul Krugman, and Anthony J. Venables. 1999. *The Spatial Economy*. The MIT Press: Cambridge, Massachusetts.

Hanson, G and A. Harrison. 1999. "Trade Liberalization and Wage Inequality in Mexico," *Industrial and Labor Relations Review* 52: 271–88.

Jian, T., Jeffrey Sachs, and Andrew Warner. 1996. "Trends in Regional Inequality in China." National Bureau of Economic Research working paper, No. 5412.

Kanbur, Ravi and N. Lustig. 2000. "Why is Inequality Back on the Agenda?" *Proceedings of the Annual World Bank Conference in Development Economics*, World Bank.

Kanbur, Ravi and Xiaobo Zhang. 1999. "Which Regional Inequality: Rural–Urban or Coast–Inland? The Evolution of Rural-Urban and Inland-Coastal Inequality in China from 1983 to 1995," *Journal of Comparative Economics* 27: 686–701.

Kanbur, Ravi and Xiaobo Zhang. 2001. "Fifty Years of Regional Inequality in China: A Journey Through Revolution, Reform and Openness," London: Centre For Economic Policy Research (CEPR) Discussion Paper 2887.

Khan, Azizur Rahman and Car Riskin. 2001. *Inequality and Poverty in China in the Age of Globalization*, Oxford University Press.

Kwiatkowski, D., P. C. B Phillips, P. Schmidt, and Y. Shin. 1992. "Testing the Null Hypothesis of Stationarity Against the Alternative of a Unit Root: How Sure Are We That Economic Time Series Have a Unit Root?" *Journal of Econometrics*, 54: 159–78.

Li, Xiao-Ming. 2000. "The Great Leap Forward, Economic Reforms, and the Unit Root Hypothesis: Testing for Breaking Trend Functions in China's GDP Data," *Journal of Comparative Economics* 27: 814–27.

Lin, Justin Yifu. 1992. "Rural Reforms and Agricultural Growth in China," *American Economic Review*, 82: 34–51.

Lin, Justin Yifu and Dennis T. Yang. 2000. "Food Availability, Entitlement and the Chinese Famine of 1959–61," *Economic Journal*, 110: 136–58.

Lin, Justin Yifu, Fang Cai, and Zhou Li. 1996. *The China Miracle: Development Strategy and Economic Reform*, Hong Kong: The Chinese University Press,.

Lyons, Thomas P. 1991. "Interprovincial Disparities in China: Output and Consumption, 1952–1987," *Economic Development and Cultural Change*, 39: 471–506.

Phillips, P. C. B. and S. Ouliaris. 1990. "Asymptotic Properties of Residual Based Tests for Cointegration," *Econometrica*, 58: 165–93.

Qian, Yingyi and Gérard Roland. 1998. "Federalism and the Soft Budget Constraint," *American Economic Review*, 88: 1143–62.

Rozelle, Scott. 1994. "Rural Industrialization and Increasing Inequality: Emerging Patterns in China's Reforming Economy," *Journal of Comparative Economics*, 19: 362–91.

Shorrocks, Anthony F. 1984. "Inequality Decomposition by Population Subgroups," *Econometrica*, 52: 1369–85.

State Statistical Bureau (SSB). 1999. *Comprehensive Statistical Data and Materials on 50 Years of New China (Xin Zhongguo wushinian Tonji Ziliao Huibian)*, Beijing: China Statistical Publishing House.

—— various years. *China Statistical Yearbook (Zhongguo Tongji Nianjian)*. Beijing: China Statistical Publishing House.

Tsui, Kai-yuen. 1991. "China's Regional Inequality, 1952–1985," *Journal of Comparative Economics*, 15: 1–21.

—— 1998. "Factor Decomposition of Chinese Rural Income Inequality: New Methodology, Empirical Findings, and Policy Implications," *Journal of Comparative Economics*, 26: 502–28.

Wei, Shang-Jin and Yi Wu. 2001. "Globalization and Inequality: Evidence from China," Center for Economic Policy Research Discussion Paper, No. 3088, December.

Wood, A. 1997. "Openness and Wage Inequality in Developing Countries: The Latin American Challenge to East Asian Conventional Wisdom," *World Bank Economic Review*, 11: 33–57.

Yang, Danis Tao. 1999. "Urban-Based Policies and Rising Income Inequality in China," *American Economic Review* (Paper and Proceedings), 89: 306–10.

Yang, Danis Tao and Cai Fang. 2000. "The Political Economy of China's Rural–Urban Divide," Center for Research on Economic Development and Policy Reform Working Paper No. 62, Stanford University.

Zhang, Xiaobo and Ravi Kanbur. 2001. "What Difference Do Polarisation Measures Make? An Application to China," *Journal of Development Studies*, 37: 85–98.

Zhang, Xiaobo and Kevin H. Zhang. 2003. "How Does Globalisation Affect Regional Inequality within a Developing Country? Evidence from China," *Journal of Development Studies*, 39: 47–67.

Zhang, Tao and Heng-fu Zou. 1998. "Fiscal Decentralization, Public Spending, and Economic Growth in China." *Journal of Public Economics*, 67: 221–40.

7 Economic liberalization with rising segmentation in China's urban labor market[*]

Sylvie Démurger, Martin Fournier,
Li Shi, and Wei Zhong

Abstract

The massive downsizing of the state-owned sector and the concomitant impressive growth of the private sector at the end of the 1990s have altered the nature of the Chinese labor market. The introduction of market mechanisms has contributed to increasing labor turnover and competitiveness in market wages. Using two urban household surveys for 1995 and 2002, this paper analyzes the evolution of labor market segmentation in urban China, by applying an extended version of Oaxaca–Blinder decomposition methods. During the seven-year period, the sharp increase in real earnings for all workers shows substantial differences across ownership, economic sectors, and regions. We find strong evidence of a multi-tiered labor market along these three major lines and highlight increasing segmentation within each of the three dimensions, the gap between the privileged segments of the labor market and the most competitive segments widening over time.

7.1 Introduction

Since the launching of the policy of reform and opening-up in the late 1970s, both rural and urban labor markets in China have changed dramatically. By allowing market mechanisms to play a greater role in wage-settings and labor mobility to reappear, economic liberalization has revived incentive mechanisms and improved the efficiency of labor allocation across sectors, enterprises, and regions[1]. Despite the loosening enforcement of the *hukou* system[2] that seriously impedes rural–urban migration, rural and urban labor markets remain highly segmented. Within both urban and rural labor markets, various rigidities also remain and reforms are still uneven and incomplete. In particular, restrictions on labor mobility across sectors and ownership in the urban labor market have remained quite strong until the mid-1990s (Knight and Song 1995; Zhao 2002; Chen et al. 2005).

Labor market segmentation arises when labor market is made up of several segments with distinct rules for wage determination and a limited mobility of labor between segments. In China, where the so-called "iron rice bowl" of lifetime employment in state-owned enterprises was the norm until it was completely dismantled in 1994 (Knight and Song 2005), the issue of the public sector efficiency may be of special importance. A multi-tiered labor market in which wages are not only determined by skill differentials, but also by different institutional arrangements may have strong implications in terms of both labor allocation across sectors and income distribution among workers. In the case of China, Zhao (2002) and Chen et al. (2005) found that the payment of high non-wage benefits in state-owned enterprises prevented labor from moving out of the state sector in the mid-1990s.

Urban employment in China has increased from 95 million in 1978 to 265 million in 2004, but from the mid-1990s onward, the employment situation in most cities started to deteriorate, with the number of jobs not increasing as fast as the labor force, and thus leading to rising unemployment in urban areas[3]. Although the official registered unemployment rate in urban areas stands at 4.2 percent (8.27 million people in 2004), actual unemployment is estimated to be much more severe, especially when unemployment in the form of laid-off workers (*xiagang*) is considered (Lai 2005). While the exact number of laid-off workers remains largely unknown, estimates provided by the National Bureau of Statistics indicate that there would have been 70 to 80 million workers laid off between 1998 and 2002 from public and non-public enterprises[4] (Li and Bai 2005).

Overall, the basic patterns in urban employment that have emerged are related to enterprise ownership, sector, and regional location. First, urban unemployment mainly comes from urban state-owned industrial enterprises. While total employment in urban areas has increased over the years, employment in state-owned units has steadily decreased since the mid-1990s, from 112.6 million in 1995 down to 70 million in 2004. The reduction of employment in state-owned and collectively owned units has been partly compensated by the increase of employment in the private sector, the foreign sector, and new enterprises ownership types.[5]

Second, the sharp decrease in employment mainly took place in the most competitive sectors, such as manufacturing, where the number of employed people dropped by 15 percent between 1995 and 2002.[6] In contrast, sectors with a state monopoly status such as banking and insurance, and real estate increased their employment by 23 percent and 48 percent respectively over the same period. Third, the regional distribution of urban employment and unemployment is also quite uneven. Northeast provinces, which have been among the hardest hit provinces by the layoff policy, are those that have experienced the sharpest drop in urban employment between 1995 and 2002 (−28 percent). In other regions, the employment level has remained the same, except in the western region where the share of total urban employment increased from 18 to 21 percent.

Over the last decade, there has been a large number of works on the changes in China's wage structure.[7] This paper analyses labor market segmentation in urban China by focusing on earnings differences within three different dimensions: enterprises' ownership, economic sector, and regional location. We use an original dataset derived from two urban household surveys conducted by the Chinese Academy of Social Sciences (CASS), which provide detailed information on labor income as well as on individual and household characteristics for urban *hukou* holders in 1995 and 2002. To assess the extent of labor market segmentation, we first estimate Mincerian earnings equations for each category of enterprises (defined by ownership, sector, or location). We then propose an extended form of Oaxaca-Blinder decomposition methodology to decompose for each dimension the observed earnings differentials into three components: the distribution of individual characteristics, differences in working time, and what can be interpreted as a pure "segment effect." Comparisons of segmentation magnitudes across ownership, sector, and region, and between the two years are expected to provide a broader view on recent changes across the various segments of the Chinese urban labor market.

7.2 Major reforms in China's urban labor market

During the pre-reform period, there was virtually no labor market in China. Job allocation and wage-settings in state-owned enterprises (SOEs) were determined within the central plan and a key function held by SOEs was to provide employment to the entire working-age population. The main features of this centrally determined wage structure were the following.[8] First, the wage determination system was characterized by rigidity with low-level wages and a distribution of wages based on an egalitarian principle. Promotion and wage increases were mostly driven by seniority. Second, SOEs were not only labor providers, but they also provided a number of social welfare benefits, including housing, medical care, pensions, etc., which aimed at compensating for low base wages. Third, with the employment assignment system and the strictly controlled movement of the population within the *hukou* system, labor mobility across sectors and regions was strongly limited.

Economic reforms launched from the end of the 1970s led to important changes within the state sector (Table 7.1). In a first step, more autonomy in decision-making for employment and wages has been granted to SOEs managers, who were now allowed to retain a share of their profit and use it to give bonus wages to their employees. Bonus wages aimed to provide incentives to employees and increase the overall productivity of SOEs. Their amount was also meant to reflect both enterprise and individual performances (Coady and Wang 2000; Meng 2000). However, given high supervision costs, bonuses have often been distributed on an egalitarian basis within work units, and the evaluation of their impact remains controversial.

The industrial reforms also allowed the emergence of a new private sector, composed of domestic private enterprises,[9] individual enterprises (*getihu*), domestic joint ventures (*lianying qiye*), foreign-invested enterprises, and shareholding companies (*gufenzhi qiye*). Although domestic private enterprises

Table 7.1 Main steps in China's urban labor market reform

1978	Introduction of a retirement system in urban areas (60 years old for men / 50 years old for women with no less 10 years of working experience).[10]
1979	Reintroduction of bonuses and piece wages to improve labor productivity.
1982	Encouragement of development of self-employment and individual firms[11].
1983	Introduction of the labor contract system to cover new entrants into state and collective sectors.[12] Introduction of a "job–holding without pay" scheme.
1984	More authority given to enterprises to determine wage and introduction of a floating wage system linked to enterprise performance and profitability.[13]
1986	New regulations promulgated, including *Temporary Regulations on Labor Contract System of State-owned Enterprises, Temporary Regulations on Dismissal of Lawbreaking Worker in State-owned Enterprises, Temporary Regulations on State-owned Enterprises Workers, Temporary Regulations on State-owned Enterprises Recruitment of Workers, Temporary Regulations on Laid-off Workers of State-owned Enterprises.* Law enabling enterprises to lay-off employees. Launching of an unemployment insurance scheme (July).
1987	New regulations on fixed-term contracts, calling for the extension of contracts to incumbent workers.
1990	Restrictions on migration of rural labor force to reduce employment pressure in urban areas.[14]
1991	Reform of the pension system.[15]
1992	*Labor Union Law* (April). More authority given to state-owned enterprises in the manufacturing sector in terms of recruitment and lay-off of workers as well as in setting wages and bonuses.[16]
1993	*Regulations on Reallocation of Surplus Staff and Workers of State-Owned Enterprises*, to define layoff (*xiagang*) conditions (firing procedures, amount of retired money, etc.). *Regulations on the Minimum Wage of State-Owned Enterprises* (November).
1994	Regulations on bankruptcy of state-owned enterprises and setting-up of re-employment centers.[17] Introduction of rules on interregional movement of rural labor force, including a number of cards such as the Employment Card and the Temporary Resident Card.[18] *Regulations on Wage Control of Joint-Stock Companies* (December).
1995	*Labor Law of the PRC* (effective on Jan. 1st), making labor contracts mandatory in all industrial enterprises, including TVEs. Working time legally set at no more than eight hours a day and no more than 44 hours a week on average in the state sector.[19] Implementation of the re-employment project, providing preferential policy for firms employing unemployed workers and surplus laborers.[20]
1997	Acceleration in the implementation of the laid-off policy.[21]
1998	Introduction of new re-employment policies such as encouraging development of private and individual enterprises, tax exemptions for firms employing laid-off workers.[22] Regulations issued by the Ministry of Public Security to loosen the control on *hukou* registration.

1999	*Regulations on Unemployment Insurance*, to help transform the laid-off subsidy system into an unemployment insurance system.
	Regulations on Security of Minimum Livelihood for Urban Residents, to provide income program for poor urban households (September).
2000	More authority given to enterprises in wage setting and allowing managers to set higher wage for themselves.[23]
	Provisional Regulations on Collective Negotiation in Wage Setting (issued by MOLSS, November).
2001	Pilot implementation of the New Social Security Scheme in some cities.[24]
2003	Drop of some restrictions to rural–urban migration, including abolishment of various cards and fees charged on migrant workers.[25]

Sources: Cai 2005; Fleisher and Yang 2003; Meng 2000; MOLSS and Literature Research Office of CCCPC 2002; Zhang et al. 2005.

suffered from restricting policies such as overtax, strict regulation, limited access to loans and skilled employees in the 1980s, the share of the non-public sector in employment grew steadily from 0 in 1978 to 17 percent in 1995, 45 percent in 2002, and 53 percent in 2004.[26]

Starting from the mid-1990s, other important changes have taken place on the Chinese urban labor market, the most radical being the laid-off policy (*xiagang*) implemented in state-owned and urban collective enterprises, first in Shanghai only in 1993 and then extended nation-wide in 1997. Given the growing burden of substantial redundant labor in the state sector, the goal of this policy was to lay off a quarter or more of its workers within 4 years (1997–2000) (Appleton et al. 2002). This policy has had a strong impact on employment in the public sector, falling from 112.6 million in 1995 to 71.6 million in 2002 in SOEs and from 31.5 million to 11.2 million in urban collective enterprises.

The second most important change is the wage reform, which was launched in 1994 and grants enterprises more autonomy in setting wages and bonuses. Consequently, the average wage in the state-owned sector has increased substantially, especially in the government sector. Between 1998 and 2002, average earnings in state-owned units have grown by 107 percent in real terms, with an annual growth rate of 10.9 percent. However, the wage reform has also widened the earnings gap between workers and managers, between skilled workers and unskilled workers, and between enterprises making profits and those making losses. During the last two years of Zhu Rongji's administration, salaries in the government sector were raised again by 60 percent, in order to narrow the income gap between civil servants and white-collar workers employed in the non-public sector.[27]

The last major change on the Chinese urban labor market over 1995–2002 is related to rural–urban migration. The policy of city governments for rural migration varies, but the general trend is that employment policies concerning rural migrants was tight up to the end of the 1990s and started to loosen at the beginning of the new century.[28] The participation of rural migrants in the urban labor market has had a great impact on wage levels and unemployment among employees with urban *hukou*. Rural migrant laborers are very competitive against local urban workers for unskilled jobs, and this puts pressure on the wage level for unskilled workers on the urban labor market, particularly for those whose wage setting is the most strongly related to market mechanisms (Cai 2005; Li and Bai 2005).

7.3 A first look at the data

7.3.1 Data

The data used in this paper come from two nationally representative household income surveys for 1995 and 2002. The surveys are part of the China Household Income Project (CHIP) coordinated by the Institute of Economics, Chinese Academy of Social Sciences, with assistance from the National Bureau of Statistics (NBS).[29] Household samples were drawn from the large sample used by the NBS.[30] The two urban surveys cover the same provinces and cities, and almost the same number of households.[31] Although the number of samples in each province is not exactly proportional to its actual population, the two figures are highly correlated, more households being selected from more populated provinces. The 1995 urban data include 6,931 households and 21,694 individuals, and the 2002 urban data 6,835 households and 20,632 individuals. The distribution of households among provinces can be found in Table 7.2.

The two urban surveys only cover urban *hukou* holders and thus exclude a potentially important segment of the urban labor market: the rural–urban migrants. In a changing environment where rural–urban migration is gathering momentum, limiting our study to only urban residents might be misleading. We acknowledge this potential shortcoming in our study, which does not allow for the evaluation of how migration is affecting the urban labor market and wage differentials.

Our sample is restricted to individuals aged 16 to 60 who declared working at least part of the year and earning (positive) wages. Owners of private or individual enterprises are not considered here since wages cannot be disentangled from profit in their case. Laid-off workers are also excluded, which leaves us with a sample of 10,898 employees in 1995 and 9,537 employees in 2002.

The earnings variable is defined as the sum of cash labor compensations and income in kind. Cash labor compensations include the basic salary as well as bonuses, allowances (except those given while "waiting for a job," *xiagang*) and subsidies (including housing, medical, childcare, and regional subsidies), other wages (including overtime wages and wages for special circumstances), and other income from work unit (except hardship allowances). Hence, our earnings variable includes some non-monetary benefits

Table 7.2 Distribution of sampled households for urban surveys (1995 and 2002)

Province	1995		2002	
	Number of cities	*Number of sampled households*	*Number of cities*	*Number of sampled households*
Beijing	1	500	1	500
Shanxi	7	650	7	650
Liaoning	5	700	5	700
Jiangsu	9	800	9	750
Anhui	6	500	6	500
Henan	8	600	8	700
Hubei	7	742	7	700
Guangdong	8	546	8	550
Chongqing	–	–	2	300
Sichuan	7	848	6	600
Yunnan	9	648	8	650
Gansu	3	400	3	400
Total	69	6,934	69	7,000

Source: 1995 and 2002 CHIP survey data.

(e.g. housing, medical care, child care, and regional subsidies), although it does not fully account for all fringe benefits provided by the public sector (such as implicit contribution to pensions, health insurance, or preferential housing rents). Finally, hourly earnings are defined as the ratio between earnings and the number of declared hours worked in a year.

An important component of earnings differentials in China may lie on differences in living standards between different cities. To account at least partially for this factor, earnings are adjusted for provincial purchasing power differences by using Brandt and Holz (2006) urban provincial-level spatial price deflators (the reference being nationwide prices in 2002). In the analysis presented below, earnings are thus expressed in "inter-provincial purchasing power parity," which we believe can be considered as more comparable than non-deflated data usually considered in the literature. Among the consequences of using this purchasing power parity adjustment is that it leads to a reduction in earnings differentials between some regions as compared to the official NBS *China Statistical Yearbooks* data.[32] It is especially the case for the comparison between municipalities and other regions, since the cost of living in municipalities is much higher.

We focus on the evolution of earnings differentials in various components of the labor market, and consider three different dimensions, namely ownership, economic sector, and geographical location, for each of which, we define several categories.

Five categories of *enterprise ownership* are considered: state-owned enterprises (SOEs); urban collective enterprises (UCEs); private enterprises

(PIEs); foreign-invested enterprises (FIEs); and government agencies or institutions (GAIs). In the course of the 1995–2002 period, new categories of enterprises have emerged, notably share-holding corporations (from both the state and others). In our definition of state-owned enterprises, SOEs at the central or provincial level are included as well as local publicly owned enterprises, and for 2002, state share-holding companies. Private enterprises comprise private or individual enterprises, and for 2002, other share-holding companies.

Economic sectors are categorized according to their openness to competition, and are grouped into four categories: competitive sectors, oligopolistic sectors, public services, and government agencies. The competitive sectors are manufacturing, construction, commerce and trade, and food services. The oligopolistic sectors are real estate, public utilities, and finance and insurance. Real estate[33] is considered as "oligopolistic" for two reasons. First, there are huge structural barriers to entry in this sector, because it requires a large amount of investment. Second, access to land in China is quite closely related to relationship with the government at any level. Both public utilities and finance and insurance are considered oligopolistic sectors because they were not (or hardly) open to the private sector in 2002.

The third economic sector considered here ("public services") includes health care, sport and social welfare, education, culture and arts, and scientific research. We separate public services from government agencies in the sector dimension because they are different in terms of wage settings. Indeed, while government agencies' wages are paid only by the government, public services can get additional funding from the market, which may substantially affect wage settings behaviors.

Some economic sectors (mining, geological prospecting and irrigation administration; transportation, storage, post office, and communication; and for social services) could not be clearly classified as defined above. We omitted these sectors from our analysis.

For the third dimension, *regional location*, we have five regions: coast, center, west, northeast, and metropolises. As the household income surveys do not cover all Chinese provinces, the five regions are represented by a subsample of provinces. Beijing is representative of province-level metropolitan cities. Guangdong and Jiangsu are representatives of coastal provinces. Henan, Anhui, Hubei, and Shanxi are representatives of central provinces. Gansu, Sichuan, and Yunnan are representatives of western provinces, and Liaoning is representative of northeastern provinces.[34]

Ideally, we would like to consider the three dimensions highlighted above simultaneously since they are obviously correlated. Among the most prominent correlations, Table 7.3 shows that (1) oligopolistic sectors mostly consist of SOEs and GAIs, (2) private and foreign enterprises are mainly found in the competitive sector as well as in the coastal region, and (3) SOEs are overrepresented in the northeast region. However, for practical reasons, it is not possible to consider the three dimensions together. This is because the

Table 7.3 Correlation between the three segments

7.3.1 Ownership / Sector

Ownership	Sector Competitive	Oligopolistic	Public service	Government	Total
1995					
SOEs	88.45	4.49	4.93	2.14	100
	69.85	38.04	16.62	9.19	52.26
UCEs	91.51	6.05	2.44	0	100
	21.11	14.99	2.41	0	15.26
PIEs	84.15	12.57	3.28	0	100
	2.07	3.31	0.34	0	1.62
FIEs	94.7	4.55	0.76	0	100
	1.68	0.86	0.06	0	1.17
GAIs	11.82	8.88	42.06	37.24	100
	5.3	42.8	80.57	90.81	29.68
Total	66.17	6.16	15.49	12.17	100
	100	100	100	100	100
2002					
SOEs	82.41	10.2	5.68	1.71	100
	49.39	58.01	9.2	3.75	34.28
UCEs	90	4.51	5.49	0	100
	10.92	5.19	1.8	0	6.94
PIEs	91.03	4.78	4.19	0	100
	33.1	16.48	4.12	0	20.79
FIEs	84.49	7.49	8.02	0	100
	3.76	3.16	0.96	0	2.54
GAIs	4.57	2.92	50.12	42.4	100
	2.83	17.16	83.92	96.25	35.44
Total	57.2	6.03	21.16	15.61	100
	100	100	100	100	100

7.3.2 Ownership / Region

Ownership	Coast	Center	Region West	Municipality	Northeast	Total
1995						
SOEs	17.07	35.68	27.21	7.8	12.24	100
	46.68	55.15	53.39	58.31	60.41	53.8
UCEs	28.83	31.91	24.05	3.47	11.73	100
	20.89	13.07	12.5	6.88	15.34	14.26
PIEs	50	22.62	19.05	3.57	4.76	100
	1.99	0.51	0.55	0.39	0.34	0.78
FIEs	55.07	10.87	13.77	12.32	7.97	100
	3.61	0.4	0.65	2.21	0.94	1.29
GAIs	17.67	35.97	30.22	7.76	8.38	100
	26.83	30.86	32.91	32.21	22.96	29.87
Total	19.67	34.81	27.42	7.19	10.9	100
	100	100	100	100	100	100

(Continued overleaf)

Table 7.3 (*Continued*)

Ownership	Coast	Center	Region West	Municipality	Northeast	Total
2002						
SOEs	17.32	36.61	25.22	8.93	11.93	100
	33.49	39	34.76	40.95	40.48	37.12
UCEs	25.96	26.55	24.48	4.57	18.44	100
	10.09	5.69	6.79	4.22	12.59	7.47
PIEs	23.83	30.96	26.94	5.38	12.9	100
	24.14	17.29	19.47	12.93	22.96	19.46
FIEs	30.33	22.27	12.32	25.59	9.48	100
	3.67	1.49	1.06	7.35	2.01	2.32
GAIs	16.34	37.85	30.35	8.32	7.14	100
	28.61	36.54	37.91	34.56	21.95	33.63
Total	19.2	34.84	26.92	8.09	10.93	100
	100	100	100	100	100	100

7.3.3 Sector / Region

Sector	Coast	Center	Region West	Municipality	Northeast	Total
1995						
Competitive	20.81	35.47	27.01	5.74	10.98	100
	69.52	65.08	65.45	59.13	72.89	66.46
Oligop.	25.1	33.47	23.85	7.67	9.9	100
	7.89	5.78	5.44	7.44	6.19	6.26
Public serv.	17.65	36.09	28.84	8.79	8.62	100
	13.55	15.22	16.07	20.84	13.16	15.28
Government	14.97	42.01	29.8	6.76	6.47	100
	9.04	13.92	13.04	12.58	7.76	12.01
Total	19.89	36.23	27.42	6.45	10.01	100
	100	100	100	100	100	100
2002						
Competitive	21.54	34.92	27.6	5.94	10	100
	65.34	54.41	56.75	46.91	62.63	57.34
Oligop.	15.96	46.12	19.07	8.2	10.64	100
Public serv.	15.79	40.88	27.23	8.49	7.61	100
	5.03	7.47	4.07	6.73	6.93	5.96
	17.54	23.33	20.51	24.55	17.46	21
2002						
Government	14.55	34.65	33.14	10.09	7.57	100
	12.09	14.79	18.66	21.82	12.99	15.7
Total	18.9	36.8	27.88	7.26	9.15	100
	100	100	100	100	100	100

Source: Authors' calculations using the 1995 and 2002 CHIP survey data.

methodology requires the estimation of earnings equations by subcategories, and if we were to consider each subcategory (e.g. SOEs in the competitive sector in the coastal region) we would have too few observations. Consequently, in the following analysis, the three dimensions will be analyzed separately, though keeping in mind that they are overlapping.

The main characteristics of employees by dimension and over time are shown in Tables 7.4, 7.5, and 7.6. A first general comment on the evolution between 1995 and 2002 is that both average age and education level have increased over time, while the share of long-term contracts has sharply decreased from 96 percent to below 80 percent.

Comparisons by ownership (Table 7.4) show that government agencies and foreign-invested enterprises employ better-educated workers than other

Table 7.4 Descriptive statistics on individual characteristics by ownership

	All	SOEs	UCEs	PIEs	FIEs	GAIs
1995						
# obs.	10,730	5,775	1,534	84	138	3,199
%	100	53.82	14.30	0.78	1.29	29.81
Male (%)	53.34	55.83	40.81	52.38	54.35	54.83
Age	38.39	38.42	38.02	32.07	30.96	39.00
Years of education	10.79	10.47	9.25	9.29	11.07	12.15
Communist (%)	25.12	21.51	11.54	4.76	10.14	39.32
Coast (%)	26.91	24.92	32.40	53.57	67.39	25.41
Long term tenure (%)	96.32	98.32	92.12	7.50	59.26	98.57
2002						
# obs.	9,081	3,371	678	1,767	211	3,054
%	100	37.12	7.47	19.46	2.32	33.63
Male (%)	56.69	60.99	43.51	55.80	59.24	55.21
Age	40.41	41.17	41.36	38.58	35.15	40.78
Years of education	11.52	11.18	10.06	10.48	12.30	12.75
Communist (%)	29.88	28.36	19.32	14.20	14.22	44.04
Coast (%)	27.30	26.25	30.53	29.20	55.92	24.66
Long term tenure (%)	77.11	88.42	72.57	38.17	56.40	89.64

Source: Authors' calculations using the 1995 and 2002 CHIP survey data.

Notes:
1. The sample includes individuals aged 16 to 60, who declared working at least a part of the year and earning (positive) wages. Owners of private or individual enterprises are not considered.
2. Education and Experience are the number of years of education and work experience declared by the respondent.
3. "Coast" dummy includes Beijing, Guangdong, and Jiangsu.
4. Long-term tenure includes both permanent workers and long-term contract workers, as opposed to temporary or short-term contract workers.
5. Ownership categories are: state-owned enterprises (SOEs), urban collective enterprises (UCEs), private or individual enterprises, (PIEs), foreign-invested enterprises (FIEs), and government agencies or institutions (GAIs).
6. Tables for different dimensions (ownership, sector and regions) may show slightly different average total values and due to attrition on categorical variables.

sectors in 1995 and 2002. As compared with private and foreign sectors, workers in the public sector are older and more often party members, with long-term tenure, but they are less likely to be located in coastal provinces. It is noteworthy that the most educated workers are found in public administration, with an average number of years of education (above 12) much higher than in any other type of enterprise for 1995 and 2002. Finally, the regional distribution of the private sector has equalized over time, which may reflect the development of the private sector at the turn of the century all over China, including inland provinces.

As for differences by sectors (Table 7.5), employees in the competitive sector are less likely to be educated (especially in 2002), party members, and working in SOEs. They are also less likely to have long-term contracts in 2002. Consistent with the ownership dimension, we can observe that it is in public services and in government agencies that the level of education is the highest.

Finally, regional differences (Table 7.6) show that workers in municipalities tend to have much better characteristics than in other regions in terms of

Table 7.5 Descriptive statistics on individual characteristics by sectors

	All	Competitive	Oligopolistic	Public services	Government
1995					
# obs	9,665	6,343	607	1,466	1,249
%	100	65.63	6.28	15.17	12.92
Male (%)	52.42	52.40	48.60	46.04	61.81
Age	38.33	38.00	36.08	40.21	38.89
Years of education	10.78	10.16	10.68	12.32	12.18
Communist (%)	24.80	18.97	22.73	28.17	51.48
SOE (%)	81.95	75.07	81.38	97.41	98.96
Coast (%)	26.93	27.29	33.77	26.74	22.02
Long term tenure (%)	96.24	95.60	92.32	98.89	98.30
2002					
# obs	8,195	4,752	706	1,560	1,177
%	100	57.99	8.62	19.04	14.36
Male (%)	54.31	52.61	58.50	50.32	63.98
Age	40.44	40.37	39.19	40.65	41.20
Years of education	11.57	10.69	11.87	13.07	12.96
Communist (%)	30.24	21.74	29.04	34.17	60.07
SOE (%)	74.92	61.99	86.54	93.27	95.84
Coast (%)	27.41	28.83	28.33	24.55	24.89
Long term tenure (%)	74.44	64.80	81.59	89.87	88.73

Source: Authors' calculations using the 1995 and 2002 CHIP survey data.

Notes:
1. See Table 7.4.
2. See text for a full definition of sectors.
3. The lower number of observation is due to the omission of unclear sectors. See text for details.

Table 7.6 Descriptive statistics on individual characteristics by regions

	All	Coast	Center	West	Municipality	Northeast
1995						
# obs	10,898	2,170	3,778	2,991	779	1,180
%	100	19.91	34.67	27.45	7.15	10.83
Male (%)	53.18	53.13	53.81	51.92	54.30	53.73
Age	38.37	38.45	37.52	38.71	40.24	38.87
Years of education	10.78	10.48	10.76	10.71	11.86	10.87
Communist (%)	25.00	23.64	24.80	26.38	31.19	20.51
SOE (%)	82.35	71.57	85.07	84.75	89.73	82.46
Long term tenure (%)	96.14	92.86	97.21	96.72	95.45	97.69
2002						
# obs	9,537	1,812	3,300	2,576	799	1,050
%	100	19.00	34.60	27.01	8.38	11.01
Male (%)	56.09	54.86	57.06	55.16	54.07	58.95
Age	40.38	40.57	39.58	40.54	42.46	40.58
Years of education	11.50	11.33	11.61	11.26	12.26	11.44
Communist (%)	29.62	28.81	30.18	30.55	29.29	27.24
SOE (%)	75.23	70.09	79.33	77.76	77.60	63.24
Long term tenure (%)	74.87	69.87	80.92	76.99	68.46	64.29

Source: Authors' calculations using the 1995 and 2002 CHIP survey data.

Notes:
1. See Table 7.4.
2. See text for a full definition of regions.

education, experience (higher age), and party membership (for 1995). On the contrary, workers in coastal provinces are less educated and less likely to be party members (with a lower share of SOEs), which may be consistent with the non-skilled labor-intensive outward-oriented light industrial structure of these provinces. For the Northeast region, the downsizing of the state-owned sector has been particularly large between 1995 and 2002; the share of SOEs employment of 63 percent in 2002 is the lowest across regions. The share of employees with long-term contracts has also dropped most radically in the northeast, from the highest in 1995 (nearly 98 percent) to the lowest in 2002 (64 percent).

7.3.2 The evolution of earnings differentials by categories

Descriptive statistics on earnings differentials and earnings composition across the three dimensions are given in Tables 7.7, 7.8, and 7.9.[35] In terms of ownership (Table 7.77), workers at government agencies and institutions have gained a lot, with a doubling in earnings. This huge increase resulted in a changing sign of the observed earnings differential with foreign-invested enterprises in 2002. Hence, while foreign-invested enterprises were providing

Table 7.7 Descriptive statistics on individual characteristics by ownership

	All	*SOEs*	*UCEs*	*PIEs*	*FIEs*	*GAIs*
1995						
Total annual earnings	6,155	6,178	4,878	5,199	8,148	6,667
c.v.	*0.51*	*0.51*	*0.57*	*0.81*	*0.74*	*0.45*
Gap to average earnings		*1.00*	*0.79*	*0.84*	*1.32*	*1.08*
Basic wage	3,821	3,833	3,240	4,614	6,531	3,942
c.v.	*0.56*	*0.53*	*0.59*	*0.89*	*0.92*	*0.49*
Bonus	983	1,067	703	257	847	991
c.v.	*1.64*	*1.58*	*2.14*	*5.19*	*1.86*	*1.55*
Subsidies	1,115	1,032	627	76	460	1,556
c.v.	*1.07*	*0.98*	*1.16*	*3.50*	*1.91*	*0.97*
Income in kind	99	99	69	105	86	113
c.v.	*2.72*	*2.62*	*3.76*	*4.56*	*2.53*	*2.49*
Hourly wage	2.89	2.88	2.36	1.96	3.45	3.15
c.v.	*0.65*	*0.66*	*0.82*	*0.86*	*0.73*	*0.54*
Hours worked per week	43.7	44.0	43.5	56.6	47.2	42.8
c.v.	*0.17*	*0.16*	*0.23*	*0.27*	*0.19*	*0.15*
2002						
Total annual earnings	11,071	10,840	7,630	8,286	13,305	13,547
c.v.	*0.66*	*0.62*	*0.61*	*0.92*	*0.66*	*0.53*
Gap to average earnings		*0.98*	*0.69*	*0.75*	*1.20*	*1.22*
Basic wage	9,128	8,985	6,709	7,141	11,081	10,838
c.v.	*0.63*	*0.58*	*0.59*	*0.89*	*0.61*	*0.53*
Bonus	1,049	1,149	549	595	1,372	1,290
c.v.	*2.41*	*2.23*	*3.75*	*3.40*	*2.12*	*2.15*
Subsidies	673	526	255	166	524	1,231
c.v.	*2.94*	*2.93*	*3.40*	*4.36*	*4.01*	*2.26*
Income in kind	130	119	94	139	333	131
c.v.	*7.68*	*6.81*	*3.11*	*11.19*	*9.02*	*3.43*
Hourly wage	5.38	5.31	3.64	3.66	6.16	6.79
c.v.	*0.88*	*0.84*	*0.66*	*1.08*	*0.71*	*0.79*
Hours worked per week	43.7	42.3	43.5	50.1	44.6	41.4
c.v.	*0.23*	*0.19*	*0.23*	*0.29*	*0.22*	*0.19*

Source: Authors' calculations using the 1995 and 2002 CHIP survey data.

Notes:
1. The sample includes individuals aged 16 to 60, who declared working at least a part of the year and earning (positive) wages. Owners of private or individual enterprises are not considered.
2. The earnings variable is defined as the sum of the basic wage, bonuses, allowances and subsidies, other wages, and income in kind.
3. Earnings are deflated using the urban provincial-level spatial price deflators calculated by Brandt and Holz (2006). Base = nationwide prices in 2002.
4. The gap to average earnings is calculated as average total earnings for enterprise category *i* divided by average total earnings for all categories of enterprises (reported in column 1).
5. Ownership categories are: state-owned enterprises (SOEs), urban collective enterprises (UCEs), private or individual enterprises, (PIEs), foreign-invested enterprises (FIEs), and government agencies or institutions (GAIs).
6. C.V. = coefficient of variation.

Table 7.8 Descriptive statistics on individual characteristics by economic sectors

	All	Competitive	Oligopolistic	Public services	Government
1995					
Total annual earnings	6,089	5,824	6,428	6,815	6,419
c.v.	*0.51*	*0.52*	*0.59*	*0.41*	*0.47*
Gap to average earnings		*0.96*	*1.06*	*1.12*	*1.05*
Basic wage	3,792	3,740	3,624	4,038	3,848
c.v.	*0.55*	*0.57*	*0.58*	*0.48*	*0.49*
Bonus	961	929	1,354	1,005	886
c.v.	*1.66*	*1.68*	*1.81*	*1.33*	*1.69*
Subsidies	1,098	889	1,243	1,597	1,503
c.v.	*1.07*	*1.03*	*1.20*	*0.88*	*1.02*
Income in kind	99	91	113	105	123
c.v.	*2.76*	*2.93*	*2.37*	*2.81*	*2.23*
Hourly wage	2.85	2.73	2.97	3.23	3.00
c.v.	*0.63*	*0.67*	*0.69*	*0.52*	*0.52*
Hours worked per week	43.7	43.9	44.3	42.9	43.1
c.v.	*0.17*	*0.18*	*0.18*	*0.15*	*0.15*
2002					
Total annual earnings	10,910	8,860	13,086	14,410	13,245
c.v.	*0.67*	*0.71*	*0.66*	*0.56*	*0.49*
Gap to average earnings		*0.81*	*1.20*	*1.32*	*1.21*
Basic wage	8,959	7,544	10,534	11,069	10,930
c.v.	*0.64*	*0.69*	*0.61*	*0.53*	*0.52*
Bonus	1,036	777	1,514	1,601	1,042
c.v.	*2.46*	*2.84*	*2.20*	*1.98*	*2.08*
Subsidies	672	327	730	1,207	1,320
c.v.	*2.96*	*3.65*	*2.94*	*2.18*	*2.21*
Income in kind	132	101	309	120	165
c.v.	*7.90*	*7.22*	*9.12*	*3.74*	*3.54*
Hourly wage	5.30	4.13	6.41	7.33	6.64
c.v.	*0.87*	*0.81*	*0.69*	*0.93*	*0.63*
Hours worked per week	43.8	45.5	41.6	41.7	41.1
c.v.	*0.24*	*0.26*	*0.18*	*0.20*	*0.18*

Source: Authors' calculations using the 1995 and 2002 CHIP survey data.

Notes:
1. See Table 7.7.
2. See text for definitions of economic sectors.

the highest total earnings in 1995, the huge earnings increase in government agencies and institutions moved them up to the first rank with wages similar to foreign-invested enterprises in 2002.[36] On the other hand, urban collective enterprises as well as private and individual enterprises have seen their relative

Table 7.9 Descriptive statistics on individual characteristics by regions

	All	Coast	Center	West	Municipality	Northeast
1995						
Total annual earnings	6,151	7,558	5,409	5,851	7,495	5,812
c. v.	*0.51*	*0.55*	*0.47*	*0.44*	*0.48*	*0.49*
Gap to average earnings		*1.23*	*0.88*	*0.95*	*1.22*	*0.94*
Basic wage	3,824	4,072	3,656	3,693	4,366	3,874
c. v.	*0.56*	*0.63*	*0.50*	*0.51*	*0.70*	*0.52*
Bonus	981	1,831	645	773	1,558	639
c. v.	*1.64*	*1.53*	*1.27*	*1.31*	*1.02*	*1.59*
Subsidies	1,111	1,357	845	1,217	1,365	1,070
c. v.	*1.07*	*1.26*	*1.04*	*0.88*	*0.87*	*0.93*
Income in kind	99	108	115	78	106	78
c. v.	*2.72*	*2.85*	*2.32*	*2.76*	*2.75*	*3.84*
Hourly wage	2.89	3.54	2.56	2.74	3.43	2.71
c. v.	*0.65*	*0.66*	*0.67*	*0.62*	*0.52*	*0.54*
Hours worked per week	43.7	44.0	43.5	43.8	43.7	43.4
c. v.	*0.17*	*0.19*	*0.18*	*0.16*	*0.16*	*0.16*
2002						
Total annual earnings	10,919	13,376	9,782	10,435	12,691	10,090
c. v.	*0.66*	*0.75*	*0.61*	*0.57*	*0.62*	*0.62*
Gap to average earnings		*1.23*	*0.90*	*0.96*	*1.16*	*0.92*
Basic wage	9,022	10,251	8,423	8,664	10,233	8,736
c. v.	*0.64*	*0.72*	*0.58*	*0.59*	*0.71*	*0.58*
Bonus	1,011	1,780	677	878	1,396	769
c. v.	*2.45*	*2.14*	*2.33*	*2.28*	*2.24*	*2.64*
Subsidies	656	1,071	361	748	902	454
c. v.	*2.98*	*2.77*	*3.10*	*2.32*	*3.02*	*3.01*
Income in kind	129	222	129	71	150	97
c. v.	*7.66*	*9.40*	*3.32*	*3.60*	*5.23*	*3.87*
Hourly wage	5.30	6.54	4.71	5.11	6.29	4.76
c. v.	*0.89*	*0.98*	*0.83*	*0.86*	*0.79*	*0.65*
Hours worked per week	43.8	43.7	44.3	44.1	41.3	43.8
c. v.	*0.24*	*0.24*	*0.25*	*0.25*	*0.20*	*0.22*

Source: Authors' calculations using the 1995 and 2002 CHIP survey data.

Notes:
1. See Table 7.7.
2. See text for definitions of regional variables.

position deteriorating, the largest gap with other enterprises jumping from 67 to 78 percent and 57 to 64 percent respectively between 1995 and 2002.

In terms of economic sectors (Table 7.8), the difference between the competitive and the non-competitive sectors (oligopolistic, public services, and government) has turned larger over time, with the earnings gap in favor of non-competitive sectors increasing from a range of 10 to 17 percent to 48 to 63 percent. A somehow similar change, with much lower amplitude though, has also taken place across non-competitive sectors, with the largest gap between two non-competitive sectors increasing from 6 percent in 1995 to 10 percent in 2002.

Furthermore, coefficients of variation (c.v.) on total earnings indicate a more equitable distribution of earnings in the public sector (SOEs and GAIs) as compared to the private/competitive sectors for both years. The earnings composition has also changed over time, the most notable change being the sharp reduction in the share of subsidies provided by SOEs (which comes from a 50 percent reduction of the absolute amount in SOEs). Consequently, while the public sector was offering much higher subsidies than the private sector in 1995, it is no longer the case in 2002, except in public administration.[37]

At the beginning of economic reform, the earnings difference between coastal provinces and inner provinces was extremely small.[38] Then, as indicated in Knight et al. (2001), a significant divergence in earnings growth across provinces in urban areas arose between 1988 and 1995. Our data (Table 7.9) indicate that no further divergence across the different geographical regions can be observed between 1995 and 2002 when earnings are adjusted by regional living costs. The relative differences between coastal provinces and central and western provinces were slightly reduced over the period, but the premium offered by the former still stands at 37 percent compared with central provinces and 28 percent compared with western provinces. The comparison between municipalities and other regions shows that taking account of differences in living costs sharply lowers the premium in favor of municipalities, especially compared with coastal provinces.

Lastly, the comparison of the number of hours worked per week shows a longer working time in the private sector than in the public sector for the two years, despite a reduction in the number of hours worked in both private or individual enterprises and foreign-invested enterprises in 2002. The comparison across economic sectors confirms that workers in public services and in government agencies work less, but it also shows that working time in the competitive sector has increased over time while it has decreased in the oligopolistic sector, leading to a quite important gap between competitive and non-competitive sectors in 2002 (about four hours per week). Regional comparisons do not reveal strong differences in working time across regions, except for a sizeable reduction in hours worked in municipalities between 1995 and 2002, which is not observed in other regions.

7.4 Methodology

In order to analyze earnings differentials between individuals belonging to different segments in the labor market (across ownership, sector, or region), we use an extended version of Oaxaca-Blinder decompositions (Blinder 1973; Oaxaca 1973) to evaluate the contribution of three complementary factors: differences in mean endowments of workers across segments, differences in hours worked, and a pure "segment effect."

7.4.1 Modeling total earnings

Let w_s^i represent hourly earnings for individual i belonging to segment s. w_s^i depends on two sets of arguments: individual characteristics (x_s^i), and a set of segment specific parameters corresponding to the earnings model linking individual characteristics with observed earnings (β_s).

$$w_s^i = W(x_s^i ; \beta_s) \tag{1}$$

Symmetrically, let h_s^i represent the number of hours worked by individual i belonging to segment s. h_s^i also depends on two sets of arguments: individual and household characteristics determining labor supply (z_s^i), and a set of segment specific parameters (γ_s).

$$h_s^i = H(z_s^i ; \gamma_s) \tag{2}$$

The total individual income (I) derived from segment s can be expressed as:

$$
\begin{aligned}
I_s^i &= w_s^i \cdot h_s^i \\
&= W(x_s^i ; \beta_s) \cdot H(z_s^i ; \gamma_s)
\end{aligned} \tag{3}
$$

7.4.2 Decomposition of observed earnings differentials

Using equation (3), the observed average earnings gap between two segments s and S can be decomposed as follows:

$$
\begin{aligned}
\bar{I}_s^i - \bar{I}_S^i &= \overline{W}(x_s^i ; \beta_s).\overline{H}(z_s^i ; \gamma_s) - \overline{W}(x_S^i ; \beta_S).\overline{H}(z_S^i ; \gamma_S) \\
&= \overline{W}(x_s^i ; \beta_S).\overline{H}(z_s^i ; \gamma_S) - \overline{W}(x_S^i ; \beta_S).\overline{H}(z_S^i ; \gamma_S : \textit{Difference in} \\
&\quad \textit{endowments} \\
&\quad + \overline{W}(x_s^i ; \beta_S).\overline{H}(z_s^i ; \gamma_S) - \overline{W}(x_s^i ; \beta_S).\overline{H}(z_S^i ; \gamma_S) : \textit{Difference in hours} \\
&\quad \textit{worked} \\
&\quad + \overline{W}(x_s^i ; \beta_s).\overline{H}(z_s^i ; \gamma_s) - \overline{W}(x_s^i ; \beta_S).\overline{H}(z_s^i ; \gamma_S) : \textit{"Segment effect"}
\end{aligned} \tag{4}
$$

This decomposition provides an evaluation of what would be the observed average earnings gap under the following conditions:

(i)   If workers observed in different categories were facing the same conditions in the determination of remuneration and of hours worked, the wage difference reflects pure difference-in-endowments effect.

(ii) If workers observed in different categories were facing the same conditions in the determination of remuneration and were endowed with the same characteristics, the wage difference reflects pure difference-in-hours worked effect.

(iii) If workers observed in different categories were facing the same conditions in the determination of hours worked and were endowed with the same characteristics, the wage difference reflects pure "segment effect."

7.4.3 Implementation and robustness issues

The practical implementation of the method consists of three steps. First, earnings equations and hours worked equations are estimated separately for each segment (see Appendix). Second, estimated coefficients are used to predict hourly earnings and hours worked for each individual and each segment. Third, each of the effects presented in equation (4) is evaluated by averaging over individuals the corresponding observed or counter-factual earnings values.

7.4.3.1 Earnings equations

Decomposition results presented below correspond to the specification for earnings equation estimations detailed in Appendix A and B. The common explanatory variables for hourly earnings functions are effective number of years of education; a dummy variable if the individual has received vocational education; effective years of work experience and the square of this variable; a dummy variable for "big cities;" and a dummy variable for acquisition of the current urban residence permit (*hukou*). Regional dummies are used as additional explanatory variables in the ownership and sector dimensions.

Selectivity bias in enterprise type and industrial sector choices may affect the estimated coefficients from earnings equations and thus decomposition results. In the absence of any credible exogenous instrument in the data, we proceeded without corrections for selection bias. In any case, our decomposition findings are robust to changes in both specification and estimation methods.[39] However, it should be stressed that, although labor has been administratively allocated in China up to 1995 and labor mobility remained quite low until this date, selection may definitely be a more important issue in 2002. While the development of labor market has allowed mobility to increase, SOE-restructuring has led to a selective laying-off of workers. Our dynamic interpretations in terms of segmentation changes might thus be partly driven by selection mechanisms.

7.4.3.2 Decomposition: path-dependence

A general issue concerning Oaxaca–Blinder decompositions concerns path-dependence (Fournier 2005). Indeed, evaluated effects a priori depend on the benchmark population structure or coefficient vector chosen to run micro-simulations. In our work, each possible evaluation is considered and used as a robustness test for our decomposition results[40]. Moreover, since decomposition results obtained from this type of analyses strongly depend on estimation quality, a bootstrap procedure has been implemented over the whole procedure (estimation, simulation, and decomposition).[41] The following decomposition tables include the corresponding 95 percent confidence intervals.

7.5 Decomposing the evolution of earnings differentials by categories

Tables 7.10, 7.11, and 7.12 document the changes in relative remunerations across enterprises of different ownership/sector/region in urban China, by applying the extended Oaxaca-Blinder decomposition method presented above. Differentials are reported both in mean value and in percentage of the lowest earnings, the stars indicating the statistical significance of estimated effects. For example, the "Endowment effect" figures reported on the first row of Table 10 read as follows. Of the 1,299 yuan observed average earnings gap between SOEs and UCEs in 1995, 352 yuan can be attributed to better characteristics observed in SOEs, which would lead, other things equal, to a 7 percent average earnings gap against UCEs (instead of the 27 percent observed differential).[42]

7.5.1 Ownership structure

In the first column of Table 7.10, observed earnings differences across enterprises of various ownership show a general increasing trend between 1995 and 2002, the only (noteworthy) exception being between FIEs and GAIs[43]. The evolution has been in favor of both FIEs and GAIs, and at the expense of UCEs. In the middle, employees in SOEs have seen their earnings gap increased compared to UCEs, but their situation has deteriorated compared to GAIs. The most striking result from Table 7.10 is the growing importance (and significance) of segmentation as the most prominent explanatory factor for the general increasing trend in earnings differences across ownership.

Earnings differentials in favor of the foreign sector in 1995 have increased over time compared to the emerging domestic private sector, but decreased compared to the public sector. The deteriorating position of FIEs as compared to GAIs mainly comes from changing segmentation patterns (from 14 percent in favor of FIEs to a non-significant 5 percent in favor of GAIs), although a higher working time in FIEs gives them a premium over GAIs (5 percent). Compared to SOEs, the observed decrease in earnings differential mainly comes from decreasing segmentation in favor of FIEs (from 23 percent to 16 percent). A stronger segmentation in favor of FIEs can be found when compared to UCEs and PIEs. The earnings gap between FIEs and UCEs (67–74 percent) comes from the conjunction of a strong and increasing segmentation (40–51 percent), better characteristics (17–20 percent) and a longer (although reducing) working time in FIEs. For the comparison with PIEs, figures for 1995 must be taken with caution since estimations do not perform very well for this year, and the number of observations in this particular category are small (see Appendices 7.A1 and 7.B1). However, it is instructive to examine earnings differentials in 2002. The comparison with FIEs shows a strong segmentation: the premium in favor of FIEs would be 65 percent in 2002 if there were no differences in characteristics and hours worked with PIEs. However, longer working time in PIEs reduces the gap by 11 percentage points on average.

In 1995, the earnings differential between the public sector and urban collectives was all in favor of the former (27 percent for SOEs and 37 percent for GAIs), and was explained by the conjunction of both better endowments of workers in the public sector and a rather strong segmentation against urban collectives (respectively 17 and 27 percent). Interestingly, the huge increase in the earnings gap between GAIs and UCEs over time (reaching 78 percent in 2002) can be attributed to a much stronger segmentation (65 percent) but also, and rather importantly, to a widening gap in terms of workers endowments, with an increase of the wage premium due to better characteristics from 9 percent to 18 percent. On the opposite, changes in hours worked are reducing the gap in 2002 between UCEs and both SOEs and GAIs, but with quite a small impact (respectively 3 percent and 6 percent).

In 2002, the comparison between PIEs and the public sector also shows high earnings differentials against PIEs, the premium in favor of the public sector ranging from 31 percent to 64 percent. Again, these gaps are driven by a strong segmentation phenomenon (50–78 percent), which cannot be compensated by longer hours worked in the private sector though this last effect is quite high and significant (18–21 percent).

The decomposition analysis presented here highlights three main phenomena on the ownership dimension, which are of importance to understand the evolution of the labor market in urban China. First, workers in the public sector, especially government agencies and institutions, are still very much privileged as compared to other segments of the labor market. Second, the foreign sector has reinforced its position through a sustained high wage policy. Third, the emerging domestic private sector and the collective sector have seen their relative position deteriorating. These results show that despite the increasing importance of market mechanisms within the private sector, active

Table 7.10 Decomposition of observed earnings gaps by ownership

1995			Observed differences				Endowment effect				Segmentation effect				Hours worked effect			
(A)	(B)		(B)–(A)		5%	95%			5%	95%			5%	95%			5%	95%
SOE	UCE	(yuan) (%)	-1,299 -27	***	-1,454 –	-1,147 –	-352 -7	***	-498 -10	-215 -4	-811 -17	***	-968 -20	-641 -13	-136 -3	***	-241 -5	-56 -1
SOE	PIE	(yuan) (%)	-979 -19	***	-1,623 –	-189 –	-578 -11	ns	-3,950 -79	1,391 28	-1,228 -24	ns	-3,692 -74	3,587 69	827 16	*	-502 -10	1,968 39
SOE	FIE	(yuan) (%)	1,970 32	***	1,250 –	2,797 –	303 5	ns	-500 -8	1,500 24	1,394 23	***	251 4	2,496 41	273 4	*	-184 -3	606 10
SOE	GAI	(yuan) (%)	490 8	***	388 –	593 –	133 2	***	41 1	220 4	532 9	***	379 6	656 11	-175 -3	***	-234 -4	-120 -2
UCE	PIE	(yuan) (%)	321 7	ns	-309 –	1,005 –	-485 -10	ns	-5,256 -108	1,492 31	-279 -6	ns	-2,713 -57	4,440 95	1,084 22	***	146 3	1,952 41
UCE	FIE	(yuan) (%)	3,270 67	***	2,572 –	4,070 –	823 17	***	236 5	1,828 38	1,958 40	***	1,016 21	2,969 61	490 10	***	112 2	845 18
UCE	GAI	(yuan) (%)	1,789 37	***	1,648 –	1,909 –	445 9	***	202 4	676 14	1,336 27	***	1,069 22	1,595 33	9 0	ns	-117 -2	179 4
PIE	FIE	(yuan) (%)	2,949 57	***	2,020 –	3,933 –	1,712 33	ns	-2,301 -40	5,953 123	1,833 35	ns	-4,521 -89	5,771 118	-596 -12	*	-2,390 -47	1,224 23
PIE	GAI	(yuan) (%)	1,468 28	***	678 –	2,139 –	-640 -12	*	-2,887 -56	3,420 68	3,028 58	**	-1,649 -40	5,447 109	-919 -18	*	-2,475 -47	634 12
FIE	GAI	(yuan) (%)	-1,481 -22	***	-2,325 –	-749 –	-155 -2	ns	-1,365 -21	1,120 17	-943 -14	***	-2,377 -36	-5 0	-383 -6	ns	-904 -14	394 6

2002			Observed differences				Endowment effect				Segmentation effect				Hours worked effect			
(A)	(B)		(B)−(A)		5%	95%			5%	95%			5%	95%			5%	95%
SOE	UCE	(yuan)	−3,210	***	−3,521	−2,788	−913	***	−1,240	−598	−2,552	***	−2,957	−2,119	256	***	93	451
		(%)	−42				−12		−16	−8	−33		−40	−27	3		1	6
SOE	PIE	(yuan)	−2,554	***	−2,932	−2,243	128	ns	−980	1,416	−4,163	***	−5,861	−2,678	1,481	***	921	2,318
		(%)	−31				2		−12	17	−50		−72	−32	18		11	28
SOE	FIE	(yuan)	2,465	***	1,589	3,512	165	ns	−802	1,222	1,746	***	610	2,770	554	***	97	938
		(%)	23				2		−7	11	16		6	25	5		1	9
SOE	GAI	(yuan)	2,707	***	2,450	2,998	411	***	113	727	2,476	***	2,131	2,853	−180	***	−364	−43
		(%)	25				4		1	7	23		19	26	−2		−3	0
UCE	PIE	(yuan)	656	***	279	1,019	1,182	***	544	1,849	−1,552	***	−2,563	−619	1,026	***	758	1,394
		(%)	9				16		7	24	−20		−33	−8	13		10	18
UCE	FIE	(yuan)	5,675	***	4,843	6,953	1,526	***	272	3,110	3,857	***	2,346	5,460	292	*	−242	948
		(%)	74				20		4	41	51		31	74	4		−3	12
UCE	GAI	(yuan)	5,917	***	5,567	6,256	1,398	***	638	2,140	4,952	***	4,256	5,821	−433	***	−826	−141
		(%)	78				18		8	28	65		55	77	−6		−11	−2
PIE	FIE	(yuan)	5,019	***	4,111	6,100	515	ns	−1,574	2,342	5,403	***	3,974	6,728	−899	***	−1,811	−338
		(%)	61				6		−19	28	65		47	81	−11		−22	−4
PIE	GAI	(yuan)	5,261	***	4,925	5,683	543	ns	−1,396	2,083	6,434	***	5,452	7,490	−1,716	***	−3,068	−915
		(%)	64				7		−17	26	78		65	90	−21		−37	−11
FIE	GAI	(yuan)	242	ns	−957	1,092	248	ns	−1,047	1,439	712	ns	−631	2,189	−717	***	−1,321	−146
		(%)	2				2		−8	11	5		−5	17	−5		−10	−1

Source: Authors' calculations using the 1995 and 2002 CHIP survey data.

Notes:

1. Percentages are calculated as a percentage of the lowest wage.
2. Decompositions based on regressions results presented in Appendices 7.A and 7.B.
3. Confidence intervals and significance test are derived from a 300 replications bootstrap procedure: * indicates that the estimated effect is statistically significant at 20 percent, ** at 10 percent and *** at 5 percent.
4. Ownership categories are: state-owned enterprises (SOEs), urban collective enterprises (UCEs), private or individual enterprises, (PIEs), foreign-invested enterprises (FIEs), and government agencies or institutions (GAIs).
5. Earnings are deflated using the urban provincial-level spatial price deflators calculated by Brandt and Holz (2006). Base = nationwide prices in 2002.

Table 7.11 Decomposition of observed earnings gaps by sectors

1995			Observed differences				Endowment effect				Segmentation effect				Hours worked effect			
(A)	(B)		(B)−(A)		5%	95%			5%	95%			5%	95%			5%	95%
Comp	Olig	(yuan)	604	***	373	880	71	ns	−137	288	503	***	195	771	30	ns	−83	147
		(%)	10		–	–	1		−2	5	9		3	13	1		−1	3
Comp	Publ. Serv.	(yuan)	992	***	859	1,107	358	***	152	605	722	***	443	935	−88	***	−170	−6
		(%)	17		–	–	6		3	10	12		8	16	−2		−3	0
Comp	Govt	(yuan)	595	***	459	695	281	***	61	432	438	***	268	681	−124	***	−198	−58
		(%)	10		–	–	5		1	7	8		5	12	−2		−3	−1
Olig	Publ. Serv.	(yuan)	387	***	103	662	545	***	217	1,005	−8	ns	−519	399	−150	**	−285	5
		(%)	6		–	–	9		3	16	0		−8	6	−2		−4	0
Olig	Govt	(yuan)	−9	ns	−287	258	470	**	−53	1,041	−348	ns	−1,080	243	−131	**	−276	31
		(%)	0		–	–	7		−1	16	−5		−17	4	−2		−4	1
Publ. Serv.	Govt	(yuan)	−396	***	−556	−247	−40	ns	−189	120	−361	***	−546	−191	4	ns	−89	101
		(%)	−6		–	–	−1		−3	2	−6		−9	−3	0		−1	2

2002

(A)	(B)		Observed differences			Endowment effect			Segmentation effect			Hours worked effect		
			(B)–(A)	5%	95%		5%	95%		5%	95%		5%	95%
Comp	Olig	(yuan)	4,227 ***	3,796	4,771	-125 ns	-916	444	5,241 ***	4,699	5,829	-890 ***	-1,408	-506
		(%)	48	–	–	-1	-10	5	59	53	66	-10	-16	-6
Comp	Publ. Serv.	(yuan)	5,550 ***	5,138	5,868	615 ***	195	1,058	5,628 ***	5,343	5,829	-693 ***	-1,111	-371
		(%)	63	–	–	7	2	12	64	60	66	-8	-13	-4
Comp	Govt	(yuan)	4,385 ***	4,017	4,735	884 ***	120	1,467	4,411 ***	3,883	5,002	-910 ***	-1,436	-509
		(%)	50	–	–	10	1	17	50	44	57	-10	-16	-6
Olig	Publ. Serv.	(yuan)	1,323 ***	725	1,839	592 **	-70	1,166	645 **	-70	1,389	86 ns	-178	351
		(%)	10	–	–	5	-1	9	5	-1	11	1	-1	3
Olig	Govt	(yuan)	159 ns	-313	668	1,155 ***	456	1,926	-891 ***	-1,775	-19	-105 ns	-347	155
		(%)	1	–	–	9	3	15	-7	-14	0	-1	-3	1
Publ. Serv.	Govt	(yuan)	-1,165 ***	-1,608	-750	766 ***	139	1,428	-1,684 ***	-2,108	-1,172	-246 ***	-483	-7
		(%)	-9	–	–	6	1	11	-13	-16	-9	-2	-4	0

Source: Authors' calculations using the 1995 and 2002 CHIP survey data.

Notes: See Table 7.10 and text for a full definition of sectors.

policies launched at the end of the 1990s to raise government wages have had a strong impact in terms of segmentation, which confirms that earnings in the public sector remain highly protected. It should be stressed that there might also be a sizeable selection effect at stake here since the downsizing of the state sector has led to the privatization of the least dynamic enterprises, the Chinese authorities still controlling large profit-making SOEs where employees remain strongly protected.

7.5.2 Economic sectors

The decomposition results by economic sectors presented in Table 7.11 also highlight quite a strong and rising segmentation between competitive and protected sectors. In 1995, segmentation against the competitive sectors contributed to more than half of the total average earnings differences. In 2002, the main reason why the competitive sectors provided much lower wages than the rest of the sectors (between 48 percent and 63 percent) almost exclusively comes from the segmentation effect, which is strongly reinforced as compared to 1995, and ranges from 50 percent to 64 percent.

By the end of the 1990s, SOEs began to retreat from the competitive sector, while strengthening their position in noncompetitive sectors, especially in the oligoplistic sector. SOEs downsizing and massive lay-offs are the main reasons for the surge in unemployment at the end of the 1990s, but our decompositions indicate no change in terms of the relative wage level for the remaining employees in the oligopolistic sector. The comparison between the competitive sector and the oligopolistic sector even reveals no significant differences in workers' characteristics, the only determinant explaining the large difference being the segmentation effect.

These findings can be analyzed in terms of profit sharing within oligopolistic sectors (Li and Bai 2005; Knight and Li 2005). Moreover, institutional explanations lie in the increased autonomy in wage settings and increased wages for civil servants provided by the Chinese government over the period. This has allowed the oligopolistic sector and public services to redistribute rents to employees, while the competitive sector has been facing growing competition.

Not only the wage level, but also working hours have changed under the pressure of competition. During the period, working time has increased in the competitive sectors while at the same time, the non-competitive sectors somewhat reduced their working hours. Given this differentiated evolution, changes in hours worked are partly hiding the magnitude of the evolution. Indeed, if workers in the competitive sectors were not working longer, the observed differences of 48 percent to 63 percent would be even larger by 8 to 10 percentage points. Hence, if there were no segmentation and only differences in the hours worked, the earnings level for similar workers in competitive sectors would be higher than the oligopolistic sectors, and quite close to public services and government jobs.

Within the non-competitive sector, observed earnings differences also turned larger in 2002. For both years, endowments in the oligopolistic sector are slightly lower than in the other two sectors. This is especially the case for the comparison with public services, in which endowments (9–5 percent) are significantly higher than in the oligopolistic sector and drive a major part of the observed earnings gap (6–10 percent). Antithetically, public services show small endowment differences with the government sector in 1995, but benefit from a favorable segmentation effect (6 percent), which turned even larger in 2002 (13 percent). This somewhat surprising segmentation phenomenon may be explained by the fact that in public services, wages are derived partly from the government, and partly from the market. The marketization of this sector has allowed workers in public services to get rising extra wage income (bonus, subsidy, etc.) on top of wages provided by the government.

The sector decomposition confirms and completes some of the findings from the ownership analysis, with a rising segmentation over 1995–2002 in favor of the non-competitive sectors. Three facts can be highlighted here to explain observed earnings differences and evolutions over the period studied: (1) increasing competition within the competitive sector; (2) increasing concentration of large SOEs within oligopolistic sectors; and (3) increasing protection of government jobs.

7.5.3 *Regional segmentation*

Consistent with the findings in the other two dimensions, regional decompositions show a trend of rising segmentation (Table 7.12). Regional disparities, especially between coastal provinces and other regions remain large, the highest gap still being close to 40 percent in 2002. A sizeable part of the observed earnings gap between regions can be attributed to a more rapid economic growth and huge capital inflow in the coastal region, and to inadequate labor mobility between regions. As illustrated in many studies (e.g. Knight and Yueh 2006), labor mobility is still limited for urban local workers subject to various institutional obstacles even at the end of 1990s, while regional mobility among rural migrant workers increased over time.

Table 7.12 shows that the share of regional differences resulting from segmentation, particularly between coastal region and other regions, is remarkably large in the two years and became stronger in almost each pair of regions. Segmentation explains the major part of the observed earnings difference between the coastal and central region (35–41 percent), between the coastal and western region (28 percent), and between the coastal and northeast region (40–1 percent).

A remarkable change between 1995 and 2002 is the deteriorating relative position of central provinces. This change may be rooted in the fact that the region has been disregarded in the strategy of regional development of the

Table 7.12 Decomposition of observed earnings gaps by regions

1995

(A)	(B)		Observed differences (B)−(A)	5%	95%	Endowment effect	5%	95%	Segmentation effect	5%	95%	Hours worked effect	5%	95%
Coast	Centre	(yuan)	−2,149 ***	−2,293	−1,984	−215 ***	−312	−117	−1,908 ***	−2,047	−1,764	−27 ns	−81	27
		(%)	−40	−	−4	−4	−6	−2	−35	−38	−32	−1	−2	1
Coast	West	(yuan)	−1,707 ***	−1,861	−1,547	−104 **	−239	21	−1,664 ***	−1,853	−1,472	61 **	−6	122
		(%)	−29	−	−2	−2	−4	0	−28	−32	−25	1	0	2
Coast	Municip	(yuan)	−63 ns	−287	176	640 ***	71	1,290	−844 ***	−1,492	−175	141 ns	−95	379
		(%)	−1	−	9	9	1	17	−11	−20	−2	2	−1	5
Coast	N–E.	(yuan)	−1,746 ***	−1,975	−1,545	519 ***	134	870	−2,337 ***	−2,838	−1,936	72 *	−19	195
		(%)	−30	−	9	9	2	15	−40	−50	−33	1	0	3
Centre	West	(yuan)	442 ***	355	529	131 ***	52	225	251 ***	156	347	60 ***	13	104
		(%)	8	−	−	2	1	4	5	3	6	1	0	2
Centre	Municip	(yuan)	2,086 ***	1,857	2,263	790 ***	383	1,182	1,199 ***	756	1,668	97 *	−29	233
		(%)	39	−	−	15	7	22	22	14	31	2	−1	4
Centre	N–E.	(yuan)	403 ***	238	563	723 ***	317	1,121	−382 *	−832	93	62 *	−36	174
		(%)	7	−	−	13	6	21	−7	−15	2	1	−1	3
West	Municip	(yuan)	1,644 ***	1,429	1,840	791 ***	373	1,204	814 ***	347	1,316	39 ns	−63	158
		(%)	28	−	−	14	6	21	14	6	22	1	−1	3
West	N–E.	(yuan)	−39 ns	−185	124	633 ***	360	923	−663 ***	−986	−343	−9 ns	−105	95
		(%)	−1	−	−	11	6	16	−11	−17	−6	0	−2	2
Municip	N–E.	(yuan)	−1,683 ***	−1,914	−1,419	−585 ***	−1,018	−156	−994 ***	−1,495	−509	−105 *	−262	36
		(%)	−29	−	−	−10	−17	−3	−17	−26	−9	−2	−4	1

2002			Observed differences				Endowment effect				Segmentation effect				Hours worked effect			
(A)	(B)		(B)–(A)		5%	95%			5%	95%			5%	95%			5%	95%
Coast	Centre	(yuan)	−3,594	***	−3,903	−3,153	142	ns	−255	509	−3,967	***	−4,156	−3,654	231	***	85	424
		(%)	−37				2		−3	5	−41		−43	−38	2		1	4
Coast	West	(yuan)	−2,941	***	−3,453	−2,554	−202	ns	−591	231	−2,879	***	−3,413	−2,337	141	**	−2	288
		(%)	−28				−2		−6	2	−28		−33	−22	1		0	3
Coast	Municip	(yuan)	−685	***	−1,248	−177	1,808	**	−61	4,305	−2,312	***	−4,987	−799	−181	ns	−631	193
		(%)	−5				14		−1	34	−18		−39	−6	−1		−5	2
Coast	N–E.	(yuan)	−3,285	***	−3,720	−2,879	731	**	−144	1,681	−4,178	***	−4,559	−3,722	162	*	−124	433
		(%)	−33				7		−1	17	−41		−46	−37	2		−1	4
Centre	West	(yuan)	653	***	361	1,006	−313	***	−517	−91	1,050	***	659	1,475	−84	*	−199	36
		(%)	7				−3		−5	−1	11		7	15	−1		−2	0
Centre	Municip	(yuan)	2,909	***	2,341	3,418	723	ns	−791	2,178	2,670	***	1,341	4,077	−484	***	−832	−87
		(%)	30				7		−8	22	27		14	41	−5		−9	−1
Centre	N–E.	(yuan)	309	**	−46	670	173	ns	−243	634	222	ns	−354	832	−86	ns	−287	98
		(%)	3				2		−3	7	2		−4	9	−1		−3	1
West	Municip	(yuan)	2,256	***	1,760	2,735	1,362	*	−247	2,894	1,191	*	−528	2,958	−298	***	−600	−23
		(%)	22				13		−2	28	11		−5	28	−3		−6	0
West	N–E.	(yuan)	−344	***	−822	0	597	***	211	1,028	−995	***	−1,584	−371	54	ns	−183	261
		(%)	−3				6		2	10	−10		−16	−4	1		−2	3
Municip	N–E.	(yuan)	−2,600	***	−3,227	−2,060	−997	***	−1,782	−180	−2,056	***	−3,100	−1,134	452	***	184	721
		(%)	−26				−10		−18	−2	−20		−31	−11	5		2	7

Source: Authors' calculations using the 1995 and 2002 CHIP survey data.

Notes: See Table 7.10 and text for a full definition of regions.

central government. However, despite declining relative earnings and increasing segmentation against workers in the region, central provinces have improved their relative position in terms of endowment in 2002. All endowment effects against central provinces in 1995 (ranging from 2 to 15 percent) reversed or became no longer significant in 2002. This may be because skilled and well-educated laid-off workers from closed SOEs had to take jobs that were previously filled by unskilled and poorly educated workers. The better-endowed people remained active while low-endowed people were forced to exit the labor market.

On the opposite, the position of the western region in terms of segmentation has improved somewhat between 1995 and 2002. One possible interpretation is that the Western Development Strategy has raised the relative level of earnings in western provinces, allowing then to maintain their relative position with respect to coastal provinces (around 30 percent earnings gap) in a context of growing regional segmentation.

The northeastern provinces, represented by Liaoning, deserve special attention. The relative earnings in the northeast region slightly decreased compared to other regions except municipalities between 1995 and 2002, which is reflected in rising observed earnings gaps between the northeast region and other regions. Concerning segmentation phenomena, the evidence is mixed: stable segmentation in favor of coastal provinces (40–1 percent), western provinces (10–11 percent), and municipalities (17–20 percent) on one hand, and decreasing segmentation in favor of central provinces (7 percent in 1995 to nonsignificant in 2002) on the other hand. This pattern can be at least partly explained by a declining endowment effect against the northeast region due to selection mechanisms. With the massive lay-offs and closures of some large scale enterprises, the absence of local re-employment opportunities caused better educated employees (e.g. professionals, technician and skilled workers) to move to other provinces.

Regional decompositions provide further evidence of rising segmentation on China's urban labor market and complement the other two dimensions by highlighting quite large regional disparities and the unequal distribution of gains or burdens related to changes in the labor market at the turn of the century. They also stress the importance of the Chinese government's regional policies in alleviating burdens in some regions (e.g. western provinces) and redistributing the benefits of economic development. In this context, central provinces appear to be by far the greatest (relative) looser in the recent reform process, facing increasing segmentation, even as compared to western and northeastern provinces.

7.6 Conclusion

This paper analyzes the evolution of labor market segmentation for urban *hukou* holders between 1995 and 2002. During the seven-year period, real earnings in urban China have increased sharply (+78 percent) and for all workers, with substantial differences across ownership and sectors, and to a lesser extent, regions. As a result, earnings differentials across enterprises have changed dramatically and sometimes induced a re-ranking.

Our decomposition results show strong evidence of a multi-tiered labor market along three major lines, segmentation arising across enterprise ownership (up to 78 percent), economic sectors (up to 64 percent), and regions (up to 41 percent). They also highlight increasing segmentation over time within each of these three dimensions. In particular, the gap between the privileged segments of the labor market (e.g. SOEs and oligopolitistic sectors) and the most competitive segments (e.g. private enterprises and competitive sectors) has widened between 1995 and 2002. Our results confirm the Knight and Song (2003) findings that

> the market forces operating in the growing private sector and the relative immunity of the state sector from those forces generated greater wage segmentation among types of ownership [between 1995 and 1999], and provincial differences in the place of reform and in economic growth created spatial segmentation in wages that could not be removed by the equilibrating movement of labor (Knight and Song 2003, 616).

In the view of the massive layoffs in the state-owned sector at the end of the 1990s and the concomitant impressive growth of the private sector, one might have expected segmentation not to increase so sharply given the growing importance of market mechanisms and competition in the urban labor market. However, the clear distinction found between a "protected" well-paying segment and a "competitive" segment mostly made of the emerging private sector stresses a strongly segmented labor market in 2002. More specifically, our findings suggest that there are two directions toward which the urban labor market in China is moving. On one hand, economic liberalization has brought various benefits to the labor system, including better signals for a more efficient allocation of labor and improved incentives for efforts thanks to enhanced rewards to effort. On the other hand, various institutional as well as market-based elements have prevented equalization of marginal products, and thus reduction in earning differences. Major explanations for the strong and rising magnitude of segmentation between 1995–2002 can be found in migration restrictions and in active government policies towards the public sector, but certainly in efficiency-wage related behavior in the foreign sector.

The observed increasing spatial segmentation reflects the still extremely low mobility of labor among urban dwellers, which represents a major obstacle to the formation of competitive market wages in urban areas. Even though regional mobility for rural–urban migrant workers has increased over time and the effectiveness of institutional barriers such as the *hukou* system has progressively declined, various institutional obstacles remained to labor mobility for urban residents even at the end of the 1990s. As a result, market mechanisms favoring wages convergence could not operate properly. The evidence found here supports Knight and Song (2005) findings of a "three tier" labor market in 1999, which consists of "privileged" urban residents never made redundant during the SOEs downsizing process, retrenched urban workers, and rural–urban migrants. The upper segment is employees in the public sector and/or the oligopolistic sectors, while the second segment is consistent with a more competitive private sector characterized by short-term contracts and by downward pressures on wages coming from the third segment (the rural–urban migrants). It must be remembered that our empirical analysis is only based on data collected for urban *hukou* holders, i.e. local urban residents. Consequently, it does not encompass the whole labor market in cities where huge inflows of rural–urban migrants are potentially key components of the urban labor market.

Contrary to European economies in transition, where studies found a wage premium in favor of the private sector after economic liberalization (Adamchick and Bedi 2000; Lokshin and Jovanovic 2003), our results highlight earnings differences in favor of the public sector in China after controlling for workers' characteristics and working time. Hence, even during the most recent period, the Chinese government has kept its influence on the urban labor market through wage income increases for civil servants and by maintaining the relative income of workers in SOEs, as well as by targeting specific provinces. Compared to European economies in transition, the Chinese government has taken active policies through wage adjustments to narrow the income gap between civil servants and white-collar workers employed in the non-public sector and thus keep skilled workers in the public sector. In this respect, the observed segmentation structure helps the public sector to retain skilled workers. It also reduces incentives for moonlighting and thus compromises the overall efficiency of the public sector, which have been observed in Poland or Yugoslavia (Adamchick and Bedi 2000; Lokshin and Jovanovic 2003).

The existence of segmentation in the labor market may also be interpreted in terms of efficiency wage theory, especially for the comparison between FIEs and domestic (public and private) enterprises, and to some extent between coastal provinces and other regions. In this line of thought, higher earnings received in FIEs may be interpreted as means to facilitate workers' cooperation, to boost their effort-intensity, and more generally, to improve the average quality of job applicants. Since FIEs in China face greater difficulties in employee supervision due to language barriers and cultural differences, they may be willing to pay wages above market rates to solve part of these difficulties and to protect their investment in employees' screening, hiring, and training. Following this approach, economic liberalization and growing market participation may be consistent with the payment of wages exceeding a pure competitive level.

If these two last points may provide some economic rationale to high and even rising segmentation, increasing segmentation associated to a non-uniform move of enterprises toward the payment of competitive market wages may yield further sources of income inequality. Indeed, evidence shows that during the seven-year period, the structure of wages has become more unequal.[44] As highlighted by Khan and Riskin (2005), the concentration ratio for urban wages increased by 68 percent between 1995 and 2002. Our results confirm this trend and the potential perverted effects of a multitiered urban labor market on income inequality.

Finally, there are good reasons to believe that the observed increasing segmentation may be only a temporary phenomenon. Indeed, given the process of SOEs downsizing, ownership structure may lose importance in the end. At the same time, the growing importance of the private sector might be expected to put more pressure on the urban labor market in the future by bringing in stronger competition and challenging the privileged situation of employees in the public and oligopolistic sectors. Similarly, population movements across provinces and regions are also on the rise and may re-balance regional disparities in the end.

7A Appendix

Appendix 7.A1 Hourly wage functions by ownership, Year: 1995

	SOEs		UCEs		PIEs		FIEs		GAIs	
	Women	*Men*	*Women*	*Men*	*Women*	*Men*	*Women*	*Men*	*Women*	*Men*
Education	0.015	0.025	0.002	0.018	-0.245	-0.069	0.052	0.074	0.021	0.013
	3.11	*5.56*	*0.17*	*1.46*	*-2.02*	*-0.57*	*1.2*	*1.53*	*3.54*	*3.2*
Work Exp.	0.069	0.045	0.074	0.062	0.178	0.111	0.028	0.026	0.052	0.044
	10.05	*11.07*	*5.78*	*6.05*	*2.23*	*1.49*	*1.04*	*1.1*	*8.11*	*9.02*
(Work Exp.)^2	-0.00128	-0.00065	-0.00172	-0.00123	-0.00491	-0.00332	0.00001	-0.00027	-0.00086	-0.00061
	-7.06	*-6.67*	*-4.39*	*-5.01*	*-1.51*	*-1.23*	*0.01*	*-0.4*	*-5.46*	*-6.05*
Central Province	-0.055	-0.023	0.024	-0.025	0.523	-0.173	0.593	0.338	-0.127	-0.066
	-2.17	*-1*	*0.53*	*-0.41*	*0.76*	*-0.31*	*1.97*	*1.32*	*-4.56*	*-3.21*
Coastal Province	0.153	0.216	0.312	0.275	2.351	0.409	0.758	0.527	0.205	0.226
	4.92	*8.64*	*6.41*	*4.93*	*4.16*	*0.77*	*2.72*	*2.2*	*6.07*	*7.73*
Big city	0.130	0.135	0.156	0.116	1.716	0.841	0.364	-0.086	0.010	0.057
	6.08	*6.95*	*4.06*	*2.34*	*3.14*	*3.11*	*2.27*	*-0.56*	*0.37*	*2.57*
Communist	0.147	0.076	0.080	0.178	-0.361	0.924	-0.089	-0.061	0.003	-0.014
	5	*3.6*	*1.16*	*2.42*	*-0.46*	*2.73*	*-0.37*	*-0.29*	*0.09*	*-0.66*
Vocational School	-0.057	-0.016	-0.128	-0.104	-0.634	-0.340	0.064	-0.139	-0.176	-0.107
	-2.07	*-0.59*	*-2.52*	*-1.62*	*-1.01*	*-0.68*	*0.29*	*-0.56*	*-3.64*	*-2.75*
Change in *hukou*	-0.065	0.043	-0.074	0.013	-1.802	-0.946	0.050	0.089	-0.087	0.032
	-1.67	*1.48*	*-1.25*	*0.17*	*-2.7*	*-1.6*	*0.28*	*0.45*	*-2.34*	*1.54*
Constant term	-0.138	-0.025	-0.139	-0.134	0.137	0.083	-0.756	-0.343	0.168	0.288
	-1.54	*-0.35*	*-0.92*	*-0.72*	*0.09*	*0.05*	*-1.62*	*-0.51*	*1.65*	*3.74*
# obs.	2551	3224	908	626	40	44	63	75	1445	1754
R^2	0.21	0.20	0.19	0.19	0.53	0.35	0.35	0.21	0.25	0.26

Note: T-statistics in italics.

Appendix 7.A2 Hourly wage functions by ownership, Year: 2002

	SOEs		UCEs		PIEs		FIEs		GAIs	
	Women	*Men*	*Women*	*Men*	*Women*	*Men*	*Women*	*Men*	*Women*	*Men*
Education	0.041 *4.95*	0.044 *7.26*	0.034 *2*	0.018 *0.98*	0.117 *5.06*	0.096 *6.35*	0.052 *2.29*	0.103 *4.24*	0.068 *10.71*	0.048 *9.33*
Work Exp.	0.061 *5.82*	0.045 *7.43*	0.040 *2.52*	0.048 *2.91*	0.019 *1.11*	0.048 *3.27*	0.051 *1.76*	0.043 *2.12*	0.050 *6.48*	0.037 *6.65*
(Work Exp.)^2	−0.0013 *−4.69*	−0.0009 *−5.97*	−0.0008 *−1.98*	−0.0009 *−2.63*	0.0000 *0.08*	−0.0006 *−1.63*	−0.0013 *−1.51*	−0.0004 *−0.87*	−0.0009 *−4.33*	−0.0005 *−4.13*
Central Province	−0.112 *−2.68*	−0.014 *−0.46*	−0.192 *−2.33*	0.061 *0.68*	−0.212 *−2.11*	−0.151 *−1.47*	0.476 *2.17*	0.263 *1.79*	−0.198 *−5.44*	−0.102 *−3.46*
Coastal Province	0.105 *2.15*	0.174 *4.93*	0.088 *0.96*	0.191 *1.83*	0.311 *3.27*	0.447 *4.73*	0.558 *2.43*	0.272 *2.08*	0.178 *4.19*	0.167 *4.6*
Big city	0.176 *4.96*	0.109 *4.12*	0.132 *1.98*	0.278 *3.87*	0.297 *3.65*	0.374 *4.65*	0.174 *1.12*	0.210 *1.63*	−0.033 *−0.97*	0.126 *4.47*
Communist	0.135 *3.08*	0.136 *4.54*	0.253 *2.73*	0.164 *2.06*	0.387 *3.25*	0.279 *3.16*	0.523 *2.65*	−0.138 *−0.71*	0.052 *1.37*	0.116 *4.06*
Vocational School	0.094 *1.84*	0.052 *1.55*	0.133 *1.22*	0.135 *1.11*	−0.065 *−0.55*	0.162 *1.68*	0.151 *0.8*	−0.135 *−0.87*	0.021 *0.59*	0.004 *0.14*
Change in *hukou*	−0.166 *−2.72*	−0.077 *−1.74*	−0.096 *−0.91*	0.158 *1.74*	−0.190 *−1.35*	0.058 *0.39*	0.254 *0.84*	0.039 *0.24*	0.043 *0.85*	0.065 *2.14*
Constant term	0.203 *1.69*	0.394 *3.99*	0.246 *1.14*	0.198 *0.73*	−0.956 *−3.31*	−1.071 *−5.02*	−0.299 *−0.77*	−0.399 *−1.16*	0.247 *2.24*	0.539 *5.55*
# obs.	1315	2056	383	295	781	986	86	125	1368	1686
R^2	0.15	0.13	0.12	0.12	0.17	0.16	0.18	0.23	0.19	0.18

Note: T-statistics in italics.

Appendix 7.A3 Hourly wage functions by economic sector, Year: 1995

	Competitive		Oligopolistic		Public Services		Government	
	Women	*Men*	*Women*	*Men*	*Women*	*Men*	*Women*	*Men*
Education	0.017	0.023	0.043	0.056	0.026	0.021	0.019	0.011
	3.62	*5.12*	*2.22*	*3.35*	*4.04*	*3.1*	*1.65*	*2.07*
Work Exp.	0.058	0.045	0.064	0.059	0.052	0.059	0.044	0.032
	9.33	*11.3*	*4.03*	*5.01*	*6.74*	*6.06*	*3.51*	*4.41*
(Work Exp.)^2	−0.0011	−0.0007	−0.0013	−0.0010	−0.0008	−0.0009	−0.0006	−0.0004
	−6.2	*−7.22*	*−2.65*	*−3.46*	*−4.51*	*−3.86*	*−2.09*	*−2.68*
Central Province	−0.035	−0.046	−0.080	−0.058	−0.104	−0.002	−0.102	−0.081
	−1.39	*−2.01*	*−0.76*	*−0.77*	*−3.03*	*−0.07*	*−1.99*	*−2.81*
Coastal Province	0.211	0.208	0.322	0.239	0.190	0.231	0.262	0.242
	7.45	*8.46*	*2.82*	*2.62*	*4.8*	*5.77*	*3.83*	*5.25*
Big city	0.159	0.159	0.136	−0.064	0.049	0.079	−0.099	0.078
	7.9	*8.19*	*1.63*	*−0.8*	*1.62*	*2.41*	*−1.81*	*2.29*
Communist	0.145	0.091	0.188	0.031	−0.002	0.003	0.073	0.023
	4.89	*4.19*	*1.79*	*0.4*	*−0.06*	*0.08*	*1.41*	*0.72*
Vocational School	−0.065	−0.055	−0.260	−0.088	−0.120	−0.195	−0.222	−0.025
	−2.45	*−2.03*	*−2.15*	*−0.84*	*−2.03*	*−2.88*	*−2.25*	*−0.51*
Change in *hukou*	−0.065	0.034	−0.204	0.030	−0.006	0.057	−0.228	−0.029
	−1.64	*1.17*	*−1.48*	*0.31*	*−0.13*	*1.54*	*−3.69*	*−1.01*
Constant term	−0.115	−0.002	−0.281	−0.292	0.052	0.014	0.215	0.402
	−1.4	*−0.03*	*−0.99*	*−1.2*	*0.47*	*0.11*	*1.06*	*3.69*
# obs.	3019	3324	312	295	791	675	477	772
R^2	0.18	0.19	0.28	0.25	0.28	0.33	0.29	0.24

Note: T-statistics in italics.

Appendix 7.A4 Hourly wage functions by economic sector, Year: 2002

	Competitive		Oligopolistic		Public Services		Government	
	Women	Men	Women	Men	Women	Men	Women	Men
Education	0.071	0.071	0.043	0.036	0.068	0.058	0.054	0.031
	7.42	9.82	2.12	2.56	7.32	6.63	3.81	3.94
Work Exp.	0.056	0.049	0.098	0.042	0.046	0.042	0.065	0.036
	6.66	6.81	4.93	3.1	4.34	4.48	4.82	3.69
(Work Exp.)^2	−0.0011	−0.0008	−0.0020	−0.0006	−0.0007	−0.0006	−0.0014	−0.0005
	−4.4	−4.74	−3.74	−1.83	−2.72	−3.07	−3.88	−2.44
Central Province	−0.116	−0.035	−0.296	−0.176	−0.260	−0.154	−0.151	−0.096
	−2.57	−0.79	−3.25	−2.28	−4.85	−3.3	−1.91	−2.23
Coastal Province	0.219	0.261	0.050	0.182	0.162	0.083	0.010	0.177
	4.72	6.03	0.5	2.11	2.68	1.4	0.13	3.31
Big city	0.173	0.320	0.246	0.009	0.081	0.165	−0.015	0.106
	4.76	9.32	3.06	0.14	1.7	4.01	−0.24	2.52
Communist	0.231	0.196	0.130	0.155	0.168	0.142	0.016	0.154
	5.19	5.96	1.39	2.04	3.2	2.84	0.25	3.25
Vocational School	0.073	0.042	0.018	0.172	0.030	0.023	0.078	−0.014
	1.39	0.97	0.17	2.58	0.64	0.53	1.11	−0.37
Change in hukou	−0.083	−0.021	−0.172	−0.022	−0.056	0.081	−0.100	0.065
	−1.25	−0.33	−1.13	−0.26	−0.77	1.51	−0.9	1.62
Constant term	−0.460	−0.437	0.099	0.674	0.294	0.439	0.377	0.732
	−3.56	−3.73	0.34	3.09	1.86	2.68	1.65	4.58
# obs.	2252	2500	293	413	775	785	424	753
R^2	0.15	0.15	0.27	0.18	0.21	0.19	0.14	0.17

Note: T-statistics in italics.

Appendix 7.A5 Hourly wage functions by region, Year: 1995

	Coast		Centre		West		Municipality		North-East	
	Women	*Men*	*Women*	*Men*	*Women*	*Men*	*Women*	*Men*	*Women*	*Men*
Education	0.022	0.028	0.025	0.027	0.030	0.024	0.020	0.035	0.037	0.025
	3.31	*4.09*	*3.62*	*5.2*	*4.41*	*4.05*	*1.16*	*2.83*	*3.83*	*2.51*
Work Exp.	0.061	0.060	0.056	0.049	0.066	0.041	0.047	0.022	0.044	0.036
	5.66	*9.74*	*9.2*	*8.91*	*6.92*	*6.79*	*2.58*	*2.38*	*4.55*	*4.04*
(Work Exp.)²	-0.00129	-0.00107	-0.00092	-0.00068	-0.00110	-0.00047	-0.00076	-0.00030	-0.00079	-0.00052
	-3.93	*-7.81*	*-5.54*	*-5.39*	*-4.75*	*-3.64*	*-1.65*	*-1.54*	*-3.01*	*-2.46*
Big city	0.117	0.106	0.120	0.103	0.147	0.127	0.000	0.000	0.397	0.339
	2.91	*3.02*	*3.93*	*3.83*	*5*	*5.02*	*0.000*	*0.000*	*7.52*	*5.33*
Communist	0.202	0.161	0.102	0.073	0.061	0.007	0.149	0.103	0.074	0.095
	3.64	*4.62*	*2.77*	*2.86*	*1.7*	*0.29*	*2.64*	*2.09*	*1.43*	*1.77*
Vocational School	-0.157	-0.044	-0.124	-0.062	-0.099	-0.098	0.025	0.004	-0.127	-0.037
	-3.32	*-0.98*	*-3.19*	*-1.64*	*-2.36*	*-2.41*	*0.28*	*0.06*	*-2.32*	*-0.58*
Change in *hukou*	-0.119	-0.025	-0.077	0.056	-0.021	0.041	-0.115	-0.005	-0.095	0.098
	-1.84	*-0.61*	*-1.82*	*2.02*	*-0.4*	*1.19*	*-1*	*-0.06*	*-1.01*	*1.19*
Constant term	0.232	0.128	-0.164	-0.104	-0.292	0.050	0.163	0.427	-0.378	-0.097
	2.21	*1.18*	*-1.63*	*-1.26*	*-2.4*	*0.46*	*0.5*	*2.51*	*-2.53*	*-0.58*
# obs.	1017	1153	1745	2033	1438	1553	356	423	546	634
R²	0.16	0.21	0.19	0.18	0.20	0.21	0.15	0.10	0.27	0.16

Note: T-statistics in italics.

Appendix 7.A6 Hourly wage functions by region, Year: 2002

	Coast		Centre		West		Municipality		North-East	
	Women	*Men*	*Women*	*Men*	*Women*	*Men*	*Women*	*Men*	*Women*	*Men*
Education	0.099	0.074	0.092	0.083	0.078	0.088	0.080	0.075	0.119	0.069
	8.15	*8.86*	*8.52*	*10.08*	*9.04*	*11.93*	*4.34*	*5.28*	*4.77*	*5.83*
Work Exp.	0.069	0.051	0.053	0.040	0.051	0.060	0.061	0.050	0.013	0.018
	5.77	*5.12*	*4.42*	*4.62*	*4.96*	*5.99*	*3.83*	*4.28*	*0.97*	*1.85*
(Work Exp.)^2	−0.00136	−0.00089	−0.00078	−0.00051	−0.00069	−0.00085	−0.00167	−0.00087	0.00016	−0.00018
	−4.15	*−3.92*	*−2.17*	*−2.5*	*−2.6*	*−3.71*	*−4.14*	*−3.2*	*0.46*	*−0.76*
Big city	0.198	0.327	0.122	0.134	0.111	0.232	0.000	0.000	0.101	0.160
	3.28	*7.16*	*2.63*	*3.26*	*2.51*	*5.52*	*0.000*	*–*	*1.15*	*2.05*
Communist	0.322	0.324	0.108	0.209	0.197	0.258	0.207	0.124	0.093	0.189
	4.61	*6.32*	*2.08*	*5.25*	*4.19*	*6.7*	*2.37*	*1.84*	*1*	*3.14*
Vocational School	0.109	0.017	0.162	0.070	0.157	0.132	−0.113	−0.104	0.097	0.072
	1.54	*0.29*	*3.06*	*1.79*	*2.89*	*3.34*	*−1.23*	*−1.37*	*1.16*	*1.21*
Change in *hukou*	−0.215	0.025	−0.051	0.050	0.098	0.048	0.014	0.117	0.205	0.019
	−2.81	*0.42*	*−0.67*	*1.05*	*1.27*	*0.76*	*0.06*	*1.1*	*1.68*	*0.14*
Constant term	−0.447	−0.021	−0.655	−0.337	−0.382	−0.631	0.096	0.211	−0.676	0.195
	−2.49	*−0.14*	*−4.07*	*−2.3*	*−2.7*	*−4.38*	*0.35*	*0.97*	*−1.88*	*1.1*
# obs.	818	994	1417	1883	1155	1421	367	432	431	619
R^2	0.25	0.22	0.15	0.14	0.19	0.23	0.12	0.14	0.23	0.13

Note: T-statistics in italics.

Appendix 7.B1 Hours worked functions by ownership, Year: 1995

	SOEs		UCEs		PIEs		FIEs		GAIs	
	Women	*Men*	*Women*	*Men*	*Women*	*Men*	*Women*	*Men*	*Women*	*Men*
Education	-0.189	7.237	4.002	-30.707	42.989	-57.875	7.051	-111.28	1.223	6.970
	-0.05	*1.41*	*0.21*	*-1.85*	*0.29*	*-0.69*	*0.28*	*-2.03*	*0.24*	*1.26*
Age	-12.75	2.60	-16.21	-64.51	-63.88	-369.23	16.64	-3.49	9.42	5.11
	-1.36	*0.34*	*-0.73*	*-2.75*	*-0.43*	*-2.80*	*0.26*	*-0.08*	*1.06*	*0.55*
(Age)²	0.151	-0.052	0.243	0.783	0.983	4.531	-0.341	0.215	-0.118	-0.083
	1.20	*-0.58*	*0.81*	*2.62*	*0.47*	*3.06*	*-0.42*	*0.37*	*-1.02*	*-0.78*
Communist	3.68	52.24	-38.94	-55.99	369.48	-1011.9	-54.86	249.54	10.27	36.67
	0.19	*3.48*	*-0.61*	*-0.89*	*0.70*	*-3.41*	*-0.28*	*1.28*	*0.55*	*2.05*
Married	-20.16	65.44	-113.11	103.73	495.47	986.98	-48.33	-164.16	18.27	-22.27
	-0.62	*1.70*	*-1.52*	*1.00*	*1.47*	*2.17*	*-0.20*	*-0.78*	*0.39*	*-0.35*
Square root of household size	807.2	-551.2	-1215.6	-13.3	7546.3	11043.6	-716.1	733.2	311.8	-85.2
	2.60	*-1.55*	*-1.61*	*-0.02*	*0.88*	*3.46*	*-0.22*	*0.22*	*0.81*	*-0.21*
Dependent elderly in the household	26.23	31.33	8.45	45.34	-115.39	103.58	-82.00	230.73	-29.49	-9.02
	0.81	*1.55*	*0.17*	*0.59*	*-0.24*	*0.50*	*-0.69*	*1.19*	*-1.06*	*-0.23*
Household size	-184.5	153.6	347.3	66.8	-1728.1	-2544.8	316.8	-228.1	-67.0	23.5
	-2.27	*1.62*	*1.75*	*0.30*	*-0.77*	*-3.46*	*0.36*	*-0.26*	*-0.65*	*0.22*
Average education of adult hh members	-6.46	-13.80	-18.13	5.13	-27.79	17.09	-42.88	39.56	2.54	2.59
	-1.37	*-2.83*	*-1.37*	*0.38*	*-0.35*	*0.34*	*-1.50*	*1.00*	*0.47*	*0.36*
Average age of adult hh members	-1.348	-2.475	-3.439	-4.821	-1.084	33.592	8.252	-18.644	0.997	1.757
	-1.03	*-1.59*	*-0.98*	*-1.28*	*-0.05*	*1.78*	*0.89*	*-1.69*	*0.68*	*0.78*
Child of hh head	-17.95	57.97	-138.23	-85.63	654.07	-262.67	-176.79	357.07	47.94	-2.05
	-0.43	*1.38*	*-1.64*	*-0.78*	*1.42*	*-0.50*	*-0.79*	*1.36*	*1.05*	*-0.03*

	(1)	(2)	(3)	(4)	(5)	(6)	(7)	(8)	(9)	(10)
Vocational school	−6.43	23.27	63.22	−99.56	353.90	515.52	280.08	−205.21	41.84	99.81
	−0.37	*1.13*	*0.99*	*−1.39*	*0.62*	*1.43*	*1.29*	*−1.13*	*1.56*	*3.33*
Change in *hukou*	12.79	47.83	41.07	−18.35	−95.82	295.29	−197.25	114.39	−39.35	−10.16
	0.55	*2.14*	*0.70*	*−0.29*	*−0.24*	*0.74*	*−1.41*	*0.83*	*−1.68*	*−0.48*
Big city	−13.01	−40.41	−79.68	−58.00	−474.62	−607.03	−47.13	−15.81	−22.34	17.43
	−1.02	*−2.96*	*−2.55*	*−1.25*	*−1.38*	*−2.34*	*−0.36*	*−0.15*	*−1.32*	*0.90*
Coastal Province	−23.659	−0.631	91.032	−9.099	−149.21	259.689	33.716	234.191	−21.663	−58.345
	−1.33	*−0.03*	*2.00*	*−0.18*	*−0.51*	*0.84*	*0.24*	*1.06*	*−0.93*	*−2.35*
Central Province	−37.467	−31.587	23.360	−25.180	475.089	−70.934	−50.924	−147.87	4.407	−13.147
	−2.65	*−1.99*	*0.58*	*−0.45*	*1.31*	*−0.18*	*−0.25*	*−0.67*	*0.25*	*−0.66*
Constant term	1787.6	2814.6	3811.6	3710.3	−4966.1	−3184.6	2564.1	2965.1	1554.0	2043.4
	5.25	*7.79*	*4.32*	*4.28*	*−0.52*	*−0.75*	*0.93*	*0.85*	*3.85*	*5.11*
# obs.	2551	3224	908	626	40	44	63	75	1445	1754
R^2	0.02	0.02	0.03	0.05	0.35	0.66	0.32	0.32	0.01	0.01

Note: T-statistics in italics.

Appendix 7.B2 Hours worked functions by ownership, Year: 2002

	SOEs		UCEs		PIEs		FIEs		GAIs	
	Women	Men	Women	Men	Women	Men	Women	Men	Women	Men
Education	-2.623	-6.517	7.968	-17.404	-26.030	-34.807	-87.406	-34.854	-6.396	3.376
	-0.39	*-1.03*	*0.52*	*-0.84*	*-1.60*	*-2.64*	*-1.94*	*-1.32*	*-0.97*	*0.58*
Age	-33.04	14.01	13.23	9.14	-27.65	-25.44	13.24	-41.59	-12.15	0.12
	-2.18	*1.35*	*0.40*	*0.27*	*-0.99*	*-0.94*	*0.18*	*-0.84*	*-0.94*	*0.01*
$(Age)^2$	0.417	-0.182	-0.240	-0.301	0.429	0.273	-0.180	0.527	0.109	0.015
	2.16	*-1.52*	*-0.55*	*-0.71*	*1.11*	*0.84*	*-0.18*	*0.90*	*0.65*	*0.10*
Communist	43.55	-18.48	-123.21	5.04	-94.20	-188.15	-37.36	-51.00	-5.31	-11.22
	1.77	*-0.92*	*-1.97*	*0.06*	*-1.17*	*-3.25*	*-0.28*	*-0.47*	*-0.25*	*-0.54*
Married	-41.46	74.44	-121.30	1.98	89.66	11.47	143.08	68.85	28.94	45.58
	-0.89	*1.27*	*-0.94*	*0.02*	*0.77*	*0.08*	*0.54*	*0.41*	*0.65*	*1.10*
Square root of household size	830.6	326.9	-11.4	-283.1	-649.2	-2062.2	-3905.6	1659.4	335.0	173.4
	1.49	*0.64*	*-0.01*	*-0.20*	*-0.49*	*-1.66*	*-1.30*	*0.62*	*0.92*	*0.41*
Dependent elderly in the household	26.26	-9.56	-137.58	-45.28	30.03	-22.32	-472.73	-178.08	-5.97	-24.96
	0.64	*-0.24*	*-2.10*	*-0.45*	*0.39*	*-0.31*	*-1.73*	*-1.18*	*-0.17*	*-0.76*
Household size	-195.6	-71.8	2.5	131.1	224.2	595.5	1183.7	-434.7	-92.2	-73.2
	-1.27	*-0.50*	*0.01*	*0.36*	*0.61*	*1.78*	*1.40*	*-0.60*	*-0.95*	*-0.66*
Average education of adult hh members	-4.20	0.54	-12.69	1.53	-13.37	-5.80	36.21	-18.39	-0.33	-9.18
	-0.53	*0.08*	*-0.72*	*0.06*	*-0.80*	*-0.37*	*0.72*	*-0.55*	*-0.05*	*-1.34*
Average age of adult hh members	-0.694	0.007	7.532	8.863	-9.613	-6.966	-3.581	-14.226	2.493	-3.547
	-0.28	*0.00*	*1.65*	*1.35*	*-1.75*	*-1.50*	*-0.21*	*-1.54*	*1.26*	*-1.74*
Child of hh head	34.37	53.30	-2.65	-340.70	163.02	-55.38	433.34	250.16	-57.24	126.82
	0.50	*0.85*	*-0.02*	*-2.33*	*1.19*	*-0.48*	*0.93*	*1.07*	*-1.07*	*2.53*

Vocational school	−68.22	6.03	−41.95	−82.20	−64.17	−64.33	−60.35	133.34	−16.86	−27.71
	−2.56	*0.27*	*−0.62*	*−0.90*	*−0.96*	*−1.05*	*−0.48*	*1.30*	*−0.81*	*−1.41*
Change in *hukou*	49.48	90.66	102.41	118.24	168.87	104.17	−138.86	343.96	32.29	6.76
	1.08	*2.67*	*1.07*	*1.24*	*1.96*	*1.19*	*−0.70*	*1.32*	*1.06*	*0.29*
Big city	−16.38	−10.46	−122.68	−64.23	−23.11	−109.65	−130.13	−108.69	48.57	15.15
	−0.74	*−0.54*	*−2.35*	*−1.01*	*−0.40*	*−2.12*	*−0.85*	*−1.11*	*2.13*	*0.67*
Coastal Province	−124.08	−6.923	70.339	−23.539	−119.96	−117.79	169.409	−120.25	−79.970	14.648
	−4.29	*−0.26*	*0.97*	*−0.23*	*−1.81*	*−1.94*	*0.77*	*−0.66*	*−3.14*	*0.51*
Central Province	−13.107	10.842	155.477	−22.931	27.400	65.043	99.163	−255.05	19.988	16.797
	−0.48	*0.49*	*2.48*	*−0.26*	*0.42*	*1.06*	*0.50*	*−1.55*	*0.84*	*0.79*
Constant term	2094.7	1561.8	1899.7	2493.8	3984.6	5691.7	5808.3	2661.1	2058.0	2167.1
	3.68	*3.01*	*1.77*	*1.64*	*3.02*	*4.66*	*2.25*	*0.97*	*5.11*	*4.18*
# obs.	1315	2056	383	295	781	986	86	125	1368	1686
R²	0.05	0.01	0.07	0.04	0.06	0.08	0.29	0.22	0.02	0.01

Note: T-statistics in italics.

Appendix 7.B3 Hours worked functions by economic sector, Year: 1995

	Competitive		Oligopolistic		Public Services		Government	
	Women	*Men*	*Women*	*Men*	*Women*	*Men*	*Women*	*Men*
Education	-3.304	0.331	3.612	-38.315	-3.807	2.302	11.438	10.413
	-0.51	*0.06*	*0.26*	*-1.50*	*-0.52*	*0.28*	*1.66*	*1.09*
Age	-11.48	-3.88	-29.77	-10.85	14.21	19.11	3.28	-14.77
	-1.07	*-0.47*	*-1.30*	*-0.40*	*1.05*	*1.14*	*0.22*	*-1.00*
(Age)^2	0.137	0.029	0.464	0.205	-0.198	-0.219	-0.026	0.074
	0.94	*0.29*	*1.55*	*0.61*	*-1.13*	*-1.14*	*-0.12*	*0.43*
Communist	-17.45	19.14	3.37	14.31	11.33	38.76	17.16	67.69
	-0.82	*1.18*	*0.04*	*0.30*	*0.44*	*1.22*	*0.58*	*2.32*
Married	-65.51	76.88	-105.26	-325.50	-30.87	-78.56	20.32	225.64
	-1.93	*1.91*	*-1.30*	*-1.94*	*-0.50*	*-0.92*	*0.42*	*1.46*
Square root of household size	336.5	-591.5	-1334.6	-519.1	-137.5	-644.0	-105.1	913.7
	1.00	*-1.66*	*-1.22*	*-0.77*	*-0.28*	*-1.05*	*-0.18*	*1.16*
Dependent elderly in the household	3.79	14.27	83.33	34.58	-31.20	36.01	-71.99	-92.81
	0.13	*0.53*	*1.82*	*0.51*	*-0.63*	*0.72*	*-1.79*	*-1.49*
Household size	-57.3	177.4	397.3	136.5	74.5	201.4	20.9	-229.2
	-0.64	*1.87*	*1.34*	*0.80*	*0.58*	*1.23*	*0.13*	*-1.14*
Average education of adult hh members	-5.57	-10.22	-10.27	3.90	1.92	15.82	-8.99	-2.01
	-1.00	*-2.01*	*-0.79*	*0.21*	*0.25*	*1.42*	*-1.01*	*-0.19*
Average age of adult hh members	-1.065	-1.728	-9.993	-7.324	2.816	0.062	-0.033	6.875
	-0.68	*-1.13*	*-2.69*	*-1.66*	*1.34*	*0.02*	*-0.01*	*1.87*
Child of hh head	-72.49	64.99	-15.21	-149.58	2.53	-16.50	61.38	28.96
	-1.66	*1.41*	*-0.16*	*-1.14*	*0.04*	*-0.18*	*0.94*	*0.18*

Vocational school	17.95	12.59	37.77	−83.85	−1.83	166.32	47.46	85.32
	0.75	*0.60*	*0.62*	*−0.90*	*−0.05*	*2.50*	*0.99*	*1.58*
Change in *hukou*	1.91	32.19	93.33	43.52	−48.79	−1.20	17.12	−11.46
	0.07	*1.40*	*1.30*	*0.62*	*−1.38*	*−0.03*	*0.47*	*−0.33*
Big city	−31.47	−59.26	−49.41	108.56	−38.72	13.83	20.12	27.52
	−2.32	*−3.99*	*−1.01*	*1.93*	*−1.77*	*0.47*	*0.67*	*0.84*
Coastal Province	32.838	29.734	58.594	−2.980	−37.314	−84.781	−9.381	−39.783
	1.94	*1.96*	*1.08*	*−0.05*	*−1.42*	*−2.64*	*−0.29*	*−1.18*
Constant term	2217.1	2921.8	4225.6	3748.1	1927.7	2142.5	2138.6	1197.0
	5.68	*8.07*	*3.79*	*5.05*	*3.59*	*3.46*	*4.00*	*1.55*
# obs.	3019	3324	312	295	791	675	477	772
R^2	0.02	0.03	0.08	0.08	0.02	0.03	0.01	0.03

Note: T-statistics in italics.

Appendix 7.B4 Hours worked functions by economic sector, Year: 2002

	Competitive		Oligopolistic		Public Services		Government	
	Women	Men	Women	Men	Women	Men	Women	Men
Education	-18.246	-19.778	10.465	-4.982	12.067	3.859	-6.475	-10.598
	-2.17	*-2.71*	*0.79*	*-0.42*	*1.17*	*0.36*	*-0.82*	*-1.42*
Age	-24.89	-22.42	9.52	17.11	-12.38	-9.83	-54.07	2.19
	-1.63	*-1.55*	*0.39*	*0.82*	*-0.66*	*-0.45*	*-2.03*	*0.15*
$(Age)^2$	0.316	0.225	0.222	-0.192	0.141	0.154	0.654	-0.069
	1.57	*1.34*	*-0.71*	*-0.78*	*0.56*	*0.58*	*1.86*	*-0.41*
Communist	-37.99	-102.61	-27.80	-50.79	-57.21	-36.28	53.95	-7.25
	-1.25	*-3.97*	*-0.72*	*-1.06*	*-1.79*	*-1.15*	*1.45*	*-0.23*
Married	-74.71	10.93	132.44	78.83	24.66	10.40	9.74	68.10
	-1.46	*0.16*	*1.23*	*0.65*	*0.34*	*0.13*	*0.12*	*1.34*
Square root of household size	-687.2	-1640.7	1453.9	2061.1	1027.8	-605.5	-227.0	976.3
	-1.08	*-2.23*	*1.95*	*1.92*	*1.78*	*-0.62*	*-0.32*	*2.05*
Dependent elderly in the household	-65.03	-45.31	-91.37	-8.25	78.14	-7.88	-21.70	-34.08
	-1.65	*-1.05*	*-1.20*	*-0.10*	*1.04*	*-0.13*	*-0.39*	*-0.80*
Household size	241.2	478.7	-366.0	-501.1	-326.6	124.4	122.7	-269.6
	1.34	*2.36*	*-1.89*	*-1.73*	*-2.05*	*0.46*	*0.65*	*-2.25*
Average education of adult hh member	-12.06	-8.60	-2.25	18.66	-16.46	-10.66	4.33	-2.51
	-1.38	*-0.99*	*-0.17*	*1.31*	*-1.28*	*-0.86*	*0.38*	*-0.27*
Average age of adult hh members	-5.105	-5.044	6.682	1.035	0.912	-5.934	3.568	1.217
	-1.89	*-1.97*	*1.53*	*0.22*	*0.24*	*-1.79*	*0.83*	*0.46*
Child of hh head	75.25	-21.98	89.46	107.29	-80.34	98.08	-137.99	20.41
	1.18	*-0.28*	*0.71*	*0.93*	*-0.87*	*1.01*	*-1.24*	*0.28*
Vocational school	-50.17	10.25	-41.33	-66.01	-57.01	-63.16	56.49	15.47
	-1.70	*0.33*	*-0.85*	*-1.55*	*-1.96*	*-2.12*	*1.40*	*0.54*

	(1)	(2)	(3)	(4)	(5)	(6)	(7)	(8)
Change in *hukou*	100.93	86.65	5.47	66.39	73.87	45.76	14.87	-9.52
	2.11	*2.08*	*0.07*	*1.10*	*1.61*	*1.16*	*0.38*	*-0.30*
Big city	-46.82	-134.44	-17.01	62.16	14.50	-21.55	-23.12	47.72
	-1.76	*-5.50*	*-0.37*	*1.23*	*0.49*	*-0.65*	*-0.57*	*1.41*
Coastal Province	-130.508	-39.563	-81.650	-87.988	-82.749	43.092	-10.280	-10.137
	-5.14	*-1.57*	*-1.90*	*-1.89*	*-2.49*	*1.00*	*-0.22*	*-0.27*
Constant term	3830.3	4837.8	227.9	-503.7	1625.9	3249.3	2991.9	1344.0
	6.01	*6.72*	*0.25*	*-0.46*	*2.44*	*3.15*	*4.46*	*2.38*
# obs.	2252	2500	293	413	775	785	424	753
R^2	0.06	0.06	0.07	0.05	0.03	0.02	0.04	0.02

Note: T-statistics in italics.

Appendix 7.B5 Hours worked functions by region, Year: 1995

	Coast		Centre		West		Municipality		North-East	
	Women	*Men*	*Women*	*Men*	*Women*	*Men*	*Women*	*Men*	*Women*	*Men*
Education	-6.264	-23.347	7.369	6.381	5.667	7.753	9.641	0.575	-18.242	8.579
	-0.57	*-2.69*	*1.00*	*1.08*	*0.76*	*1.02*	*0.94*	*0.04*	*-1.64*	*0.80*
Age	-11.534	6.296	-19.792	-19.536	6.024	8.235	-20.964	39.445	2.323	-11.361
	-0.72	*0.49*	*-1.77*	*-1.89*	*0.48*	*0.77*	*-1.72*	*1.43*	*0.10*	*-0.53*
(Age)^2	0.174	-0.081	0.249	0.238	-0.089	-0.125	0.231	-0.481	-0.025	0.143
	0.79	*-0.55*	*1.69*	*1.89*	*-0.51*	*-0.98*	*1.41*	*-1.65*	*-0.09*	*0.54*
Communist	-69.536	-36.777	-20.465	35.000	0.357	56.788	92.100	82.706	22.086	-5.994
	-1.75	*-1.36*	*-0.84*	*1.79*	*0.02*	*2.81*	*2.11*	*1.67*	*0.50*	*-0.15*
Married	-31.415	-23.390	-51.422	93.395	-50.179	66.056	10.205	-34.288	-14.583	62.072
	-0.50	*-0.32*	*-1.08*	*1.57*	*-1.01*	*1.16*	*0.26*	*-0.20*	*-0.19*	*0.84*
Square root of household size	-892.9	-821.5	869.8	-252.3	816.7	231.8	440.8	-1325.6	-773.4	-1775.1
	-1.97	*-1.54*	*1.64*	*-0.55*	*2.01*	*0.56*	*0.74*	*-0.95*	*-1.03*	*-1.69*
Dependent elderly in the household	-50.132	-6.811	-10.238	7.812	61.673	21.094	50.098	24.713	15.994	-9.675
	-1.30	*-0.15*	*-0.29*	*0.24*	*1.54*	*0.56*	*1.73*	*0.43*	*0.15*	*-0.19*
Household size	291.4	236.6	-213.7	60.9	-195.6	-44.2	-138.1	341.1	266.3	492.1
	2.39	*1.66*	*-1.56*	*0.51*	*-1.81*	*-0.41*	*-0.87*	*0.93*	*1.26*	*1.79*
Average education of adult hh members	-10.829	1.177	-5.540	-8.647	-9.496	-14.536	-13.949	8.784	7.141	-6.209
	-1.22	*0.13*	*-0.76*	*-1.35*	*-1.51*	*-2.25*	*-1.55*	*0.50*	*0.52*	*-0.50*
Average age of adult hh members	0.477	-1.544	-1.936	-3.920	0.313	-0.090	-2.366	0.689	-0.421	-0.083
	0.19	*-0.71*	*-0.91*	*-1.82*	*0.16*	*-0.04*	*-1.12*	*0.14*	*-0.14*	*-0.02*
Child of hh head	75.484	148.396	-87.927	130.582	-38.511	43.248	-80.981	33.353	0.554	-26.255
	1.23	*1.85*	*-1.52*	*2.00*	*-0.61*	*0.58*	*-2.03*	*0.26*	*0.01*	*-0.30*

	(1)	(2)	(3)	(4)	(5)	(6)	(7)	(8)	(9)	(10)
Vocational school	58.201	−44.194	51.005	78.304	21.001	37.609	−28.868	−29.766	5.420	52.365
	1.17	*−1.18*	*1.75*	*2.77*	*0.77*	*1.02*	*−0.64*	*−0.52*	*0.16*	*1.19*
Change in *hukou*	30.322	44.688	31.066	23.456	−38.681	−9.469	−109.763	101.950	22.055	−3.420
	0.73	*1.38*	*0.98*	*0.93*	*−1.30*	*−0.35*	*−1.85*	*1.06*	*0.57*	*−0.05*
Big city	−49.381	−42.404	−26.139	−13.340	−29.187	−17.176	—	—	−60.718	−99.489
	−1.91	*−1.67*	*−1.29*	*−0.72*	*−1.56*	*−0.76*	—	—	*−2.19*	*−2.25*
Constant term	3227.2	3156.1	1788.4	2880.1	1371.2	1843.8	2418.4	2631.6	2857.8	3993.7
	6.16	*5.55*	*3.29*	*6.55*	*3.01*	*4.04*	*4.27*	*2.17*	*3.51*	*3.82*
# obs.	1017	1153	1745	2033	1438	1553	356	423	546	634
R^2	0.07	0.07	0.01	0.02	0.02	0.06	0.03	0.03	0.05	0.03

Note: T-statistics in italics.

Appendix 7.B6 Hours worked functions by region, Year: 2002

	Coast		Centre		West		Municipality		North-East	
	Women	Men	Women	Men	Women	Men	Women	Men	Women	Men
Education	-24.680	-15.043	-29.159	-16.376	-1.805	-22.933	12.724	-32.527	-27.263	-7.632
	-1.76	-1.27	-3.02	-1.96	-0.20	-3.03	0.96	-2.51	-2.00	-0.71
Age	-32.931	-8.793	-30.722	15.195	-28.039	-40.128	-27.231	1.933	-15.592	4.233
	-1.39	-0.37	-1.47	0.93	-1.41	-2.11	-1.04	0.10	-0.57	0.16
$(Age)^2$	0.385	0.045	0.377	-0.175	0.373	0.429	0.129	-0.072	0.237	-0.104
	1.25	0.16	1.31	-0.89	1.45	1.99	0.41	-0.32	0.71	-0.36
Communist	-28.556	-86.791	-27.940	-122.885	-58.873	-123.171	20.700	30.892	-107.644	-79.280
	-0.72	-2.11	-0.87	-4.67	-1.88	-4.36	0.39	0.59	-2.08	-1.93
Married	32.192	47.179	-36.532	33.559	-47.063	19.562	171.904	-94.527	11.022	-73.636
	0.36	0.50	-0.52	0.45	-0.68	0.19	1.39	-0.87	0.11	-0.43
Square root of household size	-559.1	513.4	-154.5	-490.2	850.9	-975.2	-1008.2	390.0	-1777.0	-1902.1
	-0.70	0.63	-0.18	-0.64	1.20	-0.92	-0.66	0.43	-1.39	-1.33
Dependent elderly in the household	-84.368	-93.597	-11.294	-64.155	-62.999	20.735	-38.608	146.980	51.046	26.550
	-1.39	-1.64	-0.22	-1.44	-1.10	0.28	-0.62	1.52	0.78	0.44
Household size	176.2	-105.7	83.4	148.4	-191.9	286.9	221.3	-110.7	479.5	521.5
	0.84	-0.48	0.35	0.71	-0.89	0.98	0.60	-0.45	1.40	1.32
Average education of adult hh members	0.906	-17.912	2.403	-9.288	-27.228	-11.040	-4.438	27.861	-13.005	-11.400
	0.07	-1.41	0.25	-1.00	-2.50	-1.20	-0.31	1.50	-0.90	-0.84
Average age of adult hh members	0.379	-0.467	0.376	-3.966	-6.141	-6.354	8.063	-3.504	-10.772	-2.938
	0.11	-0.13	0.11	-1.24	-1.62	-2.02	1.63	-0.84	-2.64	-0.61
Child of hh head	95.840	-42.404	-10.068	89.408	23.018	-51.560	-92.786	-45.695	111.619	-168.735
	0.87	-0.51	-0.14	1.02	0.23	-0.44	-0.62	-0.49	0.98	-1.24

Vocational school	−47.683 *−1.07*	−3.256 *−0.08*	−108.498 *−3.92*	−67.207 *−2.49*	−76.243 *−2.40*	−45.343 *−1.58*	34.987 *0.74*	88.532 *1.72*	15.963 *0.38*	−35.430 *−0.89*
Change in *hukou*	112.556 *1.90*	−65.124 *−1.40*	85.118 *1.97*	45.600 *1.40*	−15.019 *−0.26*	51.905 *1.23*	25.631 *0.28*	247.411 *1.50*	−72.604 *−0.56*	201.230 *1.83*
Big city	−40.351 *−1.16*	−99.741 *−2.90*	11.917 *0.37*	−8.247 *−0.29*	−10.235 *−0.31*	−65.638 *−2.17*	0.000 —	0.000	91.759 *1.57*	19.450 *0.37*
Constant term	3499.4 *3.71*	2413.3 *2.57*	3188.2 *3.99*	2823.1 *3.71*	2452.1 *3.59*	4654.7 *4.53*	3452.4 *2.32*	2123.9 *2.26*	4842.9 *3.65*	4400.7 *3.39*
# obs.	818	994	1417	1883	1155	1421	367	432	431	619
R^2	0.05	0.06	0.05	0.05	0.04	0.07	0.07	0.05	0.08	0.04

Note: T-statistics in italics.

Notes

* Paper presented at the Asian Economic Panel meeting held in Seoul (March 20–21, 2006). The authors are grateful to discussants and participants for helpful comments.

1 The labor mobility from agricultural to non-agricultural sectors has been pointed out as a significant source of economic growth in China since the beginning of the reforms (Cai 2005).

2 The household registration system (*hukou* system) was established in 1958 to restrict migrations both between rural and urban areas and across regions. The main institutional barrier to mobility was the exclusion of rural residents from the urban welfare system then established, which provided housing, medical care, education, childcare, and pension to urban residents (Cheng and Selder 1994).

3 Except as otherwise indicated, all macroeconomic data on employment in China are official data from the National Bureau of Statistics (NBS).

4 The sum of laid-off workers at the beginning of 1998 with newly added laid-off workers during the period from 1998 to 2002 amounts to 27 million (NBS 2003, 134). According to Li and Bai (2005), the number of workers laid-off from other types of enterprises would be roughly 50 million. Within state-owned enterprises, the laid-off policy has been implemented largely in small-scale enterprises owned by local governments, which have suffered financial losses (Dong 2003).

5 These include shareholding corporations, limited liability corporations, cooperative units, and others.

6 Again, these changes are to be related with the laid-off policy, which has been mainly implemented in industries facing strong competition, such as manufacturing and construction. For instance, the number of on-post staff and workers in state-owned enterprises in manufacture fell sharply from 33.3 million in 1995 to 9.8 million in 2002 (NBS 2003, 23).

7 A main area of research analyzes various aspects of labor market segmentation in China, by focusing on earnings gaps between different groups of workers: rural migrants and urban residents (Knight *et al.* (1999), Meng and Zhang (2001), Maurer-Fazio and Dinh (2004)), men and women either in rural China (Meng and Miller 1995, Meng 1998, Ho et al. 2002, Rozelle et al. 2002, Dong et al. 2004) or in urban China (Qian 1996; Gustafsson and Li 2000; Liu et al. 2000; Hughes and Maurer-Fazio 2002; Maurer-Fazio and Hughes 2002; Liu et al. 2004; Bishop et al. 2005; Démurger et al. 2007; Ng 2005) and workers in enterprises of different ownership (Zhao 2001, 2002; Dong and Bowles 2002; Chen et al. 2005).

8 A detailed description of the pre-reform wage-setting system is given in Meng (2000, Chapter 2). See also Lin et al. 2001, and Knight and Song 2005).

9 In 1988, the State Council issued the *Tentative Stipulations on Private Enterprises* (TSPE) to govern the registration and management of private firms. This document defined a private firm as "a for-profit organization that is owned by individuals and employs more than eight people." Firms that hired eight employees or less can be registered as individual enterprises (*getihu*). The TSPE identified three types of private firms: those under sole ownership, partnerships, and limited liability companies.

10 See State Council's *Provisional Measures for Retirement and Quit of Workers*, issued on June 2, 1978.

11 *Sixth Five-Year Plan of China Economic and Social Development*, ratified by the People's Congress on December 10, 1982.

12 See *Statement of the Ministry of Personnel and Labor on Active Implementation of Labor Contract*, issued on February 22, 1983.

13 *The Central Committee of Chinese Communist Party's Resolution on Economic Institutional Reform*, issued on October 20, 1984.

14 See State Council's *Notice on Effective Work for Urban Employment*, issued on April 27, 1990.

15 See State Council's *Resolution on Reform of Pension System for Enterprise Workers*, issued on June 26, 1991.

16 See *Regulations on Transform of Operation Mechanism of State-owned Industrial Enterprises*, issued by the State Council on July 23, 1992.

17 See State Council's *Notice on Some Issues Related to Trial Implementation of Bankruptcy for State-owned Enterprises in Selected Cities*, November 25, 1994.

18 See *Provisional Regulations on Employment of Rural Labor Force between Provinces*, issued by the Ministry of Labor, November 17, 1994.

19 See State Council's *Regulations on Work Time of Workers*, issued on March 25, 1995.

20 See *Report of the Ministry of Labor on Implementation of the Re-employment Project*, Submitted to the State Council on March 27, 1995.

21 See State Council's *Complementary Notice on Some Issues Related to Trial Implementation of Merge and Bankruptcy for State-owned Enterprises and Re-employment of Workers in Selected Cities*, March 2, 1997.

22 See CCCPC and State Council's *Notice on Security of Basic Livelihood of Laid-off Workers from State-owned Enterprises and Emphasis on Re-employment*, June 9, 1998.

23 See *Guidelines for Further Deepening Distribution System in Enterprises*, issued by the MOLSS, November 6, 2000.

24 See State Council's *Complementary Notice on Pilot Plan for Perfecting Social Security System in Urban Areas*, December 25, 2000.

25 See *Notice on Better Services and Management of Employment for Rural–Urban Migrant Workers*, issued by the State Council, January 5, 2003.

26 The Company Law promulgated in November 1993, provided the legal framework for the development of limited liability companies and shareholding companies.

27 The second objective of this wage adjustment was to stimulate sluggish economic growth. However, while the relative wage in the government sector rose significantly, the macroeconomic effect of the wage adjustment remained quite limited.

28 In 1998, the Ministry of Public Security issued new regulations relaxing control over *hukou* registration. In particular, those who join their parents, spouses, and children in cities can now be registered with urban *hukou* (Cai and Wang 2003).

29 The China Household Income Project is an internationally joint research project established in 1987, and sponsored by the Institute of Economics, the Chinese Academy of Social Sciences, the Asian Development Bank, and the Ford Foundation. Additional support was provided by the East Asian Institute, and Columbia University (Riskin, Zhao, and Li 2000). Up to now, three household income surveys have been conducted – 1988, 1995, and 2002. The output of the project based on the first two surveys can be found in Griffin and Zhao (1993) and Riskin, Zhao and Li (2001).

30 The sampling method of NBS is briefly explained in NBS 2002, 318.

31 The 11 provinces included in the urban survey are Anhui, Beijing, Gansu, Guangdong, Henan, Hubei, Jiangsu, Liaoning, Shanxi, Sichuan, and Yunnan.

32 See Démurger et al. (2006) for an evaluation of the impact of using deflators on measures of spatial inequality.

33 There is some inconsistency for the definition of "real estate" between 1995 and 2002. Indeed, in 1995, "real estate" also includes "social services" (such as law

companies, housekeepers, re-employment centers, etc.) while in 2002, they are split into two separate categories. We chose not to add-up these two categories for 2002 since social services are mostly competitive. However, we believe that the bias of including social services into real estate in 1995 should not be too large since this sector was still marginal in 1995.

34 For our purpose, it is more appropriate to consider Liaoning's characteristics as representative of a fifth category of provinces, namely northeastern provinces rather than coastal provinces. Indeed, Liaoning province is quite different from coastal provinces in terms of industrial and ownership structure. Its industrial structure is strongly influenced by strategic choices that have been made during the central planning period, with a predominance of heavy industry sectors, and thus central SOEs. Moreover, it has been one of the most badly hit provinces by the laid-off policy from the end of the 1990s, which has had strong implications in terms of employment structure.

35 All the data discussed in the remaining of this paper are deflated, using Brandt and Holz (2006) urban provincial-level spatial price deflators as explained above.

36 The observed difference in 2002 is not statistically significant.

37 In 1995, there were still some institutional limitations on wage settings. This can be seen clearly from basic wages, which were quite similar across different sectors with the main determinants of earnings differences being income outside basic wage.

38 In fact, average earnings in the western region were even higher than that in the coastal region. For instance, in 1978, it was 696 yuan in the eight western provinces (Sichuan, Guizhou, Yunnan, Shaanxi, Gansu, Qinghai, Ningxia, and Xinjiang) and 666 yuan in the eight coastal provinces (Tianjin, Liaoning, Shanghai, Jiangsu, Zhejiang, Fujian, Shandong, and Guangdong) (NBS 1999, 139).

39 In particular, results obtained through the two-step method proposed by Dubin and McFadden (1984), with sector choice and enterprise choice modeled as multinomial Logit and local shares of employment in various sectors used as instruments, led to similar results for all aspects considered in this paper.

40 Each effect can be evaluated in six different ways, depending on the choice of reference populations and coefficient vectors as well as on the choice of the sequence in which different effects are evaluated.

41 By resampling from the original data, the nonparametric boostrap method allows for the derivation of confidence intervals for all statistics obtained through the microsimulation procedure presented above.

42 Both figures are statistically significant at the 5 percent level as shown by corresponding confidence intervals provided under the "5%" and "95%" headings.

43 The FIE-GAI gap vanished from 22 percent in favor of FIEs in 1995 to a low and non-significant 2 percent in favor of GAIs.

44 However, Khan and Riskin (2005) and Démurger et al. (2006) have shown that urban household disposable income inequality has been slightly but significantly decreasing over the period.

References

Adamchick, Vera A., and Arjun S. Bedi. 2000. "Wage Differentials between the Public and the Private Sectors: Evidence from an Economy in Transition," *Labour Economics*, 7(2): 203–24.

Appleton, Simon, John Knight, Lina Song, and Qingjie Xia. 2002. "Labor Retrenchment in China: Determinants and Consequences," *China Economic Review*, 13(2–3): 252–75.

Bishop, John A., Feijun Luo, and Fang Wang. 2005. "Economic Transition, Gender

Bias, and the Distribution of Earnings in China," *Economics of Transition*, 13(2): 239–59.

Blinder, Alan S. 1973. "Wage Discrimination: Reduced Form and Structural Estimates," *Journal of Human Resources*, 8(4): 436–55.

Boeri, Tito and Katherine Terell. 2002. "Institutional Determinants of Labor Reallocation in Transition," *Journal of Economic Perspectives*, 16(1): 51–76.

Brandt, Loren, and Carsten A. Holz. 2006. "Spatial Price Differences in China: Estimates and Implications," Forthcoming in *Economic Development and Cultural Change*, 55(1).

Cai, Fang. 2005. "Reform of Labor Policy in China: A Perspective of Political Economy, in *CHINA: An Economics Research Study Series – Volume 4: Reforming China*," Institute of World Economics and Politics, Chinese Academy of Social Sciences, EDS, Singapore: Marshall Cavendish Academic.

Cai, Fang and Wang Dewen. 2003. "Migration as Marketization: What Can we Learn from China's 2000 Census Data?" *The China Review*, 3(2): 73–93.

Chen, Yi, Sylvie Démurger, and Martin Fournier. 2005. "Earnings Differentials and Ownership Structure in Chinese Enterprises," *Economic Development and Cultural Change*, 53(4): 933–58.

Cheng, Tiejun and Mark Selden. 1994. "The Origins and Social Consequences of China's Hukou System," *The China Quarterly*, 139: 644–68.

Coady, David P. and Limin Wang. 2000. "Equity, Efficiency, and Labor-market Reforms in Urban China: The Impact of Bonus Wages on the Distribution of Earnings," *China Economic Review*, 11(3): 213–31.

Démurger, Sylvie, Martin Fournier, and Yi Chen. 2007. "The Evolution of Gender Earnings Gaps and Discrimination in Urban China: 1988–1995," forthcoming in *The Developing Economies*, 45(1).

Démurger, Sylvie, Martin Fournier, and Shi Li. 2006. "Urban Income Inequality in China Revisited (1988–2002)," forthcoming in *Economics Letters*.

Dong, Xiao-yuan. 2003. "China's Urban Labor Market Adjustment: A Summary of Literature Review." Available at http://info.worldbank.org/etools/docs/library/74068/china/readings/oct28/dong28engl.pdf.

Dong, Xiao-yuan and Paul Bowles. 2002. "Segmentation and Discrimination in China's Emerging Industrial Labor Market," *China Economic Review*, 13(2–3): 170–96.

Dong, Xiao-yuan, Fiona MacPhail, Paul Bowles, and Samuel P. S. Ho. 2004. "Gender Segmentation at Work in China's Privatized Rural Industry: Some Evidence from Shandong and Jiangsu," *World Development*, 32(6): 979–98.

Dubin, Jeffrey A. and Daniel L. McFadden. 1984. "An Econometric Analysis of Residential Electric Appliance Holdings and Consumption," *Econometrica*, 52(2): 345–62.

Falaris, Evangelos M. 2004. "Private and Public Sector Wages in Bulgaria, *Journal of Comparative Economics*," 32(1): 56–72.

Fleisher Belton, M. and Dennis T. Yang. 2003. "Labor Laws and Regulations in China," *China Economic Review*, 14(4): 426–33.

Fournier, Martin. 2005. "Exploiting Information from Path Dependency in Oaxaca–Blinder Decomposition Procedures," *Applied Economics Letters*, 12(11): 669–72.

Giles, John, Albert Park, and Fang Cai. 2006. "How has Economic Restructuring Affected China's Urban Workers?" *The China Quarterly*, 185: 61–95.

Griffin, Keith, and Zhao Renwei. 1993. *The Distribution of Income in China*. London: Macmillan.

Gustafsson, Björn and Li Shi. 2000. "Economic Transformation and the Gender Earnings Gap in Urban China," *Journal of Population Economics*, 13(2): 305–29.

Hausman, Jerry. 1978. "Specification Tests in Econometrics," *Econometrica*, 46: 1251–71.

Ho, Samuel P. S., Xiaoyuan Dong, Paul Bowles, and Fiona MacPhail. 2002. "Privatization and Enterprise Wage Structures during Transition: Evidence from Rural Industry in China," *Economics of Transition*, 10(3): 659–88.

Hughes, James and Margaret Maurer-Fazio, 2002. "Effects of Marriage, Education and Occupation on the Female/Male Wage Gap in China," *Pacific Economic Review*, 7(1): 137–56.

Khan, Azizur R. and Carl Riskin, 2005. "China's Household Income and its Distribution, 1995 and 2002," *The China Quarterly*, 182: 356–84.

Knight, John and Li Shi. 2005. "Wages, Firm Profitability and Labor Market Segmentation in Urban China," *China Economic Review*, 16(3): 205–28.

Knight, John, Li Shi, and Zhao Renwei. 2001. "A Spatial Analysis of Wages and Incomes in Urban China: Divergent Means, Convergent Inequality," in *China's Retreat from Equality: Income Distribution and Economic Transition*, Carl Riskin, Zhao Renwei, and Li Shi, eds, New York: M. E. Sharpe.

Knight, John and Lina Song. 1995. "Towards a Labor Market in China," *Oxford Review of Economic Policy*, 11(4): 97–117.

——. 2003. "Increasing Urban Wage Inequality in China: Extent, Elements and Evaluation," *Economics of Transition*, 11(4): 597–619.

——. 2005. *Towards a Labour Market in China*, Oxford: Oxford University Press.

Knight, John, Lina Song, and H. Jia. 1999. "Chinese Rural Migrants in Urban Enterprises: Three Perspectives," in *The Workers' State Meets the Market: Labor in China's Transition*, Sarah Cook and Margaret Maurer-Fazio, eds, London: Frank Cass.

Knight, John and Linda Yueh. 2006. "Job Mobility of Residents and Migrants in Urban China," In *Unemployment, Inequality and Poverty in Urban China*, Li Shi and Hiroshi Sato, eds, London: RoutledgeCurzon.

Lai, Pingyao. 2005. "China's Economic Growth: New Trends and Implications," in *CHINA: An Economics Research Study Series – Volume 4: Reforming China*, Institute of World Economics and Politics, Chinese Academy of Social Sciences, eds, Singapore: Marshall Cavendish Academic.

Li, Shi and Bai Nansheng. 2005. *China Human Development Report – Development with Equity*, Beijing: UNDP and China Development Research Foundation.

Lin, Justin Y., Fang Cai, and Zhou Li. 2001. *State-owned Enterprise Reform in China*, Hong Kong: Chinese University Press.

Liu, Pak-Wai, Xin Meng, and Junsen Zhang. 2000. "Sectoral Gender Wage Differentials and Discrimination in the Transitional Chinese Economy," *Journal of Population Economics*, 13(2): 331–52.

Liu, Pak-Wai, Junsen Zhang, and Shu-Chuen Chong. 2004. "Occupational Segregation and Wage Differentials between Natives And Immigrants: Evidence from Hong Kong," *Journal of Development Economics*, 73: 395–413.

Liu, Pak-Wai, Junsen Zhang, and Ching Yi Kung. 2004. "What Has Happened to the Gender Wage Differential in Urban China During 1988–1999?" Available at http://econrsss.anu.edu.au/pdf/china-abstract-pdf/Zhang-Kung.pdf

Lokshin Michael M. and Branko Jovanovic. 2003. "Wage Differentials and State Private Sector Employment Choice in Yugoslavia," *Economics of Transition*, 11(3): 463–91

Maurer-Fazio, Margaret and Ngan Dinh. 2004. "Differential Rewards to, and Contributions of, Education in Urban China's Segmented Labor Markets," *Pacific Economic Review*, 9(3): 173–89.

Maurer-Fazio, Margaret and James Hughes. 2002. "The Effects of Market Liberalization on the Relative Earnings of Chinese Women," *Journal of Comparative Economics*, 30(4): 709–31.

Meng, Xin. 1998. "Male–female Wage Determination and Gender Wage Discrimination in China's Rural Industrial Sector," *Labour Economics*, 5(1): 67–89.

Meng, Xin. 2000. *Labour Market Reform in China*, Cambridge, UK: Cambridge University Press.

Meng, Xin and Paul Miller. 1995. "Occupational Segregation and its Impact on Gender Wages Discrimination in China's Rural Industrial Sector," *Oxford Economic Papers*, 47(1): 136–55.

Meng, Xin and Junsen Zhang. 2001. "The Two-Tier Labor Market in Urban China – Occupational Segregation and Wage Differentials between Urban Residents and Rural Migrants in Shanghai," *Journal of Comparative Economics*, 29: 485–504.

Mincer, Jacob. 1974. *Schooling, Experience, and Earnings*. New York: National Bureau of Economic Research.

Ministry of Labor and Social Security (MOLSS) and Literature Research Office of CCCPC. 2002. "Selected Important Documents of Labor and Social Security in the New Period," Beijing: Publishing House of MOLSS.

National Bureau of Statistics (NBS). 1999. *Comprehensive Statistical Data and Materials on 50 Years of New China*, Beijing: China Statistics Press.

National Bureau of Statistics (NBS). 2002, 2003. *China Statistical Yearbook*, Beijing: China Statistics Press.

National Bureau of Statistics (NBS) and Ministry of Labor and Social Security (MLSS). 2003. *China Labor Statistical Yearbook*, Beijing: China Statistics Press

Ng, Ying Chu. 2005. *Gender Earnings Differentials and Regional Economic Development in urban China, 1988–1997*. Available at http://www.wider.unu.edu/research/2004–2005/2004–2005–6/agenda/3–1_Ying%20Chu%20Ng_Gender%20Earnings_English.pdf

Oaxaca, Ronald L. 1973. "Male-Female Wage Differentials in Urban Labor Markets," *International Economic Review*, 14(3): 693–709.

Qian, Jieyong. 1996. "Gender Wage Differentials in Urban China in the 1990s," PhD. Dissertation. Binghamton: State University of New York.

Riskin, Carl, Renwei Zhao, and Shi Li. 2000. "Chinese Household Income Project, 1995 [Computer file]," ICPSR version. Amherst, MA: University of Massachusetts, Political Economy Research Institute [producer], 2000. Ann Arbor, MI: Inter-university Consortium for Political and Social Research [distributor].

——. 2001. *China's Retreat from Equality – Income Distribution and Economic Transition*, London: M. E. Sharpe.

Rozelle, Scott, Xiaoyuan Dong, Linxiu Zhang, and Andrew Mason. 2002. "Gender Wage Gaps in Post-reform Rural China," *Pacific Economic Review*, 7(1): 157–79.

——. 2002. "Earnings Differentials between State and Non-State Enterprises in Urban China," *Pacific Economic Review*, 7(1): 181–97.

Zhang, Junsen, Yaohui Zhao, Albert Park, and Xiaoqing Song. 2005. "Economic Returns to Schooling in Urban China, 1988 to 2001," *Journal of Comparative Economics*, 33: 730–52.

Zhao, Yaohui. 2001. "Foreign Direct Investment and Relative Wages: The Case of China," *China Economic Review*, 12(1): 40–57.

8 The evolution of income inequality in rural China

Dwayne Benjamin, Loren Brandt, and John Giles [*]

Abstract

In this paper we analyze trends in income inequality and the distribution of income in rural China from 1987 to 1999. We find an uneven, but long-run increase in inequality in rural China, and show that nearly half of the rural population was not much better off in 1999 than at the start of the period. We rule out geography as the most important factor for explaining income differences, and the increases that occurred over time. Much more important were growing differences between households living in the same village, province or region. We also find that access to non-agricultural incomes from local wage employment and family businesses contributes to inequality, but that employment outside the county in which a household lives and accessed through temporary migration is relatively equalizing. Finally, we document important strengths and weaknesses of the primary dataset used for our analyses relative to other data sources available for study of inequality and poverty in rural China.

8.1 Introduction

China has recorded impressive growth over the past twenty years, with a commensurate increase in average living standards.[1] However, there is mounting concern that increases in inequality indicate many are being left behind, and not sharing in the fruits of development.[2] Indeed, most well-behaved social welfare functions rank unequal distributions below equal ones with the same mean income levels. An important question is whether recent increases in inequality are sufficiently high to offset general rises in average income: Is rising inequality an uncomfortable, but otherwise innocuous price to pay when the rising tide is raising all boats? Not necessarily, as there is additional concern that high levels of inequality may slow economic transition, and hinder future growth.[3]

One striking feature of the current discussion of inequality in China is the absence of well-documented facts about temporal changes in the patterns and structure of the income distribution, and inequality. To some extent, this reflects lack of access to nationally representative data, so that China has been cited as an exception to global trends in our understanding of inequality in the developing world.[4] Certainly, the level of basic knowledge about China's income distribution pales in comparison to attention paid to developed countries like the U.S., or other developing countries like Taiwan, Thailand, or India. Furthermore, China is simply bigger and more complicated so that summaries of inequality may be less meaningful than those of other economies. Still, simple impressions of inequality have emerged from the existing literature: First, inequality has gone up during the transition; second, that this is largely driven by widening inter-provincial income differences; and third, that in rural areas, the development of non-farm opportunities has provided uneven rewards for households, and is an important underlying source of inequality.[5]

Our objective in this paper is to fill in gaps in our understanding of inequality in rural China. The centerpiece of our work is a nationally representative household survey that has been collected by the Research Centre for Rural Economy (RCRE) under the Ministry of Agriculture in China continuously from 1986 to the present, and covers most of the reform period.[6] By using a common household survey across years, we are able to address a number of important methodological and measurement issues associated with describing inequality at a point in time, and comparing inequality across time periods. By employing additional, different data sets, we are also able to explore the sensitivity of our conclusions to use of our primary data set. We further provide simple decompositions of inequality by space (village, province, and region) and source of income (e.g. farm and non-farm) that yield important insights about the evolution of inequality.

Ideally, we would like to attribute changes in inequality to various factors associated with economic transition (moving to a market economy) and development (e.g. growth of a non-farm sector).[7] This is difficult, however, as both processes are potentially confounded in a common trend, and almost certainly intertwined anyway. Moreover, some of the recent rise in inequality appears to be a by-product of collapsing agricultural prices, and not the consequence of a "Kuznets-like" structural process.[8] While far from perfectly integrated with world markets, crop prices in China fell by more than a third between 1996 and 2000, mirroring large drops in world prices.[9] Since many households in rural China are still dependent on crop production for a substantial portion of their incomes, they have experienced absolute, not just relative declines in their standard of living. While we cannot explain the drop in crop prices, we show that it is clear that if prices remain low, without offsetting rapid development of the more equalizing sources of non-farm income, many in the countryside will remain poor, with commensurate political and migration pressures. In fact, we may now be observing China in a state of transition, with low returns to agriculture (as currently structured) a catalyst for a more rapid secular shift away from farming. Whether the Chinese economy is flexible enough to facilitate this transformation, or public policy sufficiently nimble and focused on the human cost of this potentially massive adjustment, remain important open questions.

We first briefly review the existing literature on rural inequality, highlighting several data and conceptual issues that we focus on in our work. We then describe our main data set, based on a panel of villages surveyed by RCRE. Included is a discussion of issues arising in the consistent measurement and definition of income and consumption from 1987 to 1999. We summarize various features of the income distribution for selected years in this time span, and show that while average incomes have undeniably risen, so has inequality. Of particular concern, we show that after initially rising, the absolute living standards of the poor declined considerably from 1995 to 1999, so that they approach income levels of 1987. Moreover, as much as half of all households were not unambiguously better off in 1999 than in 1987: the rising tide did not lift all boats. After describing the overall distribution, we then present a spatial decomposition, where we challenge the popular perception that inequality in rural China is primarily a geographic phenomenon. In fact, most inequality is local. Our final exercise breaks down total income by source, where we see that the increase in inequality is driven by the combination of falling farm incomes with rising local non-farm incomes. Wage incomes from temporary migrant employment, by contrast, are actually correlated with reductions in inequality. In the final section, we offer some interpretation of these results, and outline questions for future research.

8.2 Previous studies

There is an extensive literature concerned with the evolution of inequality in rural China since the onset of reform in the late 1970s. The primary focus has been on: (i) estimating the level of inequality and its changes over time; (ii) and identifying underlying sources of inequality and its changes. Our purpose here is not to offer a comprehensive literature review of this work. We will be very selective, with an eye to major findings, and some of the limitations that have informed our analyses with the RCRE data. At the risk of some simplification, however, the general consensus is that inequality has increased significantly over time. Motivated by the contrasting economic performance of rich and poor provinces, much of this increase is attributed to spatial differences linked to regional factors, and the highly uneven rate of growth of the non-agriculture sector in the countryside.

Data collected by the National Bureau of Statistics (NBS) have been the sole source of estimates of long-run trends in rural income inequality using household-level data. These data are not in the public domain, and details of construction of the NBS's income estimates and Gini's is sketchy. Nonetheless, Bramall's (2001) summary of NBS trends shows an increase in the national Gini coefficient for rural China of almost fifty percent, from 0.24 in 1980, to 0.31 in 1990, to 0.34 in 1995, and finally to 0.35 in 1999. The only estimates of rural inequality that are remotely comparable to those of the NBS are for 1988 and 1995 using data collected as part of the China Income Project (or "CIP", see Khan and Riskin, 1998). Covering a smaller sample of provinces and households, and based on a modified NBS household survey instrument and definition of income, these data suggest both higher levels of overall inequality and a more rapid increase over a subperiod, with the Gini coefficient rising from 0.34 in 1988 to 0.42 in 1995.

Numerous studies stress the spatial aspects of this rise in rural inequality. A majority of these, however, use provincial-level or subprovincial per capita averages, as opposed to household level survey data. Only 4 out of 16 recent papers summarized by Gustafsson and Li (2002), for example, used household-level data. Papers using regionally aggregated data have been interested in looking at trends in inter-provincial inequality, or have used provincial-level data to analyze inter-regional trends. There are two obvious limitations of these analyses. First, they underestimate inequality because they ignore any differences arising from household differences within administrative units. And second, conclusions about trends and role of contributing factors to inequality such as township and village enterprises are valid only insofar as most rural inequality arises from differences in mean incomes across these units.

A few studies have employed household-level data to decompose rural inequality into spatial components. Benjamin et al. (2002) showed (for a single point in time) that within-village inequality dominated cross-region inequality, although their study had limited geographic coverage. Gustafsson and Li (2002), using the CIP data for 1988 and 1995, provide the most comprehensive study exploring inequality across space and time. Their analysis suggests that the contribution of spatial differences at the county or provincial level was significant, and rising between 1988 and 1995. Differences in the counties (but not provinces) from which households were surveyed in the two years however pose some problems for interpretation.

Finally, a number of other studies (Hare 1994; Khan and Riskin 1998; Tsui 1998; Kung and Lee 2001) have used household data to look at the role of the emerging non-agricultural sector in explaining inequality. These studies emphasize the potential role played by the changing structure or composition of income in generating higher inequality. Several authors have also stressed the role played by political power and connections in facilitating access to new opportunities (Cook 1998; Morduch and Sicular 2002; and Nee 1992). With the exception of Benjamin et al. (2002), these studies do not separate or net out the spatial dimensions of income composition, but they do confirm the significant contribution of non-agricultural income sources to income inequality. Interpretation is handicapped, however, in the way that alternative income sources are often lumped together. For example, wage income from local and non-local sources are usually aggregated, while total wage income is sometimes combined with income from family-run businesses. Insofar as these sources of income are less than perfectly correlated with each other, grouping them together hides important aspects of emerging inequality and their links to household attributes and the external economic environment with which these households interact.

8.3 Data

The data used for our analyses come from annual household surveys conducted by the Survey Department of the Research Center on the Rural Economy (RCRE) in Beijing. Household-level surveys from over 100 villages in nine provinces (Anhui, Gansu, Guangdong, Henan, Hunan, Jiangsu, Jilin, Shanxi, and Sichuan) are matched with corresponding village-level data.[10] In each province, counties in the upper, middle and lower income terciles were selected, from which a village was then randomly chosen. Subject to the limits of this stratification, the RCRE sample should reasonably capture both inter- and intra-provincial income variations. Depending on village size, between 40 and 120 households were randomly surveyed in each village. The survey spans the period 1986 to 1999, and includes between 7,000 and 8,000 households per year.

RCRE originally intended a longitudinal survey, following the same households over time. While there is a significant panel dimension to the household sample, nearly one-third of households were lost to attrition during the period 1986–1999, much of which is a product of village attrition that occurred during two two-year gaps when RCRE was unable to conduct the survey in 1992 and 1994 because of funding difficulties. RCRE replaced lost villages by "comparable" villages in the same counties. Households lost through attrition were replaced (at least in principle) on the basis of random sampling.

The survey collected detailed household-level information on incomes and expenditures, education, labor supply, asset ownership, land holdings, savings, formal and informal access to credit, and remittances.[11] In common with the NBS *Rural Household Survey*, respondent households keep daily diaries of income and expenditure, and a resident administrator living in the county seat visits with households once a month to collect information from the diaries. The large number of households surveyed from each village and the lengthy span of the survey enables us to track the evolution of consumption, incomes and inequality during a time of changing market access and development in rural China. Of particular importance for our purposes, we are able to track a panel of villages, even where there has been household attrition. This will allow us to maintain geographic comparability over the entire period.[12]

A variety of definitions are worth clarifying, and further details related to attrition issues are provided in the Appendix 8A.I. First, household membership is defined on the basis of residency and registration.[13] Second, income is calculated as the sum of net income (gross revenue less current expenditures) from agriculture, farming sidelines (e.g. animal husbandry and livestock), family-run businesses, plus wage income, and transfers. We calculate the value of farm output that is not sold, and thus largely consumed (or stored) by the household, at market prices.[14] Household income is also gross of taxes and fees. Third, our measure of consumption includes non-durable goods expenditure, plus an imputed flow of services from household durable goods and housing.[15]

We deflate all income and expenditure data into 1986 prices using the NBS rural consumer price index for each province. For some key results we explore the sensitivity to geographic differences in price levels. In those cases we spatially deflate using a cross-province CPI deflator constructed by Brandt and Holz (2004), based on expenditure weights from the NBS rural household survey. The spatial CPI adjusts for systematic differences in price levels across provinces (at a point in time), because price levels and incomes are positively correlated, possibly exaggerating differences in living standards across regions. Finally, RCRE's sampling is not proportional to provincial population. For example, the number of households surveyed in Sichuan is nearly the same as that surveyed in Gansu, despite the fact that Sichuan has a rural population that is nearly five times larger. Therefore, we use provincial rural population (by year) to weight all calculations.[16]

In order to establish the robustness of our conclusions to various permutations of sample selection, we carried out our analyses on three different data sets. The first, or "full," sample includes every household (panel, attritted, and replacement) in each survey year. The second accounts for the fact that inequality measures may be sensitive to outliers (at both ends of the distribution), and this "trimmed-full" sample drops extreme outliers among households.[17] The third sample is a "balanced-panel," comprised of the 4352 households for which we have data for every year of the survey. As it turns out, our results are consistent across all three data samples. To minimize tables, we restrict our reported results to those from the "trimmed-full" data set.

8.4 Results

8.4.1 Income distribution over time

We begin by summarizing the evolution of average income and consumption per capita over the span of our sample in Table 8.1. To keep the table manageable, we report results for four evenly spaced years – 1987, 1991, 1995, and 1999 – that reflect the patterns in the more complete sample.[18] Mean household per capita incomes were 578 (RMB) in 1987, the beginning of our selected years.[19] Average incomes dropped slightly through 1991, and rose sharply to 772 in 1995. The average annual growth rate over the 1991–95 period was an impressive 5.3 percent, reinforcing the optimism of the expansion that followed the retrenchment between 1989–1991. This growth, which was broad-based in the rural economy, proved to be short-lived, as average

Table 8.1 Per capita income and consumption: levels and growth selected years, RCRE

	Spatial Deflator?	1987	1991	1995	1999	Implied Growth Rate
Income	No	578	551	772	712	0.019
	Yes	567	538	760	699	0.019
Consumption	No	410	402	548	508	0.019
	Yes	402	392	541	497	0.019
Observations		7,983	7,903	6,738	6,987	

Notes: This table shows mean real per capita household income and consumption (in constant 1986 RMB yuan) for selected years. The implied growth rate is defined as the average annual compound growth rate that would turn 1987 incomes to 1999 levels. The spatially deflated rows adjust for regional price differences using the price deflator in Brandt and Holz (2004), and described in the data appendix.

per capita incomes actually fell to 712 by 1999. A sharp reversal in farm prices and cropping incomes following the increase between 1993 and 1995 underlies much of this decline. Setting aside the cyclical variation in growth, the average rate of growth from the beginning to the end of the sample was 1.9 percent. An important question is whether the decline in average incomes was disproportionately borne by the poor, as this would certainly worsen the distributional consequences of rising inequality.

Our results for consumption closely mirror those for income, both in terms of the cyclical patterns, and the implied growth rate over the entire period. Given that the only overlap in the two series is home-produced consumption, it is reassuring that these two otherwise independent measures of welfare track each other so closely (though this may be less assuring for those who believe that consumption should be much smoother than income). In levels, consumption is approximately three-quarters of income. Some of this gap probably reflects measurement error, but it also reflects genuinely high rates of savings, and the fact that incomes are measured before deduction of taxes and other fees.

In Table 8.1 we also show results for spatially deflated mean income and consumption. Spatial deflation makes no difference for this exercise. This is not surprising, as the aggregate numbers do not provide much scope for differential provincial price levels to affect the evolution of the average. The deflator is more likely to matter when we compare incomes across regions, as when we examine inequality.

How do the RCRE numbers compare to other data sources from China? The only other data set that spans this period is the nationally representative – and publicly unavailable – NBS rural household survey. In Figures 8.1 and 8.2, we plot average incomes and consumption for each year of the RCRE survey along with the corresponding NBS rural averages reported in

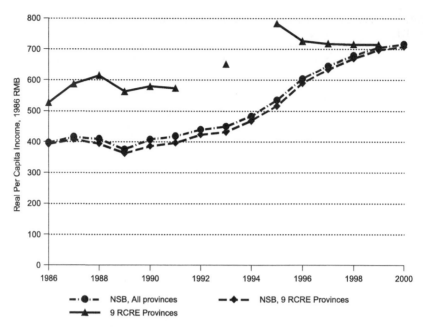

Figure 8.1 Comparing income trends in the RCRE and NBS surveys.

Notes: This figure compares real per capita household income levels and trends in the RCRE surveys with corresponding numbers reported in the NBS yearbooks. The NBS results are shown for all provinces, as well as the same nine provinces in the RCRE sample. All figures are deflated to 1986 RMB yuan.

statistical yearbooks. We do not make this comparison assuming that the NBS are the gold standard (nor are the RCRE data for that matter), but they are the only nationally representative data collected on an annual basis that could be used for this type of analysis.

Up through 1995, the basic patterns in the RCRE and NBS income series are very similar, with the notable difference that the RCRE incomes are consistently much higher than those of the NBS. The higher relative incomes of the RCRE erode by 1999, when the mean incomes in the two surveys actually converge. Thus, the RCRE data show a flatter time series, and a correspondingly lower growth rate. Despite the differences in the magnitude of the trend between 1987 and 1999, both series suggest that growth was fastest in the period 1991–1995, with a significant attenuation (or decline) from 1997–1999. The consumption estimates, on the other hand, line up better in both levels and growth. The difference in the rate of growth of consumption between the two series over the period from 1987 to 1999 is less than half of that for incomes.

One possible source of difference is that the RCRE provinces are not nationally representative. Including only the RCRE-subset of provinces in the NBS data (which come at the provincial level), means from the

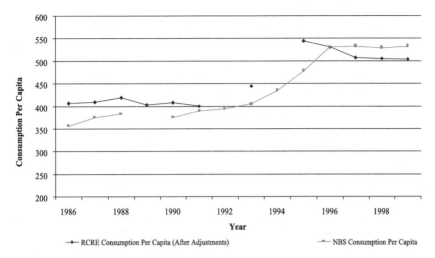

Figure 8.2 Comparing consumption trends from the NBS and RCRE surveys.

Notes: This figure compares real per capita household consumption levels and trends in the RCRE surveys with corresponding numbers reported in the NBS yearbooks. The NBS results are shown for all provinces and reflect household expenditures on durable and non-durable consumer items. The RCRE consumption series values grain at market prices and uses a flow value durable and housing consumption. All figures are deflated to 1986 RMB yuan.

RCRE-subset of provinces almost perfectly track national means. Alternatively, the two surveys may differ in terms of the kinds of households that are sampled. We do not have access to the NBS dataset, but we can line up common indicators calculated from the 1996 Agricultural Census and RCRE surveys as a check. We find that 92.8 percent of RCRE households and 90.8 percent of households in the agricultural census had positive income from agriculture, but that a slightly higher number of individuals per household were primarily engaged in non-agricultural activities in the RCRE survey. Using the information from the 1990 Census and 1996 Agricultural census as benchmarks, it is difficult to argue that the RCRE survey oversampled agricultural households, but RCRE households were slightly larger than the nine-province agricultural census average by 0.45 individuals.[20]

In Appendix 8A.II, we consider the consequences of significant differences in the calculation of income and consumption. Differences in the treatment of taxes and fees, the valuation of income from home-production, and depreciation on fixed assets loom important. For years prior to 1990, these three factors are the source of slightly more than 60 percent of the difference, with most of this due to taxes and fees and the valuation of home-production. It has been suggested (Chen and Ravallion 2004) that after 1990 NBS began to value in-kind components of income at market prices as we do over the entire period in our RCRE estimates. Still, significant differences persist. The gap in per capita income actually widens between the two series after 1990, peaking in 1995, before eventually disappearing altogether. In the case of the consumption series, valuing the in-kind component consistently between the two series also helps narrow the gap prior to 1990, but we observe similar differences in behavior to that for the income series after 1990.

We believe that continued differences in how in-kind income and consumption are actually being valued between the two surveys provide an explanation for some of the gap between 1990 and 1996. As detailed more carefully in Appendix 8A.II, NBS adjusted in-kind valuation procedures three times during the 1990s, but only in a single year, 1997, did they use market prices. From 1991 to 1996 non-marketed grain was valued at the average contract price (this was the average of two administratively determined prices, namely, the quota and above-quota price) if this price existed, otherwise enumerators were instructed to use market prices. The weighted average contract price in use between 1990 and 1996 was well below the market price, and for this reason, explains some of the difference between the two series. In 1997 agricultural commodities consumed in-kind were valued at market prices; and then from 1998 onward, commodities (grain, meats and other crops) not marketed by the households and consumed in-kind were valued at 85–90 percent of the market price, depending on the commodity.[21]

As emphasized originally by Chen and Ravallion (1996), differences in the valuation of home-consumed grain can substantially affect estimates of income and consumption. Changes in the market versus quota price, or the formula used to apply them, will further bias any estimated trends. As we compare trends in the RCRE and NBS during the 1990s, we know from NBS documentation that in-kind valuation was not done at market prices, probably underestimating incomes in the early 1990s, and exaggerating income growth. That said, there may yet remain differences in the RCRE and NBS sampling frames that we cannot detect on the basis of comparable observables. Since the NBS data are not publicly available, it is not possible to further calibrate the residual differences between average incomes in the two surveys at the beginning of our sample.

8.4.1.1   Changes in inequality over time

Table 8.2 provides measures of income and consumption inequality that highlight a variety of distributional characteristics. We begin with the Gini coefficient for income, arrayed in the first row. The Gini increased from 0.32 in 1987 to 0.37 in 1999, an increase of 0.05 or 16 percent. Is this increase economically significant? There are few benchmarks for comparison, though it is worth noting that inequality measures evolve slowly over time, and a 16 percent increase is large.[22] Of particular note, almost all of this increase was over the short period between 1995 and 1999. Combined with the decline in average incomes in the late 1990s, it should come as no surprise that

Table 8.2 Per capita income and consumption inequality various measures and selected years, RCRE

	1987	1991	1995	1999
Income				
Gini (NOT Spatially deflated)	0.32	0.33	0.33	0.37
Gini (Spatially Deflated)	0.29	0.30	0.30	0.35
Other measures of inequality:				
Variance of Logs	0.57	0.60	0.59	0.73
Atkinson (Sensitivity=2)	0.28	0.32	0.33	0.97
Atkinson (Sensitivity=1)	0.16	0.17	0.17	0.21
Atkinson (Sensitivity=.5)	0.08	0.09	0.09	0.12
Percent Below Half Cont Mean	0.14	0.17	0.17	0.22
Percent Below 1987 Half Cont Mean	0.16	0.19	0.06	0.14
90th/10th Split	4.06	3.98	3.93	5.24
Consumption				
Gini (NOT Spatially deflated)	0.25	0.27	0.27	0.31
Gini (Spatially Deflated)	0.22	0.24	0.25	0.29
Other measures of inequality:				
Variance of Logs	0.44	0.47	0.47	0.55
Atkinson (Sensitivity=2)	0.18	0.20	0.21	0.26
Atkinson (Sensitivity=1)	0.09	0.11	0.11	0.14
Atkinson (Sensitivity=.5)	0.05	0.06	0.06	0.08
Percent Below Half Cont Mean	0.08	0.09	0.10	0.16
Percent Below 1987 Half Cont Mean	0.08	0.10	0.03	0.08
90th/10th Split	3.09	3.21	3.29	4.07

Notes: This table provides various distributional summary statistics corresponding to the mean per capita income and consumption levels reported in Table 8.1. We show (1) The Gini coefficient, repeated for spatially undeflated and spatially deflated levels; (2) The variance of log per capita income and consumption; (3) The Atkinson Index, calculated with three inequality aversion parameters (decreasing in aversion for 2.0, 1.0, and 0.5); (4) The proportion of households with incomes below one-half the contemporaneous mean income (i.e. the 50 percent of mean income that year); (5) The proportion of households below one half the mean income level for 1987 (an approximation to a constant "poverty line"); and (6) The ratio of the 90th to the 10th percentiles.

concerns over inequality have intensified. In the second panel we show the results for consumption, where the Gini rises from 0.25 to 0.31 over the complete sample. As is usually the case, the Gini for consumption is lower than income, but the trend and over all time-pattern is basically the same. If anything, the increase in consumption inequality was slightly larger in percentage terms. Measuring welfare either way, it appears that inequality went up over this period, especially since 1995.

In Figure 8.3 we place the RCRE results beside those from the NBS, where the NBS Gini's are drawn from Bramall (2001). The NBS numbers show inequality rising from 0.24 in 1980, to around 0.3 in 1990, slightly lower than in the RCRE sample, and ending at 0.35 in 2000. As with the RCRE data, the

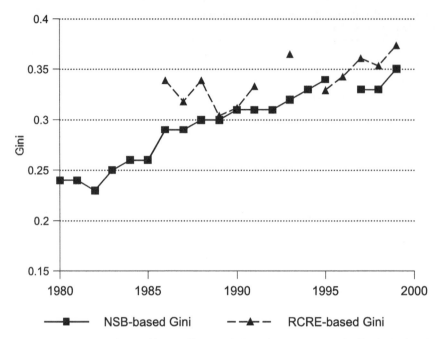

Figure 8.3 A comparison of inequality trends based on RCRE and NBS households Surveys.

Notes: This figure compares the Gini coefficients for household per capita income that we calculated using the RCRE, with Gini coefficients based on the national sample NBS data. The NBS results come from Bramall (2001).

NBS data thus show a Gini rising by about 0.05 points over the 1990s, though the increase is much smoother. Some of these differences, especially the sharp drop in inequality exhibited by the RCRE data between 1993 and 1995, can also be linked to differences in the valuation of the in-kind component of income. Other slight differences in the magnitudes of the Gini in particular years can potentially be attributed to differences in sampling, sample sizes, stratification, or other differences in the survey instrument, however, both the trends and magnitude of the increase in inequality are similar in the two surveys. Thus, while the NBS and RCRE data differ in detail, they paint a similar overall picture for the evolution of rural household welfare over the 1990s.

Returning to Table 8.2, in the second row we apply the spatial price deflator to household income. As expected, the magnitude of the Gini drops. Higher income areas appear less well off once account is taken of the higher prices faced by consumers in these provinces. The magnitude of the drop is 0.02 to 0.03, but spatial deflation does not materially affect our conclusions about the overall trend in inequality: In other words, we cannot deflate away the increase in inequality and attribute it to widening gaps in regional nominal (versus real) incomes.

While the Gini shows an increase in inequality, is there any sensitivity of our conclusions to our particular choice of inequality measure? The next four rows of the table present inequality measures for the variance of log income and the Atkinson index evaluated at three different inequality aversion parameters (ranging from 2.0 to 0.5 in decreasing magnitude of inequality aversion). While these measures can be used for comparison with other studies, the main purpose they serve for us is to confirm the rise in inequality, especially between 1995 and 1999. Most worrying, the Atkinson index with high inequality aversion increases from 0.28 to 0.97 over this four-year period! This suggests that the bottom part of the income distribution did especially badly.

A direct comparison of Lorenz curves yields a non-parametric comparison of changes in inequality, possibly avoiding the need to choose any of the inequality measures in Table 8.2. We show the Lorenz curves for 1987, 1995, and 1999 in Figure 8.4. Panel A shows the curves for the entire sample, while panel B provides a close-up view of the bottom part of the distribution (from Panel A). The 1999 Lorenz curve lies outside that for 1987 over the entire distribution, suggesting that for any inequality measure we choose, 1999 will look more unequal. Unambiguous comparisons for other pairs of years are not possible since the Lorenz curves cross. However, for much of the distribution the 1999 curve also lies outside that for 1995, while the curves for 1987 and 1995 are almost indistinguishable, with a slight advantage at lower incomes for households in 1987.[23]

8.4.1.2   Changes in relative and absolute poverty

Increases in inequality are less worrisome if incomes are increasing for the entire income distribution and the welfare of the poor is improving even as inequality is increasing. We next investigate changes in both relative and absolute inequality to understand how changes have occurred at the lower end of the income distribution. In the next two rows of Table 8.2 we switch from overall measures of inequality to considerations of relative inequality between rich and poor, and poverty. First we present the proportion of households with incomes below half the contemporaneous mean.[24] Essentially, this is a "relative poverty line" set at 50 percent of the mean income for the year: this poverty line moves with average incomes and while it does not tell us much about absolute poverty, it provides another useful way of characterizing the distribution of income.

The proportion of the sample below half the contemporary mean income increases from 16 percent in 1987 to 22 percent by 1999, with most of the jump occurring after 1995. These results suggest that the increase in inequality reflects a worsening of the relative position of low-income households: Using this relative measure, the rich are getting richer and the poor are

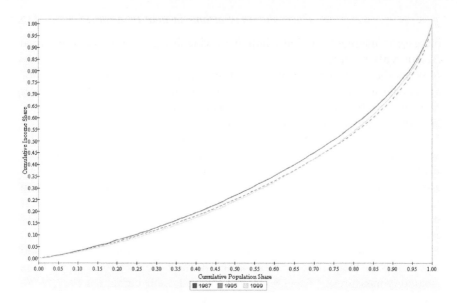

Panel A: The full picture

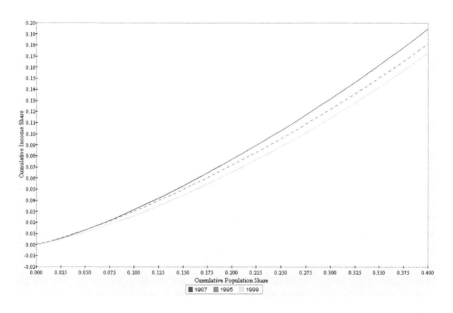

Panel B: The bottom 40 percent (from Panel A)

Figure 8.4 Lorenz curves for per capita income, selected years.

Notes: This figure shows the Lorenz curves for the distribution of real household per capita income for selected years, using the RCRE survey data. The top panel shows the entire curves (with the reference 45-degree line), while the bottom panel "magnifies" the curves, focusing on the poorest 40 percent of households. The 1999 curve lies beneath the 1987 and 1995 curves for much of the distribution, and the difference between the curves is statistically significant (see Appendix IV, Table 8A.3).

getting relatively poorer. A stronger point about absolute changes in poverty can be made when we keep the "poverty line" constant at half 1987 mean levels (in real terms), thus allowing us to track progress on the elimination of poverty with a constant benchmark. The poverty rate worsens between 1987 and 1991, which comes across as the worst year for the poor. The best year was 1995, with half as many people "poor" as in 1987. By 1999, however, the poverty rate (so-measured) has returned to essentially the same level as 1987, doubling in just four years from the level in 1995. Despite an increase of average incomes by 25 percent between 1987 and 1999, the fraction of people below the 1987 "poverty line" is nearly the same.

Use of half the contemporary mean, or any poverty line is somewhat arbitrary, and for this reason we pursue two additional exercises using the full distribution of income per capita: we examine cumulative distribution functions and Generalized Lorenz curves. Cumulative distribution functions (CDFs), shown for income per capita in 1987, 1995, and 1999 in Figure 8.5, permit using any common poverty line applied to the three years to compare poverty rates. For example, if we chose the 1987 half-contemporaneous mean of 290 RMB per capita as our poverty line, we can recover the poverty rates from Table 8.2: approximately 6 percent of people have incomes below 290 in 1995, compared to 14 percent in 1999 and 16 percent in 1987. The CDF for 1995 lies everywhere below the one for 1987 and so the distribution from 1995 first-order stochastically dominates the 1987 distribution. This implies that for any poverty line we might select, there will be less poverty in 1995 than in 1987. For other pairs of years, however, the CDFs cross, thereby complicating comparisons.

We use Davidson and Duclos' (2000) approach to estimate the critical poverty lines where CDFs cross and the point at which the stochastic dominance of one distribution over the other will switch. Comparing the 1999 distribution to the 1987 distribution, we find that for poverty lines above 226 RMB per capita the 1999 distribution dominates the 1987 distribution, and we would judge there to have been a fall in head count measures of poverty. For lower poverty lines, however, the 1987 distribution dominates and we would find an actual increase in poverty. A critical value of 226 RMB lies well below the rural poverty line of 302 Yuan RMB (in 1986 RMB) estimated by Ravallion and Chen (2004), and we may conclude that the number of individuals living in poverty has declined even as the living standards of the very poor may have worsened.[25]

8.4.1.3 Welfare comparisons using Generalized Lorenz curves

A second representation of welfare that incorporates inequality is captured by the Generalized Lorenz curves shown in Figure 8.6. The Lorenz curves from Figure 8.4 are multiplied by average annual per capita income. A Lorenz curve illustrates the share of the pie going to lower income percentiles, while the generalized Lorenz curve adjusts for the size of the pie.[26] In Panel A we

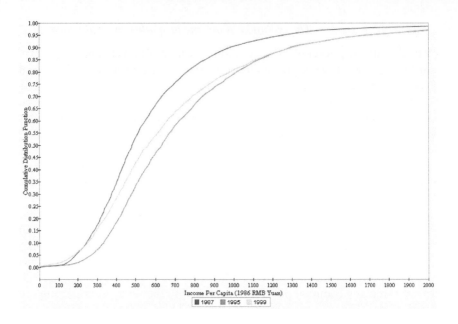

Panel A: The full picture

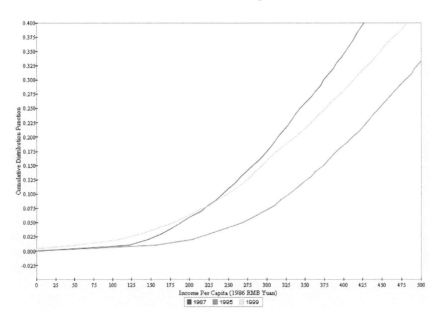

Panel B: The bottom 40 percent (from Panel A)

Figure 8.5 The CDF of per capita household income, selected years.

Notes: This figure shows the Cumulative Distribution Function (CDF) for the distribution of real household per capita income for selected years, using the RCRE survey data. The top panel shows the entire curves, while the bottom panel "magnifies" the curves, focusing on the poorest 40 percent of households. The critical poverty line when comparing the 1999 and 1987 distributions is 226 RMB/capita with a standard error of 36.3. These figures and significance of critical poverty lines were calculated using DAD (Duclos et al. 2004).

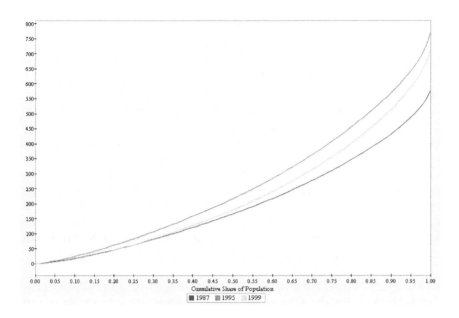

Panel A: The full picture

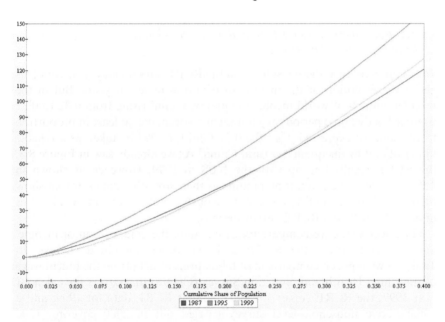

Panel B: The bottom 40 percent (based on Panel A)

Figure 8.6 Generalized Lorenz curves of per capita household income, selected years.

Notes: This figure shows Generalized Lorenz curves for distribution of real household per capita income for selected years, using the RCRE survey data. The top panel shows the entire curves, while the bottom panel "magnifies" the curves, focusing on the poorest 40 percent of households. Tests of statistical difference between the curves are shown in Appendix IV, Table 8A.4.

see that the curve for 1995 lies strictly above the other years, indicating that the distribution from 1995 Generalized Lorenz (second-order stochastic) dominates those from 1987 and 1999. At the top end of the distribution, the 1999 distribution is second best, as richer households are better off than those from 1987. What is most striking, however, is the plight of the bottom quarter of the income distribution. The Generalized Lorenz Curves cross around 0.23, suggesting that the lower 23 percent were actually worse off in 1999 than in 1987. The difference in Generalized Lorenz Curves is only statistically significant for the bottom 5 percent of the population, however, suggesting that deterioration in living standards is only significant for the very poor.[27] On the other hand, the 1999 Generalized Lorenz curve is unambiguously above the 1987 curve for only the upper 50 percent of the distribution. These results then are consistent with the bottom half being no better off, and the poorest five percent of households being worse off, after 12 years of economic growth.

Finally, the bottom panel of Table 8.2 shows the matching results for consumption. As with the Gini's and mean incomes, the picture based on household per capita consumption is essentially the same as the one based on income.

8.4.1.4 Robustness of results to sampling and data issues: evidence from other data sources

Taken on their own, these results from the RCRE surveys may raise concerns about the evolution of the income distribution in recent years. But in the broader context of world income inequality, a Gini rising from 0.32 to 0.37 over such a dynamic period may not seem so dramatic, at least in proportion to the concern expressed. Can the 0.37 Gini for 1999 be taken as a reliable upper bound for inequality in rural China? As we already saw in Figure 8.3, the RCRE results line up with the NBS in 1999. However, as shown in Table 8.3, this conclusion is premature, as there are other data sets that show higher levels of inequality, and simultaneously point to potential weaknesses in both the NBS and RCRE survey designs.

For select years, we compare mean incomes, the composition of income, and inequality using the RCRE and two other household surveys. In Table 8.3 we report a comparison of tabulations of data from the fourth wave of the China Health and Nutrition Survey (CHNS) that covers the calendar year 1997; the RCRE survey for 1997; similar RCRE data for 1999; and a collaborative household-level survey carried out in 2000 covering 1200 households in 6 provinces (the CCAP 2000 survey).[28] We break income down into that from farming, farm sidelines (forestry, livestock, and fisheries), wage income, family-run businesses, and a residual category, "other," which is largely comprised of private and public transfers. We report total per capita income, per capita income by source, and the percentage of households in each of the surveys that report non-zero income from each source. For the

Table 8.3 Comparison of surveys: levels of income and inequality

Survey:	CHNS		RCRE				CCAP			
	1997		1997		1999		2000a		2000b	
	Mean	% not 0	Mean	% not 0	Mean	% not 0	Mean	% not 0	Mean	% not 0
Income, by source:										
Agriculture	816	78.7	624	96.1	507	94.8	606	90.4	607	90.9
Livestock	92	50.0	212	77.8	182	75.2	211	75.2	211	76.4
Wages	764	37.3	748	64.9	851	68.0	892	62.4	893	62.5
Other	386	51.8	148	86.0	150	80.3	155	52.6	155	34.0
Family Business	418	21.9	522	54.5	494	50.1	796	29.7	534	28.2
Total Income	2,477	97.9	2,255	100.0	2,184	99.9	2,667		2,370	
Inequality: Gini	0.43		0.36		0.37		0.50		0.44	

Notes: This table compares levels, composition, and inequality of per capita income for three data sets (surveys) at similar (though not identical) points in time. All reported values are in nominal (undeflated) terms. For each data set, we report mean values of per capita income by source, as well as the percentage of households with non-zero observations ("% not 0"). The three primary data sets are China Health and Nutrition Survey (CHNS) for 1997; (2) The RCRE for 1997 and 1999; and the Chinese Centre for Agricultural Policy (CCAP) survey for 2000. Results from the CCAP survey are shown for 2000a, a data set that includes all households with positive income, and for 2000b, based on the same sample, but excluding the top one percent of per capita income households. Further details are available in the Data Appendix.

CCAP 2000 survey we report two tabulations: (1) based on the full sample; and (2) based on the full sample, but dropping the top one percent of households (in terms of per capita income). The second tabulation is performed in order to address the possibility that the NBS and RCRE surveys may be under sampling higher income households in rural areas. One caveat to our comparisons is that there is only limited overlap across the surveys in terms of the provinces sampled. As we saw in Figure 8.1, the RCRE provinces are not peculiar compared to national averages, but there will still be limits to comparability of the other surveys. First note the comparison of the RCRE with the CHNS for 1997. The structure of income (mean incomes by source) is similar in the two surveys, with slightly higher (by less than 10 percent) income in the CHNS. To some extent, this reflects a slightly higher fraction of suburban households in the CHNS rural sample (notice the slightly smaller proportion of farmers in the CHNS). Most notable, however, is the higher level of inequality reflected in the CHNS, with a Gini of 0.43.

The most striking gap is between the 1999 RCRE and the CCAP for 2000, with average incomes higher by 22 percent in the CCAP survey. Rural income growth was relatively flat between 1999 and 2000, so the difference cannot be attributed to economic growth.[29] Moreover, the rural CPI was falling over this period, and so the differences in real income are even slightly more pronounced than the nominal figures that we report. Much higher reported income from family run businesses in the CCAP 2000 data appears to be the source of most of the difference. Mean per capita income from family businesses was 796 in the 2000 survey, but only 494 for the 1999 RCRE. This difference represents 62.5 percent of the gap in mean incomes between the two surveys.

A comparison of inequality measures based on these surveys reveals an even more substantial difference in the two surveys, with the CCAP survey suggesting a Gini of 0.50, which is much higher than that for the RCRE (or other surveys). But a comparison with a slightly "trimmed" version of the CCAP 2000 survey identifies the likely source of the problem. Official surveys often exclude the richest households who often earn substantial incomes from family-run businesses.[30]

The most revealing comparison is made between the trimmed and untrimmed versions of the CCAP sample. Dropping the top one percent of households lowers mean household per capita income from 2667 to 2370, or eleven percent, and bringing it closer in line with the RCRE and CHNS estimates. Incomes by source also line up very well between the RCRE and CCAP trimmed samples. Almost all of the drop in mean incomes, and resulting improvement in correspondence of the surveys, comes from the decline in average incomes from family-run businesses. The Gini coefficient also falls considerably, from 0.50 to 0.44, more in line with the inequality reflected in the CHNS. If we drop the top three percent, the Gini falls slightly more, to 0.42.

This exercise highlights several important points. First, measured inequality in rural China is sensitive to the top tail of the income distribution. To the extent that the RCRE (or NBS) surveys miss the very richest households (possibly because they are not "representative") overall inequality will be understated.[31] Second, poor measurement of family-run business income alone can lead to a significant misrepresentation of the level of inequality. The CHNS and CCAP surveys thus suggest that NBS and RCRE-based estimates of the level of inequality are too low (possibly by as much as 0.10 Gini points). To the extent that family-run businesses have been increasing in importance over the reform period, the RCRE and NBS likely understate the upward trend in inequality. The results in Table 8.2 and Figure 8.3 probably provide a lower bound of the extent to which inequality has risen. Combined with the results from RCRE for roughly the lower 90 percent of the income distribution, we are confident in concluding that there has been some stagnation of rural welfare, and perhaps erosion, over the latter half of the 1990s.

8.4.2 Decompositions by geography

The role of widening regional income differences and their contribution to increasing inequality is a common theme in the literature on inequality in China.[32] Rising disparities between localities, especially provinces (inland versus coastal, for example), are often seen as the most important source of the rising income differences, as some provinces are better situated to take advantage of market liberalization and new off-farm opportunities. At the outset of the reforms, spatial differences may have also been present due to differences in per capita land endowments, access to urban markets, and the level of development of commune and brigade-run enterprises. With decline in importance of restrictions on migration created by China's residential registration system (the *hukou* system) and opening up of markets for migrant labor, however, we expect a decline in the importance of region in overall inequality. Our sample, which includes the rapidly growing coastal provinces of Guangdong and Jiangsu and slower growth interior provinces of Sichuan and Gansu, seems reasonably well suited to look for these differences and their trends.

There are a number of approaches one can take in decomposing inequality across regions. Unfortunately, the Gini coefficient is not readily (or neatly) decomposed. Gustaffson and Li (2002) report spatial decompositions for the decomposable Mean Log Difference and Theil inequality indices. We adopt a simpler strategy, decomposing the variance of log income inequality index. This entails estimating the following regression:

$$\ln y_i = D_L' \gamma + u_i \tag{1}$$

where D_L is a vector of dummy variables indicating the location of individual i.[33] The R-squared from this regression indicates the proportion of the variation (or variance) of $\ln y_i$ that is explained by the location dummies. The remainder is the (within-location) residual variance of log income, and a measure of the degree to which household income cannot be explained by the average income of its neighbors.

Table 8.4 reports the results of this exercise for income and consumption per capita with location defined at three levels of aggregation. We estimate the equation above separately using region, province and village-level dummies, and also distinguish between spatially deflated and undeflated household income and consumption per capita.[34] For comparability, we also report the results from decomposing the Theil by region.

In the first row of Panel A in Table 8.4, we see the proportion of inequality as measured by the variance of log income explained by "region" declined from 0.19 in 1987 to 0.15 in 1995, and to 0.12 in 1999. Using the Theil, the results are very similar. There are limits to comparability, but we also discuss our results in light of Gustaffson and Li's. Their results for the proportion of Mean Log Difference (MLD) (which is similar to the variance of logs) explained by region are 0.12 for 1987, and 0.27 in 1995. Our results thus differ in both level and trend. Some of this difference may be driven by differences in measurement of income.[35] Sampling might also be an issue. The provinces used in the two studies are not the same, however, the regions are similarly defined. More significantly, the RCRE subsample is comprised of a panel of counties (82 of the 103 villages in the subsample in 1999 had been in the sample since 1987), while the data used by Gustafsson and Li are drawn from a different set of counties in the two periods. This introduces a dimension of non-comparability across time-periods for studies based on the Khan and Riskin subsample of NBS data, the potential bias of which is difficult to assess *ex-ante*.

Turning to province-level results, the difference in patterns between studies is also apparent, though less pronounced. Here, we find the proportion of income inequality explained by province declined from 0.24 to 0.18 between 1987 and 1995, and further to 0.15 by 1999. By contrast, Gustafsson and Li start out with a similar proportion explained by province in 1987 (0.24), but their proportion rises to 0.32 by 1995.

In Figure 8.7, we explore possible differences between the RCRE and NBS household surveys (the basis of the samples used by Gustafsson and Li). Our objective is to compare the amount of province-level inequality present in the two data sets. For the RCRE, we calculate overall Gini-coefficients assuming everyone in a province earns the same income (provincial mean income). The national Gini is constructed on the basis of these inter-provincial income differences (weighted by rural population). For the NBS, we use provincial mean incomes from Statistical Yearbooks of China to calculate similar national Gini coefficients, weighting mean incomes by provincial rural population, and effectively attributing everyone in a province the same income. This procedure sets within-province inequality to zero, and calculates the implied Gini arising from differences in provincial mean incomes alone. The basic pattern in Figure 8.7 is similar to the one we saw in Figure 8.2: the

Table 8.4 Contribution of location to income and consumption inequality RCRE, selected years

	1987	1991	1995	1999
Contribution to Variance				
Dependent variable: ln (Income Per Capita)				
without spatial deflator				
Contribution of region	0.186	0.162	0.154	0.120
Contribution of province	0.237	0.218	0.183	0.153
Contribution of village	0.500	0.466	0.413	0.424
with spatial deflator				
Contribution of region	0.069	0.063	0.062	0.047
Contribution of province	0.133	0.105	0.085	0.077
Contribution of village	0.431	0.389	0.344	0.373
Dependent variable: ln (Consumption Per Capita)				
without spatial deflator				
Contribution of region	0.190	0.184	0.162	0.181
Contribution of province	0.278	0.246	0.189	0.231
Contribution of village	0.560	0.529	0.507	0.525
with spatial deflator				
Contribution of region	0.051	0.063	0.064	0.085
Contribution of province	0.137	0.102	0.083	0.117
Contribution of village	0.474	0.439	0.442	0.454
Contribution to Theil-T Index				
Dependent Variable: Income Per Capita				
Without Spatial Deflator				
Contribution of region	0.043	0.054	0.048	0.069
Contribution of province	0.163	0.122	0.085	0.122
Contribution of village	0.490	0.452	0.441	0.456
With spatial deflator				
Contribution of region	0.080	0.090	0.063	0.065
Contribution of province	0.114	0.126	0.078	0.092
Contribution of village	0.398	0.402	0.374	0.401
Dependent Variable: Consumption Per Capita				
without spatial deflator				
Contribution of region	0.218	0.220	0.182	0.186
Contribution of province	0.283	0.273	0.213	0.241
Contribution of village	0.539	0.539	0.507	0.508
with spatial deflator				
Contribution of region	0.047	0.068	0.055	0.062
Contribution of province	0.137	0.114	0.080	0.106
Contribution of village	0.446	0.433	0.424	0.419

Notes: This table shows the fraction of variation of real log per capita income (and consumption) attributed to location. This is simply the R-squared from a regression of log per capita income on a set of location dummies. The decompositions are reported with or without the income variable spatially deflated. The effect of location is reported at three levels of aggregation: (1) the village (103 villages); (2) Province (nine provinces, as described in the Data Appendix); and (3) Region, defined as West (Gansu, Shanxi, and Sichuan), Central (Anhui, Henan, and Hunan) and East (Guangdong, Jiangsu, and Jilin).

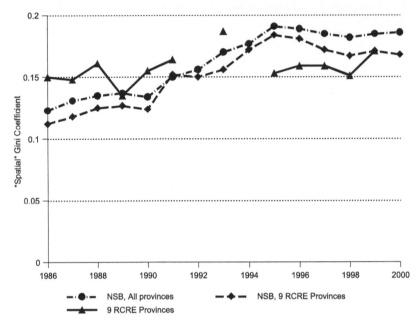

Figure 8.7 Comparing inter-provincial inequality in the RCRE and NBS surveys.

Note: This figure compares the amount of implied inter-provincial inequality in the RCRE and NBS surveys. Inter-provincial inequality is calculated on the basis of attributing everyone in a given province with the mean per capita income, and calculating the implied Gini with provincial population weights. This "simulation" exercise is conducted for all provinces in China using NBS-reported mean provincial incomes; for the subset of provinces covered by the RCRE sample (but using NBS mean incomes); and for the RCRE sample.

level of inequality is almost the same in the two surveys, but the slope is slightly steeper in the NBS. The NBS shows an especially steep increase in spatial inequality between 1988 and 1995 (Gustafsson and Li's sample years), compared to the RCRE. Both series show a significant flattening of this trend since 1995, with the NBS showing actual declines in spatial inequality from the mid-1990s to 2000. In Figure 8.7, we also note that the RCRE subset of provinces had a slightly lower level of spatial inequality than the full national sample, but not enough to render the RCRE provinces unrepresentative. In summary, while there is disagreement about the initial level of spatial inequality (as we saw in Figure 8.2) and the size of the increase up through 1995, the two data sources essentially agree on the magnitude of spatial inequality, and especially the relative decline since the mid 1990s.

Returning to the RCRE data source, our results suggest that the role of provincial rural income differences has declined over time. Another way to illustrate this point is to look at the behavior of provincial mean incomes and within-province inequality. In Figure 8.8 we plot average provincial growth rates against the initial (1987) level of income. There is no obvious pattern

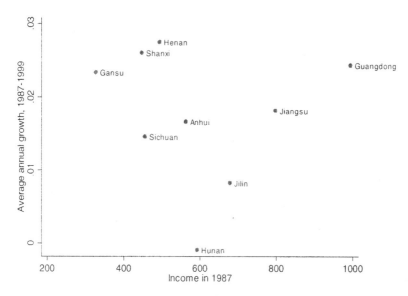

Figure 8.8 Growth in per capita income by initial per capita income, RCRE provinces.

Notes: This figure arrays average annual growth rates for incomes by province (based on RCRE data) by "initial income," that is, mean provincial income in 1987.

here, and results are sensitive to a single observation, notably Guangdong. Excluding Guangdong, this figure suggests some degree of income convergence, with poorer provinces growing more rapidly over the 1987–1999 period. This is consistent with a narrowing of inter-provincial inequality. But of course, we cannot just exclude Guangdong in painting the complete picture. Nonetheless, Figure 8.8 provides no evidence that provincial income levels were diverging.

In Figure 8.9 we plot within-province Gini's from 1999 against the provincial Gini for 1987. We also show a 45-degree line in order to benchmark the inequality levels in the two years. Here we see that inequality rose in all provinces except Gansu, and in Jilin rose to over 0.40. Again, this is consistent with the decompositions that show that within-province inequality became more important between 1987 and 1999. Furthermore, excluding Jilin, we see that the plot suggests provinces with lower inequality in 1987 had higher increases of inequality to 1999, implying convergence of Gini's across provinces.

Next, in the third row of Table 8.4 we show the fraction of inequality explained by village. Here, we see the proportion fall from approximately 0.50 in 1987 to 0.40 in 1999: Most of the inequality in our sample occurs within, as opposed to across villages.[36] An obvious question is whether 0.50 represents a half-full or empty glass, in terms of the role played by geography. Nothing in

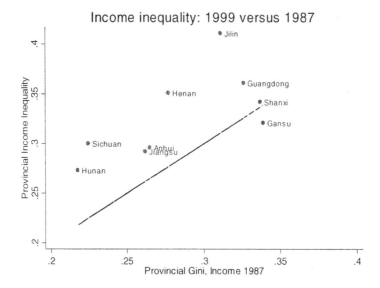

Figure 8.9 Changes in provincial inequality, 1987 to 1999.

Notes: This figure plots the provincial Gini for per capita income in 1999 (calculated with the RCRE data) versus the provincial Gini for 1987. The 45-degree line serves as a reference, whereby points lying above the 45-degree line correspond to increases in provincial inequality between 1987 and 1999.

our conclusions diminishes the fact that location is an important (perhaps the single most important) determinant of household income. Furthermore, even a diminution of the role played by village is consistent with persistence of low incomes within and across villages, such as one would expect with geographic poverty traps as identified by Jalan and Ravallion (2002). Instead, we view our results as pointing to the significant role played by within-village differences in incomes as a contributing factor in overall inequality, and correspondingly draw attention to those factors that generate inequality within villages.

Finally, in Table 8.4 we evaluate the impact of spatial deflation on the decompositions. Accounting for inter-provincial price differences cuts the share explained by province or region in half. This suggests that the inter-provincial income gaps overstate the differences in the standards of living across provinces, however, the absolute bias is declining over time. Spatial deflation has a much smaller effect on the role of village in the decompositions, but this is to be expected since the spatial deflator uses provincial level prices. Nonetheless, by 1999, between village differences accounting for spatial price differences are the source of only about a third of overall inequality.

In Figures 8.10, 8.11, and 8.12 we explore the evolution of village-level

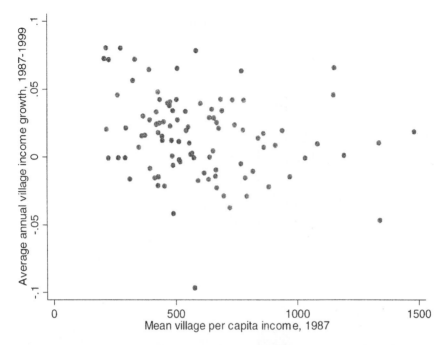

Figure 8.10 Within-village growth versus initial village income.

Notes: This figure arrays average annual growth rates for incomes by village (based on RCRE data) by "initial income," that is, mean village income in 1987. The points in this figure can be used to estimate a "convergence" regression. Such a regression yields Growth = 0.14–0.02 lnY87 (t=2.9).

inequality. First, in Figure 8.10 we show that there is evidence of convergence of income levels across villages (poorer villages tended to grow more rapidly between 1987 and 1999). All else equal, this convergence reduces the role of village in explaining inequality (as we saw in Table 8.4). Figure 8.11 shows histograms for the village-level Gini's, clearly showing the shift upwards of within-village inequality. This shift is also readily apparent in Figure 8.12, where we see that a majority of villages experienced increases of their income Ginis, with a considerable fraction experiencing increases over 0.10, though village sample sizes are small enough to warrant a caution on placing too much stock on a single Gini. As with the provincial-level inequality measures, it appears that there is convergence of inequality levels, whereby low-inequality villages experienced greater increases in inequality.

The broad conclusion from the spatial income-inequality decompositions is that (1) no more than half (and probably less) of total inequality is driven by income differences between villages, and (2) the role of geography has remained relatively constant, and likely declined in recent years. There is little evidence to suggest that widening spatial differentials account for a

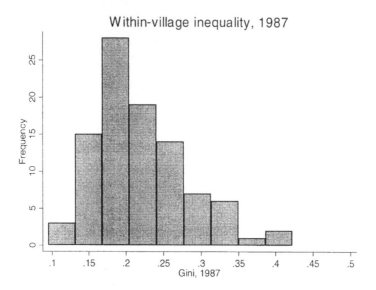

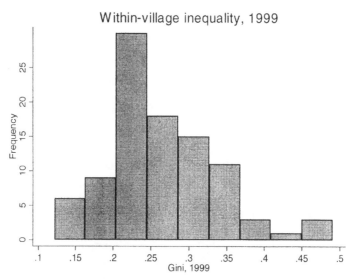

Figure 8.11 Evolution of within-village income inequality.

Notes: These histograms report the frequency of various magnitudes of village-level Gini coefficients, for 1987 and 1999.

disproportionate share of the increase in rural inequality. In terms of understanding the sources of inequality, this should serve to turn more attention towards local village and township institutions related to governance and investment in public goods, and local variation in the distribution of endowments (like skills, education, and land) and their returns.

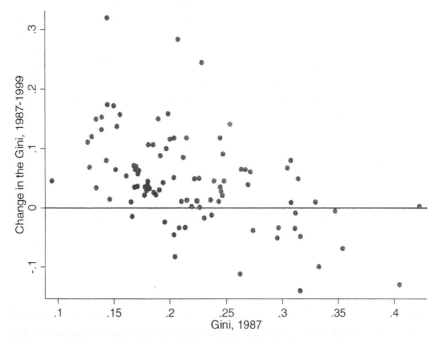

Figure 8.12 Changes in village inequality versus initial inequality.

Notes: This figure plots the changes in village-level inequality between 1987 and 1999 (based on the village-level Gini) versus the initial level of inequality (the Gini in 1987). This figure illustrates "convergence" of inequality levels across villages.

8.4.3 Decompositions by source

Why has inequality gone up within villages? Answering this question requires an understanding of the evolution of institutions across villages that map household endowments into family income, and is a significant research enterprise in itself. Our more limited objective here is to sketch some of the correlates of within-village inequality, particularly those related to the composition of household income. Previous studies have emphasized the role of non-farm income in contributing to rising inequality.[37] We can use the RCRE data to confirm the role of non-farm income, to evaluate finer details of the composition of subcomponents of non-farm income, and most importantly, to gauge trends in the role played by income composition in explaining increases in overall inequality.

The key tools in our analysis are descriptive statistics of the structure of income, and Shorrocks (1982, 1983) decompositions. The Shorrocks decomposition tells us the proportion of total inequality that can be attributed to inequality of income source k. It is a purely descriptive tool, and there are limits to the extent that one can attribute a causal interpretation to the co-efficients. For example, it is difficult to use the results to simulate the impact of an increase in the inequality of a particular income source on total inequality, without further specifying the nature of the increase in inequality of that income source. However, as we shall see, even within the limits of interpretation the decompositions are illuminating.

As an outline of the procedure, consider a decomposition of the mean of household income, based on household i's income, y_i:

$$y_i = \sum_{k=1}^{k} y_{ik} \tag{2}$$

which is the sum of K subcomponents of income y_{ik}. Clearly, mean household income can be written:

$$\bar{Y} = \bar{Y}_1 + \bar{Y}_2 + \ldots + \bar{Y}_k \tag{3}$$

A one-percent increase in mean income from source k will lead to a W_k proportionate increase in $\bar{Y}$, where W_k is the share of income from source k. Decomposition of the sources of mean income is thus straightforward, and decomposition of inequality is designed analogously. We wish to estimate S_k, the proportion of inequality attributable to the inequality of income source k:

$$I(Y) = \sum_{k=1}^{k} S_k I(Y_k) \tag{4}$$

where $I(Y)$ is the index of inequality for total income Y, and $I(Y_k)$ is the index of inequality for income source k. Shorrocks showed that for any additively decomposable measure of inequality, S_k is estimated by:

$$\hat{S}_k = \frac{\text{cov}(y_{ik}, y_i)}{\text{var}(y_i)} \tag{5}$$

So, S_k captures the degree to which income source k is correlated with total income. In this sense, it measures the degree to which particular income sources are earned by the rich or poor. If an income source is earned primarily by the rich, then the decomposition will attribute a larger share of total income inequality to inequality of income earned from that source. How can we interpret these S_k? One benchmark is zero: if an income source is negatively correlated with total income, then it is earned disproportionately by the poor, and no inequality (indeed a negative share) of total income is correlated with that income source. Presumably, marginal increases of inequality of that source of income (maintaining the same correlation with total income) would further reduce overall inequality. Very few sources of income will have negative S_k. Another helpful benchmark is the mean share of income from that source, or W_k. If $S_k > W_k$, then inequality of income source k contributes more to inequality than it does to mean income, $\bar{Y}$, which we denote as a disproportionate effect on inequality. In other words, if income from family businesses comprise 10 percent of average income, but 20 percent of inequality, we will conclude that family business income has a disproportionate effect on inequality.

As a matter of computation, $\hat{S}_k$ can be estimated by the following regression:

$$y_{ik} = \beta_{0k} + \beta_{1k}\, y_i + u_{ik} \tag{6}$$

as $\beta_{1k} = \hat{S}_k$. This regression presentation also aids in interpretation: all we are estimating is the correlation of a particular source of income y_{ik} with total income, y_i. Once we broaden our objective to the estimation of this correlation, we can also recognize the possible impact of measurement error: overestimates of income from a particular source will lead to an overstatement of the correlation with total income, and β_{1k} will be overstated. This overstatement for income source k will spill over to the other β_{1k}, leading to an underestimate of their contribution. One simple way to address this possibility is to estimate the regression by two-stage least squares, using another indicator for total income as an instrument for y_i. An obvious candidate is total household consumption, which should not suffer from the same type of measurement error as the y_{ik}. Aside from the instrumental variables interpretation, this procedure can be viewed as exploring the sensitivity of our conclusions concerning the correlation of income from a particular source with whether a household is rich or poor, to alternative definitions of rich and poor, based on income or consumption. As a final refinement on the Shorrocks procedure, we compare decompositions with and without village dummies. Inclusion of village dummies allows us to decompose within-village inequality, and to net out the possible effect of variation of income sources across villages, and this link to cross-village inequality.

We begin with a description of mean incomes by source, reported in Table 8.5. In 1987, agricultural income (crop income) comprised 40 percent of total income. The largest subcomponent was grain income, at 30 percent of total household income. Adding income from agricultural sidelines (fish, forestry, and especially livestock) raises the broadly defined share of agriculture to 53 percent, over half of family income. Family business, mostly in commerce and services, comprised 16 percent of income, while wage income was the second largest overall component, at 25 percent. Most wage income was earned locally, within the village.

Table 8.5 The composition of income in 1987 compared to 1999 (in 1986 RMB)

	1987			1999			Growth
	Mean	Share	% > 0	Mean	Share	% > 0	
Total Income	578	1.000	1.000	714	1.000	0.999	0.018
Agricultural Income	229	0.397	0.981	158	0.222	0.942	−0.031
Grain Income	175	0.303	0.978	113	0.158	0.926	−0.037
Cash Crop Income	46	0.080	0.812	30	0.042	0.564	−0.036
Fruits, Tea and Dates	8	0.014	0.248	15	0.022	0.257	0.056
Agricultural Sidelines	74	0.129	0.955	68	0.095	0.764	−0.007
Forest Products	17	0.029	0.333	10	0.014	0.185	−0.043
Livestock	54	0.093	0.950	50	0.069	0.746	−0.007
Aquaculture	4	0.007	0.125	8	0.012	0.058	0.062
Family Businesses	91	0.157	0.616	162	0.227	0.501	0.048
HH Industry	27	0.048	0.135	44	0.061	0.073	0.039
Construction	6	0.010	0.072	11	0.016	0.046	0.056
Transportation	17	0.030	0.065	26	0.037	0.076	0.036
Commerce, Service & Trade	25	0.042	0.126	57	0.079	0.172	0.070
Other Family Business Income	16	0.027	0.395	24	0.034	0.251	0.036
Wage Income	145	0.251	0.711	276	0.387	0.680	0.054
Local Wage Income	85	0.147	0.452	79	0.111	0.257	−0.006
Temporary Migrant	46	0.080	0.390	175	0.245	0.505	0.111
Local Gov't Employment	14	0.024	0.069	22	0.031	0.049	0.038
Family Transfers	29	0.050	0.525	34	0.048	0.495	0.016
Government Transfers	4	0.008	0.651	6	0.008	0.708	0.022
Other Income	5	0.009	0.138	8	0.012	0.110	0.040

Notes: This table compares the composition of income in 1987 to 1999. Real per capita income is shown for detailed subcategories of income, along with the share of income ("Share") accounted for, and the proportion of households with non-zero income from that source. The last column reports the implied annual growth rate of income for that source. Note that wage income is divided between "Local" wage income, and "Temporary Migrant." Temporary migrant employment includes both commuters returning home on weekends and longer-term temporary migrants, and in most cases involves employment outside of the township.

This structure of income changed dramatically by 1999. Most notable is the absolute decline in the amount of income from agriculture. Grain income alone dropped from 175 yuan in 1987 to 113 in 1999.[38] This 35 percent decline can be attributed primarily to the collapse in grain prices described earlier in the paper. Other sources of agricultural income – with the minor exception of income from fruit – declined to the extent that the overall share of farm income declined to 32 percent of total income, a drop of twenty percentage points from 1987. What is especially important to note is that the decline in this share is NOT due to merely increasing relative importance of non-farm income, but an absolute decline in levels of agricultural income. Moving down the column, we see improvements in income from family businesses, in absolute terms from 91 to 162 yuan, and from 16 to 23 percent as a share of total income. But the largest improvements in family income came from wage earnings, especially wages earned by temporary migrants. The wage earnings of temporary migrants include household members still resident in the village, but who commute outside the village to work and return on weekends, as well as wage earnings brought home by locally registered household members who work outside the village for a substantial portion of the year. The RCRE survey does not permit a further disaggregation. Clearly, however, locally earned wages have become less important in both relative and absolute terms, while employment opportunities outside the village and accessed through migration have become a more important source of labor earnings.

The Shorrocks decompositions are presented in Table 8.6. As a general summary, controls for location rarely matter, indicating that composition of income matters within-villages much the same way as across villages. Furthermore, the OLS and 2SLS estimates generally agree, at least in terms of broad conclusions, and we focus on 2SLS results in our discussion.

For 1987, we find that agricultural income, while disequalizing, contributed less to overall inequality than its share of total income (19 percent versus approximately 40 percent). The same applied to agricultural sidelines, so that only 21 percent of total inequality was attributed to inequality of agricultural income, even while this source accounted for 53 percent of total income. Non-farm family businesses contributed most to inequality compared to their share of income (27 percent compared to about 16 percent), followed by wage income (31.6 percent compared to 25.1 percent). Within the wage category, local wages were relatively disequalizing, while wages from employment outside the village were relatively equalizing.

The results for 1999 are significantly different, and even more different than the change in average composition would suggest. First note that inequality of agricultural income contributed only 3.5 percent of overall income inequality. Even adding livestock and other sidelines, the overall contribution of farming income to inequality was 6.3 percent. It would seem that to the extent that the machinery of redistribution (village-controlled land reallocations, for example) is directed towards minimizing inequality of farm income, it is misdirected. Inequality of non-farm family business income contributes more to inequality in 1999 than 1987, though this is not surprising given its increased importance as a source of income. Perhaps the most striking result of the decompositions is the large share – 47.5 percent, or almost half – of total inequality attributed to wage earnings. Local wage earnings, while they have declined in magnitude, are relatively unequally distributed, and disproportionately earned by higher income households. Inequality of wage earnings from temporary migrants outside the village

Table 8.6 Shorrocks decompositions RCRE, 1987 and 1999

	1987				1999			
	(1) Share	(2) OLS	(3) 2SLS	(4) 2SLS	(5) Share	(6) OLS	(7) 2SLS	(8) 2SLS
Village Dummies?	N/A	NO	NO	YES	N/A	NO	NO	YES
Agricultural Income	0.397	0.126	0.190*	0.171	0.222	0.045	0.035*	0.040
Grain Income	0.303	0.050	0.090*	0.099	0.158	0.002	0.004	0.021
Cash Crop Income	0.080	0.050	0.075*	0.061	0.042	0.026	0.022	0.008
Fruits, Tea and Dates	0.014	0.026	0.026	0.011	0.022	0.017	0.009*	0.011
Agricultural Sidelines	0.129	0.074	0.106*	0.104	0.095	0.061	0.028*	0.038
Forest Products	0.029	0.009	0.025*	0.033	0.014	-0.002	-0.006*	0.007
Livestock	0.093	0.047	0.062*	0.064	0.069	0.036	0.013*	0.019
Aquaculture	0.007	0.018	0.019	0.007	0.012	0.027	0.021	0.012
Family Businesses	0.157	0.345	0.232	0.268	0.227	0.438	0.391*	0.409
HH Industry	0.048	0.140	0.092*	0.115	0.061	0.213	0.169*	0.175
Construction	0.010	-0.004	0.000	-0.002	0.016	0.015	0.011	0.002
Transportation	0.030	0.077	0.027	0.020	0.037	0.062	0.031*	0.017
Commerce, Service & Trade	0.042	0.109	0.093	0.121	0.079	0.122	0.154*	0.203
Other Family Business Income	0.027	0.023	0.020	0.015	0.034	0.026	0.026	0.012
Wage Income	0.251	0.373	0.376	0.316	0.387	0.400	0.475*	0.401
Local Wage Income	0.147	0.298	0.310	0.270	0.111	0.150	0.204	0.170
Temporary Migrant	0.080	0.062	0.044	0.009	0.245	0.206	0.214	0.133
Local Gov't Employment	0.024	0.013	0.023*	0.037	0.031	0.045	0.057*	0.098
Family Transfers	0.050	0.076	0.090	0.122	0.048	0.043	0.056*	0.094
Government Transfers	0.008	0.000	0.000	0.008	0.008	0.002	0.004	0.009
Other Income	0.009	0.007	0.005*	0.010	0.012	0.011	0.010	0.009

Notes: The table shows Shorrocks decompositions, described in th text. Household per capita income by source is regressed on total per capita income. Columns 2 and 6 show OLS coefficients of income per capita, and columns 3 and 7 show the same coefficients, but with income per capita instrumented by consumption per capita, as a "control" for measurement error in income. Asterisks indicate where the OLS and 2SLS coefficients are significantly different (using a standard Hausman test) and thus that the 2SLS coefficients are to be preferred. Columns 4 and 8 show 2SLS results with village dummy variables added to control for the possible geographic differences of income composition. For reference, the share of income by source is reported (and is the same as in Table 8.5).

explains 21.4 percent of overall inequality, but this is actually lower than its share of total income. To this extent, access to these wage opportunities is relatively equalizing. Note also that this is one example where controls for village dummies make some difference, as the within-village contribution (13.3 percent) is less than the total contribution, reflecting spatially uneven development of labor markets for temporary migrants.

Taken together, these decompositions highlight two important sources of inequality, especially when we compare 1999 to 1987. First is the sharp decline of the relatively equalizing source of income from farming. Second is the relative increase in disequalizing income from non-farm family businesses, and the failure of non-farm labor markets to provide income opportunities for low income households that offset the collapse of agricultural income. Past emphasis on the role of non-farm income as a source of inequality was only partially correct: these results suggest that given the recent trajectory of farm income, efforts to improve the rural distribution of income should be placed on improving access to non-agricultural employment for low income households. Increasing agricultural incomes – at least in an equalizing way – are unlikely to improve overall income distribution, if for no other reason than agricultural incomes are only weakly associated with overall income, and they are also very low.

8.5 Discussion and conclusions

There is certainly a risk of over-simplification in attempting to summarize our key findings. After all, the core underlying data are based on household surveys with about 8000 observations per year for twelve years, and such measures as the Gini coefficient are summaries themselves that obscure the complexities of income distributions. That said, our analysis points to an uneven, but long-run increase in inequality in rural China, and our estimates may actually underestimate the magnitude of the increase. Especially worrisome is the deterioration in performance in the last half of the 1990s, which left as much as half of the population not much better off in 1999 than twelve years earlier, and the bottom 5 percent worse off.

The most obvious next question is why this deterioration has occurred: have economic reforms failed? Have market reforms created an economy that disproportionately rewards winners and heavily penalizes losers? Our results provide preliminary answers to these questions. First, we rule out geography as the most important factor for understanding the dispersion of incomes: at any point in time, more than half (and as much as two-thirds) of inequality is due to inequality between neighbors within a village, not differences in income between rich and poor villages. Furthermore, we find that the importance of spatial income differences at the regional, provincial and village level is declining over time. If most inequality is within-villages, then this should turn our attention to determinants of within-village inequality, such as village-level institutions, market development, and the distribution of household endowments. An important avenue for future research is to document the joint evolution of village incomes and the distribution of village income, including a careful assessment of causal linkages between village growth and inequality, as well as other correlates of village-level growth and inequality. For example, very little is known about the role of education and the potential interaction of human capital with market development and access to non-farm opportunities.[39] Efforts to design appropriate social safety nets and to improve local tax policy in rural areas need to be informed by a better understanding of the ways in which local institutions and markets influence prospects for reductions in poverty and inequality, and improve the growth prospects of the local economy.

Second (like previous researchers), we confirm that non-agricultural incomes are an important source of inequality. Indeed, to the extent that studies use NBS-like data (including the RCRE), both the level and trend of this source of inequality may be understated. But it would be a mistake to conclude that runaway income growth in non-farm income drives the winner-loser divergence in rural areas. Certainly, inequality driven by households at the very top of the income distribution is associated with lucrative family businesses. However, access to non-agricultural employment – possibly in other people's family businesses, and in particular, employment outside the home county and accessed through migration – seems to be relatively equalizing. Rising inequality and falling incomes at the lower end of the distribution are driven by inability of poorer households to earn income from non-agricultural sources.

This conclusion is emphasized by our third key finding that the failure for living standards to improve since 1995 for as much as half of the rural population in our sample is driven by falling agricultural incomes. Given that output has not generally fallen, most of the decline in incomes can be attributed to sharply falling crop prices. An important area of future research thus concerns the determinants of farm prices. Are the low prices in the last half of the 1990s a transitory shock, reflecting temporary global market conditions? This may be the case, as crop prices have shown some recovery beginning in 2003. Or are they low more permanently, because improvements in farm productivity and entry into WTO have changed the terms of trade between agricultural and non-agricultural goods within China? If crop prices are likely to be low (though possibly fluctuating) in the near future, then this raises a number of difficult policy questions. Almost all rural income-support policies are based on guaranteeing households access to land on an approximately per capita basis, through village land allocation. While this provides households a means to feed themselves, when crop-prices are low (absolutely, and relative to non-agricultural prices), the real value of this income support is quite low. Whatever the possible merits of this in-kind transfer for minimizing poverty, it has obvious limitations as a redistribution mechanism. With low returns in agriculture, a land policy that attempts to equalize farm incomes will have only a weak impact on overall inequality, given the small and declining share of income earned in agriculture.

Finally, our results show that before the big picture can be fully understood, there are a number of critical data and measurement issues to be confronted. An important starting point would be improved access to NBS household survey data, so that richer cross-time and cross-space comparisons can be made. Although our results on the stagnation of income growth and poverty reduction in the late 1990s are broadly consistent with the NBS-based findings of Ravallion and Chen (2004), significant differences in results from the two studies remain. Unfortunately, lack of access of researchers to the NBS data makes it difficult to understand all of the factors underlying these differences (e.g. sampling issues or in-kind income valuation). As good as the RCRE data are, it would be helpful to broaden participation in the evaluation of poverty and inequality policy by opening up the NBS to more users. In addition, our comparison with other surveys shows the importance of measuring income from family businesses in understanding overall inequality, especially at the top end of the distribution. Combined with insights from other (more comprehensive) studies, a richer set of questions should be included in the NBS surveys to track this important source of income.[40] Even with their current limitations, however, results based on the RCRE survey should raise some alarm at the fate of the poor in rural China, both for their own sake, as well as for the sustainability of future reforms.

8.A Appendices

Appendix 8A.I: Data

8A.I.1 RCRE village locations: Province and region

The data for the analyses of this paper come from nine provinces of the Research Center for Rural Economy (RCRE) village and household surveys. Basic information on sampling within province and region is provided in Table 8A.1. We follow the literature in grouping provinces into regions. On average, RCRE surveyed households in 30 villages in both the western and the eastern region, and 45 villages of the central region. Management of the survey was delegated to provincial offices, which made decisions regarding within-province sampling rates. In each province, equal numbers of poor, medium and rich counties were selected, from each of which a village of average socioeconomic status was surveyed. At the village level, between 10 and 20 percent of households, or roughly 30–130 households, were then randomly selected.[41]

Table 8A.1 Basic statistics on sample by province and region

Region/Province	Year						
	1987	1989	1991	1993	1995	1997	1999
Western Region							
Number of Villages	32	34	34	34	31	30	30
Avg HHs/Village	424.2	452.6	525.0	471.2	493.5	503.4	508.9
Avg Sampled HHs/Village	56.1	56.4	55.7	53.0	55.7	55.3	55.1
Central Region							
Number of Villages	48	48	49	44	44	44	44
Avg HHs/Village	313.4	332.0	353.2	367.0	405.3	408.2	403.6
Avg Sampled HHs/Village	72.2	72.1	72.5	63.3	63.7	63.9	63.4
Eastern Region							
Number of Villages	31	30	30	29	26	31	29
Avg HHs/Village	455.7	451.9	475.7	508.0	457.3	461.1	503.4
Avg Sampled HHs/Village	87.6	80.6	82.1	72.7	74.8	70.8	75.2
Overall Total							
Number of Villages	111	112	113	107	101	105	103
Avg HHs/Village	385.1	400.7	437.4	438.3	445.7	451.0	462.0
Avg Sampled HHs/Village	71.9	69.6	70.0	62.5	64.1	63.5	64.2

Note: Province-by-province annual information on attrition are available by request.

8A.1.2 Attrition of households and villages from the RCRE surveys

RCRE first fully implemented the national survey in 1986, doubling the number of villages in 1987. Since then, there has been relatively little change in the number of sampled villages. Attrition of villages from the survey has occurred, however, primarily for two reasons. First, RCRE's mandate is to use the survey to study agricultural production and factors influencing changes in agricultural productivity. Over the period from 1986 to 1999 four villages in Jiangsu and two in Guangdong were dropped and replaced because they were no longer engaged in agricultural activities. Second, attrition has also occurred as a result of disagreements between county or village leaders and provincial administrators of the survey. Of the 103 villages in the survey at the end of 1999, 82 have been in the survey since 1987. A significant share of village attrition occurred during gaps when the survey was not conducted in 1992 and 1994. Much less change in villages (and households) occurred during the periods without gaps from 1987 to 1991 and 1995 to 1999, for which 98 and 97 villages, respectively, were in the sample for all five years. In principle, dropped villages were to be replaced by a representative village in the same county.

Attrition has also occurred at the household-level (a detailed table is available upon request), and averages roughly five percent per year. Considerably more attrition came during the two-year gaps, and is largely associated with the loss of entire villages. Our estimate of attrition is also conservatively high. Households with the same household identifier in two successive years, but with significant differences in demographic structure, characteristics of housing or economic activities, were treated as separate households. In these cases, we treat the year t household as a new observation and consider the year $t-1$ household to have dropped from the sample. For the entire period between 1987–1999, we have a full panel of 4352 households. For the two subperiods, namely, 1987–1991 and 1995–1999, panel size is 6691 and 5796 households, respectively.

8A.I.3   The sample used in our analyses

In the sample used in our analyses, we trim extreme outliers from the dataset because we suspect coding errors or errors in which fixed investment is inappropriately coded as an operating cost in the household budget. To identify potential outliers, we first calculate median income and consumption per capita in each village for each year. We then drop households if the absolute value of the difference between household reported income per capita and village median income per capita for the year is greater than five times village median income. We apply the same criteria to household consumption per capita. In each year, less than one tenth of one percent of households were dropped under these criteria; altogether, 382 observations were dropped over the 1987–1999 period.

Our "Full trimmed" sample is thus this trimmed household sample, with all available observations, including panel, attritted, and replacement households. We also performed the analysis with the panel households only ("Trimmed Panel"), which would be most sensitive to possible biases introduced by attrition, and our results did not differ significantly.

8A.I.4   How representative is the RCRE household survey?

The subsample of the RCRE household survey covers between seven and eight thousand households across 100 villages in nine provinces. Given that the Ministry of Agriculture, which is presumably interested in agricultural production, carries out the survey, one might worry that agricultural households are over sampled and that this might lead to considerable bias. In order to consider this potential source of bias, we compare publicly available information from abstracts of the 1990 Population Census and the 1996 Agricultural Census with RCRE data in Table 8A.2. With respect to comparisons with the Population Census in 1990, there are no indices that are directly comparable for 1990 with either the RCRE or NBS rural household surveys. RCRE was not yet asking individual laborers to identify their primary activity. The Population Census for 1990 reports that of the population living in rural counties and holding rural registration, 92 percent reported agriculture as their primary activity. Yet this is not directly comparable to the

Table 8A.2 Comparison of RCRE nine-province sample to census information and NBS rural household survey

A. 1990 Population Census, 1990 RCRE Household Survey, 1990 NBS Rural Household Survey

	1990 Population Census (Rural Counties)	*1990 Population Census (Nine RCRE Provinces)*	*1990 Nine Province RCRE Sample*	*1990 Rural Household Survey*
Share of Households that . . .				
Specialize in Agriculture[1]	–	–	0.640	–
Specialize in Non-Agricultural Activities[2]	–	–	0.135	–
Have Positive Income from Agriculture	–	–	0.960	–
Share of Rural Registered Laborers with . . .				
Agriculture as main activity[3]	0.920	–	–	–
Non-Agriculture as main activity[3]	0.080	–	–	–
Average Household Size[4]	3.99	4.00	4.93	4.84
Average Laborers Per Household	–	–	2.85	2.92

1 Defined here as more than 50 percent of working days in agriculture.
2 Defined here as less than 20 percent of household working days in agriculture.
3 Information on main activities comes from 1990 Population Census (NBS 1993) summary tables on activities of rural registered residents from rural counties.
4 Note that in the census household size and labor force information can be broken down by rural counties, but individuals living in the (urban) county seat and county towns are grouped together with rural households, so these averages are not perfectly comparable with the RCRE household survey and NBS rural household survey.

B. 1996 Agricultural Census, 1996 RCRE Household Survey, 1996 NBS Rural Household Survey

	1996 National Agricultural Census	*1996 Agricultural Census (Nine RCRE Provinces)*	*1996 RCRE Nine Province Survey*	*1996 NBS Rural Household Survey*
Share of Households that . . .				
are Purely Agricultural	0.593	0.574	0.538	–
are Purely Non-Agricultural	0.097	0.092	0.072	–
have Positive Income from Agriculture	0.903	0.908	0.928	–
Average Household Size	4.086	4.051	4.495	4.420

Average Laborers/HH with				
Agriculture as Main Activity	1.988	1.966	1.969	–
Non-Agriculture as Main Activity	0.638	0.662	0.756	–
Average Laborers/HH	2.626	2.629	2.725	2.840

Note: The 1996 NBS Rural household survey samples from the same population covered in the 1996 Agricultural Census; see NBS (1997) for discussion of who is surveyed in the Agricultural Census and NBS (2000) for discussion of the NBS rural household survey sample frame. Both include all households that live and work in rural areas, including both households with official rural registration, and households living in the rural area for more than a year but lacking rural registration. Both include productive and non-productive households, and all households in rural areas regardless of whether productive activity is in agriculture or non-agricultural activities.

RCRE and NBS surveys, because both of these surveys sample households based on residence and registration, not registration alone. Average household size in the Population Census is smaller by nearly one individual, but from the publicly available abstracts, we are grouping urban households of rural counties together with rural households. Since these urban households were subject to much tighter family-planning restrictions, their inclusion will reduce average family size.

A better sense of sampling can be achieved using the 1996 Agricultural Census Abstract (NBS, 1997). The NBS rural household survey samples from the same population covered in the 1996 Agricultural Census.[42] Both include all households that live and work in rural areas, including households with official rural registration and households living in the rural area for more than a year but lacking rural registration. Both include productive and non-productive households, and all households in rural areas regardless of whether productive activity is in agriculture or non-agricultural activities. We present information on seven indices that can be calculated in a comparable fashion from the 1996 Agricultural Census and the 1996 RCRE household survey. In addition, we also include average household size and the number of individuals of working age per household from summary statistics of the NBS rural household survey for 1996.

From these rough comparisons, it is difficult to argue that the RCRE surveys systematically over-sample agricultural households, but it does appear that average household size is slightly higher for the RCRE survey. At the same time, however, average household size in the RCRE and NBS household surveys is nearly identical, suggesting either differences in definition of household membership between these surveys and the census or the possibility that both of these surveys have a slight bias toward surveying larger households with more working-age laborers per household.

While we note that 2 percent more households from the RCRE nine provinces report positive income from agriculture, 3.6 percent fewer households report that they are purely agricultural than in the Agricultural Census. Further, the average number of laborers per household reporting agriculture as their primary activity was nearly identical across the RCRE surveys and the census.

Finally, while we are unable to breakdown primary activity for the NBS rural household survey we do know that the share of income from agriculture was consistently higher in the NBS survey than in the RCRE survey. In 1997, for example, the share of net per capita rural income from cropping in the NBS data is 45.1 percent compared to 27.7 percent in the RCRE data. This was the one year that NBS valued non-marketed commodities at market prices, and this income result is inconsistent with more pronounced over-sampling of agricultural households by RCRE.

Recall that when comparing the RCRE survey with the CHNS and CCAP surveys above in section 8.4.1 we suggested that it is likely that both the RCRE and NBS surveys tend to under sample high income non-agricultural households. We believe that this likely source of potential bias affects both the NBS and RCRE surveys. Neither NBS nor RCRE report refusal rates for participation in their surveys, and given the onerous amount of work necessary to maintain daily diaries, we believe it reasonable that households with a higher opportunity cost of time opt out of the survey. The 2000 CCAP survey was conducted with great attention to keep refusal rates down, and not surprisingly seems to include the upper tail of a distribution that is missing from the NBS and RCRE household surveys. When the wealthiest one percent of households from the CCAP is dropped, the estimated gini coefficient falls considerably, and when the top three percent is dropped, the gini approaches the lower values found in the RCRE and NBS surveys.

Given that the RCRE survey has a significant panel component of house-holds that have been in the survey since 1986, one may also expect that the aging of the panel households may make RCRE somewhat less representa-tive over time. The extent of this bias, however, is very difficult to gauge without full access to both datasets.

8A.I.5 Issues in the calculation of household income and consumption per capita

Grain crops remain an important component of household production, yet in the RCRE survey grain produced for own consumption or stored is valued at prices reflecting the quota price rather than the market price. Up through the mid-1990s, quota prices were well below market prices. For this reason, income from grain production and consumption out of home production are both likely biased downward. To deal with this problem in our analyses, we re-value the household's non-marketed grain (and grain consumption out of own production) at average village market prices.

Household income is the sum of income from all household-managed activities (farming, agricultural sidelines, and non-agricultural activities), local wage employment, migrant remittances, formal transfers from the village and subsidies from higher levels of government, and informal transfers from friends or family (but excluding borrowing). Consumption is calculated as the sum of expenditures on food and non-durable goods purchased during the year, the value of home-produced goods consumed, the value of the flow of services from the household's stock of durable goods and housing, and the value of services (education, health care and other) purchased by the household during the period. Nominal values are converted into 1986 RMB using the provincial rural CPI from National Statistical Bureau yearbooks.

8A.II.5.2 CONSUMPTION (DURABLES AND HOUSING)

Our measure of household consumption per capita includes the value of the flow of services from the stock of consumer durables and housing. The RCRE surveys provide estimates of the original value of housing and durable goods, and report current expenditures on durables and new investment in expanding houses. To value the flow of services from housing and durables, we must first use this information to come up with a reasonable estimate of the current value of housing and durables, and then estimate the flow value of consumption.

Durable Goods. We assume that durable goods (and production assets) were accumulated in equal portions over the years between 1978 and the first year that the household appeared in the survey. We assume further that durable goods and production assets have a useful life of seven years (we checked robustness using 5- and 10-year lives), and that the non-depreciated portion of the durable good maintains its "real" value. For each year we depreciated one-seventh of the current value of the good, appreciated the remaining value of the good using a rural provincial capital goods price index, and added the new durables accumulated during that year. From this annual value of the stock of durables, we assume that the household consumes one-seventh of the existing stock of durable goods during the current year.

Housing. We assume that housing is consumed over a twenty-year period. For the initial year of the survey and for the first year that a new household appears in the survey, we value the housing stock using information from other households in the village on the real cost per square meter of living area in new housing constructed in the village in year $t-1$, t and $t+1$, and the livable floor space of the household. For each succeeding year we subtract one-twentieth of the estimated value of the house (as depreciation), appreciate the remaining 19/20ths of the value of the house using the rural capital goods price index, and add on the real value of new additions to the house made during the year. The current flow consumption of housing is one-twentieth of this current year value of housing.

8A.I.6 Discussion of CHNS and CCAP surveys and sample sizes in Table 8.4

The CCAP rural household survey was carried out in the six provinces of Liaoning, Hebei, Shanxi, Sichuan, Hubei and Zhejiang and covers the year 2000. Altogether, 1200 households in 60 villages were surveyed, or 20 households per village. In each province, counties were stratified on the basis of the gross value of agricultural and industrial output, and one county selected from each of the five quintiles. Within each county, townships were similarly stratified, and a township selected from both the upper and bottom-half of the distribution. A village was then randomly selected from each of the townships. Within each village, households were randomly selected on the basis of the most recent village household registry. Household membership was defined in a manner analogous to that used by the RCRE survey.

Details on the CHNS survey can be found on the CHNS website, http://www.cpc.unc.edu/projects/china/

8A.I.7 Spatial deflator

In order to control for absolute differences in price levels facing households across provinces, we deflate rural incomes and consumption using a spatial deflator constructed by Brandt and Holz (2004) for 1990. Using the NBS rural household survey expenditure data, they construct a single nationwide consumption basket that includes food, clothing, articles daily use, energy, services, housing, and durable goods. The basket is then priced using provincial-level price data. The range across the nine provinces in 1990 in the absolute price level is more than fifty percent (Guangdong, 1.37, and Sichuan, 0.87).

Appendix 8A.II: Understanding differences between the RCRE and NBS surveys

In principle, there is a range of plausible explanations for observed differences between the NBS and RCRE series, including: sampling strategy (both at the village and household levels), survey design, and differences in how income and consumption are defined and measured. Without actual access to the NBS data, information on survey implementation, and criteria used in the data "cleaning" and organization process, there are many issues that we cannot confront. Still, we are able to consider potential differences that remain in the way that income and consumption are defined. In section 8A.I.4 above, we considered the possibility that biases could be caused by over-sampling of agricultural households in the RCRE surveys. If we compare the few indicators that can be calculated in a comparable manner across surveys, it is not obvious that an explicit focus on agricultural households by the Ministry of Agriculture is driving the bias. Other types of sampling bias may be likely as a result of the panel nature of the RCRE dataset, or initial sampling design, but these are more difficult to assess without full access to both data sources.

One of the important differences between the two series shown in Figures 8.A1 and 8.A2 lies in the valuation of in-kind income (and consumption). In constructing consumption and income from the RCRE surveys, we valued both in-kind income and consumption in all years at market prices. In contrast, prior to 1990, the NBS valued in-kind components at prices that were at or near the quota price; subsequently, they used a higher set of prices. While Ravallion and Chen (2004) suggest that NBS started valuing in-kind income and consumption at market prices in 1990, official documentation of the rural household survey appears to indicate otherwise (NBS, 2000).[43] From 1991 to 1996 NBS instructed survey teams to use an "average contract price" to value non-marketed grain from own production. This average contract price was the weighted average of the quota price and the above quota price for sales over quota to the local grain bureau. Both of these prices were administratively determined. Survey teams were further instructed to use weighted average market prices only if there were no local administrative prices (meaning no local crop procurement).[44] It was not until 1997 that NBS instructed survey teams to value all non-marketed agricultural commodities at market prices. However, this was revised in 1998 with instructions to

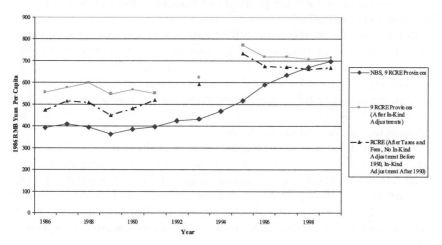

Figure 8A.1 Differences between RCRE and NBS.

Income Per Capita Series

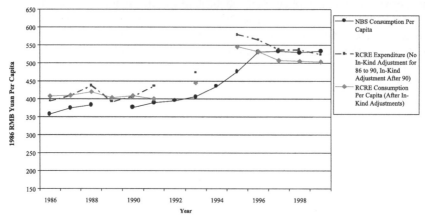

Figure 8A.2 Differences between RCRE and NBS.

Consumption Per Capita Series

value grain and meat products at 90 percent of the market price and other non-marketed commodities at 85 percent of market price.

An NBS official involved with the rural household survey since 1989 verified that the official documentation cited above (and translated in Appendix 8A.III) accurately reflected the survey protocol for the rural household survey during the 1990s. This official also volunteered an additional source of downward bias in income and consumption growth between 1991 and 1995: Some localities used the same weighted average quota and above quota sales' price calculated in 1990 for purposes of valuing in-kind income for years between 1991 and 1995.[45]

Relative to the RCRE data, NBS treatment of the in-kind component likely results in an underestimate of incomes and consumption prior to 1990, and an overestimate of growth in incomes or consumption if one calculates average annual growth rates for 1987 to 1999 period. Given that grain income was valued at a price still systematically related to the quota price after 1990, we expect the difference in average income to be correlated with the gap between the market and the quota price.

Two other differences in the income series lie in the treatment of taxes and fees and depreciation on fixed assets, both of which are subtracted from the NBS series. We concentrate on earned income and do not subtract off taxes because we are focusing on earnings ability of households, and taxes would confound the issue. Second, recorded depreciation expenses are notoriously arbitrary, so we have depreciated assets ourselves as discussed in Appendix 8A.I above.

To examine the extent to which our adjustments to the RCRE series may be driving differences, we do two things. First, we subtract off taxes and fees, as well as depreciation on fixed assets for all years. Second, we use the quota price in the valuation of in-kind grain income in the RCRE data for 1986 to 1990. For all years after 1990, the lack of a consistent method for valuing non-marketed commodities makes it impossible for us to mimic the method of valuation used by the NBS, so we use the market price to value the in-kind components. Figure 8A.1 presents RCRE income and expenditure series calculated in a manner consistent with the calculations purportedly followed in the NBS series prior to 1990.

8A.II.1 Implications for income

From 1986–1990 differences between the two surveys in the treatment of taxes and fees and the valuation of in-kind income is the source of approximately half of the differences in per capita income between the two series. Depreciation explains an additional 10 percent of the gap. For years after 1990, tax and fees, and depreciation are the source of roughly 25 percent of the gap in the years just after 1990, and nearly the entire gap by 1999. Significant differences persist however between the two series, which is not too surprising given that NBS was valuing in-kind income at the weighted average of two administrative prices until 1997. The gap in per capita income widens between the two series, peaking in 1995, before eventually disappearing after 1997.

Adjustments to valuation of grain during the early period help to narrow some of the differences in growth implied by the two series, but a significant difference remains. With the adjustment, the difference between the two series in annual growth in per capita incomes declines from 2.8 percent (4.6 – 1.8 percent) to 2.2 percent (4.6 – 2.4 percent).

8A.II.2 Implications for consumption

In general, the consumption series line up better than do the income series both in terms of levels and growth, however there are differences. First, the NBS consumption series is really an expenditure series. Valuing consumption from in-kind income consistently and looking at expenditures eliminates much of the difference in per capita consumption differences for years prior to 1990. This also helps to narrow the difference in the growth rate in expenditure between the two series from 1.3 percent (2.9 – 1.6 percent) to 0.8 percent (2.9 – 2.2 percent). As we saw in the case of the income data, however, there is a widening gap in per capita expenditure between the two series from 1991 to 1995, followed by elimination of the gap. We believe that for the purposes of our analyses, however, consumption is a more appropriate measure than expenditure.

8A.II.3   Can documented differences in valuation of in-kind income explain the gap between RCRE and NBS averages after 1990?

We believe that some of the gap in both the consumption and income series after 1990 reflects the fact that the NBS valued in-kind grain at a price that remained well below the market price. Brandt and Holz (2004) also discuss the issue of grain pricing by the NBS in some detail. With the change in NBS method of valuing non-marketed grain in 1990, they find that the new average implicit price at which the NBS valued grain increased from 0.378 to 0.513 yuan per kg. This is still only modestly higher than the average state procurement price of 0.5 yuan per kg, and considerably below the average market and state-guidance prices of nearly 1.0 yuan per kg. Given that we know from NBS documentation that the rural household survey teams are using average unit sales prices calculated from the quota and above quota administrative prices, this implies a weighted average price that will be well below the market price if the above quota price is close to the expected market price.

Indirect confirmation that imputed prices were well below market is suggested by differences in the behavior of farm incomes between 1993 and 1995 in the NBS and RCRE samples. Over this period, crop prices increased by slightly more than 90 percent. Farm input prices increased by approximately 50 percent, while the rural CPI increased by 45 percent. Assuming that value-added in farming is 60 percent, ceteris paribus, this should result in an increase in real farm incomes from cropping of 50 percent.[46] This is more or less what we see in the RCRE data, however, the increase in the NBS data is less than half of this. Much of the difference between the two series in the growth of per capita incomes from 1993–1995 can be linked to the more rapid growth in crop income in the RCRE data.

Given NBS treatment of in-kind incomes after 1990, we expect the bias in income estimates to depend on the gap between the quota and market price, which tended to be highly cyclical. In fact, we find a strong positive correlation (0.92) between the size of gap between the two income series, and our estimate of the ratio of the market-to-quota price, which is as high as 1.46 in 1995, and then falls below 1 by 1997. After 1997, the NBS series is directly related to the market price, and we observe some convergence in the income and consumption series.

Finally, biases introduced by NBS approaches to valuation of in-kind income may also help to explain some of the slight differences in the behavior of the Gini coefficient over time between the two series. The NBS income Gini coefficients rise monotonically. The RCRE data suggest modest growth prior to 1995, and then a significant increase over the next four years. One interpretation for this behavior is that the much higher valuation of in-kind income in the RCRE data for the years 1993–1995 is helping to dampen the effect of dis-equalizing growth in wage and business incomes. The effect is temporary, however, and once farm prices begin to fall, we see the sharp increase in inequality associated with falling farm incomes.

Appendix 8A.III: Testing for statistical significance in differences of Lorenz Curves, CDFs and generalized Lorenz Curves

We test for the statistical significance of the difference between Lorenz Curves and Generalized Lorenz curves using DAD, a distribution analysis software developed by Duclos, Araar, and Fortin (2004). We present estimated differences between Lorenz Curves and Generalized Lorenz Curves at different cumulative population shares in Tables 8A.3 and 8A.4, respectively. In the discussion of Section 8.4.1 we consider differences between curves to be statistically significant when the difference between curves is greater than twice the standard deviation of the differences.

In Figure 8.5, we also use DAD to find a critical poverty line of 226 RMB per capita. This is where the 1999 CDF of income per capita crosses the 1987 CDF from above. The standard deviation of this critical poverty line is 36.3.

Table 8A.3 Do Lorenz curves for income per capita differ significantly?

(Standard error of difference in parentheses)

Cumulative Population Share (%)	Difference 1999 LC – 1987 LC	Cumulative Population Share (%)	Difference 1999 LC – 1995 LC
1	−0.0018 (0.0005)	1	−0.0012 (0.0006)
2	−0.0030 (0.0007)	2	−0.0024 (0.0009)
3	−0.0039 (0.0009)	3	−0.0034 (0.0011)
4	−0.0048 (0.0012)	4	−0.0044 (0.0013)
5	−0.0056 (0.0015)	5	−0.0053 (0.0015)
10	−0.0095 (0.0028)	10	−0.0097 (0.0024)
25	−0.0206 (0.0066)	25	−0.0194 (0.0049)
50	−0.0374 (0.0125)	50	−0.0290 (0.0082)
75	−0.0427 (0.0167)	75	−0.0296 (0.0097)
90	−0.0331 (0.0162)	90	−0.0175 (0.0086)
95	−0.0257 (0.0142)	95	−0.0092 (0.0071)
99	−0.0108 (0.0069)	99	0.0001 (0.0041)
100	0.0000 (0.0000)	100	0.0000 (0.0000)

Table 8A.4 Do generalized Lorenz curves for income per capita differ significantly?
(Standard error of difference in parentheses)

Cumulative Population Share (%)	Difference 1999 GLC – 1987 GLC	Cumulative Population Share	Difference 1999 GLC – 1995 GLC
1	−1.0571 (0.3471)	1	−0.8666 (0.4722)
2	−1.5522 (0.5445)	2	−1.8624 (0.6417)
3	−1.8577 (0.7120)	3	−2.7566 (0.7784)
4	−2.0672 (0.8837)	4	−3.6421 (0.9120)
5	−2.2014 (1.1067)	5	−4.5068 (1.0757)
10	−2.3117 (2.1502)	10	−8.7575 (1.8195)
25	0.3612 (5.2284)	25	−20.1981 (3.9434)
50	13.1336 (10.5384)	50	−37.1695 (8.2987)
75	44.7752 (16.2268)	75	−52.0422 (14.7880)
90	81.1552 (20.8501)	90	−55.7593 (20.1826)
95	99.3007 (23.5031)	95	−55.4198 (22.3429)
99	122.7926 (28.5704)	99	−55.2562 (24.2397)
100	135.5869 (32.5647)	100	−58.7977 (25.4232)

Notes

*   We are grateful for helpful comments and suggestions from Carsten Holz, Martin Ravallion, Sangui Wang and two anonymous referees. Benjamin and Brandt thank the Social Sciences and Humanities Research Council of Canada for financial support. Giles gratefully acknowledges financial support from the National Science Foundation (SES-0214702) and the Intramural Research Grants Program at Michigan State University.

1 Annual series from the National Bureau of Statistics (NBS) suggest an average GDP per capita growth rate of 8.2 percent from 1980 and 2000 (NBS 2003). Rawski (2001) among others have criticized China's recent GDP statistics, but few dispute the considerable growth that China has experienced since the onset of reforms.

2 The World Bank (2003) Beijing office notes concerns about the consequences of increasing inequality for support for continued economic reform, and the new leadership in Beijing openly voices concerns about potential adverse consequences of rising inequality (Hutzler 2003).

3 See Aghion, Caroli and Garcia-Penalosa (1999) for a review of the growth-inequality relationship from the perspective of new growth theory; Banerjee and Duflo (2003) for a cross-country growth regression analysis; and Dayton-Johnson and Bardhan (2002) for an analysis of the impact of inequality on common property management in village settings.

4 See Deaton 2005.

5 See, for example, Gustafson and Li 2002; Meng 2004; Morduch and Sicular 2002; Rozelle 1994).

6 There were gaps in the panel in 1992 and 1994 when the survey was not conducted.

7 This simple (and optimistic) two-factor attribution of the sources of inequality during Chinese transition is outlined in Benjamin and Brandt (1999).

8 For the original discussion, see Kuznets 1955.

9 As an example, the price of rice in the United States fell from $463.97 per metric ton in 1996 to $367.36 per ton in 2000, a nominal decline of about twenty percent.

10 The complete RCRE survey covers over 22,000 households in 300 villages in 31 provinces and administrative regions. RCRE's complete national survey is 31 percent of the annual size of the NBS Rural Household Survey. By agreement, we have obtained access to data from 9 provinces, or roughly one third of the RCRE survey.

11 One shortcoming of the survey is the lack of individual level information. However, we know the number of dependents and individuals working, as well as the gender composition of household members.

12 Of the original 110 villages surveyed in 1987, 82 were among the 103 villages surveyed in 1999.

13 It includes individuals in the household with rural registration (*hukou*) plus a small number of individuals with non-rural registration, but who live in the village full-time. This definition of household membership differs slightly from that of the World Bank's Living Standard Measurement Survey, which for other than the household head, bases membership on the actual number of months of residency in the house.

14 RCRE's surveys follow pre-1990 NBS conventions and value non-marketed grain at quota prices. We follow an approach used by Chen and Ravallion (1996) to recalculate the value of non-marketed grain at market prices. This is discussed in more detail in Appendices A and B.

15 In order to convert the stock of durables into a flow of consumption services, we assume that current and past investments in housing are "consumed" over a twenty-year period, and that investments in durable goods are consumed over a period of seven years. We also annually "inflate" the value of the stock of durables to reflect the increase in durable goods' prices over the period.

16 Specifically, weight =[(Province Rural Population)/(Number of Households Sampled in Province)]*(Household Size).

17 The lowest income households actually have negative incomes. These are typically households that have high gross incomes, but also high business-related expenses. The problem of measurement error for these households is especially severe. We discuss our procedure for eliminating outliers in Appendix 8A.I, Section 7.3. In each year, less than one-tenth of one percent of households were dropped from the panel.

18 Results for Tables 8.1 and 8.2 (our main results) for the complete sample of annual observations, and for the different samples (panel and non-panel) are available from the authors by request. Some information for other years is presented in Figures 8.1 and 8.2 below.

19 RMB is the abbreviation for "Renminbi," the name of the Chinese currency. The

unit of account is the "yuan" (equal to one RMB). In 1986, the official exchange rate was 3.45 yuan per dollar.

20 Appendix 8A.I discusses this sampling issue in more detail and a comparison between RCRE and Agricultural Census indicators is shown in Appendix Table 8A.II.

21 Appendix 8A.II (Section 8) provides a more detailed discussion of in-kind valuation procedures and implications for trends in the NBS rural household survey. A translation of the relevant part of the document can be found on Giles' website (www.msu.edu/~gilesj) as well as excerpts from the original Chinese language document.

22 See Deininger and Squire (1996) for a discussion of the evolution of inequality over a broad range of countries.

23 We use the Davidson and Duclos (2000) procedure implemented in the DAD software package (Duclos, Araar, and Fortin 2004), and test for significance of the difference in Lorenz curves at different points. We find that the 1999 Lorenz curve is significantly below the 1987 Lorenz curve along the entire distribution, and that it is significantly below the 1995 curve for the lowest 90 percent of the distribution. A summary of results of the tests of significance is presented in Appendix IV, Table 8A.3.

24 See Jenkins (2000) for an example of using the "half-contemporaneous mean" in summarizing the evolution of the distribution of income in the UK.

25 Ravallion and Chen (2004) estimate a poverty line of 850 RMB Yuan per capita in 2002, which is equal to 302 RMB Yuan per capita in 1986 values. This is actually quite close to the half 1987 mean income per capita value of 290 RMB Yuan per capita. For this poverty line, the 1999 distribution dominates the 1987 distribution.

26 The Generalized Lorenz Curve was introduced by Shorrocks (1983). See also Foster and Shorrocks (1988), Atkinson (1987), and Deaton (1997) for more general discussions relating Generalized Lorenz Curves to stochastic dominance, welfare rankings, and poverty.

27 See Appendix IV, Table A.4 for tests of the difference between Generalized Lorenz curves.

28 The 2000 survey was a collaborative effort involving Bai Nansheng (formerly of the RCRE), Loren Brandt, Scott Rozelle (UC-Davis), and Zhang Linxiu (Chinese Center for Agricultural Policy, or CCAP). See the Data Appendix for further details.

29 The NBS rural household survey data show an increase in nominal per capita net incomes from 2210 to 2254, or an increase of less than 2 percent.

30 Refusal rates are likely to be higher among households with a high opportunity cost of time, and neither RCRE nor NBS report refusal rates. By design, both surveys are also less successful in accurately estimating household incomes from family-run businesses. For example, both the RCRE and CHNS surveys simply ask respondents for total revenue and expenditures from family businesses, and while enumerated, we believe that the distinction between fixed and variable costs is often lost in the enumeration process. In general, this is among the most difficult source of income to enumerate accurately, and thus often the noisiest (Vijverberg and Mead 2000). It is also believed to drive rural inequality, so under-estimation of this income source may significantly lead to understatement of the level of inequality. Considerable effort was placed in the CCAP 2000 survey on minimizing problems stemming from inaccurate reporting of non-farm business income, both in terms of random sampling of households within villages, and a more careful enumeration of the balance sheets of family businesses.

31 The record-keeping requirements of the RCRE and NBS surveys also suggest that they likely under-enumerate low-income, illiterate households. The Gini is slightly

less sensitive to the lower tail. In the context of the CCAP survey, dropping the lower 10 percent of households reduces the Gini by only several points.

32 Kanbur and Zhang (1999) provide an excellent overview of the literature on regional inequality, highlighting inland versus coastal, and urban versus rural dimensions. See also Gustaffson and Li 2002.

33 For example, for a provincial-level decomposition, this will be a set of provincial dummies.

34 We define three regions as: West (Gansu, Shanxi, and Sichuan), Central (Anhui, Henan, and Hunan), and East (Jilin, Jiangsu, and Guangdong).

35 For example, the NBS-based estimates may not fully reflect the effect of the increase in agricultural prices in the mid-1990s on incomes, inequality, and spatial differences.

36 Gustaffson and Li do not report results for village, as their finest unit of location is the county. With this caveat, they find that 40 percent of inequality was across counties in 1988, rising to 50 percent by 1995. While trends are opposite ours, the basic magnitude is similar. Also note that the NBS data show a decline in inter-provincial inequality from 1995 to 1999 (Figure 8.6), so more recent numbers from the NBS might line up more closely.

37 See Benjamin et al. (2002) for a survey of these studies.

38 While the 1987 to 1999 trend suggests a straight decline of grain income from 175 to 113 RMB per capita, grain income peaked at 257 RMB per capita in 1995, and declined rapidly between 1995 and 1998.

39 Benjamin, Brandt, Glewwe, and Li (2002) show exploratory results that suggest that the combination of rising education levels and the development of non-farm employment opportunities can reduce inequality, and furthermore, that the effect of the distribution of education on overall income distribution depends on local development of markets.

40 See Vijverberg and Mead (2000), for example.

41 Our sample originally included Zhejiang province. An examination of county gross value of output and mean rural per capita income revealed that a disproportionate number of the surveyed counties in the province were from the upper-third of the distribution. Thus, they were unlikely to represent well the distribution of income within Zhejiang, leading to biased estimates of inequality across regions. Sampling of counties in other provinces appears to be consistent with RCRE's guidelines.

42 See NBS (1997) for documentation of who is surveyed in the Agricultural Census, and NBS (2000) for documentation of the NBS rural household survey sample frame.

43 A translation of these sections of the authoritative NBS document and a scan of Chinese language originals are available from Giles' website (www.msu.edu/ ~gilesj/).

44 Wang, Xia, and Liu (1996) also point out that up through 1995, NBS policy was to use a weighted average of the quota price (called *tonggou jia* during the 1990s) and above-quota/negotiated price (*chaoguo jia*).

45 Loren Brandt interview with an NBS Division Chief conducted on December 18, 2004.

46 A rough conservative estimate based on information from the 2000 CCAP survey discussed in the paper is 60 percent value added.

References

Aghion, Philippe, Eve Caroli, and Cecilia Garcia-Penalosa. 1999. "Inequality and Economic Growth: The Perspective of the New Growth Theories," *Journal of Economic Literature* 37(4): 1615–60, December.

Atkinson, A. B. 1987. "On the Measurement of Poverty," *Econometrica*, 55(4): 749–64.

Banerjee, Abhijit V. and Esther Duflo. 2003. "Inequality and Growth: What Can the Data Say?" Journal of Economic Growth, 8(3): 267–99.

Benjamin, Dwayne and Loren Brandt. 1999. "Markets and Inequality in Rural Contemporary China: Parallels with the Past," *AER Papers and Proceedings*, May.

Benjamin, Dwayne, Loren Brandt, Paul Glewwe, and Guo Li. 2002. "Markets, Human Capital and Income Inequality in an Economy in Transition: The Case of Rural China," in *Inequality Around the World*, Richard Freeman, ed., Palgrave-MacMillan, Houndsmills, Basingtoke, Hampshire.

Bramall, Chris. 2001. "The Quality of China's Household Income Surveys," *China Quarterly* 167: 689–705, September.

Brandt, Loren and Carsten Holz. 2004. "Spatial Price Differences in China," Department of Economics, University of Toronto, manuscript.

Chen, Shaohua and Ravallion, Martin. 1996. "Data in Transition: Assessing Rural Living Standards in Southern China," *China Economic Review*, 7(1): 23–56.

Cook, Sarah. 1998. "Work, Wealth and Power in Agriculture: Do Political Connections Affect Returns to Household Labor?" in *Zouping in Transition: The Process of Reform in Rural North China*, Andrew G. Walder, ed., Cambridge, Mass.: Harvard University Press.

Davidson, Russell and Jean-Yves Duclos. 2000. "Statistical Inference for Stochastic Dominance and for the Measurement of Poverty and Inequality," in *Econometrica*, 68(6): 1435–64, November.

Dayton-Johnson, Jeff and Pranab Bardhan. 2002. "Inequality and Conservation of the Local Commons: A Theoretical Exercise," *Economic Journal*, 112(481): 577–602, July.

Deaton, Angus. 1997. *The Analysis of Household Surveys: A Microeconometric Approach to Development Policy*, Johns Hopkins University Press for the World Bank.

Deaton, Angus. 2005. "Measuring Poverty in a Growing World (or Measuring Growth in a Poor World)," *Review of Economics and Statistics*, 87(1): 1–19, February.

Deininger, Klaus and Lyn Squire. 1996. "New Data Set Measuring Income Inequality," *World Bank Economic Review*, 10(3): 565–91, September.

Duclos, Jean-Yves, Abdelkrim Araar, and Carl Fortin. 2004. "DAD 4.3: A Software for Distributive Analysis / Analyse Distributive," MIMAP Programme, International Development Research Centre, Government of Canada and CREFA, Universite Laval.

Foster, J. E. and A. F. Shorrocks. 1988. "Poverty Orderings," *Econometrica*, 56: 173–7.

Gustafsson, Bjorn and Li Shi. 2002. "Income Inequality within and across Counties in Rural China 1988 and 1995," *Journal of Development Economics*, 69(1): 179–204, October.

Hare, Denise. 1994. "Rural Nonagricultural Activities and Their Impact on the Distribution of Income: Evidence from Farm Households in Southern China," *China Economic Review*, 5(1): 59–82, Spring.

Hutzler, Charles. 2003. "For China's Poor Regions, a Kinder, Gentler Beijing – Incoming Leadership Makes A Priority of Those Ignored By Headlong Liberalization," *The Wall Street Journal*, p. A13, February 25.

Jalan, Jyotsna and Martin Ravallion. 2002. "Geographic Poverty Traps? A Micro

Model of Consumption Growth in Rural China," *Journal of Applied Econometrics*, 17(4): 329–46, July–August.

Jenkins, Stephen P. 2000. "Modelling Household Income Dynamics," *Journal of Population Economics*, 13(4): 529–67, December.

Kanbur, Ravi and Xiaobo Zhang. 1999. "Which Regional Inequality? The Evolution of Rural–Urban and Inland–Coastal Inequality in China from 1983 to 1995," *Journal of Comparative Economics*, 27(4): 686–701, December.

Khan, Azizur Rahman and Riskin, Carl. 1998. "Income and Inequality in China: Composition, Distribution and Growth of Household Income, 1988 to 1995," *China Quarterly*, 154: 221–53, June.

Kung, James and Yiu-fai Lee. 2001. So What If There Is Income Inequality? The Distributive Consequence of Nonfarm Employment in Rural China," *Economic Development and Cultural Change*, 50(1): 19–46, October.

Kuznets, Simon. 1955. "Economic Growth and Income Inequality," *American Economic Review*, 45: 1–28.

Meng, Xin. 2004. "Economic Restructuring and Income Inequality in Urban China," *Review of Income and Wealth*, 50(3): 357–79.

Morduch, Jonathan and Terry Sicular. 2002. "Rethinking Inequality Decomposition, with Evidence from Rural China, *Economic Journal*, 112(476): 93–106, January.

National Bureau of Statistics. 1993. *Tabulation on the 1990 Population Census of the People's Republic of China* [*Zhongguo 1990 nian renkou pucha ziliao*]. Beijing: National Bureau of Statistics Publishing House.

National Bureau of Statistics. 1997. *Abstract of the 1996 Agricultural Census of China* (English Version). Beijing: National Bureau of Statistics Publishing House, 1997.

National Bureau of Statistics. 2000. *How to Use the Statistical Yearbook* [Ruhe shiyong tongji nianjian], Chengxiang Liu, Ke Liu and Zhaofeng Jin, eds, Beijing: National Bureau of Statistics Publishing House [zhongguo tongji chuban she]. The ISBN number for this volume is: 7-5037-3380-2/C 1834, September.

National Bureau of Statistics. 2003. *China Statistical Yearbook 2003 [Zhongguo tong ji nian jian 2003]*. National Bureau of Statistics, National Bureau of Statistics Publishing House, Beijing.

Nee, Victor. 1992. "Organizational Dynamics of Market Transition: Hybrid Forms, Property Rights, and Mixed Economy in China," *Administrative Science Quarterly*, 37: 1–27.

Ravallion, Martin and Shaohua Chen. 2004. "China's (Uneven) Progress Against Poverty," World Bank, manuscript.

Rawski, Thomas G. 2001. "What Is Happening to China's GDP Statistics?" *China Economic Review*, 12(4): 347–54.

Rozelle, Scott. 1994. "Rural Industrialization and Increasing Inequality: Emerging Patterns in China's Reforming Economy," *Journal of Comparative Economics*, 19(3): 362–91, December.

Shorrocks, Anthony F. 1982. "Inequality Decomposition by Factor Components," *Econometrica*, 50(1): 193–211.

Shorrocks, Anthony F. 1983. "Ranking Income Distributions," *Economica*, 50: 3–17.

Shorrocks, Anthony F. 1983. "The Impact of Income Components on the Distribution of Family Incomes," *Quarterly Journal of Economics*, 98(2): 311–26.

Tsui, Kai-yuen. 1998. "Trends and Inequalities of Rural Welfare in China: Evidence from Rural Households in Guangdong and Sichuan," *Journal of Comparative Economics*, 26(4): 783–804, December.

Vijverberg, Wim and Donald Mead. 2000. "Household Enterprises," in *Designing household survey questionnaires for developing countries: Lessons from fifteen years of the Living Standards Measurement Study*, Margaret Grosh and Paul Glewwe, eds, vol. 2, pp. 105–37. Washington, DC: World Bank.

Wang, Sangui, Ying Xia and Xiaozhan Liu. 1996. "Criteria to Measure Poverty in China" [Zhongguo pingkun zhibiao yanjiu] in *Research on Economic and Technological Development in Agriculture [Nongye jingji yu keji fazhan yanyiu]*, China Agriculture Technology Press, Beijing.

World Bank. 2003. *China: Promoting Growth with Equity, Country Economic Memorandum*, Poverty Reduction and Economic Management Unit, East Asia and Pacific Region, Report No. 24169–CHA.

9 Rural poverty in China: problem and solution*

Gregory Chow

Abstract

This chapter describes the economic conditions of rural China regarding poverty. By dividing the problem of rural poverty into three components it explains why rural poverty is China's number one economic problem in spite of the significant improvement in the living standard of the rural population. After discussing the solution proposed by the Chinese government it raises two policy questions, one concerning a proposal to eliminate the operational functions of township governments in the streamlining of the local government structure and the second on the possibility of controlling the abuse of power by local party officials that infringes on the rights of the farmers. A comparison with the conditions in India is provided.

9.1 Introduction

China's rapid economic growth in the order of 9.4 percent per year since economic reform started in 1978 is well recognized. Many observers also agree that the momentum for further growth in the foreseeable future is assured. The large amount of wealth created and the insufficient attention given to the welfare of residents in the rural regions have created a large income gap between the urban rich and rural poor as well as opportunities of exploitation of the latter by local government and Communist Party officials. Hence the country's leaders now consider the number one economic and social problem to be rural poverty, despite the substantial improvement in the living standard of the rural population in recent years.

In section 9.2, I will examine the economic conditions of the rural population, its absolute improvement, its relative status as compared with the urban population and the increase in disparity in per capita consumption between regions. In section 9.3, I will divide the problem of rural poverty into three components and explain why it is the number one problem in spite of the improvement in the economic conditions of the poor. Section 9.4 is a description of government policy to solve the rural poverty problem. Section 9.5 discusses two policy issues concerning the government's solution, one on the policy to eliminate the functions of township governments in five years and the second on the protection of farmers' rights to keep the land contracted to them. Section 9.6 is a brief discussion of the poverty problem in India by comparison. Section 9.7 concludes.

9.2 Statistics on rural poverty and economic disparity in China

In this section I examine three kinds of statistics on rural poverty and economic disparity in China. One is the means of per capita disposable income and per capita consumption of urban and rural residents and their rates of change. The second is the change in the lower tail of income distribution of rural residents through time. The third is measures of dispersion of per capita income or consumption across provinces.

9.2.1 Trends of per capita income and consumption of urban and rural residents

Table 9.1 shows the annual per capita disposable income of urban and rural residents. The ratio of urban to rural per capita income decreased from 2.57 in 1978 to 1.86 in 1985 showing the initial benefits of agricultural reform through the household responsibility system of assigning land to individual farm households. However, the ratio increased in favor of the urban residents afterwards, rising steadily from the late 1980s until 2003 when it reached 3.23. Thus, income disparity between urban and rural residents has increased steadily since the middle 1980s.

Concerning the improvement of per capita income in real terms for the rural residents, we record the consumer price index for rural residents in the last row of Table 1 which shows an increase from 100.0 in 1985 to 320.2 in 2003. In 2003 prices, the per capita income of rural residents in 1989 was 602(3.202/1.579) or 1220.8 yuan. This amounts to an exponential rate of increase from 1989 to 2003 of (ln2622–ln1220.8)/14 or 0.0546 per year, or by 5.61 percent per year, a fairly substantial rate of increase. A similar calculation for urban residents shows per capita real income increased from

Table 9.1 Annual per capita disposable income of urban and rural residents (yuan)

Year	1978	1980	1985	1989	1997	2002	2003
Urban	343.4	477.6	739.1	1374	5160	7703	8472
Rural	133.6	191.3	397.6	602	2090	2476	2622
Income Ratio	2.570	2.497	1.859	2.282	2.469	3.111	3.231
Urban CPI	100.0	109.5	134.2	219.2	481.9	475.1	479.4
Rural CPI			100.0	157.9	322.3	315.2	320.2

Source: China Statistical Yearbook 1999 Table 10.1 for years up to 1985; *China Statistical Yearbook 2004* Table 10.1 for income data beginning 1989, Table 9.2 for the urban and rural consumer price indices (respectively with 1978 = 100 and 1985 = 100).

1374(479.4/219.2) = 3005.0 yuan in 2003 prices in 1989 to 8472 yuan, implying an exponential rate of increase of (ln8472–ln3005)/14 = 0.0740, which is
two percentage points higher than the rural figure.

On per capita consumption, Table 9.2 provides the annual per capita living
expenditure of urban and rural households for 1989, 1997, 2002, and 2003.
The ratio of urban to rural expenditure increased from 2.351 in 1989 to 3.351
in 2003, showing a very large increase similar to that in the income ratio in
Table 9.1.

In 1989 real per capita consumption in 2003 prices for rural residents was
515(320.2/157.9) = 1044.4 yuan. This gives an average exponential rate of
increase of (ln1943–ln1044.4)/14 = 0.04434 from 1989 to 2003, a very high
rate of increase by comparison with other developing countries. In 1989 real
per capita consumption in 2003 prices for urban residents was 1211(479.4/
219.2) = 2648.5 yuan. This implies an average exponential rate of increase of
(ln6511–ln2648.5)/14 = 0.06425 from 1989 to 2003, also two percentage
points higher than for rural residents.

Thus, the data show that urban/rural income and consumption disparity
has increased, but the rural residents have enjoyed a fairly substantial rate of
increase in both income and consumption, to the order of 5.5 and 4.5 percent
per year respectively, even though these are two percentage points below the
corresponding figures for urban residents.

There are some other aspects of consumption not measured in the above
statistics on per capita consumption expenditure. First, per capita education
expenditure provided by the government for urban residents was higher than
for rural residents. Second, land was available for rural residents to build their
own houses. As a result, living space per person available for rural residents in
their own housing was more than housing space for urban residents for many
years. Third, medical care for urban residents provided by the government
under an insurance system was better than for rural residents. Only 22.5
percent of rural people are covered by a rural cooperative medical care insurance system while the vast majority of urban residents receive adequate medical care, with some 80 percent of medical resources concentrated in cities. In
terms of infrastructure, supply of running water is less adequate in rural
areas. More than 60 percent of rural households do not have access to flush
toilets. Some 6 percent of villages are still beyond the reach of highways;

Table 9.2 Annual per capita living expenditure of urban
and rural households (yuan)

Year	1989	1997	2002	2003
Urban	1211	4186	6030	6511
Rural	515	1617	1834	1943
Ratio	2.351	2.589	3.288	3.351

Source: China Statistical Yearbook 2004, Table 10.1.

2 percent of villages have no electricity supply; 6 percent of villages do not have telephones. Some 150 million rural households face problems in fuel supply. However, incorporating these elements of consumption will not affect the general conclusions reached above concerning urban/rural comparisons of per capita income and consumption.

9.2.2 Percentage of rural residents with per capita income below the poverty line

Since the poverty problem may not be a problem among all rural residents but among the poorest of them, we have provided in Table 9.3 the left tail of the per capita annual income distribution of the rural residents. If we draw the poverty line in 2003 as having income below 600 yuan, we find 3.47 percent below it, or about 28 million out of a rural population of 800 million, still a substantial number of people. (The 28 million figure is consistent with the official statement in 2005 that 26 million rural people live in poverty and nearly 20 million urban people live on the government's minimum allowance). In 1990 when the rural Consumer Price Index (CPI) was about half of the 2003 CPI, the percentage of households with per capita income below 300 yuan was 8.64. In 1985, when the CPI was about a third, the percentage of households with per capita income below 200 was 12.22 percent. Thus, the percentage of the rural population remaining below the poverty line of 600 yuan in 2003 prices has decreased substantially from 12 percent in 1985, to 9 percent in 1990 and to 3.5 percent in 2003. In 1985, the Chinese farmers were by and large happy, as their economic conditions had improved significantly after the introduction of the household responsibility system of private farming.

9.2.3 Inequality in wealth distribution

As a third kind of statistics we examine the distribution of income across provinces by considering the standard deviation of the natural logarithm of

Table 9.3 Percentage of rural households in different income ranges

Income	1980	1985	1990	1995	2000	2002	2003
< 100	9.80	0.96	0.30	0.21	0.31	0.40	0.49
100–200	51.80	11.26	1.78	0.36	0.20	0.19	0.18
200–300	25.30	25.61	6.56	0.78	0.43	0.28	0.31
300–400	8.60	24.00	12.04	1.47	0.69	0.50	0.52
400–500	2.90	15.85	14.37	2.30	1.01	0.79	0.78
500–600		9.06	13.94	3.37	1.37	1.25	1.19
600–800		8.02	20.80	9.54	4.44	3.62	3.25
<800	98.4	94.76	69.79	18.03	8.45	7.03	6.72
<600	98.4	86.74	48.99	15.21	4.01	3.41	3.47
<500				11.84	2.64	2.16	2.28

rural consumption expenditure per capita, treating consumption as a measure of permanent income or wealth. In 1981 this standard deviation computed for the 28 provinces then in existence was 0.2612, as compared with 0.3475 in 1998 for the same 28 provinces (see Chow (2002, 169)). Thus, consumption inequality among provinces increased between these two years, at the average rate of (0.3475–0.2612)/17 = 0.00508 or about half of a percentage point per year. To see whether the increase in consumption disparity has slowed down, I have computed the same standard deviation for 1993, using data on page 281 of the *Statistical Yearbook of China 1994* and obtained 0.3370. The average rate of increase in the standard deviation in the five years from 1993 to 1998 is (0.3475–0.3370)/5 = 0.0021, much slower than 0.00508. Thus, the rate of increase in disparity slowed down in the late 1990s but was still in the range of two-tenths of one per cent per year. The same standard deviation for 2004 is 0.3731 (based on data in the *China Statistical Yearbook 2005*, Table 10.26 for the same 28 provinces), suggesting that the increase in dispersion has continued between 1998 and 2004 at the average rate of (0.3731–0.3475)/6 = 0.0064 per year. This agrees with the continued increase in income disparity up to the present as found in section 2.1 and shows in addition that the rate of increase in disparity was even higher in the last six years from 1998 to 2004 than in the five years from 1993 to 1998 and also in the 17 years between 1981 and 1998 (with possible errors due to the omission of Hainan, Chongqing, and Tibet in the calculations for 1998 and 2004).

A related question is whether rural per capita consumption increased in the poorest provinces and at what rate. From Chow (2002, Table 9.2), the three provinces with the lowest consumption in 1981 were Gansu, Yunnan, and Qinghai, with per capita rural consumption of 135.23, 137.75, and 141.68 respectively. From Chow (2002, Table 9.5), in 1998 these three provinces had per capita rural consumption of 939.55, 1312.31 and 1117.79 yuan. The general retail price index given in Table 9.2 of the *China Statistical Yearbook 1999* is 110.7 in 1981, 128.1 in 1985 and 370.9 in 1998; the general consumer price index for rural areas is 100.0 in 1985 and 319.1 in 1998. To approximate the increase in consumer prices for rural areas, we assume the same proportional increase in these two indices between 1981 and 1985 to obtain a value of 86.4 for the latter index in 1981. The increase between 1981 and 1998 in rural consumer prices from 86.4 to 319.1 is a factor of 3.69. The increase in the nominal value of per capita consumption is 939.55/135.23=6.95 for Gansu, 9.81 for Yunan and 7.89 for Qinghai. If we consider the two other poorest provinces as of 1998 among the original 28, namely Shanxi and Guizhou, with consumption per capita of 1056.45 and 1094.39, and consider their improvement from the 1981 values of 147.78 and 162.51 in Chow (1992, Table 9.2), we find factors of 7.15 and 6.73. Thus, Guizhou is the province having the smallest increase in rural consumption per capita between 1981 and 1998. The improvement in real consumption during this period is only a factor of 6.73/3.69 or 1.82. In terms of exponential rate of increase per year between 1981 and 1998, Guizhou experienced a rate of 0.035.

To summarize our discussion on disparity as measured by the dispersion in rural consumption per capita among provinces, the disparity has increased at the rate of about half a percentage point per year between 1981 and 1998, but the rate of increase has slowed down to 0.2 of a percentage point in the last five years of this period. There have been significant increases in the level of real consumption per capita in all provinces in the meantime. Even Guizhou, the province with the slowest rate of increase among the original 28 provinces, experienced an average exponential rate of increase of 0.035 per year.

9.3 Three components of the problem of rural poverty

I have divided the problem of rural poverty into the following three components.

The first is the income gap between the urban and rural residents. From the data presented in the previous section it is clear that the problem of rural poverty is not due to the low income level of the rural population, nor to a small rate of increase in income. Per capita income of rural residents has increased fairly rapidly, in the order of 5.5 percent per year since 1989, and the percentage of rural residents with income below the poverty line has declined rapidly. It is true that the gap in per capita income between the urban and rural residents has widened but the rate of increase in the latter has been so rapid that the rural population, on average or as judged by the poorest among them, is so much better off economically than before. If one uses income as the sole measure of rural poverty the problem has to be viewed either as (1) the deterioration of the *relative* income of the rural residents in spite of the rapid increase in absolute income, or (2) possible social discontent created during a period of improvement in income level which enables the poor to express their discontent. These two interpretations explain a part of the problem of rural poverty but are not sufficient to explain the seriousness of the current problem, which is accounted for by the following two components, the second of which is the unfavorable treatment by the central government of the rural residents as compared with the urban residents.

The inadequacy of government provision for the rural residents will be detailed in section 9.4 when government policy to remedy the situation is discussed. First, the government has spent less on infrastructure investment in rural areas than in urban areas. It invested only a limited amount to improve agricultural productivity. Second, it provided fewer welfare benefits including health care and education subsidies to rural residents. Although much labor mobility was allowed for farmers to move to urban areas to find work, those working in the urban areas are subject to discrimination under government policy (introduced in the 1950s) of separating residence status and thus the entitled benefits of the urban and rural populations. The migrating workers do not have residence permits in the cities and cannot receive the services provided, such as health care and schooling for their children. Third, although the Commune system was abolished, procurement of farm products by government agencies has continued and the procurement prices were often set below market prices. In the mean time the farmers were not allowed to sell their products to private traders as private trading and transportation of grain were prohibited. Thus, the market economy does not function in the distribution and pricing of grain for the benefit of the farmers.

The neglect of the central government in dealing with the rural problems is probably not by design but a result of the historical development of economic reform. The initial success of the privatization of farming in the early 1980s that improved the economic conditions of the farmers was a result of market forces at work and not of government intervention. The strategy of "letting some people get rich first" resulted in the income gap between the urban and rural population. The historical entitlement of welfare benefits provided to the urban population who had the required residence permits excluded the rural population – this was inherited from the period of economic planning and not a new policy favoring the urban population while the collapse of the commune system took away similar welfare benefits to the rural population. Finally, the need to deal with other important reform problems concerned with the state enterprises, the banking and financial system, and the open-door policy together with the human and financial resources required to accomplish them (including resources for the building of infrastructure for the special economic zones as a part of the open-door policy) has also contributed to the neglect of the rural population. When the Chinese government realized the seriousness of the relative poverty problem facing the farmers, perhaps valuable time had been lost. The problem is called the san-nong (three-farm) problem that covers farming, rural areas, and farmers.

The third, and very important, component of the san-nong or three-farm problem is that the farmers' rights have been violated by illegal activities of local government officials. This component is not poverty in the narrow sense of low income *per se* but is concerned with the economic welfare of the low-income farmers when their property rights are violated. The most disconcerting example is the confiscation of land from farmers for urban development while many farmers receive a compensation that is arbitrary and well below market price. Second, many farmers and other rural residents are not paid, or not paid on time, for work performed such as public work and teaching in public schools. Third, farmers are subject to illegal levies. The levies include the increase in reported acreage of the farmer's land that is subject to tax over the acreage actually used, special tax for growing commercial crops other than grain and for livestock, fees for schools, road construction and other services provided by the local government. One reason for the extra levies is the tax reform of 1994 which increased the proportion of government revenue paid to the central government (from 22.0 percent in 1993 to 55.7 percent in 2004) at the expense of provincial and local governments. Another reason is the central government's policy to assign the responsibility of providing "compulsory education" of nine years and adequate healthcare to local governments.

Concerning the violation of the farmers' right to the use and transfer of land, a Chinese official in charge of rural policy Chen Xiwen (2006, 37) writes:

> It is stipulated in our Constitution that in rural China . . . land is collectively owned by farmers but contracted to individual households. However, at the grassroots level, few officials have read this provision . . . Therefore, some grassroots officials constantly make troubles with farmers' land, causing endless land contract conflicts. Because of this, the Rural Land Contract Law was passed in March 2003 in which there are two basic regulations: (1) during the contract period, the contract granting party shall not be allowed to take back the contracted land; and (2) during the contract period, the contract-granting party shall not be allowed to adjust the contracted land. Neither regulation, however, has been well implemented.

As head of the Institute for the Study of the San-nong Problem of the Central Party School, Zeng Yesong (2004, 43) states the problem of the lack of basic rights on the part of Chinese farmers as follows:

> Farmers in many places have limited right to information. Policies of the central government fail to reach the farmers. In some provinces policy documents to reduce taxes on farmers were not distributed to them. In some places, farmers were mistreated because the matter was not handled on time. They even suffered from subjugation which forced them to report to authorities above. However, many people in the government above believed only in the officials below and not in the farmers. They found small excuse to imprison the farmers, and even persecute those who dared to report to officials above. This not only deprives the farmers of their right to speak out but also interferes with their human rights.

In a popular book, well-known Chinese authors Chen and Wu (2005, 108–9) provide a dramatic illustration of the extortion of illegal levies in a village. The village Party secretary led a group of several armed tax collectors to each house to collect a "school construction fee" of 6 yuan when all school buildings were in good condition. When one housewife did not have the money to pay, the collectors took away a television set. After returning home and finding out this incident, the husband was brave enough to visit the county Party secretary to file a complaint but he was ignored. When the village Party secretary found out about this visit, he went back to the house for a second time to take away a bicycle. This story illustrates the lawlessness and abuse of power of local Party officials, and that the "three-farm" problem is not a problem due to extreme poverty, at least in this case, since the farm household has a television set and a bicycle, but to the violation of the farmers' rights.

All through much of Chinese history local government officials considered themselves a class above the farmers, having the authority to rule over them. The abuse of power under the PRC is worse because the officials are given even more power to control the activities of the citizens. Some well-publicized stories of the abuse of power by local Party and government officials are documented in Chen and Wu (2005), who also describe the multi-level bureaucracy in the village-township-county governments that protects each's interests and positions and fails to carry out policies of the central government to benefit the farmers, a point also stated in Zeng (2004, 43) quoted above. Chapter 1 of Chen and Wu (2005) tells the story of citizens of a village sending representatives to report to the county officials the illegal levies and false financial accounting by village officials who later mistreated one of the representatives, sent policemen to put him in jail and eventually beat him to death (though perhaps not intentionally). This story collaborates with Zeng (2004, 43) on the violation of the farmers' human rights by local government and Party officials.

The abuse of power by local officials is known to be fairly widespread, as stated in the writing of the three authors quoted above and evidenced by the large number of demonstrations and protests by the farmers reported in the news media. Zhang (2006, pp. 19–20) quoted (1) statistics provided by Han (2003) that some 34 million farmers have lost their land to local government land taking and (2) statistics provided by the Ministry of Construction to show that, between January and June 2004, 4,026 groups and 18,620 individuals had lodged petitions over allegedly illicit land confiscations, compared to 3,929 groups and 18,071 individuals for the entire year of 2003.

9.4 Solution proposed by the Chinese government

Realizing these problems, the Central Government has given the agricultural sector much attention in recent years. In 1993, the "three-farm policy" was introduced to improve agricultural productivity in farming, promote economic development of rural areas and increase the income of farmers. It includes increasing capital investment in rural areas and helping the farmers to use better technology and better methods for farming, reducing corruption and misbehavior of local government officials and economic assistance to farmers. The development of the agricultural sector was the first important task mentioned in Premier Zhu Rongji's work report of March 2001 to the National People's Congress.

In February 2004, the State Council announced a set of policies to improve the living conditions of farmers that include the following:

1 support the development of agricultural production in grain-producing areas to increase farmers' incomes. This includes providing incentives to farmers, improving methods of production as well as quality of land, and increasing government investment in agriculture;

2   change the structure of agricultural production by improving output mix, management and technology;
3   develop industrial and service industries in rural areas, including the encouragement of township and village as well as private enterprises. (Township and village enterprises, perhaps involving less capital than those that flourished in the 1980s and of more primitive nature being tied to agricultural production, did not develop in the very poor regions, probably because of lack of human capital among the residents and lack of incentives on the part of local government officials to promote them;)
4   assist the farmers in moving to urban areas to find work by reducing various levies collected from them by city governments and by giving responsibility to the latter for the training of the incoming farmers and for the education of their children;
5   establish a market mechanism for the distribution and marketing of grain by allowing more distribution channels including collectives and by the promotion of farm products;
6   build infrastructure for rural areas, including water supply, roads and electricity in poor areas;
7   carry out reform in rural areas including the tax system;
8   continue to improve programs to reduce poverty by subsidies and other means;
9   strengthen the leadership of the Communist Party in putting the above policies into practice.

One important step was taken in 2005 when the Central Government decided to abolish all taxes to farmers. This policy seemed to be a good move if one compares the costs and benefits of taxing the farmers. The benefits are small, since such taxes accounted for only just over 1 percent of total government revenue. The costs of taxing farmers are much larger, as the tax increases their discontent which might lead to social instability and provides an excuse for local government officials to impose illegal levies. Although some local officials might continue to impose such levies, the policy of allowing no tax to farmers makes it more difficult for them to do so.

On February 21 2006 and for three consecutive years (according to *People's Daily Online* of February 23, 2006) the Central Committee of the Chinese Communist Party and the State Council issued its most important "Number 1 Document" on the subject of agriculture, farmers and countryside development. This document is more comprehensive and systematic than the previous two. Agriculture and rural areas are to receive higher fractions of national fiscal spending, budgetary investment on fixed assets and credits. In 2005, over 300 billion yuan ($US 37.5 billion) from the budget of the central government was allocated to support rural development, a 50 percent increase from the 2002 figure when the price level was stable. In addition to direct financial support, the government announced the abolition of agricultural tax as of January 1, 2006, which totaled 22 billion yuan ($US 2.75 billion) in the previous year. The evolution of government policies to deal with the san-nong problem between 2004 and 2006 illustrates the use of experimentation and observation in revising and improving policies, termed "crossing the river by feeling the rocks" by China's reform leader, Deng Xiaoping.

The 2006 Number 1 Document covers:

1   an infrastructure building that will include the provision of safe drinking water, clean energy supply (by the use of methane, straw gasification technology, small hydropower, solar energy, wind farm and upgrading of power grids) and the construction of country roads;
2   a national support system for agriculture and the farmers consisting of:

   a   direct subsidies to grain production (to be raised to 50 percent of the grain risk fund used to stabilize market price) and to grain farmers for the purchase of high-quality seeds and farm machinery;
   b   improvement of agricultural production and marketing;
   c   facilitating the migration of rural labor by removing discriminative restrictions on migrant workers on urban job markets and gradually providing them with a social security system, possibly with a guarantee of subsistence allowances in rural areas (insurance for occupational injuries to cover all migrant workers);
   d   an increase in funding for the rural compulsory education system, and reduction or exemption of tuition for students included in the system in western areas, to be extended to all rural areas;
   e   the training of farmers to make them well educated and technologically literate with basic knowledge in management, with 100 million to be trained by 2010, including 50 million in agricultural technology and another 50 million in other sectors;
   f   a social assistance program covering 50 million people and four areas (regular social assistance providing minimum living subsidies to poor urban and rural residence, emergency assistance for people suffering through disasters, temporary assistance to low-income migrants to urban areas, and social assistance from donations, with the total of assistance amounting to only 0.02 percent of GDP);
   g   more financial support for the new rural cooperative health care system (since rural residents, who account for some 60 percent of the nation's total population, have access to only 20 percent of the country's medical resources) both from the central and local fiscal systems in 2006, to cover almost all the rural areas in 2008. The plan is to cover 40 percent of China's counties in a new government-backed medicare cooperative program for farmers in 2006, and to promote the program to all the rural areas in the next few years. Under the plan, the government will allocate 40 yuan for every account of

farmers who each pay 10 yuan, and set up a clinic in every village in the near future;

h   rural financial reform for community financial institutions in order to provide agricultural insurance and easily accessible loans to rural households and small and medium business enterprises;

3   streamlining the functions of the multi-level government system (central, provincial, county, township, and village) by elimination of the operational functions of *township* governments within five years and in the interim changing their functions from engaging in investment and operation of their own projects and production of grain to creating a favorable environment for the farmers, while the finance of *counties* will be placed under the direct control of the provincial governments or of the villages themselves;

4   village planning that is environmentally friendly, by remodeling existing houses rather than constructing new ones, efficient use of land, energy and materials for the construction of farm housing and the preservation of ancient villages and residences.

The "three farm" policies announced above were incorporated in the 11th Five-Year Plan passed by the National People's Congress on March 14 2006 under the heading, "building a new socialist countryside" and "according to the requirement of advanced production, improved livelihood, a civilized social atmosphere, clean and tidy villages and democratic administration." The budget allocated for these policies amounted to 339.7 billion yuan from the central government in 2006 as compared with 297.5 billion yuan from the central government budget in 2005 spent on agriculture, rural areas, and farmers, the latter being an increase of 34.9 billion yuan from 2004.

In summary, the policies of the central government aim mainly at redirecting economic resources to the rural areas (items 1 and 2 listed above) and also at streamlining the structure of local governments (item 3).

9.5 Two policy issues in the solution of the Chinese government

This section raises two questions concerning the solution of the Chinese government outlined above, one on the streamlining of the local government structure and a second on the possibility of enforcing a policy to solve the third component of the three-farm problem.

The first question is concerned with item 3 of the 2006 Number 1 Document to streamline the multilevel local government structure by eliminating the operational functions of township governments in five years. The main purpose of this policy is to eliminate the taxation power of local governments at both the county and the township levels and thus to reduce the opportunity and power of corruption on the part of county and township level government officials. However, there may be difficulty in implementing this policy. Township governments have been in existence for many years and played an important role in recent Chinese history. In the form of Communes before economic reform, they provided healthcare and education and directed construction projects for the rural population. In the 1980s and early 1990s they established township and village enterprises that propelled China's rapid economic growth. A number of questions can be raised concerning the policy to eliminate the township governments in five years and to take away the financial authority of county officials.

Where would the township government officials go five years from now? Supposedly, some are due to retire and others will work in departments of the county governments above. In the interim if they are not allowed to operate enterprises, how would they find sufficient financing for their government and what incentive would they have to create a favorable environment for the farmers as they are supposed to do? Why should they be treated differently from other government officials and even university administrators who are allowed to operate enterprises to generate additional income for their units and even for themselves? Resistance by the officials in the township governments whose power is taken away and by officials in the county governments whose financial authority is taken away may present a serious obstacle to the implementation of this policy. These are natural questions to ask when such a bold move is proposed to change the local government structure. I assume that the Chinese leadership has considered these questions carefully and found solutions to them. It will be interesting to observe the implementation of this policy in the next five years.

The second issue concerning the official solution is the absence of any provision to deal with the third component of the "three-farm problem," namely, to protect the rights of the farmers to keep the land contracted to them, to be free from illegal taxation and to receive wage payments due to them. In fact illegal land seizure is the major cause of rural discontent. The government is certainly aware of this problem as stated in Chen (2006, 37) quoted above. As pointed out earlier, the National People's Congress passed the Rural Land Contract Law in 2003 which stipulates that during the contract period the contract-granting party shall not be allowed to take back the contract land or to adjust the contract land. However, the local officials who confiscated the land for economic development disobeyed this law. The strict enforcement of this law is therefore essential. As Premier Wen Jiabao stated on March 14, 2006, strict enforcement of existing policy must be strengthened to protect the farmers' rights at a time when illegitimate land seizures have fueled protests in the country side (*New York Times* 2006).

Therefore, the problem of illegal land seizure boils down to one of law enforcement. It can be considered a special case of the problem of corruption when a Party or government official takes advantage of his economic or political power to extract payment from the Chinese people. The extent of this case of corruption, as corruption in general, increases when the official has more power relative to the people being exploited and when the economic gain is higher. The degree of discontent increases when the exploited are poor and cannot afford to pay. In the present case, the extent of economic abuse is large because the peasants have very little power relative to the village Party secretary and the economic gain in using the land for economic development can be great. There is much discontent because many farmers are poor and cannot afford to give up their land without adequate compensation.

From the above observations, the problem of land seizure will become less serious if the farmers have more power to protect themselves or if the Party secretary is deprived of his power to extract money from the farmers, and if the economic gain from land seizure is reduced. The degree of discontent will be reduced as the farmers grow richer. If rural economic development succeeds, the farmers will become richer; they will have more power to protect themselves and they can more easily afford to give up their land with less compensation. The local government officials will also have more revenue from taxation but they may desire and be able to extract even more as the price of land goes up.

A key to the solution of this law enforcement problem lies in the ability to take away the power of village Party secretaries to exploit the farmers economically. The leadership in the central government and in the Communist Party has difficulty in disciplining the rank-and-file Party members who have established power locally, as shown by the failure to control the widespread corruption in China (see Chow, 2006, for a discussion of corruption). This explains partly why an explicit policy to discipline the local Party officials is not a part of the No. 1 Document in dealing with the three-farm problem. Instead, the government's approach to protecting the farmers' rights is to extend democracy in rural areas and to organize farmers' associations for self-protection, as stated in the 11th Five-Year Plan and in Zeng (2004, p. 338). The possible shortcomings of this policy are the following. First, building democracy at the grassroots level will take too long for the solution of the current three-farm problem, which is urgent. Second, providing law and order is the responsibility of the government and should not be relegated to the people's associations. Third, if currently elected village heads are not able to protect the farmers' rights, how can we expect future elected officials to do so?

An effective policy to enforce the law to protect the farmers' rights can be made up of two parts. The first part is a more strict discipline to be applied to Party officials who violated the farmers' rights to land use (or rights to compensation for unpaid wages and for illegal tax levies) and failed to provide them with suitable compensation, together with a commitment of central government to compensate by using its own funds if the local government fails to do so. In 2005, about 45,000 Party members were expelled for misbehavior. The present case of abuse of power can be treated as a most serious offense leading to the loss of Party membership. Since public democratic elections in Chinese villages are widespread, an offending party secretary can be replaced by the elected village head to serve as the chairman of the most powerful village committee. There is sufficient fund in the Central Government budget of 340 billion yuan in 2006 allocated for solving the three-farm problem to set up a guarantee, during the next few years and in cases where the local governments fail, to compensate the deserving farmers among the 34 million who lost their land.

The second part is to allow the news media to report cases of abuse to a larger extent than is the case at present. To implement the above policy of applying strict discipline, a major requirement is to be able to identify cases of abuse. There are two channels to accomplish this. First, the local courts can identify possible cases of violation that are brought to their attention. Second, the farmers can appeal to the news media if it has sufficient freedom to publish cases of violation of the farmers' rights. At the present time such freedom is restricted. It is recognized that in China the degree of freedom allowed for the news media is a very important matter for the Party leadership to decide. However, if the leadership desires to solve the third and very important component of the three-farm problem, it has to allow more freedom of the press to report cases of abuse openly. If the court realizes the existence of the two parts of the proposed policy stated above, it would tend to be fair in deciding on what the farmer deserves in each case.

One might be concerned that this policy could lead numerous farmers to file illegitimate claims, but this is unlikely to happen. Ordinary farmers are in no position to file an illegitimate claim against the more powerful Party officials; they would assert their rights only when injustice is done to them. Furthermore, the news media and the courts will render judgments and the farmers in general do not dare to take the risk of filing illegitimate claims. If the claims turned out to be too numerous to handle, one solution would be to settle them in an order based on the claimant's income, with the cases of the poorest farmers to be resolved first.

The announcement of such a policy would boost the confidence of the farmers and the Chinese people in general and would help alleviate the problem of social discontent in rural China. The determined execution of this policy would also set an example of the central government's ability to eliminate one aspect of corruption. The problem of corruption as a whole is not easy to solve but the successful exercise of discipline in one specific and important case would serve as a first step in reducing the degree of corruption. This policy could be an important addition to the policies announced by the State Council on February 21, 2006 as stated above.

Why is such a policy not a part of the 2006 No. 1 Document? Perhaps the central leadership recognizes that the violation of the farmers' rights as stated has occurred partly because local government officials need to finance economic development and other responsibilities such as the provision of compulsory education and healthcare that are assigned to them by the central government itself. If this is the case, the central government should provide more funds for such local programs, as it is currently doing to some extent, but in no case should it allow lawless behavior to spread widely. Preserving law and order is a very important function of the Chinese government and should be top of its list of priorities. Although one cannot expect that the above policy to enforce an important law to protect the rights of the farmers will be implemented successfully in all parts of China within one or two years, its successful implementation in substantial parts of the rural areas within several years will be a great step forward in solving a very important component of the san-nong problem and in "building a new socialist countryside" in China.

9.6 Comparison with India

When we compare the problem of rural poverty in China with that of India, three important propositions can be made. First, China has made much progress in solving its economic problem of poverty as compared with India. Second, in India the problem of income inequality and relative rural poverty does not exist because there has been no rapid economic growth in certain regions, at least until 2003. Third, the abuse of power by local officials and the resulting discontent of the rural population is not a serious problem in India. I will elaborate on these statements below.

Table 9.4 (see www.indiastat.com) shows the proportion of the rural and urban population below poverty line in selected years in India. The data support our first statement by showing the large proportion of both the rural and urban population remaining below the poverty line in 1999–2000 and the fairly slow reduction in these amounts through the years, unlike in the statistics shown in Table 9.3. Since the contrasts in the data are so great, the statement is valid even if the definition of poverty line is different for the two countries. Second, if these proportions are used to measure income status (instead of mean income), there does not exist a large income gap between the rural and urban population, as there does in China. Note that the fraction

Table 9.4 Incidence of poverty in India

Population below Poverty Line (as per Expert Group Methodology) in India (1973–4, 1977–8, 1983, 1987–8, 1993–4 and 1999–2000)

Sector	1973–4	1977–8	1983	1978–88	1993–4	1999–2000
Population in millions						
Rural	261.3	264.3	252	231.9	244	193.2
Urban	60	64.6	70.9	75.2	76.3	67
Total	**321.3**	**328.9**	**322.9**	**307.1**	**320.3**	**260.2**
Poverty ratio (%)						
Rural	56.4	53.1	45.7	39.1	37.3	27.1
Urban	49.0	45.2	40.8	38.2	32.4	23.6
Total	**54.9**	**51.3**	**44.5**	**38.9**	**36.0**	**26.1**

Source: Rural Development Statistics 2002–3, National Institute of Rural Development.

Note: Year: Period of fiscal year in India is April to March, e.g. year shown as 1990–1 relates to April 1990 to March 1991.

below the poverty line for the urban population is only slightly smaller than for the rural population. As of 1999–2000 India was still a very poor country as judged by the large proportion (27.1 percent for rural and 23.6 percent for urban) of its population below the poverty line.

As is well known, India did not experience a rapid economic development between 1978 and 2000. This is seen by the fairly slow reduction in the fraction of population below poverty line and by the relatively small rates of growth, relative to China, of India's per capita net state domestic product (NSDP) in constant prices in recent years as shown in Table 9.5. From the *World Development Indicator* database, one finds that for the year 2004 China's per capita GDP was 5,495 in PPP (international $) while India's was merely 3,115, showing China has gone much further in its development path than India.

On the third statement that the abuse of power is primarily a Chinese problem, one can cite a number of factors special to China. As pointed out earlier, the abuse of power by local officials who consider themselves rulers over the peasants has its root in Chinese history and the power has increased by the authority given to them by the PRC government. The peasants now have higher income and more economic resources, including the right to use public land, creating opportunities for the bureaucrats to exploit. If the economy were not rapidly growing the market value of the land for use in urban development would be much lower and less worthy of illegal confiscation. All these factors do not exist in India.

9.7 Conclusion

In this chapter I have examined three kinds of statistics on rural poverty and suggested that the problem of rural poverty has three components: income disparity, policy neglect of the central Party and government leadership and violation of the rights of the farmers by local party officials. After studying the proposed solution of the government, I have raised one set of questions concerning possible difficulties in the implementation of the government policy to take away the taxation power of county governments and to eliminate the operational functions of township governments in five years and in the interim not to allow them to operate enterprises as they have been accustomed to do. I have also suggested a policy to protect the rights of the farmers to the use of land contracted to them, to compensate them for the

Table 9.5 Growth of per capita NSDP at 1993–4 prices in India (as on November 30, 2004) from 1994–5 to 2003–4

Year	1994–5	1995–6	1996–7	1997–8	1998–9	1999–2000	2000–1	2001–2	2002–3	2003–4
India	4.9	5.2	6.1	2.6	4.4	4.3	2.4	4.5	1.8	6.5

Source: Central Statistical Organization (see www.indiastat.com).

illegal seizure of their land by severe punishment of party officials who violate these rights and by exposing the violations by giving the news media more freedom. Although the solution of the san-nong problem may take some years, economic forces will naturally enrich the farmers in the future as in the past, if social discontent does not seriously interrupt the economic process under a government policy that protects the basic rights of the farmers against infringement by the local officials.

Note

This chapter builds on my keynote address delivered at the annual meetings of Chinese Economist Society, July 1–4, 2006, Shangai, China.

Acknowledgment

I would like to thank Harvey Lam, Jianping Mei, Yan Shen, Xiaobo Zhang and participants of the Conference on Economic Development of Western China organized by George Tolley at the University of Chicago and of my lecture in the Contemporary Issues in the Chinese Economy Series sponsored by the Department of Economics and Finance of the City University of Hong Kong for helpful comments and the Center for Economic Policy Studies and the Gregory C Chow Econometric Research Program at Princeton University for financial support in the preparation of this paper.

References

Chen, Guidi and Wu Chuntao. 2005. *Zhongguo Nongmin Diaocha (China Famers Survey)*, Taipei: Dadi (Great Earth) Publishing Company (in Chinese).

Chen, Xiwen. 2006. "Conflicts and Problems Facing China's Current Rural Reform and Development," Chapter 4 in Dong, Song, and Zhang, eds, *China's Agricultural Development: Challenges and Prospects*, Hampshire: Ashgate Publishing Limited.

Chow, Gregory C. 2002. *China's Economic Transformation*, Oxford: Blackwell Publishing Company.

Chow, Gregory C. 2006. "Corruption and China's economic reform in the early 21st century," *Journal of International Business*, 20, 263–80.

Dong, Xiao-yuan, Shunfeng Song, and Xiaobo Zhang. 2006. *China's Agricultural Development: Challenges and Prospects*, Hampshire: Ashgate Publishing Limited.

Han, Jun. 2003. "Jiang Tudi Nongmin Jiti Suyou Dingjie Wei An Gufen Gongyouzhi" (Chinese Collective Land Ownership into Shareholder Ownership), *Zhongguo Jingji Shibao (China Economic Times)*, November 11, 2003 (in Chinese).

New York Times. 2006. "China's Leader Says Rapid Rise Comes with 'Acute Problems' ", reported by Jim Yardley, March 14, A5.

Zeng Yesong. 2004. *Xin Nong Lun (New Farm Treatise)*, Beijing: Xin Hua Publishing Company (in Chinese).

Zhang Xiabo. 2006. "Asymmetric Property Rights in China's Economic Growth," DSGD Discussion Paper No. 28, January, 2006, Washington, DC: International Food Research Institute, Development Strategy and Government Division.

Part III
Governance and institutions

10 Economic–social interaction in China

Assar Lindbeck[1]

Abstract

This chapter analyzes economic-social interaction in China in connection with the country's change of economic system. I define an economic system in terms of a multidimensional vector of broad institutional characteristics, and I emphasize that important features of the social development are closely related to specific changes in these various dimensions. I classify China's options for future social improvements into three broad categories: policies that improve the stability and distribution of factor income; government-created wedges between factor income and disposable income; and improvements in the quantity, quality and distribution of human services, such as education and health care.

China's highly successful economic transition during the last three decades, with an officially reported GDP growth rate of 9.5 percent per year since 1980, has been accompanied by huge and complex social change.[2] I refer, in particular, to changes in the incidence of poverty, the security and distribution of income, employment opportunities and the provision of human services such as education and health care. The development in these areas raises the issue of China's future policy options to improve social conditions; indeed, this is the basic topic of the paper. First, however, it is important to be clear about the nature of the economic transition.

10.1 The nature of the economic transition

Since the economic reforms in China imply a radical, although gradual, change of the country's economic system, it is useful to analyze the reforms in the context of a typology of economic systems. To this end, I regard an economic system as a multi-dimensional phenomenon, defined in terms of a nine-dimensional vector of broad institutional characteristics; see Figure 10.1[3] The *first two* dimensions concern ownership of firms and assets, respectively – contrasting public (government) and private ownership. The *third* dimension deals with the choice between centralized and decentralized economic

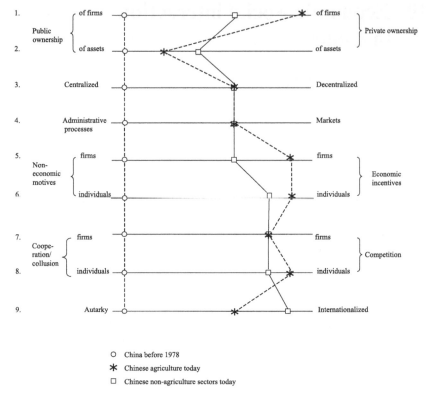

Figure 10.1 Dimensions of economic systems.

decision-making, and the *fourth* with the related choice between administrative processes and market mechanisms for transmitting information, coordinating economic decisions, and distributing goods and services among households. The *fifth* and *sixth* dimensions concern the extent to which economic behavior is influenced by non-economic motives and economic incentives, respectively – in the case of individuals as well as firms. The *seventh* and *eighth* dimensions refer to a crucial aspect of the relation between economic agents in the domestic economy: the role of competition. The *ninth* dimension, finally, concerns the relations between domestic economic agents and the outside world, contrasting autarkic and internationally integrated ("internationalized") economic systems.

I depict the initial ("standardized") position of China's economic system in the late 1970s by the vertical vector of circles to the far left in the figure. Today's position (in 2007) is schematically described by stars in the case of agriculture, and by squares for the rest of the economy. In terms of this diagram, the economic system has gradually shifted to the right in all dimensions – towards private ownership of firms and assets, decentralized decision-making of production and consumption to firms and households respectively, and increased reliance on markets, economic incentives, competition and international economic interaction (codified in China's entry into WTO in year 2001). Although each dimension is conceptually distinct from the others, several of them are strongly interdependent. An obvious example is that market mechanisms fulfill the role of coordinating decentralized decision-making by firms and households. There are also complex interrelations between ownership and other dimensions of the economic system. In particular, public ownership makes it easier, perhaps also more tempting, for politicians and public-sector administrators to centralize decision-making and restrict the operations of markets.

In the figure, I have also schematically indicated the relative magnitude of the shifts in different dimensions of the economic system. Except for the second and ninth dimensions – asset ownership and internationalization – the reforms seem, so far, to have advanced further in agriculture than in industry.[4] The reason is largely that politicians and public-sector administrators still routinely intervene in state-owned enterprises (SOEs) in industry, services and financial institutions. Needless to say, the figure is only illustrative. (When I see no specific reason for asserting that a shift is larger in one dimension than in another, or in one sector than in another, the shifts are simply depicted as having the same size in both cases.)

This disaggregation of the concept of an economic system reminds us that the traditional distinction between capitalism and socialism is too blunt for a constructive analysis of economic systems. Moreover, as will be emphasized below, important features of the social development in China in recent decades turn out to be closely related to changes in specific dimensions of the country's economic system. In this sense, contemporary suggestions of social reforms are largely triggered by, and have to be adjusted to, China's shift to a new economic system.

How, then, should today's economic system in China be labeled? Some observers call it "state capitalism." While this label may have been appropriate (outside agriculture) in the 1980s, it is rather misleading today. The bulk of production today takes place in private firms, including privately owned Town and Village Enterprises (TVEs) and firms controlled by foreign (nonmainland) owners. For instance, OECD (2005a, Table 2.1) estimates that about 60 percent of aggregate production in China in 2004 was accounted for by the private sector.[5] The term "market socialism," although recently often used by the Chinese authorities, is also misleading. After all, dominating models of market socialism – such as those developed by Oskar Lange (1938) and Abba Lerner (1934) – presuppose public ownership of firms. In some models of market socialism, such as that of Lange, prices are also supposed to be determined by the government, while most prices in China are today formed on markets, the main exceptions being natural resources and public utilities. Moreover, the label "socialism" is usually not associated with a strong reliance on economic incentives, competition, internationalization and (as in China) an apparent neglect of the distribution across households of income, education and health care.

For these reasons, it is perhaps most appropriate to simply characterize today's economic system in China as a kind of "mixed economy," although with a number of specific features, such as less private ownership of assets than of firms (in particular, in agriculture); frequent ad hoc government interventions in public-sector firms; less developed factor markets than product markets; and an important role for informal business networks, *guanxi*. The guanxi, which often also includes politicians and public-sector administrators, partly compensates for deficiencies in "the rule of law" in the country. However, the guanxi is a mixed blessing. It contributes to an insider-outsider division of the business community and, as will be emphasized below, it keeps the doors open to corruption.

10.2 Social consequences

China's economic transition since the late 1970s has been accompanied by pronounced social achievements as well as serious social problems. The sevenfold increase in per capita income for a billion of some of the poorest people in the world, and the related dramatic fall in the incidence of deep ("absolute") poverty, are perhaps the most obvious social *achievements*.[6] It is also natural to regard the increase in economic (in contrast to political) freedom of individuals as a major social achievement: the right to choose profession, employer and consumption bundle, as well as to set up a business and become an entrepreneur. However, it is also easy to identify a number of remaining, and in some cases deteriorating, social *problems* during the period of economic transition – problems that constitute a natural background to a discussion of China's policy options for improving social conditions in the country.

10.2.1 The breakdown of previous social arrangements

With only slight exaggeration, we could say that the division of tasks between the government and firms, or rather work units (*danwei*), during the *pre-reform* period was the reverse of the corresponding division in developed countries today. While the government was in charge of basic production decisions (a primitive type of input-output planning), work units functioned as mini-welfare states, or "enterprises running small societies" (Xiaoyi 1996). It is hardly surprising that the shift to competitive markets made it difficult for the work units to fulfill the assigned social obligations. Many firms could simply no longer afford to guarantee jobs, pay cash benefits (including pensions) or provide "human services" to their employees – such as health care, housing and elementary education for the employees' children. Moreover, benefits tied to specific work places do not sit well in a market economy, since an efficiently functioning labor market requires social benefits to be highly portable. The move to a competitive market, and the increased reliance on economic incentives, also meant that income-insecurity increased, including a rise in unemployment risks. Hence, while income protection deteriorated, the need for such protection increased.

As many observers have pointed out, acute social problems in urban areas were mitigated during the first phase of the economic transition thanks to the gradualist nature of the economic reforms. In particular, this helped the country avoid a "transition depression" – in contrast to what happened in most other transition economies.[7] Moreover, ad hoc selective capital transfers from the government and "social" loans from state banks functioned as stop-gap solutions helping state firms live up to at least some of their social obligations, including their "job guarantees." However, this did not only increase the volume of "soft" and, indeed, often non-performing loans, with negative consequences for the stability of financial institutions. It also accentuated the discrimination of private firms in financial markets, since the loans to state firms drained the lending to other firms, with negative consequences for the ability of domestic private firms to expand production and employment. The "double bind" – state firms constrained in shedding labor and private firms constrained in acquiring loans – implied a kind of catch-22 situation during much of the reform period. It has been difficult to remove this double bind as long as private firms are not able to expand their employment sufficiently to absorb redundant workers in state firms and workers exiting agriculture – and before new arrangements for income protection are in place. The negative consequences of these policies for the development of aggregate employment have been accentuated by China's highly capital-intensive growth strategy.[8]

The social consequences of the new role of work units were even stronger in rural than in urban areas. Indeed, the shift from agriculture communes to family farms implied that the earlier existing social arrangements in rural areas largely disappeared – in the case of income protection as well as human services, in particular, health care.

Inadvertently, during the reform period, households also indirectly helped finance the social obligations of state firms, since households' deposits in state banks (at low, and during some periods even negative, real interest rates) have been intermediated into low-interest loans to state firms. As a result, the social obligations of state firms have, in fact, been partly financed by an "inflation tax" on households' financial savings (although less so during years with low inflation). This, in turn, implies that much of the real return on household savings has been transferred to the beneficiaries of various social arrangements – much like a tax-financed pay-as-you-go system, although in this case the "tax" has been imposed on the return on savings rather than on work.

Moreover, surviving privileges for employees in state firms – in terms of wages as well as social benefits of various types – have created a pronounced insider-outsider character also for the urban labor market.[9] This character has been accentuated by the residence registration system, the urban *hukou*.

Although this system has recently become less restrictive, individuals without permanent urban residence – the "floating population" – are still a strongly disadvantaged group in urban areas. They often have particularly unpleasant and dangerous jobs and they seem to be less rewarded than others in terms of the return on their human capital (Maurer-Fazio and Dinh 2004).[10] The *new* social arrangements created during the period of economic transition have also systematically favored "urban insiders" – leaving the "floating population," many private-sector employees and rural residents behind. Indeed, as late as in 2005 most arrangements of income insurance in the country as a whole seem to have covered less than twenty percent of the workforce.[11] Moreover, since the government has only slowly taken over the financing of human services, citizens have in recent years found it necessary to finance about 55 percent of the health expenditures and about 18 percent of the spending on education from out-of-pocket money (the figures refer to 2004).[12]

Rapid, urbanization is also connected with social problems, and these are likely to be accentuated in the future. For instance, without any drastic intervention against motor traffic in cities, such as congestion fees, the traffic system is bound to not only run into serious inefficiencies but also to contribute to deterioration in the quality of city life and health due to pollution, crowding and noise. Indeed, such deterioration is already underway, but the worst is yet to come. Since the required policy interventions are politically easier when car owners are still a small minority, the political "window of opportunity" for dealing with these problems is likely to shrink in the future. It is also unavoidable that China gradually will run into other "typical" urban social problems such as high criminality, the misuse of drugs and alcohol, and a clustering of individuals with mental disorders in urban areas – not least in large cities.

Other important social changes are a direct consequence of recent changes in demography. So far, the so-called demographic burden for the active generation has diminished – partly a result of the one-child-policy.[13] However, this "demographic dividend" will turn into a "demographic deficit" from about 2010 when the share of individuals of working age will start to fall.[14] Since China is "getting old before getting rich," such demographic problems will emerge at a lower per capita income level in China than they did in today's developed and middle-income countries. While, to begin with, this burden will mainly be felt within families, in a long-term perspective (when comprehensive social insurance systems have been built up) both the pension system and public-sector arrangements for old-age care will feel the pinch of the demographic development. The aging of the population will probably also impede the long-term vitality of the economy in the future, since innovation and new entrepreneurship often thrive among young population groups. Experiences from many countries suggest that it is not easy, although not impossible, for governments to do much about the demographic situation, such as boosting fertility after it has declined substantially.[15] Recent tendencies to a softening of the one-child policy are, therefore, unlikely to drastically ameliorate the demographic situation, although the distorted proportions between newborn boys and girls (1.2 today) might be modified.

10.2.2 Distributional consequences

It is hardly surprising that China's radical change of economic system has been accompanied by a widening of the income gap in various dimensions – across regions, between urban and rural areas (from the mid-1980s) and within geographical areas. For instance, it is a commonplace that China's open-economy strategy contributed to the huge regional income gaps to the advantage of the coastal areas – an effect accentuated by the build-up of the "Special Economic Zones" (SEZs), and a concentration of infrastructure investment to these zones. Falling terms of trade for agriculture from the late 1980, and the absence of new efficiency-enhancing agriculture reforms after the shift to farm households in the early 1980s, also contributed to widen the income gap between urban and rural areas from the mid-1980s.[16] Indeed, in economic terms, China today looks less like a nation state than a *continent* with a mixture of middle-income industrial areas and some of the poorest areas in the world.[17]

It is also easy to understand that the shift to an incentive-based economic system contributed to widen the income gaps, since both the reward for success and the punishment for failure increased. Some individuals have simply been more successful than others in utilizing the new incentive system – depending on skills, energy, contacts, luck, etc. For instance, this is reflected in the large increase in the skill premium (Blanchard and Giavazzi 2005). The shift from price control and rationing to market-determined prices for basic consumer products also tended to redistribute real income to the disadvantage of low-income groups, for which such products constitute a relatively large fraction of their total consumption.

The shift of economic system also created new, and highly unevenly distributed, types of income: entrepreneurial income and capital income. The *way* firms and assets were privatized accentuated these consequences, since the ownership of firms and housing were in many cases handed over to a limited fraction of the population – at prices far below market values. Indeed, those favored by this "asset stripping" probably also had a higher than average labor income. (Of course, these distributional consequences of privatization should be compared to the contributions of the privatization process to the long-term reduction in *absolute* poverty – through the release of private entrepreneurship.)

Basically, the increased inequalities are also a result of the absence of comprehensive policy measures to counteract the distributional consequences of the shift of economic system. This helps explain why the Gini coefficient for the distribution of household income in China increased from 28 in 1981 to 43 in 2001; indeed, it may very well be as high as 50 today; for 2004, ADB

(2007) reports a Gini of 47. The wide dispersion of the overall distribution of income is also reflected in statistics on *relative* poverty, expressed, for instance, by the shares of aggregate earnings received by the poorest relative to the richest part of the population.[18]

10.2.3 Weak property rights and corruption

The earlier mentioned deficiencies in the "rule of law" have also had important social consequences during the period of economic transition. The best-known example is perhaps the expropriation of land-lease contracts held by farmers. At least 34 million farmers seem to have lost their land-lease contracts, partly or completely, between 1987 and 1991 due to the expropriation without full economic compensation (UNDP 2005, footnote 120). Such expropriations have also subsequently taken place. Thus, social concerns have been relinquished for other purposes – such as a fast rate of structural change, when land-lease contracts have been handed over to developers in industry, retailing, housing etc. (Zhang 2006). This also seems to have been a major source of corruption in rural areas, since the economic gains in connection with these transactions have often been shared between developers and local "cadres" – politicians as well as public-sector administrators; see, for instance Chow (2007). It is also difficult to avoid rampant corruption in connection with the earlier mentioned informal networks among businessmen, public sector administrators and politicians. More generally, it is difficult to get rid of corruption as long as politicians and public-sector administrators have something to sell – like permits, contracts of various types, loans and subsidies. Experiences from many countries also suggest that the absence of political democracy and a free press breed corruption (Svensson 2005 and references therein).

Asset stripping has, however, not been "all bad." Most likely, it has speeded up the shift to *decentralized* private ownership of firms and assets. This is in contrast to the development in the former Soviet Union, where the ownership of firms and assets during the transition process became concentrated to a small group of "oligarchs." However, if asset stripping and other forms of corruption become a permanent component of Chinese society, they may undermine the legitimacy of the economic system, in particular when the ensuing inequalities are unrelated to productivity-enhancing incentives. Experiences in other countries also suggest that corruption is likely to be detrimental to economic efficiency in a long-run perspective (Svensson 2005).

10.3 Options for future socially oriented policies

It is hardly surprising that new comprehensive social arrangements – for income protection and human services – did not emerge spontaneously in China through market forces, as the old arrangements broke down. Indeed, this experience is consistent with traditional economic analysis, which highlights various limitations of spontaneous market solutions in this field. However, the political leaders in China have recently been increasingly worried about the social situation in the country – worries reflected rhetoric-ally in promises to create a "harmonious society" and a "new socialist coun-tryside" in the future.[19] It is also tempting to speculate that the new emphasis on policies with social ambitions has been stimulated by apparent social unrest in the country, reflected in some 80,000 reported "social incidents" each year recently. Indeed, the actual pace of reform to improve the social situation in the country seems to have increased recently (from about 2005), in particular in the countryside.

What, then, are China's main future policy options for improving the social situation? When discussing this issue, it is useful to classify such pol-icies into three broad categories: (i) policies designed to increase in the level and stability of *factor income*, in particular among the poorest section of the population; (ii) wider *wedges* between factor incomes and disposable income; and (iii) improvement in the quantity, quality and distribution of *human services*, such as education and health care.

10.3.1 Factor-income policies

Naturally, a continuation of fast GDP growth is required not only for a further rapid increase in per capita household income; it would also facilitate further fast reduction in the incidence of serious poverty. The potential importance of the latter point is illustrated by the observation that about 25 percent of the Chinese population still live on less than $2 a day (according to World Bank calculations). However, China also has much to gain from shift-ing from its highly "extensive" to a more "intensive" growth path. Resources could then also be released for social purposes. One example of such a shift would be a change of the composition of investment from real capital assets to human capital. While fast GDP growth requires a large accumulation of capital, the present composition of investment between real capital assets and human capital is heavily tilted in favor of the former. For instance, while investment in real capital has recently been 43 percent of GDP, spending on education has only been 4.3 percent. Less capital-intensive production would also help keep unemployment down – another important social objective. Smaller inputs of energy and raw material per unit of GDP, and less destruc-tion of the physical environment, would be other important examples of a shift to a more intensive growth path. The importance of dramatic improve-ments in environmental policies in China is, of course, well known today; see, for instance, Economy (2007). Indeed, such improvement would be an auto-matic consequence of less emphasis on investment in real capital assets, in particular in heavy industry, and it could be considerably accentuated by allowing much higher user-prices for such inputs (Lardy 2006).

Most likely, generally improved working conditions for small firms, for instance through better functioning capital and credit markets, are also crucial for a major long-term improvement of factor income among people in rural areas. *Targeted* infrastructure investment in real capital assets and human capital to poor geographical areas in China are other obvious methods to boost factor income in such areas.[20] (Targeted human capital investment may take many forms – not only education but also policy actions designed to improve nutrition, sanitation and basic health services among the poor population.) Against this background, it is interesting to notice recent signals by the political leaders in China of future shifts of investment from eastern provinces to poor geographical areas in the west – the newly announced "Go West Strategy." Assuming a falling marginal return on investment in both real and human capital (at least after some point), the economic costs for the country as a whole of such a shift of the geographical allocation of investment may not be very large, provided that the new investment projects are based on reasonably careful cost-benefit analysis.[21]

Removal (or at least a further softening) of the urban *hukou* would also be expected to boost the per capita factor income of low-income groups – both among those who move to urban areas and among those who remain in the countryside (the latter effect as a result of both increased remittances from migrants and diminished labor supply in rural areas).[22] The period of Arthur Lewis-type "unlimited supply of labor" (Lewis 1954) might then be extended, at least in some urban areas. The most likely losers would be urban insiders exposed to stiffer wage competition, with an overall reduction in income inequality in the country as a whole as a result.[23] During a comparable phase of industrialization, today's developed countries in Europe also experienced a huge outflow of labor from agriculture. But a considerable share of the rural population could then migrate to other continents with ample availability of agricultural land and expanding urban labor markets. China's current agricultural population does not have the same opportunities.

Moreover, a shift to private ownership of agricultural land is likely to improve the average factor income of farmers – in a similar way as the shift from collective farms to the so-called "household responsibility system," and subsequently to family farms in the early 1980s. For instance, farmers would be encouraged to make long-term investments, including the amalgamation of land holdings, with a better exploitation of returns to scale as result. (Such results are particularly likely in the case of wheat, vegetables and animal products.[24]) Strengthened farmers' property rights – through a shift to outright ownership of land – would also improve the income security of farmers.

Thus, there seems to be a conflict between a lingering socialist ideology with respect to land ownership, on the one hand, and concern about long-term efficiency and per capita factor income among farmers, on the other hand. However, the existing distribution of political power is most likely another explanation to why ownership of land has not been privatized in China. As pointed out above, control over ownership of land is an important basis for financial gains among local politicians and public-sector administrators.

However, there may also be more altruistic arguments behind the reluctance of the Chinese authorities to privatize agricultural land. One might be that privatization could make the distribution of wealth gradually more uneven *within* the agricultural population – although the distribution of income and wealth among the Chinese population as a whole could very well become more even by such privatization. The authorities may also be afraid of massive migration to the cities. Another consideration might be that a shift to private ownership of land, and a subsequent consolidation of land hold-ings, could reduce the possibilities for migrants to urban areas to return to agriculture after having failed in the cities. There would simply be fewer family farms to receive them. This disadvantage would, however, be mitigated by the fact that private ownership of land would enable elderly farmers to transform their land into cash and, in turn, provide financial assistance to family members (probably mainly children) who did not "make it" in the cities.

In principle, price regulations are another conceivable method for influ-encing the distribution of factor income across population groups. Indeed, agricultural price regulations have been extensively used in many countries for this purpose. While developing countries have often implemented such regulations to keep down the prices of agricultural products, primarily to favor urban consumers at the expense of farmers, most developed countries have done just the opposite. There is no doubt that policies of the latter type have boosted revenues for the agricultural population, at least initially. But there are serious inherent problems in such policies. For instance, inefficient farms will survive more easily, thereby delaying the consolidation of land holdings and hence, the rationalization in the agricultural sector.

There are also well-known distributional problems associated with agri-cultural protectionism. Owners of large farms tend to be favored as compared to owners of small ones, since the latter consume a considerable fraction of the output from their farms themselves. Low-income consumers outside agri-culture are also harmed relative to other consumers, since they use a larger sharer of their income to buy agricultural products. Thus, schematically speaking, there tends to be a redistribution of income from poor consumers to relatively affluent farmers. An alternative way of supporting farmers is, of course, tax concessions or direct subsidies to agriculture production – the so-called "low-price route" used, for instance, in the United Kingdom before the country's entry into EU. One well-known advantage is that consumer prices would then be less distorted, in particular in an open economy. Another is that the burden on poor consumers would be smaller. Indeed, China has recently taken some steps along this "low-price route." I refer to the recent removal of the specific agriculture tax and experiments with pro-duction subsidies to farmers – probably partly in response to the depressing effect on the prices of many agricultural products in connection with China's accession to the WTO.

Price control in the housing market, mainly rent control, has also been frequently used in several countries to redistribute factor income across population groups. In particular, rent control may boost the income of tenants in apartment houses at the expense of landlords, at least temporarily. However, the disadvantages of such policies are also well known from experience in developed countries: excess demand for housing ("housing shortages"), black markets for rental contracts, deterioration in the quality of the housing stock, and a fall in new construction (which has often induced governments to start subsidizing housing construction). The distributional consequences among tenants are also rather dubious, since apartments in markets with a permanent housing shortage tend to be distributed through personal contacts with landlords and (capital-requiring) transactions on black markets – i.e. methods favoring high-income groups. As indicated above, after the mid-1990s, China has followed another route than increased rent control to favor (some) tenants, namely large-scale shifts from leasing contracts to ownership contracts on favorable terms, hence a privatization of apartments.

Generally speaking: if the Chinese authorities want to boost the factor income of low-income groups, it is likely that policies improving the productivity of these groups, alternatively production subsidies, are more promising instruments than price regulations. Not only are they more favorable for economic efficiency; they are also easier to target.

Obviously, not only the level but also the *stability* of the factor income of individuals is vital from a social point of view. In particular, this holds for the poorest segments of the population, since their margins in terms of misery are especially narrow. It is then natural to regard policies that smooth macroeconomic fluctuations as a first line of defense against factor income instability.[25] In so far as stabilization policies have been pursued at all in China during the last decades, they mainly seem to have taken the form of direct quantitative regulations of investment and credit flows rather than general fiscal and monetary policy incentives. One reason is probably that public-sector firms have been regarded as quite insensitive to economic incentives. However, as the economic system in China gradually becomes more incentive-oriented, stabilization policy can increasingly rely on such incentives, which would reduce the conflicts between the stabilization and the allocation "branches" of economic policies.

10.3.2 Tax/transfer arrangements

The main purpose of tax-transfer programs is, of course, to make the disposable income of households more stable and more evenly distributed than factor income. What, then, are China's basic policy options in this field? One issue concerns the choice between (fairly) generous income-insurance arrangements for a narrow group of individuals and basic (safety-net) arrangements for the population as a whole. So far, the Chinese authorities have emphasized the former alternative. So what could a strategy with a broader coverage of tax/transfer arrangements look like? From an administrative point of view, unemployment insurance and pensions (the two major systems of income insurance) could certainly be extended to basically all employees in industry and services – in urban as well as in rural areas. It is much more difficult to organize similar systems of income insurance in agriculture, since concepts such as income, unemployment and retirement are difficult to define and measure in this sector. However, improved crop-failure legislation and/or improved natural-disaster relief may to some extent fulfill similar functions. Moreover, in the case of pensions, a basic (or guarantee) lump-sum benefit should be administratively feasible not only in urban but also in rural areas. Indeed, this was the way pensions originally emerged in most of today's developed countries, in fact, even in rural areas.

There are also a number of country-specific problems in connection with China's emerging tax/transfer arrangements. One is that risk pooling often only takes place across limited geographical areas, such as a city, or possibly a province. At a first glance, this may seem to be a trivial problem, since the geographical domains of risk pooling are often more populous than many European nations. However, the composition of industries often differs strongly across geographical areas, so that payroll taxes, designed to finance the benefits, vary strongly across such areas. In particular, firms in areas with many unemployed or pensioners are exposed to much higher social costs than firms in other areas. For instance, payroll taxes are relatively high in regions with old industries, such as mining and steel, whereas they are relatively low in regions with new industries, such as banking, electronics, and civil aviation. This tends to influence the relative competitiveness of firms in a rather arbitrary way, especially if local wages do not fully adjust to the differences in the payroll taxes. The limited area of risk pooling also reduces the portability of benefits, which impedes the emergence of a national labor market. Thus, de facto fragmentation of the social arrangements across the country has created problems for both the relative competitiveness of firms in different regions of the country and the mobility of labor. Therefore, in a long-term perspective, China may have a great deal to gain from further unifying the arrangements of income insurance across the entire nation.

Like several other countries, China has in recent years also experimented with a *combination* of pay-as-you-go ("paygo" for short) and funded pension systems – so far mainly covering urban citizens. However, both types of arrangements are likely to be confronted with financial problems in the future. Since the main problem in the paygo part of the pension system is closely related to the "graying" of the population, this specific problem could, in principle, be mitigated by a gradual increase in the effective retirement age. (The formal pension age today is 60 years for males and 55 for females, with an effective retirement age of only 55 for the former.) If this reform does not suffice, it may be combined with less generous benefits and/or higher contribution rates, although higher rates may be problematic since *total* payroll taxes are already quite high in urban sectors – about 40 percent, 30 percentage points being paid by the employer.[26]

A more specific problem for China is that contributions originally paid into the funded part of the pension system have, in fact, been used to finance deficits in the paygo part of the system – the problem of "empty individual accounts." As a consequence, the funded part of the mandatory pension system, so far, merely looks like another paygo system with "notional" (book-keeping) rather than real accounts. The Chinese authorities have basically to choose between two alternative strategies for dealing with this issue. One would be to altogether abandon the idea of funded individual accounts and be content with the paygo part of the system. The other alternative would be to "recapitalize" the accounts. One possibility would then be tax-financed capital injections into the accounts. Another possibility, suggested by Pieter Bottelier (2002), would be to let the National Social Security Fund take over the shares in a number of state firms. The fund could then be instructed to gradually sell the shares on the open market, at appropriate intervals to avoid strong negative effects on share prices. The revenues from the sales could then be used to recapitalize the empty individual accounts. In this way, two birds would be killed with one stone: a restoration of the individual accounts and a speed-up of the privatization of government-owned corporations. A more modest version of this idea has, in fact, already been implemented. The collective fund in China is entitled to receive 10 percent of the proceeds from sales of shares in state-owned companies every time there is an initial public offering (IPO), or a new share issue.

A more general problem with funded mandatory pension systems is whether the government should opt for government-operated or privately-operated funds. The latter alternative is, of course, more consistent with the notion of a decentralized and competitive market economy. Government-operated funds always run the risk of being "high-jacked" by politicians who might insist that *they* should decide on the portfolio policy of the funds, appoint the members of the board of the fund(s), and perhaps also appoint board members in firms where the funds own shares. China may then slip back towards more collective control and ownership of both assets and firms. Retreats may then be induced also in other dimensions of the economic system depicted in Figure 10.1, for instance through more centralized decision-making and more command in the production sector.

The most promising way of significantly reducing the likelihood of such political intervention is probably to design a system where individuals are asked to place their mandatory pension savings in non-government funds of their own choice – although the government may continue to collect the pension contributions (taxes). Such reforms would also help create a broader and more active market for financial instruments, as a complement to the bank-dominated financial system that exists today in China. Considering China's recent tradition of government ownership and political intervention in individual firms, the risk (or "hope" among some observers) that a funded, government-created pension system will, in fact, result in a strongly nationalized economy is hardly less in China than in other countries.

10.3.3 Human services

After the breakdown of the pre-reform system of the provision of human services, the responsibility for such services has been shared among private agents, organizations affiliated with SOEs and local governments (31 provinces, 331 prefectures, 2109 counties, and 44,741 townships). In the case of *education*, the basic problem in China today is not that the services are currently provided by several different types of agents. Indeed, this pluralism on the supply side seems to have contributed to experimentation and variation in terms of curriculums and teaching methods (Hannum 1999). Many observers seem to agree that the most pressing tasks today are instead to (i) expand the number of students from low-income families in secondary and tertiary education; (ii) reduce the financial burden of parents with children in school age; and (iii) improve the quality of education at all levels. Certainly, these tasks cannot be achieved without increased resources to education from the central government, including grants to local governments in poor areas of the country. Thus, the basic problem of the education arrangements in China seems to be the *financing*.

Naturally, China, like other countries, also has to deal with a number of organizational problems in the education system. One is to determine the number of years students should follow a single track and when (and how) students should be separated according to interest and ability (dual or multiple tracks). Another problem is the trade-off between "basic skills" (reading, writing, and arithmetic) and broader, more vague "social abilities" (including preparation for civic duties and hobby activities). A third trade-off is between theoretical skills and vocational skills.

In all these dimensions, it is probably a good idea to avoid extreme solutions. For instance, there is general agreement among specialists in education that early separation of schoolchildren (as, for instance, in Germany) into different tracks (in some countries as early as the fifth grade) disfavors children from homes without an academic background. Other countries have instead chosen a single-track system that extends through the ninth grade or even further, thereby emphasizing theoretical training that prepares a large share of a cohort of youngsters (sometimes as much as one-third or even half) for university studies. While problems associated with early separation are then avoided, the highly heterogeneous classes of students in the upper grades of the secondary school system have made it necessary to limit the intellectual ambitions in theoretical education. At the same time, students who are better fitted for, and show more interest in, vocational (rather than academic) training often have difficulties following such a highly theoretical education, with pacification and a large drop-out rate as a result. Moreover, several countries that have emphasized general "social abilities" rather than basic skills now seem to regret having done so. It is also interesting to note that many of today's rich countries did emphasize basic skills when they were poor 50 or 100 years ago.

Due to the uneven possibilities of parents to finance their children's school-ing, and the uneven financial resources across local communities to offer high-quality education, China has, in fact, developed into a "multi-track" education system – in terms of years of schooling as well as quality. This threatens to create a highly polarized distribution of school achievement – across geographical areas as well as among individual households.

Like many other countries, China also has serious problems in the field of *vocational training*. Such training is today divided among SOEs, training cen-ters affiliated with such firms, schools affiliated with the Ministry of Educa-tion (MOE) and, to some extent, schools connected with the Ministry of Labor and Social Security (MOLSS).[27] However, there seem to be huge variations in the quality of this training.[28] Deficiencies in quality in many places may explain why many individuals have recently chosen to finance their vocational training themselves.[29] China is, I believe, well advised to take inspiration from the German experience with apprenticeship work at firms, combined with general education at school (i.e. two days a week at school and three on the job, or the reverse). This could be accomplished without a very early separation of students into a two-track system (like in Germany). Many youngsters uninterested in, or not qualified for, academic education would then be able to make decent livings as craftsmen, and also feel pride in their specific skills. Indeed, the fast expansion of tertiary education as compared to (secondary) vocational education in China might indicate that authorities, students and parents overestimate the future (social and private) return on the former as compared to the latter type of education.[30]

It is even easier to identify basic deficiencies in *health-care* in China. The background is multifaceted: (i) the virtual collapse of health services in rural areas (services previously provided by agricultural communes and "barefoot doctors"); (ii) the inability of many SOEs to live up to their earlier responsi-bilities also in this field; and (iii) the absence of comprehensive health services for the rapidly increasing work force in the private sector. As in the case of education, the problem is not mainly that the private sector has taken over the responsibility for a considerable fraction of the production of services – in the case of sick-care about a third (Kin et al. 2002), although partly with the help of assets (medical facilities) rented from public-sector authorities. The basic problem is rather that the public sector has reduced, and decentralized, its responsibility for the financing of health care.

Despite the fact that China has recently (in 2004) spent as much as 5.6 percent of GDP on health care (Ministry of Health 2006, Table 4.1), the deficiencies of the services are huge and well documented – a result of both inefficiencies and an uneven distribution of the services.[31] One indication of both the inefficiencies and the inequalities is that about 80 percent of the health spending in recent years has been concentrated to large and medium-sized cities (Chow 2006; UNDP 2000, 3). These allocations cannot possibly reflect the need for such services in the country as a whole. There are also serious problems of moral hazard in the health-care sector, including excessive medical examinations and unnecessary operations in many cases –required by patients or suggested by physicians; see, for instance, Eggelston et al. 2006.

As in many other countries, these inefficiencies are partly a result of the price system applied to the health sector. One example is the heavy reliance on fee-for-service, i.e., cost-plus-pricing among sick-care providers. Experiences from other countries suggest that inefficiencies and moral hazard could be mitigated by a shift to prospective indemnity payments to providers (a standardized payment for each treatment), alternatively so-called "capitation" (advance payments based on the number of individuals for which the health care provider is responsible). Indeed, there seems to be a modest development in this direction in some places in China.

Another example of inefficient pricing is that the low (controlled) prices received by health-care providers ("producers' prices") for simple treatment have induced the providers to shift resources to more sophisticated and hence more expensive treatment, where the rewards to the providers are higher. Moreover, hospitals and health clinics have in recent years financed much of their health-care provision by revenues from hefty oversubscription and excessive pricing of drugs (Hesketh and Zhu 1997; Eggleston 2006).[32] A more efficient price system in the health-care sector would, most likely, improve the allocative efficiency and favor the provision of basic health services. Clearly, considerably improved health-care in China as a whole also requires a relative shift of resources from urban to rural areas, as well as from affluent to poor urban areas. Realistically speaking, this cannot be achieved without more financial resources being transmitted from the central government to poor local governments. As in the case of education, this clearly requires an overhaul of the system of intragovernment transfers. On their way down to local governments, a considerable fraction of the money flows sent down from the central government to poor local governments has, in fact, tended to be siphoned off to powerful authorities – in more or less the same way as some Chinese rivers, which are full of water inland, turn out to be nearly dry when they reach the coast.[33] Most likely, a fast and drastic improvement of health services in rural areas also requires a re-establishment of public and/or cooperative health clinics in these areas, since the return may not be attractive enough for private entrepreneurs. Indeed, health-care reforms along these lines are to some extent underway.

As in the case of pensions, the financing of future health-care insurance in urban areas is supposed to rely on a combination of paygo financing and funding (with individual accounts), the latter being organized along similar lines as in Singapore and Malaysia.[34] Presumably, individual accounts are particularly useful for relatively inexpensive, mainly "out-patient," treatment rather than expensive hospital treatment. Costly treatment (including "catastrophic health care") would then have to be covered by the paygo (risk pooling) part of the system. The basic idea behind this mixed financing system is presumably that once the individual accounts have been depleted, the individual is supposed to pay from out-of-pocket money – until some income-related ceiling is reached, when financing from the paygo system takes over. However, the individual accounts in China already seem to have run into financial difficulties (similar to those in the pension system), thereby forcing the government to inject new money from the general budget into the paygo part of the system.[35]

In addition to the trade off between basic (relatively inexpensive) and more sophisticated (relatively expensive) health care, the authorities, of course, also have to deal with the trade-off between preventive and curative care. As for developing countries in general, both ethical and efficiency concerns make a case for increased emphasis on preventive health services for broad population groups, rather than (specialized) curative health care for a minority of the population.

Whereas preventive health care in developed countries is mainly an issue of individuals' life style (smoking habits, diet, exercise, etc.), in poor countries it is also a matter of sufficient nutrition, sanitation and efforts by the authorities to combat transmitted diseases. Not least in China, it is also an issue of reducing exceptionally serious pollution and improving often miserable working conditions (Brajer and Mead 2004; OECD 2007). This is, of course, another important example of economic-social interaction in the country.

The Chinese authorities have recently tried to address the pollution problem by quantitative regulations and graduated charges when emissions exceed certain mandated ceilings. But many SOEs do not seem to be particularly sensitive to such charges, simply because profit considerations do not dominate their objectives. (This resembles the insensitivity of state firms to monetary and fiscal incentives in the context of stabilization policy.) There have, however, been recent experiments (conducted in cooperation with the World Bank) to exert *social pressure* on firms, rather than simply relying on quantitative restrictions and economic incentives.[36] The basic idea of the latter types of policy measures is, of course, that firms' pollution behavior could be influenced by social norms, which are supposed to be upheld by the general public through its approval or disapproval. However, as in the case of corruption, the absence of politically independent media is bound to constrain the influence of the general public. In the future, when more firms in China are likely to be profit-oriented, it will be easier to pursue successful incentive-based policies to improve the environment by way of Pigouvian tax/subsidy programs, such as fees on polluters. When it comes to improvements of the work environment, experiences in today's developed countries suggest that legislation and inspection are effective tools, although experience-rated fees in work injury insurance are also potentially important.

In spite of the modest ambitions of social and environmental policies in China during the period of economic reforms, average life expectancy is rather high as compared to other countries with about the same per capita GDP. The level of adult literacy is also relatively high. Indeed, according to several cross-country evaluations, China ranks higher in terms of such aggregate "social" (or "human") variables than in terms of per capita GDP – in spite of the rather low priority given to social and environmental policies during the reform period.[37]

There are at least three ways of explaining this apparent paradox.[38] One could be that high life expectancy and widespread adult literacy, relative to the level of per capita income, were "inherited" from the pre-reform period, when widely distributed, although quite simple, health care and basic education were emphasized. As regards health, another explanation could be that China – more than other countries with a similar GDP per capita – has a recent history (after World War II) of promoting widespread sanitation and nutrition for broad population groups – factors that, on the margin, may have been more decisive for life expectancy than health care.[39] These policies seem, to some extent, to have compensated for the modest increase in per capita income during the pre-reform period. Third, serious health effects of environmental damage may only emerge after rather long time lags (several decades). It may be added that both health conditions and the provision of health services in China vary dramatically across population groups, indeed, probably even more than in most other developing countries in Asia (Eggleston 2006; Svedberg 2007).

Moreover, "general" social policies – such as social insurance, education, sick care and pollution control – are not likely to be sufficient in dealing with "new" urban social problems such as those connected with the misuse of alcohol and drugs. Much more *selective* (targeted) social interventions are necessary in these cases. Perhaps China could mitigate some such problems by promoting the emergence of small and medium-sized cities as alternatives to ever-larger mega-cities. Medium size in this case might then be interpreted as cities with less than half a million people, rather than ten to thirty million.

A more general problem concerning the provision of human services is related to difficulties in providing effective mechanisms for adjusting quantities and qualities of human services to consumers' needs and preferences. In particular, in countries where local governments have a monopoly on the provision of human services, the "exit option" is not available as a means for consumers of exerting such influence (except possibly when moving to another municipality). The "voice option," exerted via the political system, is necessarily also rather weak in most countries, since citizens' political influence basically is limited to the right to choose among policy packages offered by political parties, rather than among specific services and/or service providers. Obviously, the voice option is particularly weak in non-democratic societies, such as China. To strengthen the voice somewhat at the local administrative level, China has recently introduced elections of village leaders in some parts of the country (and in a few townships). There is some evidence that this reform has heightened the responsiveness of local authorities to the demands among citizens for public goods (Luo et al. 2007). But the extent to which such reforms will actually strengthen citizens' influence on the provision of human services would be expected to be limited without political democracy and competing political parties, and as long as centrally appointed party officials (party secretaries) have strong political power over local administrations. The absence of free media, of course, also seriously limits the advantages of local elections.

We would also expect that improved income insurance and increased tax financing of education and health care in the future would induce households to cut down on their huge savings (20–25 percent of disposable income).[40] Individuals would then not only get welfare gains through better access to health care and education (for their children) but also through better consumption smoothing over time and higher lifetime consumption (since less precautionary saving would be necessary). As a side-effect, the huge surplus in the current account of the balance of payment would fall which, most likely, would reduce protectionist tendencies toward China in the rest of the world.

10.4 Social policy trade-offs

Clearly, China's strongly growth-oriented development strategy has brought about great social achievements in terms of increased household consumption for a huge part of the poor in the world. However, to be economically and socially sustainable during future decades, it is obvious that China has to shift to a development strategy that is much less energy consuming and much friendlier to the environment and to working conditions for employees. It is also well known that China's achievements have been quite modest in terms of the distribution and security of income and the provision of human services, such as education and health care outside a group of urban insiders. Indeed, the consumption of education and health care seems to be about as unevenly distributed as other types of consumption.[41] Presumably, such policies do not only reflect the administrative difficulties of running social arrangements in rural areas; they also reflect the distribution of political powers in Chinese society.

It is tempting to speculate that risks of social unrest among disfavored population groups – rural residents as well as the "floating population" in urban areas – will generate future shifts of relative political powers in favor of these groups, and that such shifts will result in greater emphasis on social issues among the political leaders. A future move towards political democracy and free media would certainly speed up such a process, and probably also result in more energetic attempts by the authorities to fight corruption and to improve the polluted environment and today's miserable working conditions for many employees.

But what about the often asserted "grand" trade-off between more narrowly defined social policies (the distribution and stability of income, employment opportunities and the provision of human services) and "narrow" economic concerns (efficiency and growth)? The extent to which such trade offs actually emerge to a considerable extent depends on the *methods* used in social policies. Clearly, such conflicts may not be serious in the case of policies designed to boost the factor income of low-income families – for instance, through infrastructure investment in less developed regions and targeted policy measures that improve nutrition, sanitation, basic health care and education among poor families. Indeed, in some cases, such policies may be favorable also from a narrow (aggregate) economic point of view.

The risk of running into a "grand" trade-off is greater in the case of tax/transfer programs. As a rule, the more generous such programs are, the more difficult it is to avoid conflicts between social and narrow economic ambitions. However, such conflicts may to a considerable extent be mitigated by tight links between the individual's contributions and his/her expected future benefits, i.e., by creating strong actuarial elements in the systems. However, there is a dilemma here: the tighter the link, the less redistribution of lifetime income across individuals there is.

When considering China's future options in the field of social reforms (in the narrow sense of the term), there are also important lessons to be learned from recent welfare-state experiences in developed countries. The most important positive lesson is perhaps that it is possible to provide quite ambitious social arrangements without ruining the possibilities of a continuation of steady GDP growth. There are, however, also negative lessons to be learned. The most obvious one is that serious disincentive effects on work may arise as a result of *interactions* between tax wedges on labor income and "moral hazard" in connection with social insurance and social assistance. In Western Europe, such problems seem to have been particularly severe in the case of unemployment benefits, sick-absence pay, and early retirement benefits (Lindbeck, 2008). The problem is accentuated if individuals gradually develop a more "liberal" interpretation of their right to live on benefits from the government, rather than on work, i.e., if attitudes and social norms in favor of work, or against living off government benefits, are weakened. Outright benefit cheating is an extreme case. I have hypothesized elsewhere that contemporary welfare-state problems in developed countries are partly due to such changes in attitudes and social norms (Lindbeck 1995; Lindbeck, Nyberg, and Weibull 1999). Indeed, today, about 20 percent of the population of working age in Western Europe live on various types of welfare-state benefits.

In view of the modest levels of taxation and social spending in China today, the country is not likely to encounter serious disincentive problems of these types in the near future. After all, total government budget spending in China today is only about 20 percent of GDP, as compared to 40–55 percent in several countries in Western Europe. However, if welfare-state arrangements gradually become more encompassing and generous in China in the future, there is no reason to assume that the country will be immune to such problems.

Notes

1 The chapter builds on my keynote speech at the meeting of the Chinese Economist Society in Shanghai July 2006. Lindbeck (2006a) provides richer references to data

sources and the literature. I am grateful to Harry Flam, Nannan Lundin, Peter Svedberg and Solveig Wikström for useful comments on a draft of the paper. Financial support from Jan Wallander and Tom Hedelius' Research Foundation is gratefully acknowledged.

2　Some outside specialists in national accounting report lower figures for China's GDP growth rate. According to Maddison (2003) and Young (2003), 7.5–8.0 percent per year is a more realistic figure.

3　I follow a classification of economic systems in Lindbeck (1975).

4　For a discussion, see Lindbeck (2006a, 9–17).

5　In a speech to the congress of the Chinese Economists Society in Shanghai, July 3, 2006, the Deputy Finance Minister of China, Jiwei Lou, stated that private firms account for 70 percent of aggregate output.

6　The incidence of absolute poverty, defined as the fraction of the population with an income of less than (about) one dollar a day, is estimated to have fallen from about 50 percent to less than 10 percent between 1981 and 2004 (World Development Indicators 2006).

7　The so-called "dual track approach to transition" in China is an important example of gradualism. For a while, the old SOEs could count on previously agreed prices and deliveries – at the same time as a "new" economy emerged alongside the old one (Lau et al. 2000).

8　Aggregate employment growth seems to have been no more than one percent per year between 1993 and 2004; see Kuijs and Wang 2005.

9　However, the previous "job guarantees" for workers in SOEs have gradually become worth less due to large lay-offs in such firms from the mid-1990s.

10　The size of the floating population is today officially estimated at 147 million (China Population Statistics Yearbook 2006 3).

11　In 2005, unemployment insurance covered 14 percent of China's workforce, work-injury insurance 11 percent and the basic mandatory government pension scheme 17 percent (NBS, National Bureau of Statistics of China, 2006b, 43 and 201). Even the social assistance program for the poor in urban areas, the so-called *Di Bao* system ("welfare" in US terminology), is still confined to registered urban residents.

12　NBS, 2006a Tables 21–6 and 2005 Tables 12–31; Ministry of Health, 2006, Tables 4.1.

13　Broadly speaking, the fertility rate has dropped from about 6.2 in 1950–1955 to about 1.7 today, and life expectancy (at birth) has increased from about 40.8 to about 72.0 years during the same period (UN, World Population Prospects, 2006).

14　Indeed, reasonable forecasts suggest that the number of individuals of working age in 2050 will be about the same as the number of dependents (the sum of children below 18 and elderly above 60). The UNDP (2005) predicts that the population share of individuals of working age will be as low as 53 percent by 2050 – the lowest predicted share at that time among East Asian countries except Japan.

15　Although the drastic fall in fertility in China has been speeded up by the one-child policy, the time path of the fertility rate does not differ drastically from the path in other East Asian countries during comparable periods of "modernization" (UNPD, 2005).

16　In the early 1980s, the shift to family farms, like the immediately previous shift to the so-called "household responsibility system," narrowed the income gap between urban and rural areas for a while. It even contributed to an overall equalization of income in China (Ravallion and Chen 2007).

17　The level of per capita GDP is currently reported to be about seven times higher in the most developed than in the least developed province, even if we exclude the very poorest province (Guizhou); see NBS 2006a, Tables 3–9. Moreover, according to official statistics, the average income in urban areas is 3.2 times higher than in rural areas (NBS 2006b, Tables 2–27, p. 6 and Tables 2–40 p. 72).

18 While the poorest 10 percent of households seem to earn about 2 percent of aggregate disposable household income, the richest 10 percent earn about 35 percent (World Development Indicators 2006).

19 In particular, the coverage of health insurance programs seems to have increased recently, although the benefit levels are still very low. NBS (2007) and Ministry of Health (2007) report that about half the population in urban areas was protected by compulsory health insurance in 2006, and in rural areas about the same share was covered by the voluntary cooperative health program.

20 For instance, Jalan and Ravallion (2002) find that investment in both infrastructure and human capital in rural China has significantly raised the return to farmers' investment in physical assets (other factors held constant).

21 According to Bai et al. (2006), the return to real capital has generally been highest in the eastern region, followed by the central region, and lowest in the western region. However, the dispersion has decreased over time.

22 On basis of a computable general equilibrium (CGE) model, Whalley and Zhang (2007) find non-trivial redistributional effects of this type as a result of an assumed removal of the *hukou*.

23 However, a faster outflow of young people from rural areas would leave some villages and small towns with mainly elderly people and a stagnating local economy.

24 Already improvements in the transferability of land-lease contracts would facilitate such consolidation. Indeed, Wan and Cheng (2001, 191) estimate that consolidation of fragmented patches of land would raise labor productivity by as much as 12–17 percent, depending on the types of crops.

25 On basis of a dynamic simulation model of the Chinese macroeconomy, Zhang (2001) reports that temporary external shocks tend to reduce the growth path of the economy for a considerable period of time (several years). Clearly, this is not unique for China.

26 China's Social Security White Paper 2006.

27 See, for instance, Fleisher and Wang 2001; and Li 2004.

28 Li (2004) reports many examples of poor supervision, considerable disorder and inefficiencies, as well as large mismatches between the demand for skills and the availability of training opportunities for different types of skills. The number of vocational schools has fallen gradually – in total by at least 50 percent – since the early 1990s.

29 In a sample used by Li (2004), about a third of the individuals engaged in vocational training participated in programs mainly financed by out-of-pocket money.

30 The number of students in tertiary education increased by a factor of eight between 1985 and 2006, while the corresponding factor is three in the case of (secondary) vocational education. (NBS, 2006a, Tables 21–6) The population in age groups 18–21 enrolled in tertiary education was 3.4 percent in 1990, and it had increased to 21 percent in 2005 (Educational Statistics Yearbook of China 2006, 15).

31 The spending seems to be some 2–3 percentage points higher than in countries with a similar level of per capita income in Southeast Asia, except Vietnam (UNDP 2005).

32 According to Blumenthal and Hsiao (2005), as much as half of the total spending on health care consists of costs for drugs, while more normal figures in developed countries are usually 10–15 percent. Field studies suggest that only a modest fraction of the subscribed use of drugs has been medically motivated (Eggelston 2006, 1–2).

33 The distribution of per capita public spending across provinces seems to be at least as uneven as the distribution of per capita GDP, perhaps even more so (UNDP 2005, 75); OECD 2005b, Fig. 4).

34 An individual's entire contribution (two percent of the earnings) and a third of the contribution covered by the employer (six percent of the wage bill) are supposed to be paid into the individual's (funded) personal account, while the remaining two-thirds of the employer's premium are allotted to the paygo part of the system (i.e. the common "health insurance pool").

35 The payroll tax that finances health insurance is currently 8 percent of the wage rate (OECD 2005a, Table 4: 3).

36 One attempted method is to rank firms (publicly) according to their degree of environmental concern – the so-called "Green Watch Program" (Wang et al. 2004).

37 See, for instance, the Human Development Index, HDI, which is based on a number of broad economic and social indicators (UNDP 2005, 81). Another source is the China Center for Modernization Research (2005).

38 Nicholas Lardy brought this apparent paradox to my attention.

39 As we know, during the Mao period, the authorities were also responsible for the devastating famine in connection with the "Great Leap Forward" in the late 1950s and the early 1960s and the huge educational regress during the "Cultural Revolution" in the late 1960s and early 1970s).

40 The present GDP share of private consumption seems to be below 40 percent. (NBS, 2006b, Tables 3–13, p. 70. Government consumption (including government spending on education and health care) seems to be about 18 percent of GDP (NBS, 2006b, Tables 8.4 and Tables 8.5 p. 283).

41 This seems to be the case for the distribution of per capita government spending on education and health across provinces, as well as for the distribution across income classes of individuals' spending on such services through out-of-pocket money. See NBS (2006a), tables in section 10 and Tables 21–6; and China Statistical Yearbook for Regional Economy (2006), tables in section 2. See also Zhang and Kanbur 2005.

References

ADB. 2007. *Inequality in Asia Highlights*, Washington DC: Asian Development Bank.

Bai, C., C. Hsieh, and Y. Qian. 2006. "The Return to Capital in China," NBER Working Paper No. 12755, NBER: Cambridge, MA, http://www.nber.org/papers/w12755.

Blanchard, O. and F. Giavazzi. 2005. "Rebalancing Growth in China: A Three-Handed Approach," CEPR Discussion Paper No. 5403, London, http://www.cepr.org/pubs/new-dps/dplist.asp?dpno=5403&action.x=12&action.y=8&action=ShowDP.

Blumenthal, D. and W. Hsiao. 2005. "Privatization and its Discontents – The Evolving Chinese Health Care System," *New England Journal of Medicine*, 353(11): 1165–70.

Bottelier, P. 2002. "Where is Pension Reform Going in China? Issues and Option," *Perspectives*, 3(5), Overseas Young Chinese Forum, http://www.oycf.org/perspectives/17_063002/Pension_China.htm.

Brajer, V. and R. Mead. 2004. "Valuing Air Pollution Mortality in China's Cities," *Urban Studies*, 41: 1567–85.

China Center for Modernization Research. 2005. China Modernization Report – A

Study on Economic Modernization, Beijing: Chinese Academy of Sciences May 19, http://www.modernization.com.cn/cmr2005%20overview.htm.

China Population Statistics Yearbook. 2006. Beijing: China Statistics Press.

China's Social Security White Paper. 2006. China Internet Information Center, webmaster@china.org.cn

China Statistical Yearbook for Regional Economy. 2006. Beijing: China Statistics Press.

Chow, G. 2006. "An Economic Analysis of Health Care in China," mimeo, 5/27/ 06, Princeton.

——. 2007. *China's Economic Transformation*, 2nd edn, Oxford: Blackwell Publishing.

Economy, E. C. 2007. "The Great Leap Backward? The Costs of China's Environmental Crisis," *Foreign Affairs*, September/October, pp. 38–59.

Educational Statistics Yearbook of China. 2006. Beijing: China Statistics Press.

Eggleston, K., L. Ling, M. Qingyue, M. Lindelow, and A. Wagstaff. 2006. "Health Service Delivery in China: A Literature Review," World Bank Policy Research Working Paper No. 3978, Washington, DC, http://www-wds.worldbank.org/external/default/WDSContentServer/IW3P/IB/2006/08/01/000016406_2006080111 4229/Rendered/PDF/wps3978.pdf.

Fleisher, B. and Z. Wang. 2001. "Skill Differentials, Return to Schooling, and Market Segmentation in a Transition Economy: The Case of Mainland China," *Journal of Development Economics*, 73(1): 315–28.

Hannum, E. 1999. "Poverty and Basic-Level Schooling in China: Equity Issues in the 1990s," *Prospects: Quarterly Review of Comparative Education*, 29(4): 561–77.

Hesketh, T. and W. X. Zhu. 1997. "Health in China: The Healthcare Market," *British Medical Journal*, 314: 1616–20.

Jalan, J. and M. Ravallion. 2002. "Geographic Poverty Traps? A Micro Model of Consumption Growth in Rural China," Global Development Network, Washington, DC, http://www.gdnet.org/pdf/580_Jalan.pdf.

Kin, L. M., Y. Hui, Z. Tuohong, Z. Zijun, F. Wen, and C. Yude. 2002. "The Role and Scope of Private Medical Practice in China," mimeo, commissioned by UNDP, WHO and MOH China, http://www.worldbank.org.cn/english/content/Private_Medical_in_China.pdf.

Kuijs, L. and T. Wang. 2005. "China's Pattern of Growth: Moving to Sustainability and Reducing Inequality," World Bank Policy Research Working Paper No. 3767 (November) Washington D.C.: World Bank, http://www-wds.worldbank.org/external/default/WDSContentServer/IW3P/IB/2005/11/08/000016406_2005110815 4427/Rendered/PDF/wps3767.pdf.

Lange, O. 1938. *On the Economic Theory of Socialism*, Minneapolis: University of Minnesota Press.

Lardy, N. 2006. "China's Domestic Economy: Continued Growth or Collapse?," in Bergsten, F., Bates, G., Lardy, N. and Mitchell, D., eds, *China: The Balance Sheet*, New York: Public Affairs, pp. 18–39.

Lau, L, Y. Qian, and G. Roland. 2000. "Reform without Losers: An Interpretation of China's Dual Track Approach to Transition," *Journal of Political Economy*, 108(1): 120–43.

Lerner, A. 1934. "Economic Theory and Socialist Economy," *Review of Economics and Statistics*, II, pp. 51–61.

Lewis, A. 1954. *Economic Development with Unlimited Supply of Labor*, Manchester School of Economics and Social Studies, 22: 139–91.

Li, M. 2004. "Firm-based Training Programs and Workforce Developments in Mainland China," Report to World Bank Institute, Washington, DC.

Lindbeck, A. 1975. "Economic Systems and the Economics of the New Left," in *Der Streit um die Gesellschaftsordnung*, Lectures at the University of Zurich, Zurich: Schulthess Polygraphischer Verlag, pp. 91–112.

—— 1995. "Hazardous Welfare-state Dynamics," *American Economic Review*, 85(2): 9–15.

—— 2008. "Welfare State," in Durlauf, S. and L. Blume, eds, The New Palgrave, Cambridge: Palgrave-Macmillan.

Lindbeck, A., S. Nyberg, and J. W. Weibull. 1999. "Social Norms and Economic Incentives in the Welfare State," *Quarterly Journal of Economics*, 114(1): 1–35.

Luo, R., L. Zhang, J. Huang, and S. Rozelle. 2007. Elections, Fiscal Reform and Public Goods Provision in Rural China, paper presented at Chinese Economists Society, Shanghai, July 1–3, Journal of Comparative Economics, 35(3), pp. 583–611.

Maddison, A. 2003. The World Economy; Historical Statistics, Paris: OECD. http://www.theworldeconomy.org/publications/worldeconomy.

Maurer-Fazio, M. and N. Dinh. 2004. "Differential Rewards to, and Contributions of, Education in Urban China's Segmented Labor Markets," *Pacific Economic Review*, 9(3), pp. 173–189(17).

Ministry of Health 2005–2007. China Statistical Yearbook on Health, Beijing: China Statistics Press. http://www.moh.gov.cn/newshtml/18903.htm.

NBS (National Bureau of Statistics of China) 2005. *China Statistical Yearbook*, Beijing: China Statistics Press.

—— 2006a. *China Statistical Yearbook*, Beijing: China Statistics Press.

—— 2006b. *China Statistical Abstract*, Beijing: China Statistics Press.

—— 2007. http:www.stats. gov.cn/tjgb/qttjgb/qgqttgb/t20070518_402406314.htm.

OECD 2005a. *Economic Surveys: China*, Vol. 2005/13, Paris: OECD.

OECD 2005b. OECD Review of Agriculture Policies – China, Paris: OECD.

OECD 2007. OECD *Environmental Performance Reviews* – China, Paris: OECD.

Ravallion, M. and S. Chen. 2007. "China's (Uneven) Progress Against Poverty," *Journal of Development Economics*, 82(1): 1–42.

Svedberg, P. 2007. Child Malnutrition in India and China, 2002 Focus Brief on the World's Poor and Hungry People, Washington, DC: IFPRI.

Svensson, J. 2005. "Eight Questions about Corruption," *Journal of Economic Perspectives*, 19: 19–42.

UN, World Population Prospects. 2006. http://esa.un.org/unpp.

UNDP. 2000 and 2005. *China: Human Development Report*, New York: Oxford University Press.

Wan, G. and E. Cheng. 2001. "Effects of Land Fragmentation and Returns to Scale in the Chinese Farming Sector," *Applied Economics*, 33: 183–94.

Wang, H., J. Bi, D. Wheeler, J. Wang, D. Cao, G. Lu, and Y. Wang. 2004. "Environmental Performance Rating and Disclosure: China's Green Watch Program," *Journal of Environmental Management*, 71: 123–33.

Whalley, J. and S. Zhang. 2007. "A Numerical Simulation Analysis of (Hukou) Labour Mobility Restrictions in China," *Journal of Development Economics*, 83: 392–410.

World Development Indicators. 2006. World Bank, Washington, DC.

Xiaoyi, H. 1996. "Reducing State-Owned Enterprises, Social Burdens and Establishing a Social Insurance System," in Broadman, H., ed., *Policy Options for Reform of Chinese State-Owned Enterprises*, Washington, DC: World Bank, pp. 125–48.

Young, A. 2003. "Gold into Base Metal: Productivity Growth in the People's Republic of China during the Reform Period," *Journal of Political Economy*, 3(6): 1220–61.

Zhang, X. 2001. "External Shocks and the Long-term Growth of the Chinese Economy," in Lloyd, P. and Zhang, X., eds, *Models of the Chinese Economy*, Cheltenham, Edward Elgar, Chapter 9.

Zhang, X. 2006. "Asymmetric Property Rights in China's Economic Growth," Discussion Paper No. 28, International Food Policy Research Institute, Washington, DC, http://www.ifpri.org/DIVS/DSGD/dp/papers/DSGDP28.pdf.

Zhang, X. and R. Kanbur. 2005. "Spatial Inequality in Education and Health Care in China," *China Economic Review*, 16: 189–204.

11 Redefining relations between the rule of law and the market – clues provided by four basic issues in China today[*]

Weidong Ji

11.1 Main theme of a modern market economy: harmony of freedom and the rule of law

China now has a passion for liberty and is in a stage of passionate liberalism. Over the past 25 years, a frenzy of business launches has been stimulated by the relaxation of administrative control and regulation and a major release of long bottled-up popular energy. Opening to the outside world, globalization and great changes to the economic base have led to fluctuations and even collapse in the social value system. The profit motive has as a result been unfettered and is raging everywhere. The hurried inflation of individual desire at the same time to some extent facilitated unrestrained, fierce, free competition, ultimately causing China's economy to post astonishing achievements – in 2005 its GDP surpassed both those of England and France, ranking fourth in the world.[1] On the other hand however, surging desire and one-sided devotion to the GDP, together with lags in political reform and public construction, led to a series of serious problems: inequality of opportunity, the law of the jungle, lack of distributive justice, polarization of rich and poor, spreading systemic corruption, environmental deterioration, energy shortages, imbalance of basic social relations, etc., the prime indicator of which was the increase to 87,000 of cases of group conflicts (involving 15 or more people) in 2005.[2]

In just such circumstances, voices demanding distributive justice and social harmony have been growing louder. In order to maintain stability, even the government must reconsider "laissez fair freedom" and highly capricious "unplanned regulation," striving to transform the mode of economic management, and critically ranking the measures other countries have taken to adapt to the unified global market – a novel situation wherein capital and even labor can vote with their feet. Economic competition is, by this token, curbed to some extent by institutional competition. China, clearly, must now further improve its investment environment: all open, transparent, and more effective institutionalised means – punishing corruption and other crimes, or reorganizing the market order – can and should be adopted. And to coordinate relations between freedom and coercion, a complete set of legal procedures and realistic criteria of judgment is needed for the recognition of rights, the redistribution of incomes and resources and the restraint of government actions. Carrying out the rule of law has thus become the basic consensus of the present stage.

More and more people, that is to say, accept that the rule of law can play an important role in suitably moderating individual desires, creating an atmosphere of cooperation and sharing; it constitutes the institutional foundation for coordinated, sustainable economic development. In their discussions concerning the commodity economy and the merits of the marketChinese economists have already in fact raised the task of constructing a modern rule of law order to an important agenda.[3] In response to this demand, a strengthening of dialog and collaboration between legal and economic scholars is underway.[4]

11.2 Two main types of liberal theory of rule of law, their selection, and reorganization

Economists taking stock of things from classical liberal or libertarian standpoints (especially that of the Austrian school), offer two different readings of the concept of rule of law as it relates to the market.

One is the viewpoint of Ludwig von Mises. While advocating the spirit of laissez-faire, and denying the possibility of socialist economic calculation and planning, he accepted that government, given irreconcilable opposition between producers and consumers, could deal with them coercively and make trial and error adjustments up to a point; striving at the same time, by means of rational institutional design, to prevent arbitrary allocation of resources by government.[5] In other words, while state norms cannot directly promote economic development, they may in fact provide essential conditions for reducing friction, solving disputes and curbing abuses of authority. In this sense, the market structure is centralized due to the rule of law government's regulatory actions; it should have an overall integrity. This position, while different to those of Coase, who stressed the influence of demarcating rights (judicial rules) on market efficiency, and Buchanan, who stressed the influence of public choice and the constitutional order (legislative rules) on individual exchange behavior, is not substantively opposed to them.

The second viewpoint is Hayek's doctrine of spontaneous order, which forbids government intervention in toto, placing more stress on a view of the market characterized by diffuse competition, and on the evolution of traditional norms.[6] Although Hayek also emphasizes the rule of law, he in fact completely separates it from sovereign edicts, government action, "means-end" thinking, etc., and rejects institutional design, which in reality makes it easy for topics – such as how to make the state safeguard individual freedom, how to prevent planned social transformation being blocked by cultural conservatism or the tyranny of the status quo, etc. – to be for the most part removed from our field of vision. It is in fact very easy for such a standpoint to slide from spontaneous order to "lawless order."[7]

Accordingly, among basic theories proposed by modern jurists, there are two analytical frameworks with paradigmatic status on the role of the rule of law in a market economy, viz:

1   As shown by Max Weber's theory about modern bureaucracy and the rule of law, with established rights and formally rationalized implementing agencies as well as legitimacy of coercion as a starting point, provide conditions of predictability for free exchange behavior by means of the state's system of actual norms. In the present age, this kind of scheme is further elaborated, as mainly seen in Ronald Dworkin's "rights thesis" limiting judicial deliberation, and "right answer thesis" overcoming scepticism, and the "model of rules" constructed on the assumption of distinguishing principles and policies.[8]
2   Lon L. Fuller's approach is somewhat different, starting from reciprocal benefit and procedural natural law, and providing a separate moral foundation for exchange and marginal utility, as well as corresponding legal obligations.[9] Extending from this, we may find Philip Selznick's conceptions of non-state "industrial justice" and the "responsive law" which gives constant feedback about social demand. There is also Gunther Teubner's concept of hybrid laws, unifying personal autonomy and state governance,[10] which can, like that of David P. Gauthier, establish some kind of consensus-based morality.[11]

It goes without saying that the evolution of the above two concepts of good governance of market economic development have influenced value judgments and related institutional designs throughout modern legal systems. Hence not only must we take seriously the influence of the rule of law on the market economy, we also must pay attention the different influence of different models of the rule of law on different models of market economy. In other words, in current Chinese considerations of the relative positioning and functioning of the rule of law and harmonious economic development, decisions must first be made on selecting or reorganizing the different models, and for this, a set of unique local questions must be sorted out.

11.3 Four basic questions revolving around relations between rule of law and the market

Karl Polanyi once likened the mechanism of "One Big Market" to a "demonic grindstone,"[12] describing how all forms of human social solidarity and natural life are constantly ground to powder and liquid by the pressure of pursuing profit to the maximum and the dual forces of marketisation and opposition to it. Intuitive impressions obtained from the microscopic plane, are no more than manifestations of forms of competition or even "law of the jungle" modelled on commodities (for example the free buying and selling of labor), etc. Then again there are the tensions and frictions between the freedom appearing when competition intensifies, and government intervention. China's market supervision and management has up to now taken extremely tough, straightforward forms, and the relevant laws and regulations often present rigid structures, characterized by orders and bans, and striking hard with heavy sanctions. The result is the coexistence and intermeshing of two extremes, laissez-fair and mandatory directives, constantly setting up the dilemmas of "controlling it to death, then letting it run wild." In the present stage of acknowledging the legitimacy of the market economy, greatly relaxing administrative regulations and devoting efforts to developing social harmony, the state should become more nimble and diverse in managing curbs on inflation of the profit motive and distorted market development. As Coase remarked when discussing social cost, we should focus on "reciprocity of the problem,"[13] or the reciprocity behind demands for rights. Hence the need to make the institutional environment of competition present a more richly elastic structure. Implied here is a view of the rule of law which is pluralistic, dynamic, emphasises proof of validity, constantly adjusts conformity through reconsideration, corresponding to the demand for social equity (impartiality) [sic]. In other words, the normative system relevant to economic development must be transformed from a rigid to an elastic structure. This is the first group of issues which we have to face.

As early as the mid 1980s, China's economists and jurists pointed out the egregious irrationality of the government acting both as contestant and as referee. They called for business to be separated from government, for functions to be differentiated and for state power to be neutralized.[14] The problem, however, has never been solved; indeed, as globalization gets more complex it takes ever new forms. For example the government, as an active subject in the market, while providing very strong policy-type assets, is also engaged in large scale purchases; while issuing huge treasury bills, it sells state-owned stock. On the other hand, however, it must take a detached stand, and regulate the market from outside it using a range of policy and institutional measures: currency, interest rates, employment, salaries, prices, social security, etc.

In fact, while tendencies to "denationalization" are promoted by such factors as the formation of the world system of trade and finance, the increasing freedom of multinational corporations, the expanding scale of industrial and capital markets, etc., international competition over energy, technology, market share, as well as institutions and policies are constantly intensifying, lending more clout to trade protectionism as well as "re-nationalization" campaigns. The Chinese government currently emphasizes rationalizing the reward system, distributive justice, environmental protection, energy regulation and a sustainable development model which will inevitably maintain or form an opportunity structure allowing or strengthening state intervention. The government's growing financial role obliges it to situationally adjust savings, expenditure and investment, and the requirements of redistribution brings into full play its central regulatory role. The choice that is left is mainly whether state intervention adopts a democratic, centralized, or in fact dictatorial mode of policy making. The dual role of government, opposite yet complementary to participation and intervention in the market, is the second set of issues to be faced.

In the deep structure of the modern order of rule of law, boundaries and confrontations are quite vitally significant. There are explicit, rigorous dividing lines and sustained incessant conflict and resistance between what is legal and illegal, who wins and loses lawsuits, personality and property, public and private, sovereignty and human rights, national and international law. But since the impact of the two mighty currents of globalization and localization in the 1990s, many of the original demarcation lines have become ever more blurred. The transnational mobility of personnel, materials, capital and information induces simultaneous deconstruction and reconstruction, the mixing of heterogenous factors and the blending and rematching of various constituents of the legal framework. For example, contractual rights to oil field excavation, which originally had no direct connection with international security safeguard strategies, are now very easily embroiled together, leading to diplomatic conflict; corporate institutions are divided into the three different basic stages of financing mode, governance structure, and resource reorganization, each with their own respective norms, procedures, and behavioural logic. Given huge capital markets and intense international competition, however, frequent mergers can to cause corporations to change completely, leading to short-circuiting between securities transactions and corporate governance, thereby causing a melting-down of organizations and the substantive economy. Again, there are non-government organisations that replace government in providing public goods to society, criminal penalties for non-natural persons, relativization of the difference between intention and error in torts, intricate legal relationships hinging on copyright and modes of assessment of economically valuable digital information, and so forth. Our third set of issues thus involves the demolition of all old institutional barriers and normative spheres that have been highly relativized.

There is, finally, the influence of cultural values and rights consciousness. From ancient times the Chinese empire adopted a ruling strategy of minimizing laws and restricting lawsuits, laying stress on the educative role of ritual, control by people regarded as sages, village rules and folk compacts, mediation and compromise. The market as a result lacks the institutional conditions needed for the demarcation and reorganization of rights, and the rights and interests of individuals lack essential legal safeguards. Indeed, the rule of law has certain inherent flaws, requiring it to be supplemented with social justice (equity) and other ordering mechanisms. But it is precisely the rule of law, an arrangement of legitimate coercion, which can surmount particular negotiations, reciprocities and contracts, and thus strengthen the definiteness of future expectations and social relations. In other words, law may create trust which is principled, unable to be capriciously altered – indeed some which is absolutized and unbargained for [sic] – and which is extremely important to the judgment and choice of those engaging in market exchange. A hallmark of the ordering principle in today's China is that facts have precedence over norms, and reciprocity over rights; in the view of the rule of law being established before or above interpersonal relationships, even if it is not completely absent, it is extremely weak.[15] Rather than ignorance of or failure to abide by the law, the cause of this situation lies in people's understanding of or biases regarding fairness [sic], and draws on the widespread influence of state power to arbitrarily explain rules, manipulating clauses according to utilitarian goals. Each has its own moral criteria, everything is decided by trust in particularistic exchange, which creates a legal framework itself discordant, filled with inherent contradictions, and lacking actual effect. With other scholars, I carried out two questionnaire surveys of Chinese citizens' values in the 1990s. It gave us a glimpse of a psychology whereby citizens' confidence levels toward particular persons (for example, family members, leaders), and even towards the authorities (for example organs of coercion with extremely strong deterrents and compensations such as the army, the government, etc.) are quite high, while towards legal institutions (in particular towards judicial agencies whose public trust and implementation power are weak) it was rather low.[16] How lack of trust in the rule of law is to be overcome is a fourth issue which China's market economic development still offers no means of avoiding.

This essay offers preliminary analysis and discussion of this set of issues, laying particular emphasis on eight crucial measures involving institutional operability: (1) realize constructive trust [sic] in the rule of law and self-reference of the the routine system through procedural techniques; (2) establish routine expectations that embrace confidence in the sustainability of the form of property rights and to provide complete institutional safeguards; (3) feel out a third road for harmonious economic development through redistribution and "planning for the market"; (4) dampen the impact on society of intensifying domestic and foreign free competition by building a minimum social security network; (5) strengthen enterprise compliance reporting through judicial methods and a system of internal reporting; (6) look at harmonious economic development and corporate and government governance through revision of China's corporation law of and formulation of antimonopoly law; (7) harmonize the normative system through independence of trials and the superiority of judicial interpretation; (8) safeguard equilibrium between various economical relations by giving full play to the role of the community of legal professionals – specially lawyers – in open market.

11.4 Harmonious economic development in terms of rule of law and trust – fictive self-reference and long-enduring normative expectations of the property rights form

In today's China, the division of labor between trades and occupations grows ever finer, systemic structures ever more integrated, and digital networks spread confusion even while transmitting information. Given all this, the risks to individual action are constantly rising. As a result, the requirement for communication and cooperation is ever higher, and mutual trust plays an ever greater role. It must be recognized however that the conditions for forming, maintaining and strengthening trust are actually worse now than in the past, and have indeed weakened greatly. The social nexus has become slack, and certainty of the social environment and unity of thought have clearly dropped. The shadows of relativization and disquiet are fluttering everywhere. Based on actual conditions, people have to place their hopes for stability and security with the body of state power. But Chinese-style power is itself imaginary, personified, prone to ignoring principle and changing with the circumstances, to making decisions according to the subjective will of individuals: hence power itself inevitably full of indeterminacy.

In brief, trust is on the one hand very necessary, while on the other hand it is possibly deficient; thereis, paradoxically, an inverse ratio between the two. If this paradox is not eliminated, it is impossible to realize long-term economic rationality or any relevant coordination and equilibrium. How to form trust in the state's actual legal norms and judicial justice, and through the rule of law establish a universal system of trust, will be of the utmost importance to China's harmonious economy development.[17] Individuals are thus allowed to choose and reorganize their norms, is the trend of increasing complexity.[18]

When considering trust in the law, there is an unavoidable question of its fictitious nature. How can something that is fictitious be trusted? Key to explaining this question lies in, how law as legal fiction is understood. The Japanese civil law scholar Saburo Kurusu discusses related topics, seeking for example to break the myth of there only being one correct answer, and allowing a plurality of legal interpretations to coexist. The German legal sociologist Niklas Luhmann's focal point is however quite different, stressing the real need of the system to make use of the simplifying role of paradox, reducing its tendency to increasing complity. Namely: one must embark first from fiction, then disregard it, thus forming a self-referential trust mechanism.

To explain his thinking, Luhmann gives the example of a well-known story of a family dividing up the camels it owned: once upon a time a wealthy herdsman left a large herd of camels to his three sons in his will, with the proviso that they apportion them as follows: the eldest would get half of them, the second a quarter, and the third a sixth. But later the number of camels fell for various reasons, with only 11 surviving when the old man died, so that they could not be divided according to the terms of the will. When the eldest son claimed six for himself on the basis of primogeniture it was disputed by the others, who took the case to court. In the end a wise judge determined as follows: to avoid the legal difficultty of not being able to make the division according to the will, he provided a camel of his own, stipulating however that it be returned to him as soon as the case was wound up. As a result, with this token of trust, legal inheritance took place completely according to the proportions stipulated in the will, the eleven camels were assigned smoothly to the heirs, with the eldest receiving six, the second eldest three, and the third 2, while the one left over was handed back over to the judge, and everyone was happy.

Analyzing this, Luhmann points out that the borrowed camel is merely a semiotic device allowing the system to work. It betokens a certainty that is in itself useless, and is essentially part of the system's self-reference. Here, the judge's camel belongs within the system of adjudication, which, while essential, was nonessential as well, constituting a legal paradox.[19] Through this fiction, in other words, the system of adjudication could begin to operate in conditions of doubt and great uncertainty. Fiction can however be made use of in practical decisions, avoiding certain sensitive dilemmas which exist in reality, finally bring about suitable handling in the normative plane. In other words, a legal fiction is only a supplementary line for solving dilemmas of recognition and assignment of rights in the market economy, while condidence in the law must be established on the foundation the independence, finality, and self-reference of adjudication system.

If it is acknowledged that trust in the law and trial system is actually established on the basis of self-reference, it is also necessary to investigate certain questions further, such as how moments of trust (including faith in fictional abstractions, confidence in fair trials, belief in basic norms, etc) can be inserted in the system. In terms of the above instances, the outside society's trust in the entire legal system's ability to solve problems is a pivot. It goes without saying that the actual effect of the law and the quality of lawyers can affect both the judgment of this ability and the level of confidence generated by it. Moreover, lawyers' mode of handling their own belief in self-reference, and the psychic mechanism allowing litigants and the external society to believe the lawyers' behavior is really credible, are very important as well, and hence constitute another pivot of trust in the intention of the legislators and judiciary. The question remaining is, what type of institutional design is advantageous to setting up society's trust in the ability and intentions of the community of professional lawyers in China?

Speaking of the inner workings of the legal system, Fuller's distinctive views on "reliance interests" [sic] and corresponding developments in jurisprudence are especially worth reviewing. According to Fuller's theory, the law of contractual obligation should not only protect anticipated interests, but also should protect reliance interests, i.e. attempt to establish rules such that harm caused by breach of rational trust must be compensated, and the trust of those suffering harm not merely left to return to its original condition; it means in fact introducing the jurisprudence of abuse of power to the field of contracts, and legal protection of strengthened trust in contracts. This way of promoting the formation of trust in transaction activities in judicial or legislative policy will inevitably further strengthen trust in pledges as well as expand the zone of protection of anticipated interests, and enable judicial agencies to be involved in the sphere of civil law regulating on the basis of the concept of distributive justice.[20] P. S. Atiyah subsequently further developed Fuller's thesis of reliance interests, seeking to abandon the influence of moral principles, grasping the essence of the law of contract only by unifying trust behavior and pledges. Not only that, he also gives reliance a legal status superior to pledges, and seeks the the basis of the binding force of contracts in sustained relationships apart from expressions of the meanings of two litigants. This opens the door wide to the theory of relational contract based on social exchange and free planning initiated by Ian Macneil et al.[21] It can thus be seen that relationalizating and socializing the domain of civil law strengthens the inevitable trend towards trust in the inner workings of contemporary legal systems, while its most basic motive force is provided by litigants, through safeguarding their interests in regard to damage compensation, and demanding rectification of the results of spontaneous negotiation.

Social exchange can be established, however, only when the conditions or acceptable outcomes proposed by the opposite party are seen to be advantageous to oneself, and not necessarily when all are willing to carry on objectively equivalent exchange. What commonly goes by the name of equivalent exchange is thus often not really so, but only what is subjectively felt to be a worthwhile exchange ratio, roughly equivalent, or a reasonable give and take despite being of disparate value. To see this point is critically important. Just because individual effectiveness or value judgments are incapable of being quantified, and are hard to unify, the emphasis of legal institutions must be placed on safeguarding the freedom and procedural justice on value exchanges, and not too much on demanding some a priori standards given by substantive law. In other words, concrete exchange ratios can only be determined through the combination of different factors;in the process of negotiation and communication; in order to avoid social exchange being incapable of reaching balance, becoming a mere formality, or displaying corruption and fraud counterfeits, a set of inherent legal stability installations must be provided – for example, the general provisions of honesty and good faith, compensation for damage to reliance interests, various rights to sue and important procedural documents, and so on. Formally sustainable safeguards for property rights are another expression of this.

11.5 Realizing social harmony by eliminating injustice – the long-term rationality of financial redistribution and overall planning to safeguard the open market

While pursuing and realizing reliance interests in a framework of sustainable property rights and contract institutions is no doubt the dominant driving force for regulated economic development, this does not automatically enable it to eliminate resistance from society. In China today, the prime factors causing unrfest or turbulence are land requisitioning and unemployment, which touch on the survival rights respectively of the peasants and workers, whose demands cannot for the most part obtain full expression and representation, i.e. they "have nowhere to turn for help." Stamping out poverty, curbing corruption, correcting inequality, raising the levels of salaries and unemployment benefits, providing disadvantaged groups with rights to solidarity and political participation have hence become urgent tasks in building a harmonious society. The previously mentioned problems of the dual role played by government, whose participation and intervention in the market is both opposite and complementary, are prominently displayed here.

Given that social harmony presupposes social justice, the present discord must first be altered and injustice eradicated. The government, as representative of the goal of public openness and as a third party adjudicating conflicts of private interest, has an unshirkable responsibility for changing the present injustices. The government however has its own special interests as well, and its activities are implemented through these interest-motivated individuals; its ability to genuinely realize the ideal of justice depends on whether the institutional arrangements of the rule of law can effectively limit the arbitrary exercise of state power, and hold the government accountable for its actions. It is noteworthy here that there are essential differences between the moral standards of governance and the market, which if conflated would certainly cause the proliferation of endless contradictions and conflicts as well as corruption of the social structure.[22] That is to say, limits to power from the angle of fair competition are based on the morality of the market, whose standards might as well include utilitarian value judgments; while making officials accountable is based on the morality of governance, which in Professor Dworkin's words should be "trumps."

Injustice in market economic activity is generally displayed in competition that is wrongful (as when goods are fake or infererior) or brutal (as when work is underpaid or excessive). These obviously point to violation of the regulations, of the rules of the game. Insider trading in the stock market and corporate bribery of government officials, etc., are all cases in point. Compliance with the law hence becomes an important indicator of equitable competition. Not all behavior which violates the rules, however, is considered unjust. Some people for example are late paying their tax, and while this is against the rules and seen as wrong and deserving of punishment, it is not necessarily seen as unjust; whereas if it is very easy for social strata on high incomes to evade taxes, and even be protected by the relevant government agencies, people will be infuriated and condemn it as injust, as the intense argument that erupted in China in 2005 over revisions to the individual income tax laws showed quite clearly.

Thus it can be seen that in a market economy the difference between justice and injustice is related in the first place to whether public norms, above all the law, are respected; next, to whether there is equal compliance with the rules, and lastly with whether violations of the rules or inequality involves interests which relate to certain goals and even relevant to the pattern of distribution. But among these three, the most central factor is equality. The main criterion of justice therefore is equal value. Observing norms involves issues of equal rights, while reckoning interests involves issues of equal effectiveness; attention to norms involves discovering wrongful actions and mechanisms to punish them, while attention to interests involves preventing such problems as what economics terms "free riding," how to provide and safeguard public goods. Generally speaking, the concept of equality as the basis of the view of justice for the economy and society as a whole is comprised of two main meanings. First, all people must be treated impartially, and equality of opportunity for this must be safeguarded; second, corresponding different treatment of each person obtained according to characteristic differences, must carry out distributive justice for this and suitable adjustment and correction of unequal outcomes, moreover also includes free choice between plural values. Hence equality here does not mean equal subjection to state coercion, nor absolutely equal distribution, but equality of freedom realized and safeguarded by the legal system and moderate equality.

By "moderate equality" is meant a certain socially acceptable equilibrium achieved between equality of opportunity and resultative equality, including two basic aspects, the golden mean and redistributive policies. In moderate equality terms, the principle of equality of opportunity is inadequate. For, even given equality of opportunity, when small disparities in capability coexist with great disparities in income, inequalities of opportunity on the assumption of "minding one's own business" are liable to cause envy and disaffection, and people will thus develop deeper feelings of injustice; particularly because, if even fortuitous or accidental inequality can cause intense antisocial sentiment, how much more can differences between individuals' abilities and location in the social environment? If differences between people can appear even given the equal assignment of basic wealth, as advocated by theories such as John Rawls' "property-owning democracy" (sic),[23] it is actually impossible to have equality of opportunity in the true sense. It is necessary then to consider and make efforts to solve to some extent the problem of resultative equality, and to broaden the contents of the goal of equality, which is not restricted to resources, income or effectiveness, but should also include the latent capability to choose a life style autonomously.[24]

With the coming of the information age, globalization and technological democratization may cause deconstruction of the system of rank in certain countries, expanding the space for activity and influence of social powers that resist the advantaged groups, thus helping to popularizen equality as a value. But one should also note that the network structures and relational capital very easy lead to outcomes of asymmetrical distribution of resources and wealth and the winner takes all. This will intensify the polarization of rich and poor, and deepen the degree of inequality. This is the paradox of equality ecountered in the electronic and Internet era. Against this background, achieving moderate equality is a major issue worldwide.[25] Different societies have of course different specific standards of justice: it is very difficult to speak generally, or to carry on comparisons, to make a clear judgement about high and low. But this does not mean there are no general features of social justice, or generalizable value indices. Nonetheless, there are varying degrees of mutual difference between views of justice in pre-industrial, industrial and post-industrial societies, each having its own characteristics.

The basic model for realizing justice in an industrialized society might be summarized as follows: a free competitive market, together with enterprises offering long-term employment, and a government willing to intervene. Full freedom of choice is also in the picture, together with reasonable stability, fairly predictable living, and welfare that is fairly equally supplied. Its actual foundation is a well-off middle class, on the one hand opening to mobility both up and downward, giving hope of being able to make it, and on the other hand may also play the role of balancer between the value of freedom of the elite social strata and the value of equality of the grassroots. But in a postindustrial society, the situation undergoes sweeping change: the market is still one of free competition, while to some extent the long-term stability and predictivity provided by industrial organization is reduced; market activities are more and more controlled by pluralized consumption demand and short-term profit motive. Linked to this, risk, chance, fluidity, and relativity are all to varying degrees strengthened in society. In such a risk society, prior preparation and control become extremely difficult, and only the mode of ex-post determination of responsibility and judicial monitoring can be adopted to maintain a just order; hence mechanisms that assign responsibility have more vital significance for the state and society. Given this, the most essential institutional design is not a scheme opposing public to private, nor that of the welfare state, but a social safety net provided for losers in the market competition, constructed by various legal methods, i.e. widespread minimum safeguards provided to people under conditions of total dependence on the principles of free competition and self-responsibility.

China is becoming the world's factory, and at the same time one of the critical new economic sites centred on information technology. This determines that if justice is to be realized in today's China, the different requirements of industrial and post-industrial society must be satisfied at the same time. Thus, while China must seek a point of balance between "wealth" and "equality" in the process of building a harmonious society, slogans like shared or common wealth and the like cannot never again be promoted: not only are they unattainable, they may destroy the new mechanisms formed in the 25 years of reform. A more suitable policy is thought to be, assuming income disparities are admitted, to vigorously initiate the elimination of poverty. It goes without saying that in this process, redistribution is of critical importance. Given the rule of law, redistribution would comprises two basic aspects: (1) redistribution according to the princeples of public law, start from tax revenue and consideration of the fiscal budget, reorganize the legislative power, representative system and mode of administrative intervention according to special interest group liberalism and interest democracy; (2) redistribution according to the principles of civil law, protect the status parity of the vulnerable in market negotiations through the general provisions of civil law, the principles of real preoperty rights as well as the compulsory provisions of contracts, and carry out this kind of civil law redistribution in the plane of justiciability through institutions of adjudication.

We may therefore say that a socialized rule of law nation that can fully safeguard individual rights, suitably provide social welfare, and retain to the maximum the choice space of plural values is most conducive to harmonious economic development. This means China will surmount the quarrel betwen "liberal" and "New Left," devote itself to deepening reform and from this achieve balance and mutual coordination of market, government and society. In other words, we should seek a "third path," conforming to China's actual needs, between free competition and long-term rationality, namely carry out some kind "coercion for the sake of freedom" or "planning for the market" on the basis of China's special situation and conditions.

11.6 Regulated management of enterprises and fair competition – the ethical spirit of economic organizations constantly produced between hard and soft law

Whether or not a market economy can develop harmoniously is closely linked to whether the agencies playing the game observe its rules. But, as the third set of issues listed above showed, the structural changes following globalization break through existing institutional barriers. Against the background of a huge capital market and intense international competition, frequent merger activity may lead to total change in companies, short-circuiting relations between finance and corporate governance, and further causing a meltdown organizationsas well as the substantive economy. When boundaries are erased here or there, domains become extremely opposed, and the internal and external relationships of systems are constantly reintegrated, the entire situation becomes increasingly fluid and fortuitous, and the stable social order gives way to opportunism. Such extremely liberalized conditions enable the market agencies' sense of legality to weaken by the day. As is well known, in the case of for-profit enterprises, if matters are allowed to drift, one can hardly expect to have genuine fair competition, much less legitimate management of company organizations. Under just such conditions, to adapt easily to the rules and regulations, mechanisms must be constructed inside the firm which can effectively monitor and restrict the formidable powers of management. Institutional designs for corporate "compliance" [sic] have hence aroused widespread interest.[26]

While naturally centred on observing laws and regulations, "compliance" is not restricted to this, but also includes the corporation's internal rules and regulations. For example, articles of incorporation, employees' joint pledges, rules of service, confidentiality, professional ethics, etc., which relate to the prestige of providing high-quality services and high-grade management culture. In fact, according to the requirements of compliance, the standards which firms must observe comprise three levels, namely: (1) laws and orders promulgated by the state; (2) community rules and decisions formulated by the firm itself, (3) the general ethics of good faith required by the free market; these are in fact not unlike the tripartite structure of laws of the land, local rules and moral propriety of normative system of traditional China. This is clearly a comprehensive scheme of governance.

Institutional design for compliance emphasizes the enterprise as self-conscious quest for perfection on the part of the enterprise as a whole, based neither on one-sided state coercion, nor only on the personal merit of the managers, but is an organizational response to and handling of practical activity, whose substantive content is various aspects of the company working as one, which, by observing and utilizing a range of official and unofficial rules, realizes healthy operational performance and harmonious development of the sectors of the economy that concern it, maintaining the good faith and public welfare of its profit-making activities. In rule of law terms, according to the requirements of compliance, besides strictly observance of mandatory statutes, the role of directory statutes in the firm's management organization and system operation is strengthened. Correspondingly, the autonomous domain further expands; as a result, room for maneuver is also gained for adjusting and correcting the operation of state norms. A more important change is, compliant corporate governance is constrained to vertical control relations of obeying commands and following directions, but conversely also encourages the firm's internal criticisms and suggestions, as well as mutual supervision by means of reporting institutions. This also constitutes the answser to the first set of issues – how to transform the legal framework from a rigid into an elastic structure.

In US experience, the requirement of compliance in legal aspects mainly manifests in the *Federal Sentencing Guideline Manual's* criteria for punishing corporate crime. In order to prevent an overall moral slide caused by bias towards superficial sanctions on organizations, this standard-setting document establishes concrete standards for deciding the severity of penalties for corporate crimes, reflecting an institutional design mentality that combines persuasion and threat. According to the relevant provisions, all corporate crime involving management with prior criminal record and who hinder criminal detection, must carry added punishment. Otherwise, all corporations that bring regulatory institutions in to prevent illegal activity beforehand, carry on self-declaration of illegal matters, initiate confession of crimes, and show willingness to assist the judicial organs, may [be treated] with discrimination [to obtain] mitigated punishment. Not only is there lenience [in return for] confession, they may also be allowed to make reparations institutionally, a very interesting judicial policy. An important document for lenient treatment, which encourages firms to establish rules and regulations preventing illegal activity, [it is] known simply as the "compliance program," and comprises seven stages, namely: (1) formulating norms and procedures of compliance to prevent corporate crime; (2) appointing a senior manager to oversee implementation of relevant norms and procedures; (3) informing and educating staff on the relevant norms and procedures; (4) paying full attention to tasks in jurisdictional division and delegation; (5) establishing supervisory and reporting institutions; (6) adopting precautionary disciplinary measures to behavior violating the rules; (7) constantly improving relevant rules and regulations for preventing the repetition of similar problems.[27]

After the "separation of ownership and right of management" there comes the second enterprise revolution of "separation of right of management and right of supervision." Compliance requirements are also embodied in corporate governance (especially monitoring the higher management of big corporations), for example diversified institutional arrangements for legal risk management (sic), demanding fully accountability of management, rewarding internal reporting of corporate crime issues so as to form mechanisms of mutual supervision,[28] paying punitive damage for fraudulent lawsuits, promoting private lawsuit carried on for public welfare (qui tam action) (sic), and so on. In this sense it may also be said that, having kept up the "separation of ownership and management rights," a second enterprise revolution of the "separation of management and supervisory rights" is taking place. Moreover, bolstering employment safeguards and environmental protection according to the theory of stakeholders, forbids monopolistic management actions and respects intellectual property rights according to principles of free and equitable competition are other major elements in the compliance project.

Whether private or state-owned, all enterprises in China today have complex linkages with governments and banks, leading to non-transparency of enterprise and bank accounts. The efficiency of management is doubly disturbed by power emanating from state and society. If loopholes like these are not closed, the problems of investment overheating and non-performing bank loans will be hard to solve; even when the basic macroeconomic conditions are quite good – there is, for example, no marked inflation, rich financial revenues, and considerable foreign exchange reserves – once there is substantive financial liberalization, huge risks of an economic crisis possibly erupting must be faced. Another loophole is [when] reform of the stock system does not link share transactions to corporate interests, one even may say the stock market has to a great extent become purely an installation for snaring money. Meanwhile, as the main instrument restricting financial shocks induced by speculation on the part of shareholders, and preventing hostile acquisitions by international capital, one only has the state and enterprises holding large amounts (around 60 percent of stock total) of non-circulating stock as controlling shares – which strengthens long-term cooperation relations with a network architecture in which the non-circulating stock is the nexus, and floating international capital and scattered small stockholders are brought stably into the framework – constantly de-randomizing the fortuitousness produced by speculation.

While these two loopholes exist, however, managers have opportunities to turn firms into private property through various channels; it is hard to push forward plans to reduce state-owned stockholdings, and harder to implement them according to the principles of distributive justice, i.e. through public, transparent procedures; this encourages the business community to set their hearts on risky speculative capital and harbour expectations of state relief, and makes it hard for book-keeping to become more transparent; as a result, a healthy capital market serving industry never gets on the right footing. Conversely, with the structure of corporate governance and the industrial capital market never meeting the requirements of a rule of law economy, comprehensively introducing mechanisms of free competition is very likely to induce a raging tide of hostile international takeovers as well as massive losses in the substantive economy. hence on this foundation it is difficult to weaken the motive for maintaining non-circulation stock and establishing defence pacts between domestic enterprises. In brief, these difficulties together with the high risks, lend urgency to the requirement for legal management, but at the same time sets up more barriers to the enterprise compliance project.

Major revisions of China's Corporation Law made in 2005 took effect on January 1, 2006. The basic intention of the new provisions was precisely to strengthen enterprise compliance while relaxing the rules and regulations, promoting the formation, expansion and improvement of the domestic capital market by such means as rewarding investment, fully drawing in social floating capital, and protecting small shareholders' rights and interests. As regards rationalization of the structure of corporate governance, the burden of the revised corporation law was to reduce intervention in firms and apply compulsory legal norms, respecting and emphasizing the articles of incorporation and the efficacy of internal discipline, improving operational decision-making and all management procedures, expanding the role of boards of directors, introducing institutions of lawsuits [over] shareholder proxies, taking the harmonious relations of stakeholders seriously, etc. Worthy of note was that in order to prevent enterprises abusing the legal principle of limited liability, violating market rules and enterprise ethics, Article 20 of the new Corporation Law set up the institution of denial of legal personality, and, in the case of of companies that significantly harm the interests of opposite parties by illegally evading debts, expanding the scope of compensation claims to sources of wealth beyond corporately managed assets.

The goal of rationalizing the structure of governance is, assuming their operations are legal, to strengthen the competitive power of enterprises, and enhance the efficiency of economic development. As international corporate competition intensifies, institutional competition is growing in importance, making relations ever closer between corporate, stock exchange and antimonopoly law, and requiring legislative agencies to consider them – and any measures to reform them – in an all-around way. Here, antimonopoly law, which constitutes the essential condition for advancing free activities of firms, and also the criteria for strictly differentiating between harmonious economic development and monopolistic collaboration, between emphasizing the market model of cooperation for reciprocal benefit and inter-enterprise counter-competitive collusion, joint management mergers, stock inter-ownership, making concrete discrimination of the differences between collusion in management activities and regional protectionism, is worth taking especially seriously.

In considering compliance and competitive order of Chinese enterprises, there is a realistic difficulty that must be raised, namely the great influence of the dual role of government touched on our second set of issues. Debate is fierce over the major reasons for delayed passage of the draft antimonopoly law, also over limiting the extent and mode of administrative monopoly, and the resistance of vested interest groups has been very strong. When the government agencies concerned pursue economical rationality as market players, they naturally have incomparable superiority over private [*minjian*] enterprise, especially in their access to internal information and sanctions and in being able to directly control the results of competition through their advantages in altering policies. If the government arbitrarily changes the market rules and regulations in its own interests or those of official rent-seeking, it inevitably makes nonsense of any talk of corporate compliance. In this sense, limiting the exercise of power, opening up information and removing administrative monopolies are key to setting up and improving competitive mechanisms. People have perfectly good reason for being disappointed with deletion of provisions regarding administrative monopolies in the antimonopoly law, which has recently been passed in principle. Even if the complex relations between natural monopoly phenomena, the problem of externalities in technological development, the coordination of enterprise strategy behavior to break barriers of inequitable trade protectionism internationally, domestic defensive alliances against hostile acquisitions, and the requirements of independent technical collective assaults on the pass, are all brought into the field of vision, it is hard to make a plausible defence of the state in which loopholes in explicit rules have been left in the antimonopoly law.[29]

11.7 Harmonizing legal institutions – establishing true jurisdiction independence and promoting deduction, expression and integrity of lawyer discursive rights

Several truths are brought to light by the opposing opinions on the anti-monopoly law: if the rule of law is to safeguard competitive freedom and equity, it first must earn the people's trust; but if such trust in the rule of law is to be established and maintained, there can be no contradictions or personal variations between various institutions and norms, there must be continuity and coordination; in the era of globalization, the cause of legal system conformity is not restricted to domestic law itself, but must lead to the harmonization of the laws of Chinese with those of foreign countries, with international law and indeed with local norms. In brief, without harmony between various legal institutions, it is very difficult to realize economic development or the harmony of society as a whole.

Breaking administrative monopolies and orderly government retreat from the market imply fundamental changes in the basic mode of economic management and regulation: changing from *ex ante* permits and direct regulations to *ex post* judicial relief and indirect restraints. To adopt a Chinese economist's account, it is "gradually expanding the intervention of courts in market control."[30] If courts are to play the role in market competition that they ought, they must maintain strict neutrality and have final decision-making powers. This places requirements on their degree of adjudicative independence and technical standards.

As is well known, China has not adopted the system of separation of powers – all levels of courts must be responsible to and be supervised by National People's Congresses of corresponding level, expressed at the institutional level in periodic personnel appointments and dismissals by the representative and deliberative organs, and regular work reports and acceptance of interpellation by the chief Judge to the National People's Congress. Although the Supreme Court may to a some extent actually create norms through judicial interpretation, all courts must, in theory or in institutional design, uphold the principle of the supremacy of the representative and deliberative organs, and refrain from judicial examination of laws or regional rules and regulations. This logic extends to an explicit rulimg that courts are unable to carry on judicial examination of administrative regulations and administration in the abstract that formulates the rules and decisions. Moreover, while the Supreme Court may interpret legal norms, it is of course restricted to relevant judicial activities, and never interprets constitutional texts. Thus it can be seen, the key to guaranteeing adjudicative independence is expanding the scope of judicial examination to administrative action in the abstract, so as to carry on legal examination of the administrative regulations and rules, etc., and then apply constitutional scrutiny to laws and the activities of agencies of state power.[31]

The history of the judicial examination system in contemporary China might be traced to Article 5 of the Administrative Procedure Law (1989). The major feature of judicial examination as provided by this law is that the scope of legal review by courts is strictly limited to concrete administrative actions, and in Article 11 the concrete actions as the object of administrative proceedings are enumerated one by one. Clause 2 of Article 12 clearly excludes administrative regulations, rules, and decisions and orders with universal binding force from the scope of admissibility.[32] Administrative interpretations of administrative regulations, rules, and decisions and orders with universal binding force are not concrete administrative actions, much less when all abstract administrative actions to some extent bear the attributes of carrying out legal norms and making administrative interpretations of them.

Logically, therefore, courts cannot carry out examination of administrative interpretations. And what is more, in Article 1 the Administrative Procedural Law comes straight to the point, providing that the objectives of people's courts trying administrative cases also include, apart from supervision, safeguarding the functional activities of administrative agencies which, moreover, have precedence over supervision. Obviously, in China administrative interpretation is superior to judicial; this hierarchy of power relations is counter to modern principles of the rule of law, and inevitably leads to legal conflicts and normative dissonance.

It is comforting that legislatures have recently begun to revise the Administrative Procedure Law and the State Compensation Law, and one extremely important added provision in the new draft carries out the human rights provision of the 2004 constitutional amendment, stipulating that citizens are authorized to file lawsuits requesting compensation for abstract administrative actions. implying a major development of the admissible scope of administrative proceedings, and implying as well that all levels of judicial organization are authorized to examine and revise local authorities' regulations and other universal decisions, and the legality and constitutionality of instructions, and may lead to the relevant agencies undertaking to carry on legal liability for state compensation. In order to accord with the the requirements of the law after revision, and prevent local organs of power and administrative organs interfering with impartial handling of cases by administrative trial agencies, further reform will also be carried on of relevant court institutions, especially reversing the existing pattern of regional courts at all levels being restrained in such aspects as system, personnel and finance, etc., by regional National People's Congresses and governments at the same level.[33]

If judicial independence is to be genuinely realized, further efforts must be made to authorize the Supreme Court to interpret the Constitution in order to test the constitutionality of the content of legislation, without which it is very difficult for the normative system to have coherence and harmony. The question is whether at present the manpower, finances, material resources, etc, of the higher courts and Supreme Courts can objectively fully adapt to the new state pf play. Speaking only of the Supreme Court, the corps of judicial personnel after 1988 has always fluctuated between 300 and 340, with a total staff complement of some 600 people. Relative to China's 200,000 strong judicial corps, this figure is really too small. One might well summarize that the basic situation of China's judicature at present is a "big judiciary with a small Supreme Court," one that appears very abnormal, and not conducive to transforming the structure of state power or full displaying the function of judicial principles.[34]

While there are only nine grand justices in the United States Supreme Court, and only fifteen judges in Japan's, there are many personnel doing concrete service and preparatory work who are qualified judges. The office of each Chief Justice in the US Supreme Court may for example have four outstanding investigative officers. It is even said that they are in fact made up of nine law offices which have established their own schools of thought; most trial services are separately hendled by federal Appellate Courts (with a total of 153 judges according to 1,998 judicature statistical data,), Circuit Courts (642 judges), local courts (1,404 judges including bankrupt court and public security judges), as well as four levels of State courts (30,316 judges during 1998–99, including the State Supreme Courts). Judges in Japan (including *banshi* and *banshibu*) total 1,740 nationally; in the Supreme Court, some 40 people are qualified as judges, as well as some 40 law clerks and other staff members, totalling 1,000 people.[35] China's Supreme Court establishment is thus actually much smaller than that of other countries. According to its plan, starting in 2006 the Supreme Court, having resumed the authority for examining and approving the death penalty, must for the sake of its service needs increase its corps of judicial personnel by more than 300. The number of judicially qualified personnel may reach 700, and total staff numbers will inevitably exceed 1,000. Such an establishment will actually still be far from sufficient however, when tasks like the optimization of administrative trials and judicial review of constitutionality of laws and regulations, etc. are brought into its field of vision.

Of the professional legal community, which includes judges, public prosecutors and lawyers, the latter are closest to individual citizens, to the market and to society. Whether in harmonious economic development, safeguarding individual rights and interests, or regulating the normative order, lawyers play extremely important intermediary and the ordering roles. Between 1986 and 2005, Chinese lawyers multiplied, with noticeably increasing speed, by a factor of 5. However, in the overall structure of the community of professional lawyers, including judges and public prosecutors, lawyers actually still number only about 1 in 5. In 2000, the ratio of judges to lawyers in China was 2.5 to 1, just the opposite of many other countries (e.g. South Korea's 1:3, France's 1:5, Japan's 1:6, US's 1:25).[36] This pattern of government-people relations, it must be noted, where the scope and force of judicial bureaucrats and civilian defence lawyers are so incommensurate and inverted, has been kept up for fully 20 years. It has led to the appearance of certain flaws in the discursive space of law, – so that the top-down voice of commands, propaganda, education and persuasion often conceal the bottom-up voice demanding rights, and very easily distorts the feedback mechanisms of social control and adjustment. Along with the deepening of judicial reform, it is therefore necessary to adjust the internal layout of the professional legal comunity, and raise the topic of changing its top-heavy, malformed development to the political agenda.[37, 38, 39]

What has provided motivation and power in the evolution of China's lawyer system to date? For the most part, clearly, economic demand. This point is vividly reflected in early slogans such as one defining lawyers as "economic police requiring no government outlay."[40] According to precisely this logic, the Ministry of Justice in 1992 accepted the notion that legal offices are part of the service sector, and acknowledged openness and competitive mechanisms of the legal services market, and in 2004 began to allow the existence of lawyers' advertising. An undue stress on economic demands alone will inevitably, however, push legal offices willy-nilly towards profit-seeking, clearly at odds with views of social justice and the requirements of legal professionalism. In view of the need to limit the profit-seeking trend, the Ministry of Justice began as early as 1994 to lay more emphasis on the lawyer's role and duty in public welfare, and positively organized and led legal aid activities. It might in a sense also be argued that the provisions regarding legal aid duties in Article 42 of the current Legal Practioners Law, is in fact a very significant flag of the Chinese judicial administration regime, by means of mandatory norms and various accompanying measures, overcoming the bias toward legal commercialism, and at the same time upholding the ideals of legal professionalism; it may to some extent play a role analogous to the provisions safeguarding human rights in laws regarding the judiciary in other countries, because providing legal help to disadvantaged groups is also an important aspect of rights defense. Of course, Article 42 is by itself far from sufficient.

Moreover, using the lever of economic demand to drive reform and development of the judiciary, while emphasizing independent accounting systems and management benefits for legal offices, also quietly changes the resource allocation of legal services, forcing lawyers to withdraw from counties and towns, where rewards are low, and gradually concentrate in cities, whose market share is greater. While public legal service offices, legal aid centers and village and town legal service stations can to some extent ameliorate these interregional imbalances and other ill effects, by 2005 some 206 counties had in fact become "zero lawyer" regions, i.e. where legal services were nonexistent. How to safeguard various regions and social strata in respect of equal access to legal services, and forestall the emergence of corners where justice is forgotten, has clearly become an extremely urgent task in legislative work henceforth.

As is well known, in 2004 China started to adjust its economic strategy on its own initiative, as a result of which sustainable development, green GDP, the environment, reducing the gap between rich and poor, etc, have became buzzwords of the day. Given this social background, the habitus of lawyers will also to some degree change along with. For example, disputes and lawsuits over environmental damage have grown sharper, and lawyers act not only as agents in the case, they also to some extent devote themselves to writing scattered claims for rights into the institutional framework. In many fields apart from environmental lawsuits, lawyers play the role of organizers, coordinatorss or important intermediaries, in dialogue, communication and negotiation between the people and the government, and in the process of making order out of chaos. Clearly, to promote private rights, emphasize distributive justice, to establish and improve free markets and a democratic country under the rule of law, the sphere of action of lawyers should be expanded, and the interaction between professional lawyers and individual citizens should be strengthened.

11.8 Foundations of sustainable development: institutional safeguards of property right and budget deliberation procedures

Taking four basic issues in relations between the economy and the law as clues, this essay has discussed some crucial institutional conditions for harmonious social development in China, touching on "planning for the market," the settlement of property relations, procedural techniques, distributive justice, corporate compliance, freed and equitable competition, reform of the judicial system and strengthening the role of lawyers, etc. In conclusion, I would like finally to specially emphasize two major legal installations which, while part of these institutional conditions, in fact have decisive significance. One is the draft Real Property Law whose passage has been long held up in deliberation because of intense ideological debate; the other is the tentative plan for a "budget parliament" to coordinates between various special interest groups by non-politicized rational techniques.

The essence of the draft Real Property Law which has been discussed by all the people is to adapt the structure of the extant ownership system to the needs of business liberalization, legally interpreting property rights in terms both of exchange value and distributive justice, and providing full safeguards for the new property relations formed in the reform period. In terms of the Law's economic and social functions, those concerning the transfer of land utilization rights, common ownership of real estate, unification of the notarization system, and rules for land requisitioning such as relocation procedures and standards of compensation, etc., have attracted most attention. Passage of this bill may be called a sine qua non of harmonious economic development. The question whether the subject of rights to various decisions on the disposal of collective lands is the villagers' collective (a democratic decision making assembly), or rather those qualified as cultivators of the land enjoying real rights safeguards (the peasant households who operate under contract) needs to be clarified as soon as possible. Otherwise market negotiations may not lead to rational, highly efficient allocation of resources, and objections, resistance, lawsuits and even rioting against land requisitions and relocation, which are already in evidence, may well become increasingly fierce in future.

Some Chinese legal scholars argue that distributive justice and social harmony are based on public ownership, and that there are issues with the constitutionality of the present draft Real Property Law, thrusting the relevant legislation into the intersection of economic and political reform. Those pushing for maintaining the precedence of state ownership fail to see that the basic motif of twenty-first century economic globalization is undergoing deep transformation, and as regards China – above all manufacturing firms who face consumers directly – the issue of overproduction is more salient by the day. The main economic problem bothering government and society will therefore be inflation rather than stagflation, and extremely intense price wars. Under these conditions, the significance of continued dependence on financial investment to promote a boom is diminishing. And so long as there is no major war, the direct stimulation of firms by government procurement will diminish as well. Prompt withdrawal of government from the market, rapidly sharpening the multi-level competitive ability of private [*minjian*] companies themselves, and raising the technological intensity of industry as a whole are thus of the greatest importance. In the light of these major tendencies, institutional reform in the present stage must as soon as possible vigorously drive privatization and de-statification [*minyinghua*] of management, deregulating the enterprises, and not the opposite.

Even if one considers only solving concrete, actual problems and safeguarding immediate social stability, the scholars opposing the draft Real Property Law have made a serious error in judgment – trying to prevent the erosion of state assets, solve distributive injustice and eliminate social discontents by avoiding political reform and maintaining the totalitarian mode of ownership to is no different to climbing a tree to catch a fish. The root of the bad land policies lies in fact not in privatization but in the public ownership system. Because of public ownership, non-state enterprise is forced to pay heavily for utilization rights, creating abnormal rises in firms' operating costs. But the bulk of this income does not really go to the state treasury, so the state is unable to obtain the full benefit from the transfer of land which could drive structural reform of industry and radical improvement to the social security system.[41] It can thus be seen that the means of effecting a permanent cure is not to keep providing powerful minorities with rent-seeking opportunities by defending the existing pattern of public ownership, but genuinely changing the structure of property rights. As for how to strengthen the protection of state assets under the existing conditions, this is a problem in public law, which should be detached from the work of formulating the Real Property Law.

Related to the argument revolving around the Real Property Law, there are also problems like how to regulate demands among divergent interest groups, safely solve various disputes, and so on. A series of taxation, finance and allocative institutions must therefore be reformed, strengthening the deliberation and supervision by NPC delegates of the budget bill and its implementation. All levels of National People's Congress and the Political Consultative Conference might as well be transformed into a lively and transparent "budget parliament," making all the interest groups and political influences learn the skills of compromise by establishing and deliberating a pure fiscal budget, gradually enhancing the competitiveness of agencies of state power. Hallmark of the institutional design mentality of a "Budget parliament" is, first, as far as possible place the emphasis of the representative system's scope of discussion on those taxation and financial matters which effect distributive justice between different interest groups, and to some extent temporarily depoliticize other political issues – set aside disputes and wait for a suitable time to solve them later. In other words, this means the ruling party is in economic terms to genuinely safeguard fair competition (freedom principle), and distributive justice (equality principle), and taking this as prerequisite, sign a partially depoliticized or non-adversarial (social regulation principle), interest democracy type (social security principle) social contract with the people. The benchmark of such a social contract is a system of interest group liberalism,[42] but due to the partially depoliticized institutional arrangements, it would in power structure terms have two two opposite yet complementary sides – looking like social corporatist intermediation [sic], but with a more honest and effective informal negotiation style the bureaucracy and laws. The whole made up of these heterogeneous factors is the institutional arrangement of proceduralist democracy.

In brief, the market with free competition and the rule of law state should be unified. To this end I would also emphasize several basic concepts as follows:

The state of polarization between "laissez faire freedom" and "unplanned regulation" is more in need of legal norms [to act] as intermediaries, flexibility of market supervision to implant systemic confidence and universal trust in the legal system as the prerequisite, the mode of rights defence movement organised by lawyers to reduce inequitable phenomena and transform emotionalized demands gradually into rational legal language, coordinating the interest relations of different groups needs to set up two public forums – a "budget parliament" and a judicial examination system. This kind of institutional design has the possibility of better terminating the evils of "unplanned regulation" and "laissez faire freedom," and gradually developing a third path for China's harmonious economic development – achieving the harmony of freedom and equality of "planning for the market."

Notes

* Keynote address to the annual meetings of Chinese Economists Society "Governing Rapid Growth in China: Efficiency, Equity and Institutions", July 1–4, 2006, Shanghai, China.
1 According to People Net Report http://finance.people.com.cn/GB/1037/3944145.html)
2 Ministry of Public Security press conference content revealed in New China net report: http://news.xinhuanet.com/legal/2006-01/19/content_4072115.htm.
3 For example, Wu Jinglian and Wang Dingding, "Dialogue on the future of China's reforms," *Caijing* no. 11, 1998, Qian Yingyi, "The market and the rule of law," *Jingji shehui tizhi bijiao* [Comparative Economic and Social Systems], no. 3, 2000, "Government and the rule of law," *Bijiao* [Comparison] no. 5 (2003), Wu Jinglian, "Transcending 'left' and 'right': establishing a market economy with rule of law," *Hongfan pinglun* [Hongfan Law Review], no.1, 2004.
4 For legal scholars' response to the economists, see for example Liang Huixing "Struggle for a Chinese Civil Code," (Beijing: Law Press, 2002), Jiang Ping "The Market and the Rule of Law," "Hongfan Law Review" 1 (1) (2004), Liang Zhiping, ed., "State, Market and Society: Law and Development in Contemporary China" (Beijing: China University of Political Science and Law Press, 2006).
5 For Mises' doctrine of the relations between the free economy and adjustment mechanisms that use rules and directives, in particular points in common with the

market socialism models of Taylor and Lange, see Nishibe Makoto, *The Geneal-ogy of Images of the Market – Schemes Revolving around the "Economic Calcula-tion Debate"* (Tokyo: Japanese Economy Daily Press, 1996) chs 1 and 3.

6 For details see Friedriech Hayek, *Collected Works* (trans. Deng Zhenglai, Beijing: Capital University of Economics and Trade Press, 2001). One must point out that even if Anglo-American case-law can be used as a prototype to understand the concept of the "law of liberty," it seems somewhat farfetched to define such rule of law as spontaneous order. See Ji Weidong "Hayek's rule of law paradox: organism and liberty – debate with Professor Deng Zhenglai on scholarly appraisal of the spontaneous order theory" *Zhongguo shuping* [Chinese Book Review] no. 1, 2005 (resumed publication).

7 Robert C. Ellickson, *Order without Law: How Neighbors Settle Disputes* (Rep. ed., Cambridge, Mass.: Harvard University Press, 2005). Cf. Karen Clay & Gavin Wright, "Order without Law? Property Rights during the California Gold Rush," *Explorations in Economic History*, 42(2): 155–83, 2005.

8 For details, see Ronald Dworkin, *Taking Rights Seriously* (revised edn, Cambridge, Mass.: Harvard University Press, 1978), his *A Matter of Principle* (Harvard University Press, 1985), and his *Law' Empire* (Harvard University Press, 1986).

9 Lon L. Fuller, *The Morality of Law* (New Haven: Yale University Press, 1964).

10 Cf. Robert A. Kagan et al. (eds) *Legality and Community: On the Intellectual Legacy of Philip Selznick* (Lanham: Rowman & Littlefield Publishers, Inc., 2002).

11 E.g. David P. Gauthier, *Morals By Agreement* (Oxford: Clarendon Press, 1986).

12 Karl Polanyi, T*he Great Transformation: The Political and Economic Origins of Our Time* (Boston: Beacon Press, 1957), Jieze yingcheng et al., Japanese trans., "The Great Transformation: Formation And Collapse of the Market Society," (Tokyo: Dongyang Economic News Press, 1975) p. 98.

13 See Ronald H. Coase, "The Problem of Social Cost," *The Journal of Law and Economics*, 3(1): 1–44, 1960.

14 For analysis of the relevant issues, see Zhang Chunlin, *Qiye zuzhi yu shichang tizhi* [Enterprise Organization and Market System] (Shanghai: Shanghai Sanlian Book Store, 1991), Zhang Weiying, *Qiye lilun yu Zhongguo qiye gaige* [Theory of the Firm And China's Enterprise Reforms] (Beijing: Peking University Publishing House, in 1999).

15 For details, see Ji Weidong, *Changes in Modern China's Legal System* (Tokyo: Japan Review Press, 2001) Ch. 1 of Part III, "Reciprocity-based Law and its Implementation," esp. pp. 267–8 and 290–1.

16 For details, see Ji Weidong, "The Political Consciousness of China's Urbanites in the 1990s," *Kobe Law Journal*, 2(48): 191ff, 1998.

17 For a typical view from economics, see, e.g., Zhang Weiying *Information, Trust And Law* (Beijing: Sanlian Book Store, 2003). See Francis Fukuyama, *Trust: The Social Virtues and Creation of Prosperity* (New York: Free Press, 1995), Peng Zhihua (Chinese trans.), "Xinren: shehui meide yu chuangzao jingji fanrong" (Haikou: Hainan Press, 2001) discusses low confidence levels in China. For Fushan's retort, see Wang Shaoguang and Liu Xin "Foundations of trust: a rational explanation," *Sociological Research* (China), 2002 no. 3. I argue that China's principle of order does indeed emphasize trust, but the Legalist precepts of "rewards and punishments carried out rigorously and impartially" and "accumulating lesser trust to build greater" place stress on the sovereign establish-ing authority, and neglect relations of interpersonal mutual confidence in the social plane, and indeed hold that all people are "untrustworthy"; while the Con-fucian precepts that "nothing is established without trust" and "speech must be in good faith, action must bear fruit" were suitable only for instructing the common people, not for managing the elite social stratum, which was supposed to adapt to

changing circumstances; the literary intelligentsia "need not actually be in good faith." Both schools take extreme views, leaving society as a whole with no starting point for building a community of trust. Only partial, particularistic trust is left, and the integrity of universal trust is lacking; what passes in daily transactions are tokens of trust and related guarantees. When this is used as a mode of state rule, it evolves into a situation of mutual guarantee and guilt by association, of reporting on and exposing each other, with the ironic outcome of trust destrying trust. While the objective of "propriety and law acting together" is to unify the legal and relational principles of trust, it sticks at the level of the power-holders borrowing folk resources of trust to shore up their power, and no effective institutional means of fully protecting trust are adopted, while no mechanisms for trust are induced in the legal framework, to become actual norms and procedures or technical constituents. to change market-relevant laws from a rigid to a flexible structure, the mechanism of trust is clearly a very important lever and fulcrum.

18 See Yuelai Shaisanlang "Law and Fiction" (Tokyo: University of Tokyo Press, in 1999), pp. 23ff. 23.

19 Nikolas Luhmann "Returning the 12th camel: the meaning of analysis in legal sociology," in Gunther Teubner (ed.), *Luhmann: Paradoxes of Law and justice* (Kyoto: Minerva Press, 2006) pp. 2–74, sections 1–3.

20 The *locus classicus* is L.L. Fuller and William R. Perdue, Jr. "The Reliance Interest in Contract Damages," pts 1–2, *Yale Law Journal*, 46(1): 52–96, 1936, (3) 373–420, 1937. For an account of the main argument, see Tian Gui "Contract Regeneration" (Tokyo: Kobundo Press, in 1990) 119–29 page. For a more exhaustive examination see Kunihiko Yoshida "The interest theory of damage compensation in US law of contract – brief critique of 'law and society' research," *Law of the US*, 1992, pp. 245–81.

21 See P.S. Atiyah, *Essays on Contract* (Oxford: Clarendon Press, 1990), esp. pp. 73–92, 355–85. See the relevant account in Takashi Uchida, op. cit., pp. 130–42. Cf. also David Campbell and Donald Harris, "Flexibility in Long-term Contractual Relationships: The Role of Co-operation," *Journal of Law and Society*, 20(2), 166–91, 1993.

22 Cf. Jane Jacobs, *System of Survival; A Dialogue on the Moral Foundations of Commerce and Politics* (New York: Random House, Inc., 1992), Xiang Xitai (Japanese trans.), "Market Ethics, Governance Ethics" (Tokyo: Japanese Economical News service, in 2003).

23 For details, see John Rawls *Zuowei gongpingde zhengyi – zhengyi xin lun*, Shanghai: Shanghai Sanlian Book Store, 2002) sec. 4. Cf. also John Rawls, *A Theory of Justice* (rev. edn, Cambridge, Mass.: Harvard University Press, 1999) pp. xv–xvi.

24 Cf. Amartya Sen, *Inequality Reexamined* (Oxford: Oxford University Press, 1992).

25 See Keishi Saeki and Ryuyichiro Matsuhara, *Conceiving a "New Type Market Society" – Images of trusting and just eonomic society* (Tokyo: New World Society, in 2002).

26 Cf. Jay A. Sigler and Joseph E. Murphy (eds) *Corporate Lawbreaking and Interactive Compliance: Resolving the Regulation-deregulation Dichotomy* (New York: Quorum Books, 1991); Liu Lianyu "Company Governs with Company Society Responsibility" (Beijing: Chinese Politics and law University Press, 2001), Xiangyuan xinlang, "Company Law and Compliance – from "Law-abiding" to "Adaption to Social Demand" (Tokyo: Japanese Economy New Newspaper office, in 2006).

27 See US Sentencing Commission, *Federal Sentencing Guideline Manual: Sentencing of Organizations* (2004), Dove Izraeli and Mark S. Schwartz, "What Can We Learn From the U.S. Federal Sentencing Guidelines for Organizational Ethics?" http://www.itcilo.it/english/actrav/telearn/global/ilo/code/whatcan.htm, Lawrence M. Friedman, "In Defense of Corporate Criminal Liability," *Harvard Journal of*

Law and Public Policy Vol. 23: 833ff, 2000. The reference Tetsumaru Hatanaka "the American Type Strategic Gathers Gauge Management – Legal Risk Prevention And Crisis management Which Raids to Enterprise" (Tokyo: Great Article Hall, in 2001).

28 For details see Danei Shenzai, ed., "Compliance and Internal Reporting" (Tokyo: Japan Labor Research Association, 2004), Binbian Yangyilang "Internal Information Systems – Mechanism Forms and Problem Management" (Tokyo: *Dongyang jingji xinbao* Press, 2004).

29 On various legal issues of equitable competition and inequitable trade, technical innovation and technical monopoly in the context of conflicting international interests, see Shihei Yixian, *Law and Economy* (Tokyo: Yanbo Press, 1998), and the same author's *Law and Economy in the Electronic Society* (Tokyo: Yanbo Press, 2003).

30 Quoted fron Zhou Qiren, *Property And Institutional Change: Studies in China's Reform Experience* (Revised and enlarged ed.; Beijing: Beijing University Press, 2004) p. 262.

31 For details see Ji Weidong "The role of the Supreme People's Court and its evolution" Qinghua Faxue 2006 pp. 4–20. See also Ji Weidong, "Again on constitutional examination – topology of networks of power relations and the game of institutional change," *Kaifang shidai*, Issue 5: 6–23, 2003.

32 On China's unique concepts of judicial review and related institutional analyses, see also Luo Haocai and Wang Tiancheng "China's judicial review system," *Chinese and Foreign Legal Science*, 1991, Issue 6; Luo Haocai (ed.) "China's Judicial Examination System" (Beijing: Beijing University Press, 1993).

33 See He Weifang *Judicial Ideals and Institutions*, (Beijing: Chinese University of Politics and Law Press, 1998), Wang Liming, *Studies in Judicial Reform* (revised edn), (Beijing: Legal Press, 2001).

34 For details, see Ji Weidong, "Composite portrait of adjudication in China: judicial reform at the juncture of public opinion and workflow management" (Tokyo: Youpeige, 2004).

35 Based on relevant data from Guangdu Qingyu (ed.) *Comparative Legal Sociology of Legal Persons* (Tokyo: University of Tokyo publication meeting, in 2003) appendix material.

36 Ibid., see pp. 179–81.

37 Based on Ministry of Justice views on further reform of lawyers' work, *Zhongguo Lüshi*, Issue. 5: 4–9, 1992. More explicit policies on the marketisation legal of services appeared in *Fazhi ribao*, June 27, 1993.

38 "Professional Ethics of Lawyers (provisional)" (passed by the Chinese Bar association, March 20, 2004, pp. 122–32.

39 See Ji Weidong, "Social Justice Issues in China and lawyers' *pro bono* activities," Japanese Legal Aid Association (eds.), *Legal aid in Asia – lawyers' pro bono activities and applied legal education* (Tokyo: Modern Humanities Press, 2001) pp. 237–53.

40 This catchword is quite common. See, e.g. *Zhongguo Lüshi* [Chinese Lawyer] Issue 5: 3, 1993.

41 See Jiang Ping, Zhou Qiren, Bai Zhongen and Bai Nansheng, "Land dilemma to be solved," *Caijing*, No. 134 (2005); Li Jiange, Jiang Shengsan, and Liu Shouying "Deciphering Land," *Caijing*, Issue 153 (2006).

42 Two works best typifying the huge literature here are E. Pendleton Herring, *Group Representation Before Congress* (Ann Arbor, Mich.: University Microfilms International, 1929); and Robert A. Dahl, *Dilemmas of Pluralist Democracy* (New Haven: Yale University Press, 1982).

12 Political turnover and economic performance

The incentive role of personnel control in China

Hongbin Li and Li-An Zhou

Abstract

In this paper, we provide empirical evidence on the incentive role of personnel control in post-reform China. Employing the turnover data of top provincial leaders in China between 1979 and 1995, we find that the likelihood of promotion of provincial leaders increases with their economic performance, while the likelihood of termination decreases with their economic performance. This finding is robust to various sensitivity tests. We also find that the turnover of provincial leaders is more sensitive to their average performance over their tenure than to their annual performance. We interpret these empirical findings as evidence that China uses personnel control to induce desirable economic outcomes. Our study adds some basic evidence to a growing theoretical literature emphasizing the role of political incentives of government officials in promoting local economic growth.

12.1 Introduction

In the course of China's remarkable economic growth since the late 1970s, local government officials have been playing an active role in building local infrastructure, encouraging local businesses and attracting foreign investment. The strong pro-business role of Chinese local officials stands in stark contrast with the rent-seeking behavior (the "grabbing hand") of local officials in other transitional and developing countries (Krueger 1974; Frye and Shleifer 1997).

Two principal explanations have been put forward for why Chinese officials behave so differently. The first, based on what has come to be known as "market-preserving federalism," argues that the pro-business incentives given to Chinese local officials are a result of a policy of fiscal decentralization and high-powered intergovernmental fiscal revenue-sharing contracts (Oi 1992; Montinola et al. 1995; Qian and Weingast 1997; Weingast 1995; Mckinnon 1997).[1] Employing provincial-level data, Jin et al. (2000) find empirical evidence which supports the fiscal decentralization view.

However, a more recent explanation emphasizes the role of political incentives or career concerns on the part of local officials in China. According to this view, the readiness of the Chinese central government to reward and punish local officials on the basis of their economic performance motivates them to promote the local economy (Blanchard and Shleifer 2001). The reward and punishment mechanisms are made possible within the multidivisional-form (M-form) structure of the Chinese economic system, which allows yardstick competition among local officials (Qian and Xu 1993; Maskin et al. 2000). Although anecdotal evidence shows that Chinese cadres are evaluated in accordance with their economic performance (Whiting 2001), no systematic body of empirical evidence has been presented on the relationship between the career mobility of Chinese local officials and their economic performance.

In this paper, we provide empirical evidence on the relationship between the turnover of Chinese provincial leaders and their economic performance in the post-reform period. Using the ordered probit model, we find that the likelihood of promotion of provincial leaders increases with their economic performance while the likelihood of termination decreases with their economic performance. This finding is robust to various sensitivity tests. We also find that the turnover of provincial leaders is more sensitive to their average performance over their tenure than to their annual performance. We interpret these empirical findings as evidence that China uses personnel control to induce desirable economic outcomes.

Our paper draws extensively on the growing empirical literature on the political incentive of government officials both in the Chinese context and in general. Huang (1996) examines how the Chinese central government used centralized personnel control to solicit the local officials' compliance with the central macroeconomic control policy in their investments. He suggests that the central government may influence local investments by sending provincial officials with central connections or by adjusting the tenure duration of officials. Thus, in his study, China's personnel control is a device for implementing a macroeconomic stability policy. In contrast, our paper emphasizes the incentive role of centralized personnel control in motivating Chinese local officials to build up the local economy. In a study of the comparative advantage of M-form versus U-form, Maskin et al. (2000) find that the political status of a Chinese province (measured by the number of Central Committee members) is correlated with the provincial economic ranking. However, they do not establish the direct link between the career mobility of provincial leaders and their economic performance.[2] In a different political setting, Besley and Case (1996) show that the economic performance of a state relative to neighboring states has a positive impact on the re-election prospects of US governors.[3]

Our paper also relates closely to the empirical literature on the career concerns of firm managers. Both our methodology and findings are similar to those of studies on career concerns of managers in western corporations (Murphy and Zimmerman 1993; Weisbach 1988).[4] In fact, the evidence presented in this paper supports the characterization that the Chinese economy is run in such a way that provincial leaders act as middle managers of a large corporation and their internal career mobility, which is controlled by the headquarters, is closely tied to their economic performance.

Our paper also has bearing on a study by Groves et al. (1995). They show that in the 1980s, the Chinese industrial bureaus selected managers of state-owned enterprises (SOEs) on the basis of firm performance. Since Chinese SOE managers are semi-officialssituated in the bureaucratic hierarchy, this manager selection rule reflects a general shift in personnel control from the political criterion to the performance criterion since the late 1970s. While their evidence indicates that local governments were performance-conscious while selecting SOE managers, our finding about the incentive role of personnel control at the provincial level actually offers an explanation for why local governments acted this way.

The remainder of the paper is organized as follows. The following section briefly describes the institutional background pertaining to the personnel control system in China, especially during the reform period 1979–1995. Section 12.3 outlines the econometric specification. Section 12.4 describes the data. Section 12.5 presents empirical results and sensitivity tests. Section 12.6 concludes.

12.2 Internal career mobility and personnel control in China

China is a unitary state, and its political system is broadly composed of five layers of state administration: the center (*zhongyang*), province (*sheng*), prefecture (*diqu*), county (*xian*), and township (*xiang*).See Lieberthal (1995) for a comprehensive description of the Chinese political system. The Central Committee of the Chinese Communist Party (CCP) acts as the headquarter of this "multidivisional" system, which ultimately controls the mobility of government officials within the system. This highly centralized personnel control remains intact even to this day.

Provinces are the second level of China's political hierarchy. As of today, excluding Taiwan, Hong Kong, and Macau, China has 31 provincial units—four centrally administrated cities (Beijing, Shanghai, Tianjing, and Chongqing), 22 provinces and five autonomous regions.[5] A province ranks at the same level as a ministry in the central government. The top position at the provincial level is that of the provincial party secretary, followed immediately by the provincial governor. This reflects the dual presence of the communist party and government organs at each level of China's political hierarchy.[6]

China started its far-reaching economic reforms in 1978. These reforms have let provinces play a much more important role in economic management than ministries at the center which were traditionally in charge of planning and coordination, reflecting thestrategic importance of provincial leaders (Qian and Xu 1993; Huang 1996). Moreover, reforms have also empowered provincial leaders with the ultimate authority in allocating economic resources in their provinces. Their political and economic decisions greatly influence the economic performance of these provinces. For this reason, they are also held accountable for the corresponding results arising from their decisions. To a degree, provincial leaders are just like the middle-level managers in a multi-divisional corporation who are responsible for their divisional performance.

Accompanying economic reforms, China also started to reform its personnel control system at the same time. A crucial turnaround in personnel management was the wholesale change in the evaluation criteria for government officials. Political conformity, which was the only important pre-reform criterion for promotion, gave way to economic performance and other competence-related indicators. Although political loyalty remains important, three new elements were introduced into the evaluation process. Officials had to be of a young age, good education and expertise in administrative management. Above all, local economic performance became the most important criterion for higher-level officials assessing lower-level officials. One revealing indication of the importance of economic performance for local officials is their "obsession" with economic ranking among peers. Government reports or provincial yearbooks often contain detailed information on the relative rankings of the provincial performance, ranging from GDP growth, steel production, to miles of road constructed.

In 1980, for the first time in its history, the CCP officially proposed the abolition of the lifetime appointment of party and government officials and installed a mandatory retirement system. Under this new regime, provincial leaders are required to retire at the age of 65 if they are not promoted to higher positions in the central government. According to the new policy, many senior provincial leaders were urged to leave office to make way for younger people. The reform, which was implemented in 1982, led to two large waves of retirement in 1983 and 1985. However, like many other policies in China, the mandatory retirement age was not strictly enforced even until 1995, the last year of our sample period.

The economic and political reforms have made provincial leaders operate within a well-defined career structure inside the Chinese political hierarchy. The promotion opportunities that lie ahead for provincial secretaries include membership of the State Council, the vice-premiership, premiership and a membership of the Politburo or the Politburo Standing Committee. Provincial governors, at one level lower than party secretaries, can also move up to provincial party secretaryship or to equal-ranking positions in ministries or commissions at the center. Thus, a promotion in this paper means that a provincial leader moves up to one of these positions.

Apart from promotions, terminations, including retirement and demotions, can also serve as an incentive mechanism. Typically provincial leaders do not retire in the full sense immediately after leaving office unless there are exceptional circumstances, such as poor health. Before retiring officially, as a transition, they are often assigned to an honorary yet virtually powerless position, such as director of the provincial People's Congress or chairman of the provincial People's Political Consultative Conference. Some are given honorary positions on the National People's Congress or the National People's Consultative Conference. Whatever gloss may be laid on it, the loss of power is what marks the end of an official's political career. Therefore, in this paper, we define *retirement* as any departure from secretary-ship or governorship that is not followed by a lateral move or promotion. Although demotion is different from retirement, we have not been able to identify many demotions in the data. Publicly announced demotions were very rare, and a seemingly routine retirement may well disguise a dismissal. Because of the subtle difference between retirement and demotion, we group them together, and call both *terminations*.

It is worth noting that there is one peculiarity regarding the career profiles of provincial leaders. Unlike corporate managers or politicians in western societies, Chinese government officials have few options outside the internal political labor market. If a provincial leader is separated from the government hierarchy, there is virtually no avenue for her/him to find a job else-where.[7] In this sense, it may be appropriate to treat the Chinese political hierarchy as a single internal labor market without outside options. The lock-in effect, coupled with the huge difference in terms of personal benefits between staying in power and relinquishing power, greatly reinforces the incentive for Chinese officials to hold onto their power.[8]

To summarize, the following organizational features of the Chinese personnel control system are important for the purposes of this study. First, personnel control is centralized at the central government, and the economic performance of provincial leaders is a crucial indicator in personnel evaluations. Second, the M-form structure of the Chinese economic structure makes each provincial leader's performance individually distinguishable and comparable and thereby allows for a sensible link between performance and turnover. Third, government officials move up in the internal political labor market, and there is virtually no outside opportunity. Therefore, the concerns about the prospect of promotion and termination become a very important incentive mechanism to motivate provincial leaders to build up the provincial economy.

12.3 Econometric specification

Our aim in this paper is to examine the incentive role of personnel control in China by exploring the link between political turnover and economic performance. Given the fact that the crucial sources of career concerns for Chinese provincial leaders comefrom the prospect of promotion and termination, a natural approach is to examine directly how these turnover prospects relate to the economic performance they achieve while in the post.

We employ the ordered probit model to examine the probability of promotion and demotion for provincial leaders. Suppose that the central government gives each provincial leader an evaluation score, $y*$,[9] every year, and makes promotion and termination decisions based on this score. However, we do not observe such a score. We only observe the turnover of a provincial leader, or the variable y, which equals 0 for a termination, 1 for remaining at the same level (including staying in the same position and lateral moves), and 2 for a promotion. Assume that the latent evaluation score y^* is a linear function of our independent variables x, or $y^* = x\beta$, where β is a vector of coefficients. Define a_1 and a_2 as the two cutoff points of y^*, which the turnover decisions are based on. More specifically, a provincial leader is terminated ($y = 0$) if $y^* \leq a_1$, stays at the same level ($y = 1$) if $a_1 < y^* \leq a_2$, and is promoted ($y = 2$) if $y^* > a_2$. Following the notation in Wooldridge (2002), the Ordered probit model is expressed as

$$\Pr ob(y_i = 0 \mid x) = \Phi(a_1 - x\beta) \tag{1}$$

$$\Pr ob(y_i = 1 \mid x) = \Phi(a_2 - x\beta) - \Phi(a_1 - x\beta) \tag{2}$$

$$\Pr ob(y_i = 2 \mid x) = 1 - \Phi(a_2 - x\beta) \tag{3}$$

where Φ is the cumulative Normal distribution function.

Since we are more interested in the marginal effects of x on the probability of promotion and termination than the coefficients β themselves, we need to transfer the estimated β into the marginal effects. Define the probability of termination, remaining at the same level and promotion as p_0, p_1, and p_2. Following Wooldridge (2002) (p. 506), the marginal effects for the k-th variable are calculated according to the following formula.

$$\partial p_0 / \partial x_k = -\hat{\beta}_k \, \phi(\hat{a}_1 - x\hat{\beta}) \tag{4}$$

$$\partial p_1 / \partial x_k = \hat{\beta}_k \, [\phi(\hat{a}_1 - x\hat{\beta}) - \phi(\hat{a}_2 - x\hat{\beta})] \tag{5}$$

$$\partial p_2 / \partial x_k = \hat{\beta}_k \, \phi(\hat{a}_2 - x\hat{\beta}) \tag{6}$$

where ϕ is the Normal distribution function, and the variables with hats are estimated parameters from the model. In the empirical section, we report the coefficients for variables, but interpret results by calculating these marginal effects.

The key variable in x is the economic performance of a province. In this paper, we use the provincial GDP growth as the measure of provincial economic performance. As introduced in more detail in Section 12.5, we use both the annual growth rate and the weighted average growth rates during a leader's tenure as performance measures. Using these performance measures, our main hypothesis is as follows.

Hypothesis 1. *The probability of promotion (termination) for provincial leaders increases (decreases) with the provincial economic performance.*

Besides the GDP growth rate, the characteristics of leaders may affect the likelihood of promotion and termination. Leaders' personal attributes such as education, age and tenure of office are included in our estimations to control their effects on turnover.[10] Education, which is an indicator variable that equals one for leaders with college education and zero otherwise, measures a leader's human capital, and thus we expect it to have a positive (negative) effect on promotion (termination). Age has become a critical variable determining turnover, especially terminations after the age-based retirement rule was implemented in 1982. To capture the potential non-linear effect of age on the probability of turnover, and in particular the effect of the 65-years of age retirement rule, we add a dummy variable "age65" which equals one if the leader is 65 or older and zero otherwise. Tenure measures how many years a leader has been in the post. Since longer tenure without promotion may be a bad signal for the lack of ability, we expect tenure to have a negative (positive) effect on promotion (termination).

The leaders' connections with the central government could also affect the likelihood of turnover. A provincial leader's experience in the central government may allow her/him to maintain stronger connections with the center and better knowledge of the workings of central appointment procedures, which will result in better turnover prospects. The central experience can also help the leader cultivate informal connections with central leaders who can influence personnel evaluations.[11] Although central connection is so important, to the best of our knowledge, no empirical study has been undertaken that directly links this factor to the career mobility of provincial leaders. We will include central connection in our empirical analysis to examine the effect of political connections on career mobility. The central connection variable is an indictor that equals one for leaders having previous experience or holding joint-appointment in the central government, and equals zero otherwise.

Our regressions also take into consideration the effect of both provincial characteristics and cyclical policy shocks common to all provinces.[12] The development level of a province could affect the career prospects of its leaders. We use the lagged provincial per capita GDP to control for this potential effect. The provincial location could also matter in affecting a leader's likelihood of promotion. For example, starting from 1979, the central government introduced a variety of preferential economic policies that favor coastal provinces, such as Guangdong and Fujian. One may wonder whether the central government has a special preference towards those leaders in coastal areas. In order to control for the potential bias of turnover decisions in favor of certain areas, we include a set of provincial indicators in x.

Evidence shows that central policies regarding personnel management change over time. For example, our data show that there were two large waves of retirement in 1983 and 1985 after the central government implemented the mandatory retirement rules (see next section). There is also a cyclical pattern that many personnel changes occur around the time of the party congress and people's congress held every five years. To control for the effect of policy changes over time and political cycles, we include a set of year indicators in estimating the ordered probit model.[13]

To summarize, we have the following control variables in the ordered probit model that estimates the effect of economic performance on turnover: the leader's age, age 65, education, tenure, a central connection indicator, the lagged provincial per capita GDP, and a whole set of provincial and year indicators.

12.4 Data

The data used in this study cover 254 provincial leaders (provincial party secretaries and governors) who served in 28 Chinese provincial units from 1979 to 1995.[14] Information on these leaders is compiled from two books published in Chinese: *Who's Who in the Chinese Communist Party* (1997) and *The Documentation of Administration in the People's Republic of China* (1996). The dataset contains detailed personal information about these leaders, including their age, education and work experience prior to the current appointment, with special note taken of whether they have ever held a position in the central government. The data also track down the month and year in which they took and/or left office and the nature of the turnover – promotion, lateral moves, staying at the same position or retirement. Economic performance data come from the relevant issues of the China Statistical Yearbook.

Some leaders may hold multiple positions at different times, or even simultaneously. For example, 37 provincial governors were promoted to party secretaryship during the sample period. These party secretaries are treated as different persons from the time of their promotion, because the promotion has already reflected their past performance and any future evaluations need to be based on their performance in the new job. Ten party secretaries were jointly appointed as governors in the same province. In this case, we count them as party secretaries since this reflects their real political rank. In four instances, a party secretary or governor moved laterally to another province. Again, we treat them as different persons once the lateral moves have occurred. In total, we have 864 leader-year observations with complete information.

In order for us to see the disciplinary and incentive roles played by centralized personnel control, the turnover in this "internal labor market" needs to be sufficiently frequent. This is indeed the case.[15] More than 70 percent of leaders in our sample experienced turnover in the sample period. The average annual turnover rate is more than 20 percent, which is very close to that of U.S. top executives (generally around 20 percent) documented in Denis and Denis (1995) and Warner et al. (1988).[16]

To examine the trend of the turnover rate, we plot the frequencies of both promotions and terminations for each year in Figure 12.1. As seen from the figure, the termination rate is more volatile than the promotion rate. There were two large waves of retirement in 1983 and 1985 after the central government implemented the mandatory retirement rules. Many provincial

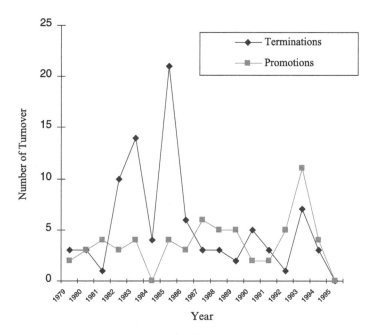

Figure 12.1 The time trend of provincial official turnover: 1979–1995.

secretaries and governors were urged to step down during that period. Compared to retirement, the incidence of promotion was relatively stable: around four incidences per year.

An important variable for the study of turnover is the age of provincial leaders. Table 12.1 shows that the average age of provincial leaders is about 60.4 years, varying from 43 to 75 years. To examine the correlation between turnover and age, we describe the distribution of turnover by age group for both the whole sample and the post-1985 subsample in Table 12.2. There are three categories of turnover: promotion, termination and remaining at the same level (including staying in the same position and lateral moves). Note first that even though there are a significant number of provincial leaders younger than 50, none of them were promoted or terminated below the age of 50. The majority of promotion cases took place for leaders between the ages of 50 and 64 for both the whole sample and the post-1985 subsample. Terminations are more evenly distributed, but peak between the ages of 65 and 67.

For the study of terminations, we need to make sure that at least some of the terminations are disciplinary terminations rather than normal retirements, in particular for the post-1985 sample. Comparing the whole sample with the post-1985 subsample (Table 12.2), we can see that forced retirement at the age of 65 indeed has a significant role. No provincial leaders were older than 68 for the post-1985 subsample. Moreover, for the post-1985 subsample,

Table 12.1 Summary statistics of variables

Variables	N	Mean	Standard deviation	Min.	Max.
Promotion	864	0.075	0.264	0	1
Termination	864	0.103	0.304	0	1
Age	864	60.37	5.82	43	75
Age 65	864	0.250	0.433	0	1
Education (college = 1, lower = 0)	864	0.618	0.486	0	1
Central connection	864	0.234	0.423	0	1
Tenure	864	3.032	2.115	1	12
Provincial annual GDP growth	864	0.104	0.060	−0.159	0.504
Average GDP growth	864	0.098	0.045	−0.159	0.296
Lagged provincial per capita GDP (one-year lag) (1000 yuan)	864	0.950	0.870	0.194	6.939

Note: The observation unit is provincial leader-year. Promotion is an indicator variable that equals one if a provincial leader (the provincial party secretary or governor) is promoted and zero otherwise. Termination includes both retirement and demotion for provincial leaders. It equals 1 if termination occurs and 0 otherwise. Average GDP growth rate is the GDP growth rate averaged over the tenure of a provincial leader. All GDP measures are calculated in 1980 constant prices. Age 65 equals 1 if a leader is 65 or older and 0 otherwise. Central connection is 1 if the leader has previous working experience or currently holds a joint appointment in the central government and 0 otherwise.

a significant number of terminations happened at exactly the age of 65 (25 percent of the termination cases). However, the forced retirement was still not strictly enforced. Even for the post-1985 subsample, for the group of leaders at age 65 or above, there are more cases of those remaining at the same level (24 cases) than terminations (21 cases). Two leaders were even promoted at the age of 66. Examining the termination cases only, a significant number of terminations (more than 40 percent of the total number) occurred beyond the retirement age of 65. The fact that some provincial leaders were terminated at the "normal" retirement age or even younger, but others stayed or were promoted at the same or older ages implies that variables other than age must have playeda disciplinary role in leader turnover. We will examine whether economic performance is such a disciplinary variable in the next section.

Table 12.1 also shows that in the period 1979–1995, China achieved a very rapid growth rate. The average annual growth rate was more than 10 percent.[17] However, the growth rate varies widely across provinces and over time with a standard deviation of six percent. The fastest growth rate (more than fifty percent) happened in Yunnan Province in 1994, while the slowest

Table 12.2 The frequency of political turnover by age

Age	Whole sample			Post-1985 subsample		
	Promotion	Termination	Same level	Promotion	Termination	Same level
40–49			35			23
50–59	28	5	296	24	3	229
60	8	1	44	7	1	40
61	4	2	47	4	2	37
62	3	4	52	3	2	35
63	7	6	49	3	3	24
64	5	4	48	2	2	23
65		12	42		8	15
66	5	13	28	2	7	7
67	2	13	21		3	2
68	1	9	13		3	
69		5	10			
70–75	2	15	25			
Total cases	65	89	710	45	32	458

Note: The observation unit is provincial leader-year.

(negative 16 percent) happened in Gansu Province, also in 1994. The large variation of the growth rate is important for us to identify how it is correlated with leader turnover.

Other independent variables are also described in Table 12.1. More than half (62 percent) of provincial leaders have a college degree, which shows that the central government indeed tried hard to promote well-educated cadres. About 23 percent of provincial leaders have connections with the center. The average tenure of office in the sample is 3.03 years, with some leaders staying as long as 12 years. Since the official term for a provincial leader is five, the average of 3.03 years indicates a considerable degree of turnover.

12.5 Turnover and economic performance: the evidence

In this section we present evidence on the impact of economic performance on the turnover of provincial leaders. We use both the annual GDP growth rate and the average GDP growth rate over a leader's tenure as performance measures. We also test how sensitive our main findings are when we use different weights in calculating the average growth rates. Finally, we conduct some sensitivity tests to make sure our findings are not mainly a result of the new retirement policy implemented in the mid-1980s.

12.5.1 Turnover and annual performance

Table 12.3 reports maximum likelihood estimation results of an ordered probit model using the entire sample that pools party secretaries and governors together. To allow for heterogeneity and serial correlation across observations, we estimate the ordered probit model with the robust standard errors option.

In the first column of Table 12.3, we report a regression with the annual GDP growth and provincial and year indicators as independent variables. Consistent with our hypothesis, the annual GDP growth rate has a positive impact on the probability of promotion and a negative impact on the probability of termination. The sign of the coefficient of annual growth rate is positive, and is significant at the five percent level. Moreover, the marginal effects of economic growth on turnover are reasonably large. The marginal effects of the annual growth rate when evaluated at the mean of the independent variables are 0.188 for promotion and −0.251 for termination.

Table 12.3 Ordered probit regressions estimating the effect of annual economic performance on the turnover of provincial leaders (whole sample)

	Dependent variable: turnover (0 = termination, 1 = same level, 2 = promotion)				
	(1)	*(2)*	*(3)*	*(4)*	*(5)*
Annual GDP growth rate	1.615** (2.05)	1.581* (1.87)	0.487 (0.52)	0.372 (0.52)	1.659** (2.03)
Age		−0.026* (−1.91)	−0.013 (−1.20)	−0.014 (−1.15)	−0.024* (−1.91)
Age 65		−0.974*** (−5.27)	−0.914*** (−5.28)	−0.975*** (−5.54)	−0.908*** (−4.85)
Education		0.154 (0.96)	0.068 (0.55)	0.155 (1.13)	0.063 (0.44)
Central connection		0.384*** (2.79)	0.337*** (2.72)	0.305** (2.24)	0.392*** (3.10)
Tenure		−0.053* (−1.74)	−0.076*** (−2.81)	−0.064** (−2.17)	−0.070** (−2.52)
Lagged per capita GDP (1000 yuan)		0.0001 (0.43)	0.0001** (2.06)	0.00001 (0.06)	0.0001** (2.25)
Provincial indicators	Yes	Yes	No	Yes	No
Year indicators	Yes	Yes	No	No	Yes
Number of observations	864	864	864	864	864
Log pseudo-likelihood	−468	−414	−448	−434	−429

Note: The numbers in parentheses are t-ratios based on robust standard errors. The significance levels of 1%, 5%, and 10% are noted by ***, **, and *.

These numbers mean that when the annual growth rate increases by one standard deviation (0.06) fromthe mean (0.10), the probability of promotion will increase by 0.011, or 15 percent of the average probability of promotion (0.075), and the probability of termination will decrease by 0.015, which is also 15 percent of the average probability of termination (0.103).

We next report a regression that includes age, age 65, tenure, education, central connection and the lagged provincial per capita GDP as control variables (Table 12.3, column 2). With these variables controlled, the annual GDP growth has about the same marginal effects on the probabilities of promotion and termination. The effects of both age and age65 are negative and significant at the one percent level. The marginal effect of age for promotion is slightly smaller in absolute value than that for termination (–0.003 versus 0.004). An increase of age by one year from the mean of 60 will decrease the probability of promotion by 0.3 percentage points, and will increase the probability of termination by 0.4 percentage points. The effect of age 65 on promotion is relatively large. Reaching the age of 65 will reduce the probability of promotion by 5.5 percentage points and will increase the probability of termination by 9.0 percentage points.

The regression also shows that the previous or current work experience in the central government increases (decreases) the probability of promotion (termination). The central connection indicator has a positive coefficient, and it is significant at the one percent level. Moreover, the magnitude of this effect is large. Having central connections increases the probability of promotion by 3.4 percentage points and decreases the probability of termination by 3.5 percentage points. This result seems to beconsistent with the argument that experience at the center helps cultivate informal connections with central leaders who can influence the personnel evaluation process. Another significant variable in column 2 is the tenure variable, the negative sign of which means that promotion (termination) is less likely for leaders with longer (shorter) tenure. One plausible interpretation for this result is that longer tenure without promotion may be a bad signal indicating lack of ability.

To test the importance of the provincial and year indicators, we report regressions without one or both sets of indicators in the last three columns of Table 12.3. Note that when we do not control the year indicators (columns 3 and 4), the coefficient of the annual GDP growth becomes very small and it is not significant in both cases. When we control the year indicators only (column 5), the coefficient of the annual growth rate becomes significant and its magnitude is similar to those in the first two columns. These tests indicate that the year effects, i.e. the effects of policy changes over time and political cycles, indeed affect our estimation of the effect of economic performance on turnover.

12.5.2 Turnover and average performance

The above analysis implicitly assumes that the central government makes decisions on the turnover of provincial leaders solely on the basis of annual economic performance. While this assumption is easy to justify empirically, it overlooks the fact that provincial leaders are appointed officially with a five-year term. While no detailed evidence is available on how the central government evaluates provincial leaders, casual observation suggests that evaluations may rely on the cumulative or multiple-yearperformance rather than simply on annual performance. The central government may prefer the average performance over several years because it is a less noisy measure than the simple annual performance, which puts too much weight on short-term shocks. Evaluations based on cumulative or average performance can average out short-term shocks.

Although the official term of a provincial leader is five years, in reality the term varies from one to twelve years (Table 12.1). In order to incorporate the effect of past performance so as to make it fit the personnel evaluation procedure discussed above, we create an average measure of the relative GDP growth rate over the tenure, T, $\tilde{g}_T$, which is defined as

$$\tilde{g}_T = \sum_{t=1}^{T} g_t$$

where T is the number of years on the post up to the point of calculation, t is the t-th year ($t = 1, 2, \ldots, T-1, T$) and g_t is the GDP growth in year t for a province. Thus, $\tilde{g}_T$ is the moving average of GDP growth from the start yearup to the current year in office, or the GDP growth rate averaged over the tenure. This measure corresponds to a personnel assessment mechanism in which there is an annual evaluation, but where the evaluation is based on both the past and current performance in the post.

Table 12.4 reports the results of regressions with the average growth rate as the performance measure. Overall, regressions using the average growth rate perform similarly to those using the annual one. Consistent with previous findings, the promotion (termination) probability of provincial leaders increases (decreases) with the average performance. Moreover, promotion and termination appear more sensitive to the average growth rate than to the annual growth rate, because both the estimated coefficients and the corresponding marginal effects of the average GDP growth rate are larger than those of annual measures reported in Table 12.3. The marginal effect of average growth on promotion is 0.408 and that on termination is −0.521 (estimated by regression 2), both of which more than double those of the annual growth. These numbers mean that when the average growth rate increases 0.06, the probability of promotion will increase by 33 percent of the average probability of promotion, and the probability

Table 12.4 Ordered probit regressions estimating the effect of average economic performance on the turnover of provincial leaders (whole sample)

	Dependent variable: turnover (0 = termination, 1 = same level, 2 = promotion)				
	(1)	*(2)*	*(3)*	*(4)*	*(5)*
Average GDP growth rate	4.727*** (4.34)	4.540*** (3.90)	1.805* (1.93)	2.132** (1.98)	3.860*** (3.67)
Age		−0.023* (−1.68)	−0.012 (−1.10)	−0.011 (−0.94)	−0.023* (−1.82)
Age 65		−0.976*** (−5.25)	−0.914*** (−5.27)	−0.976*** (−5.53)	−0.916*** (−4.86)
Education		0.187 (1.17)	0.078 (0.63)	0.182 (1.31)	0.088 (0.62)
Central connection		0.404*** (2.89)	0.343*** (2.75)	0.310** (2.26)	0.409*** (3.20)
Tenure		−0.055* (−1.78)	−0.076*** (−2.78)	−0.064** (−2.17)	−0.067** (−2.42)
Lagged per capita GDP (1000 yuan)		0.00001 (0.05)	0.0001* (1.96)	−0.00003 (−0.21)	0.0001** (2.13)
Provincial indicators	Yes	Yes	No	Yes	No
Year indicators	Yes	Yes	No	No	Yes
Number of observations	864	864	864	864	864
Log pseudo-likelihood	−462	−410	−447	−433	−425

Note: The numbers in parentheses are t-ratios based on robust standard errors. The significance levels of 1%, 5%, and 10% are noted by ***, **, and *.

of termination will decrease by 30 percent of the average probability of termination. This result is consistent with the argument that the average measure is less likely to be subject to short-term shocks than the annual measure, and thus weights more in turnover decisions made by the central government.

12.5.3 Sensitivity analysis

Although the average performance measure incorporates the effect of past performance, it assumes that each year during a leader's tenure has the same weight in the personnel evaluation. In reality, the weight on each year may not be the same. To test how sensitive the effect of economic performance on turnover is, we allow the weight to differ across years.[18] More specifically, we create a weighted measure of the GDP growth rate over the tenure T, gw_T, which is defined as

$$gw_T = \frac{\displaystyle\sum_{t=1}^{T} g_t\, r^{T-1}}{\displaystyle\sum_{t=1}^{T} r^{T-1}}$$

where r is the time-discount factor.

We allow r to take twenty different values, which start from 0 and have an increment of 0.1. For each value of r, we calculate the weighted growth rate, and use it to estimate (1)–(3). Note that both the annual growth and the average growth measuresused above are special cases of gw. The annual growth rate corresponds to the case $r = 0$, while the average growth rate corresponds to the case $r = 1$. When $r > 1$, the average performance measure has more weights in earlier years.

Regressions alternating all twenty performance measures generate the results that support Hypothesis 1. In Table 12.5, we report the marginal effects of the weighted growth rates that correspond to the twenty different discount factors on both promotion andtermination. The marginal effects on all the weighted growth rates are positive and significant. The magnitudes of the marginal effects rise with r for $r < 1.1$, reach the peak of 0.411 for promotion and −0.526 for termination at $r = 1.1$, and then start to decrease from $r > 1.2$. However, none of these marginal effects are statistically different from each other. Thus, even if the magnitude of the marginal effect of the weighted growth rate varies with the discount factor, this variation is not statistically significant. Since the average performance yields a larger marginal effect than the annual performance, we use it for the following sensitivity tests.

One possible problem with the above estimation is that many terminations in the sample were the result of forced retirement at the age of 65. Since normal retirements are not disciplinary and we are not able to differentiate disciplinary separations fromnormal retirement, our estimates of the disciplinary effect of economic performance on terminations may be biased. Results from summary statistics and regressions are mixed. On one hand, reaching the age of 65 indeed has a significant impact on turnover. On the other hand, the retirement rule was far from strictly enforced in the sample period, which means that certain variables other than age must have played a role in terminations.

We employ two methods to more rigorously examine whether the forced retirement at 65 could cause a bias.[19] First, we estimate the ordered probit model using a sample of leaders younger than 65. Since these leaders have not reached the retirement age, their promotions and terminations are most likely disciplinary. Second, we use the pre-1983 subsample to do the same estimations. Since the age-based retirement was not introduced until 1983, turnover in the pre-1983 subsample are more likely to be disciplinary.

Table 12.5 Ordered probit model estimates of the marginal effects of weighted average economic performance on the turnover of provincial leaders (whole sample)

The marginal effect on the weighted performance measure (gw_T)

$$gw_T = \frac{\sum_{t=1}^{T} g_t r^{T-t}}{\sum_{t=1}^{T} r^{T-t}}$$

The discounted factor r has 20 values as in the table; g_t is the annual GDP growth rate in year t

Promotion

Discount factor:r	0	0.1	0.2	0.3	0.4
The marginal effect on promotion	0.147* (1.83)	0.179*** (2.07)	0.212** (2.31)	0.247** (2.54)	0.281*** (2.75)
Discount factor: r	0.5	0.6	0.7	0.8	0.9
The marginal effect on promotion	0.313*** (2.95)	0.343*** (3.12)	0.367*** (3.25)	0.387*** (3.36)	0.400*** (3.43)
Discount factor: r	1.0	1.1	1.2	1.3	1.4
The marginal effect on promotion	0.408*** (3.47)	0.411*** (3.49)	0.411*** (3.48)	0.409*** (3.46)	0.405*** (3.43)
Discount factor: r	1.5	1.6	1.7	1.8	1.9
The marginal effect on promotion	0.401*** (3.40)	0.396*** (3.36)	0.391*** (3.33)	0.386*** (3.29)	0.381*** (3.26)

Termination

Discount factor: r	0	0.1	0.2	0.3	0.4
The marginal effect on termination	−0.186* (−1.86)	−0.227** (−2.12)	−0.269** (−2.39)	−0.313*** (−2.65)	−0.357*** (−2.90)
Discount factor: r	0.5	0.6	0.7	0.8	0.9
The marginal effect on termination	−0.399*** (−3.14)	−0.437*** (−3.35)	−0.469*** (−3.52)	−0.494*** (−3.66)	−0.511*** (−3.75)
Discount factor: r	1.0	1.1	1.2	1.3	1.4
The marginal effect on termination	−0.521*** (−3.81)	−0.526*** (−3.83)	−0.526*** (−3.82)	−0.523*** (−3.80)	−0.518*** (−3.77)
Discount factor: r	1.5	1.6	1.7	1.8	1.9
The marginal effect on termination	−0.513*** (−3.73)	−0.507*** (−3.69)	−0.500*** (−3.64)	−0.494*** (−3.60)	−0.488*** (−3.56)

Note: The numbers in parenthesis are t-ratios based on robust standard errors. The significance levels of 1%, 5%, and 10% are noted by ***, **, and *. The regressions we use to generate these marginal effects have the following independent variables: the average GDP growth measure corresponding to each value of r, age, age 65, tenure education, central connection, the lagged per capita GDP, and provincial and year indicators.

Regression results of both methods are reported in Table 12.6. Even though we have two much smaller samples than before (648 observations for the first subsample, and only 191 observations for the second subsample), regression results continue to support the hypothesis that the probability of promotion (termination) increases (decreases) with a provincial leader's economic performance. The average growth rate has a positive coefficient, and it is significant at at least the five percent level. The magnitudes of these coefficients and the marginal effects are even larger than those using the full sample.

In summary, regression results in Tables 12.3–12.6 show that the Chinese central government tends to promote provincial leaders who perform well economically and terminate provincial leaders who perform poorly. Regressions show that the average performance over years has a larger marginal effect on turnover than the annual performance, although the difference between the two is not statistically significant. Overall, the main finding that

Table 12.6 Ordered probit regressions estimating the effect of average economic performance on the turnover of provincial leaders (two subsamples)

	Dependent variable: turnover (0 = termination, 1 = same level, 2 = promotion)			
	Subsample for age<65		Pre-1983 subsample	
	(1)	*(2)*	*(3)*	*(4)*
Average GDP growth rate	4.891***	5.339***	5.323**	5.090**
	(3.43)	(3.53)	(2.37)	(1.98)
Age		−0.005		−0.077**
		(−0.30)		(−2.10)
Age65				−0.437
				(−1.49)
Education		0.479**		−0.639**
		(2.16)		(−2.10)
Central connection		0.310		0.293
		(1.64)		(0.77)
Tenure		−0.040		−0.020
		(−0.98)		(−0.12)
Lagged per capita GDP (1000 yuan)		−0.0003		0.001
		(−0.99)		(0.31)
Provincial indicators	Yes	Yes	Yes	Yes
Year indicators	Yes	Yes	Yes	Yes
Number of observations	648	648	191	191
Log pseudo-likelihood	−241	−234	−97	−90

Note: The numbers in parentheses are t-ratios based on robust standard errors. The significance levels of 1%, 5%, and 10% are noted by ***, **, and *.

economic performance matters for provincial leaders' career prospects is robust to various sensitivity tests.

Our findings lend support to the notion that the Chinese central government, which holds complete power in relation to personnel control, acts in a way which is very similar to the way in which the board of directors of a western corporation monitors and disciplines its managers.[20] The functioning of China's personnel control system is remarkable in that it is made possible through centralized political control by the Communist Party in an M-form economic structure.

12.6 Conclusion

In this paper, we have examined the relationship between the turnover of provincial leaders and their economic performance. We find that the likelihood of promotion (termination) of provincial leaders increases (decreases) with their economic performance. This finding supports the view that the Chinese central government uses personnel control to motivate local officials to promote local economic growth. We also find that the turnover of provincial leaders is more sensitive to their tenure-averaged performance than to their annual performance. These results support the hypothesis that the Chinese economy is run in such a way that provincial leaders act as middle managers of a large corporation and their internal career mobility is closely tied to their economic performance (Blanchard and Shleifer 2001).

China started its transition from a planned economy to a market economy with some bold reforms in the government system. In particular, it decentralized the fiscal system in 1980 so that the central and local governments shared fiscal revenues according to certain sharing contracts. The fiscal decentralization has motivated local officials to lend a "helping hand" in pushing forward local economic growth (Jin et al. 2000). Another equally important reform, the reform of the personnel management system, was carried out at almost the same time, but its significance has long been overlooked in the literature. In this sense, our findings should help to draw some attention to the role of China's internal political market which not only provides incentivesto local officials to promote economic growth, but also integrates the decentralized central-local fiscal mechanism in China.

Notes

1 Some studies relate the positive incentives given to local officials to a number of other economic factors, such as the emergence of local government ownership as a credible institutional device to avoid state predation (Che and Qian 1998) and inter-regional competition in the product and capital markets (Li et al. 2000; Qian and Roland 1998).
2 Also, their simple regression may be subject to the omitted variables bias.
3 In a related research, Besley and Case (1995) examine how re-election probabilities of US gubernatorial officials affect their choices of economic policy.

4 Also see a comprehensive survey by Murphy (1999).

5 We will call all provincial-level units provinces in the rest of the paper.

6 Because the governance structures at all levels are similar, the basic observations we obtain from provincial-level data may also apply to lower levels. Casual observations seem to support this conception (Whiting 2001).

7 This statement is valid for the sample period we study in this paper. Things have begun to change since the mid-1990s as China's private sector, relatively free from the Party's control, has grown into a large employer in the labor market.

8 Terminated provincial leaders may hold leading positions in the People's Congress or People's Consultative Conference, and they can retain certain privileges, such as having secretaries and cars. But since these positions carry no direct executive power, terminated officials have lost the major source of benefits associated with such power.

9 To simplify notation, we ignore the subscript i for a leader and t for a year.

10 Given the fact that there is a time lag between the steps taken by provincial leaders and the results of their efforts in the form of economic growth, we match provincial GDP growth with leaders in the following way: the current year's provincial GDP growth rate applies to a leader if he/she is promoted/terminated after July of this year, otherwise the previous year's GDP growth rate applies as the performance measure.

11 Local officials' connections with the central government have attracted a lot of attention in the literature of the Chinese political economy (Huang 1996; Jin et al. 2000). It is believed that provincial leaders with prior or current central experience tend to havemore attachment to the center and thereby are more compliant with central policies. Alternatively, the central experience may also indicate a lack of local knowledge, which may have a negative effect on economic performance.

12 We are very thankful to an anonymous referee for making this suggestion.

13 To control for both cyclical and provincial effects provides us a difference-in-difference estimate of the effects of performance on the likelihood of turnover. It also helps address the concerns about the effects of performance relative to national or provincial benchmarks on the probability of turnover.

14 Two provincial units, Tibet and Hainan, are excluded from the sample because Tibet assumes a very special policy status while Hainan is a spin-off from Guangdong province, only becoming a separate province in 1988. In any event, including Tibet and Hainan in the sample does not change the qualitative results.

15 Another necessary condition is that the central government has the ultimate authority to appoint or remove provincial leaders. The authority of the center is beyond any doubt, since the political system in China is highly centralized.

16 Following Denis and Denis (1995), this rate is defined as the total turnover number divided by the total number of province-years in the sample. Since each province has two top leaders, we double the total number of province-years to calculate the overall annual turnover rate.

17 The annual provincial GDP is calculated at 1980 prices.

18 We thank Roger Gordon for making this suggestion.

19 We thank an anonymous referee for suggesting both methods.

20 See Murphy and Zimmerman (1993) and Weisbach (1988) on studies of the relationship between CEO turnover and firm performance.

References

Besley, T. and A. Case. 1995. "Does Electoral Accountability Affect Economic Policy Choices? Evidence from Gubernatorial Term Limits," *Quarterly Journal of Economics*, 110: 769–98.

Besley, T. and A. Case. 1996. "Incumbent Behavior: Vote-Seeking, Tax-Setting and Yardstick Competition," *American Economic Review*, 85: 25–45.

Blanchard, O. and A. Shleifer. 2001. "Federalism with and without Political Centralization: China versus Russia. in Transitional Economics: How Much Progress?" *IMF Staff Papers*.

Che, J. and Y. Qian. 1998. "Insecure Property Rights and Government Ownership of Firms," *Quarterly Journal of Economics*, 113: 467–96.

Denis, D. and D. Denis. 1995. "Performance Changes Following Top Management Dismissals," *Journal of Finance*, 50: 1029–57.

Frye, T. and A. Shleifer. 1997. "The Invisible Hand and the Grabbing Hand," *American Economic Review*, 87(2): 354–8.

Groves, T., Y. Hong, J. McMillan, and B. Naughton. 1995. "China's Evolving Managerial Labor Market," *Journal of Political Economy*, 103: 873–92.

Huang, Y. 1996. *Inflation and Investment Controls in China*. Cambridge: Cambridge University Press.

Jin, H., Y. Qian, and B. Weingast. 2000. *Regional Decentralization and Fiscal Incentives: Federalism, Chinese style*. Mimeo. Stanford University.

Krueger, A. O. 1974. "The Political Economy of Rent-Seeking Society," *American Economic Review*, 64: 291–303.

Li, S., Li, S., and W. Zhang. 2000. "The Road to Capitalism: Competition and Institutional Change in China," *Journal of Comparative Economics*, 28: 269–92.

Lieberthal, Kenneth. 1995. *Governing China: From Revolution Through Reform*. New York and London: W. W. Norton & Company, Inc.

Maskin, E., Y. Qian, and C. Xu. 2000. "Incentives, Scale Economies, and Organization Forms," *Review of Economic Studies*, 67: 359–78.

McKinnon, R. 1997. "Market Preserving Fiscal Federalism in the American Monetary Union," in M. Blejar and T. Ter–Minassian, eds, *Macroeconomic Dimensions of Public Finance: Essays in Honor of Vito Tanzi*. London: Routeledge, pp. 73–93.

Montinola, G., Y. Qian, and B. Weingast. 1995. "Federalism, Chinese Style: The Political Basis for Economic Success in China," *World Politics* 48: 50–81.

Murphy, K. 1999. "Executive Compensation," in *Handbook of Labor Economics*, vol. 3, O. Ashenfelter and D. Card, eds, Amsterdam: North-Holland Company.

Murphy, K. and J. Zimmerman. 1993. "Financial Performance Surrounding CEO Turnover," *Journal of Accounting and Economics*, 16: 273–315.

Oi, J. 1992. "Fiscal Reform and the Economic Foundations of Local State Corporatism in China," *World Politics*, 45: 99–126.

Qian, Y., and G. Roland. 1998. "Federalism and the Soft Budget Constraint," *American Economic Review*, 88: 1143–62.

Qian, Y. and B. Weingast. 1997. "Federalism as a Commitment to Preserving Market Incentives," *Journal of Economic Perspectives*, 11: 83–92.

Qian, Y. and C. Xu. 1993. "Why China's Economic Reforms Differ: The N-form Hierarchy and Entry/Expansion of the Non-State Sector," *Economics of Transition* 1: 135–70.

Warner, J., R. Watts, and K. Wruck. 1988. "Stock Prices and Top Management Changes," *Journal of Financial Economics*, 20: 461–92.

Weingast, B. 1995. "The Economic Role of Political Institutions: Market-Preserving Federalism and Economic Development," *Journal of Law, Economics and Organization*, 11: 1–31.

Weisbach, M. 1988. "Outside Directors and CEO Turnover," *Journal of Financial Economics*, 20(1–2): 431–60.

Whiting, S. 2001. *Power and Wealth in Rural China: The Political Economy of Institutional Change.* Cambridge: Cambridge University Press.

Wooldridge, J. 2002. *Econometric Analysis of Cross Section and Panel Data.* Cambridge: The MIT Press.

13 The lessons of China's transition to a market economy

Justin Yifu Lin, Fang Cai, and Zhou Li

Abstract

China's transition from a planned economy to a market economy began at the end of 1978. The approach to reform can be characterized as piecemeal, partial, incremental, and often experimental. China's average annual rate of GDP growth has been miraculous since the beginning of the transition and is the most successful of the transition economies. It is argued that the system of central economic planning and its related problems in the transition economies have the same root – namely, the attempt to pursue a capital-intensive heavy-industry-oriented development strategy when the economy is constrained by capital scarcity. Therefore, China's approach to reform provides useful lessons for other transition economies. It is shown that the boom-and-bust cycle in the Chinese economy is the result of institutional incompatibility arising from the piecemeal and partial approach to reform.

China's transition from a planned economy to a market economy began at the end of 1978. When China started the process, the government did not have a well-designed blueprint. The approach to reform can be characterized as piecemeal, partial, incremental, and often experimental. Some economists regard this approach as self-defeating (Murphy, Schleifer, and Vishny 1992). China's average annual rate of GDP growth has been miraculous since the beginning of the transition (Lin et al. 1996) and is the most successful of the transition economies. Nevertheless, the Chinese economy has been troubled by an increasingly serious "boom and bust" cycle (see Figure 13.1).

Whether China's experience provides useful lessons for other transition economies is hotly debated. Some economists argue that China's success demonstrates the superiority of an evolutionary, experimental, and bottom-up approach over the comprehensive and top-down "shock therapy" approach that characterizes the transition in Eastern Europe and the former Soviet Union (Jefferson and Rawski 1995; McKinnon 1994; McMillan and Naughton 1992; Singh 1991; Chen et al. 1992; Harrold 1992; Perkins 1992). Other economists argue that it is neither gradualism nor experimentation but rather China's unique initial conditions-namely, a large agricultural labor

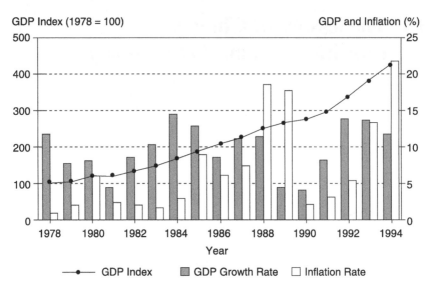

GDP Index (1978 = 100)

GDP and Inflation (%)

Figure 13.1 Economic growth and inflation in China.

Source: State Statistical Bureau (1995: 4, 8, 45).

force, low subsidies to the population, and a rather decentralized economic system that have contributed to China's success (Woo 1993; Sachs and Woo 1993; Qian and Xu 1993). According to these economists, China's experience has no general implications because China's initial conditions are unique.

In this paper, we offer a new perspective on the debate. Whether or not China's experience provides useful lessons depends on whether the nature and cause of the problems that China and other transition economies attempt to solve are similar. We argue that the system of central economic planning and its related problems in the transition economies have the same root-namely, the attempt to pursue a capital-intensive heavy-industry-oriented development strategy when the economy is constrained by capital scarcity. Therefore, China's approach to reform provides useful lessons for other transition economies. Moreover, we show that the "boom and bust" cycle in the Chinese economy is the result of institutional incompatibility arising from the piecemeal and partial approach to reform. To obtain a sustained, smooth growth, it is imperative for China to complete the transition from the planned economy to a market economy. China must shift from a traditional anti-comparative-advantage, heavy industry-oriented development strategy to a strategy that relies on the economy's comparative advantages.

The paper is organized as follows: first, we discuss China's economic development strategy before the reforms and present a simple economic model to analyze the problems associated with that strategy. Second, we provide an analytical review of China's reforms. Third, we compare China's approach to reform with the "big bang" approach. In the final section, we present some concluding remarks.

13.1 The major prereform problems in the Chinese economy

The traditional planned economic system in China was shaped by the adoption of a heavy-industry-oriented development strategy (HIODS) in the early 1950s. The system had three integrated components: (1) a distorted macropolicy environment that featured artificially low interest rates, overvalued exchange rates, low nominal wage rates, and low prices for living necessities and raw materials; (2) a planned allocation mechanism for credit, foreign exchange, and other materials; and (3) a traditional micromanagement institution of state enterprises and collective agriculture. These three components were endogenous to the choice of a capital-intensive HIODS in a capital-scarce agrarian economy, although the specific institutional arrangements adopted in China were also shaped by socialist ideology, the Chinese Communist Party's experience during the revolution, and the Chinese government's political capacity of pursuing its intended goals.[1] The relation between the development strategy and the economic system is summarized in Figure 13.2.

At the founding of the People's Republic in 1949, the Chinese government inherited a war-torn agrarian economy in which 89.4 percent of the population resided in rural areas and industry consisted of only 12.6 percent of the national income. At that time, a developed heavy-industry sector was the symbol of the nation's power and economic achievement. Like government leaders in India and in many other newly independent developing countries, Chinese leaders had the motivation of accelerating the development of heavy industries. After China's involvement in the Korean War in 1950, with its resulting embargo and isolation from western nations, catching up to the industrialized powers also became a necessity for national security. In addition, the Soviet Union's outstanding record of nation building in the 1930s,

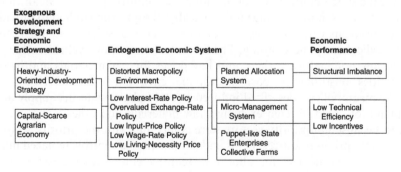

Figure 13.2 Formation of the traditional economic system in China.

in contrast to that of the Great Depression in Western market economies, provided the Chinese leadership with both inspiration and experience for adopting a HIODS. Therefore, after recovering from wartime destruction in 1952, the Chinese government set heavy industry as the priority sector of economic development. The goal was to build, as rapidly as possible, the country's capacity to produce capital goods and military materials. This development strategy was implemented through a series of Five-Year Plans.[2]

Heavy industry is a capital-intensive sector. The construction of a heavy-industry project has three characteristics: (1) it requires long gestation;[3] (2) most equipment for a project, at least in the initial stage, needs to be imported from more advanced economies; and (3) each project requires a large lump-sum investment. When the Chinese government initiated that strategy in the early 1950s, the Chinese economy had three characteristics: (1) capital was limited and the market interest rate was high;[4] (2) foreign exchange was scarce and expensive because exportable goods were limited and primarily consisted of low-priced agricultural products; and (3) the economic surplus was small and scattered due to the nature of a poor agrarian economy. Because these characteristics of the Chinese economy were mismatched with the three characteristics of heavy industry projects, spontaneous development of capital-intensive industry in the economy was impossible.[5] Therefore, a set of distorted macropolicies was required for the development of heavy industry.

At the beginning of the First Five-Year Plan, the government instituted a policy of low interest rates and overvalued exchange rates to reduce the costs both of interest payments and of importing equipment.[6] Meanwhile, to secure enough funds for industrial expansion, a policy of low input prices-including nominal wage rates for workers[7] and prices for raw materials, energy, and transportation-evolved alongside the adoption of this development strategy. The assumption was that the low prices would enable the enterprises to create profits large enough to repay the loans or to accumulate enough funds for reinvestment. If the enterprises were privately owned, the state could not be sure that the private entrepreneurs would reinvest the policy created profits on the intended projects.[8] Therefore, private enterprises were soon nationalized[9] and new key enterprises were owned by the state to secure the state's control over profits for heavy-industry projects. Meanwhile, to make the low nominal-wage policy feasible, the government had to provide urban residents with inexpensive food and other necessities, including housing, medical care, and clothing. The low interest rates, overvalued exchange rates, low nominal wage rates, and low prices for raw materials and living necessities constituted the basic macropolicy environment of the HIODS.[10]

The macropolicies described induced a total imbalance in the supply and demand for credit, foreign exchange, raw materials, and other living necessities. Because nonpriority sectors were competing with the priority sectors for the low-priced resources, plans and administrative controls replaced markets as the mechanism for allocating scarce credit, foreign reserves, raw materials, and living necessities, ensuring that limited resources would be used for the targeted projects. Moreover, the state monopolized banks, foreign trade, and material distribution systems.[11]

In that way competition was suppressed and profits ceased to be the measure of an enterprise's efficiency.[12] Because of the lack of market discipline, managerial discretion was potentially a serious problem. Managers of state enterprises were deprived of autonomy to mitigate this problem.[13] The production of state enterprises was dictated by mandatory plans and furnished with most of their material inputs through an administrative allocation system. The prices of their products were determined by pricing authorities. Government agencies controlled the circulation of their products. The wages and salaries of workers and managers were determined not by their performance but by their education, age, position, and other criteria according to a national wage scale. Investment and working capital were financed mostly by appropriations from the state budget or loans from the banking system according to state plans. The state enterprises remitted all their profits, if any, to the state and the state budget also would cover all losses incurred by the enterprises. In short, the state enterprises were like puppets. They had no autonomy in the employment of workers, the use of profits, the plan of production, the supplies of inputs, or the marketing of their products.

The development strategy and the resulting policy environment and allocation system also shaped the evolution of farming institutions in China. To secure cheap supplies of grain and other agricultural products for urban low-price rationing, a compulsory procurement policy was imposed in the rural areas in 1953. This policy obliged peasants to sell fixed quantities of their produce, including grain, cotton, and edible oils, to the state at government-determined prices (Perkins 1966, Chapter 4).

In addition to providing cheap food for industrialization, agriculture was also the main foreign-exchange earner. In the 1950s, agricultural products accounted for over 40 percent of all exports. If processed agricultural products are included, agriculture contributed more than 60 percent of China's foreign-exchange earnings until the 1970s. Because foreign exchange was as important as capital for the heavy industry-oriented strategy, the country's capacity to import capital goods for industrialization in the early stage of development clearly depended on agriculture's performance.

Agricultural development required resources and investment as much as industrial development. The government, however, was reluctant to divert scarce resources and funds from industry to agriculture. Therefore, alongside the HIODS, the government adopted a new agricultural development strategy that did not compete for resources with industrial expansion. The core of this strategy involved the mass mobilization of rural labor to work on labor-intensive investment projects, such as irrigation, flood control, and land reclamation, and to raise unit yields in agriculture through traditional methods and inputs, such as closer planting, more careful weeding, and the use of more organic fertilizers. The government believed that collectivization of agriculture would ensure these functions.

The government also viewed collectivization as a convenient vehicle for effecting the state's low-priced procurement program of grain and other agricultural products (Luo 1985). Income distribution in the collectives was based on each collective member's contribution to agricultural production. However, monitoring a member's effort is extremely difficult in agricultural production due to dimensions of time and space. The remuneration system in the collectives was basically egalitarian (Lin 1988).

The distorted macropolicy environment, planned allocation system, and micro-management institutions all made the maximum mobilization of resources for the development of heavy industry possible in a capital-scarce economy. Since most private initiative in economic activities was prohibited, the pattern of the government's investment was the best indicator of the bias in the official development strategy. Table 13.1 shows the sector shares in state capital construction investment from the First Five-Year Plan (1953–7) to the Sixth Five-Year Plan (1981–5). Despite the fact that more than three-quarters of China's population was agricultural, agriculture received less than 10 percent of state investment in the period 1953–85, while 45 percent of investment went into heavy industry. Moreover, heavy industry received a lion's share of the investments that fell under the heading "other," including workers' housing and infrastructure. As a result, the value of heavy industry in the combined total value of agriculture and industry grew from 15 percent in 1952 to about 40 percent in the 1970s (see Table 13.2).[14]

Judging from China's sector composition, the trinity of the traditional economic system-a distorted macropolicy environment, a planned allocation mechanism, and a puppet-like micro-management institution-reached its intended goal of accelerating the development of heavy industry in China. However, China paid a high price for such an achievement. The economy is very inefficient because of (1) low allocative efficiency, due to the deviation of the industrial structure from the pattern dictated by the comparative advantages of the economy, and (2) low technical efficiency, resulting from managers' and workers' low incentives to work.

Table 13.1 Sector shares of state capital construction investment

Five-Year Plan	Agriculture (%)	Light Industry (%)	Heavy Industry (%)	Other (%)
First	7.1	6.4	36.2	50.3
Second	11.3	6.4	54.0	28.3
1963–65	17.6	3.9	45.9	32.6
Third	10.7	4.4	51.1	33.8
Fourth	9.8	5.8	49.6	34.8
Fifth	10.5	6.7	45.9	36.9
Sixth	5.1	6.9	38.5	49.5
1953–85	8.9	6.2	45.0	39.9

Source: State Statistical Bureau (1987b: 97).

Table 13.2 Sector composition (current prices)

Year	Agriculture %	Light Industry %	Heavy Industry %
1952	56.9	27.8	15.3
1957	43.3	31.2	25.5
1962	38.8	28.9	32.3
1965	37.3	32.3	30.4
1970	33.7	30.6	35.7
1975	30.1	30.8	39.1
1980	30.8	32.6	36.6
1985	34.3	30.7	35.0

Source: State Statistical Bureau (1989: 11).

1   Low allocative efficiency. In the current stage of China's economic development, capital is relatively scarce and labor is relatively abundant. If
prices were determined by market competition, capital would be relatively expensive and labor relatively inexpensive. Therefore, the comparative advantages of the Chinese economy lie in labor intensive sectors. If
investments had been guided by market forces, profit incentives would
have induced entrepreneurs to adopt capital saving and labor-using technologies and to allocate more resources to labor-intensive industries. The
effects of the HIODS on the industrial structure can be illustrated by
Figure 13.3. Let us assume there are only two sectors in the economy,
namely, labor-intensive light industry and capital-intensive heavy industry. Given the endowments, OCD is the production possibility frontier.
EP represents the market-determined relative prices line, which existed
before the imposition of the HIODS. Under the undistorted relative
prices, the economy will produce OY_1 of light-industry products and
OX_0 of heavy-industry products. However, for the development of heavy
industry, the state monopolized the allocation system and used administrative measures to direct the allocation of resources. If we suppose the
target of the development strategy is to expand heavy industry from OX_0
to OX_1, then the state would need to reduce the production of light
industry from OY_0 to OY_1 to shift resources from light industry to heavy
industry. The production possibility frontier is truncated to Y_1AD. If
there is no technical inefficiency, the production mix of the economy
would locate on A, corresponding to a quantity of OY_1 light-industry
products and OX_1 heavy-industry products.[15]

As we can see from Figure 13.3, the static consequence of the strategy
is that the economy, based on the prices before distortion, suffers a loss
of "ea" in absolute magnitude or "ea/eO" in relative measure.[16] The
income loss due to allocative inefficiency implies the reduction of surplus
available for investment. If we assume that a fixed portion of the national
income is used for investment, the decline in investment would further

diminish gross investment. However, if we assume that the government's plan is to develop light and heavy industry in a fixed ratio of OX_1/OY_1 then each production cycle would repeatedly generate an income loss of "ea/eO" in relative measure. All these factors significantly dampen the growth of the whole economy. To maintain the growth rate, it is necessary to raise the accumulation rate, resulting in insufficient consumption and long-lasting low living standards for people.[17]

2   Low technical efficiency. Because profits ceased to be a measure of efficiency and the planned allocation system often failed to distribute materials in time, managers were forced to keep large reserves and had no incentive for using resources economically. Overstaffing, underutilization of capital resources, and overstocking of inventories characterized China's puppet-like state enterprises.[18] Moreover, managers had no authority over workers' wage rates and bonuses. Wages were not related to effort in the enterprise nor to the enterprise's profits; hence, workers had little incentive to work efficiently. Similarly, in the agricultural collectives, farm workers had a low incentive to work because the link between reward and effort was weak.[19] Losses resulting from these technical inefficiencies mean that production will end up at some point inside the production possibility frontier, such as point B in Figure 13.3.

Because of low allocative and technical efficiency, the Chinese economy experienced an extremely low rate of total factor productivity growth. Even with the most favorable assumptions, the World Bank (1985a) found that total factor productivity grew by only 0.5 percent between 1952–81, a quarter of the average growth rate of 19 developing countries included in the study. Moreover, the total factor productivity of China's state enterprises stagnated or fell between 1957–82 (World Bank 1985b).

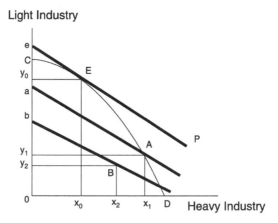

Figure 13.3 Development strategy and the truncated production frontier.

13.2 An analytical review of China's economic transition

It is unlikely that China's leaders had worked out a blueprint when they set out to reform the economic system (Perkins 1988, 601). However, retrospectively, China's transition followed a logical process that is predictable from the theoretical model described. The trinity of the traditional economic system is endogenous to the adoption of a HIODS in a capital-scarce economy. The main fault in the economic system was low economic efficiency arising from structural imbalance and incentive problems. Before the late 1970s, the government had made several attempts to address the structural problems by decentralizing the allocative mechanism.[20] However, the administrative nature of the allocative mechanism was not changed and the policy environment and managerial system were not altered; thus, the attempts to rectify the structural imbalance and improve economic incentives failed. The goals of the reform in late 1978 were to rectify the structural imbalance and improve incentives. However, what set the reforms apart from previous attempts were the micro-management system reforms that made farmers and managers and workers in state enterprises partial residual claimants. That small crack in the trinity of the traditional economic system was eventually pried open, leading to the gradual dismantlement of the traditional system.

13.3 The micro-management institution reforms

The most important change in the micro-management institution was the replacement of collective farming with a household-based system, now known as the household responsibility system. In the beginning, the government had not intended to change the farming institutions. Although it had been recognized in 1978 that solving managerial problems within the collective system was the key to improving farmers' incentives, the official position at that time was still that the collective was to remain the basic unit of agricultural production. Nevertheless, a small number of collectives, first secretly and later with the blessing of local authorities, began to try out a system of leasing a collective's land and dividing the obligatory procurement quotas to individual households in the collective. A year later those collectives brought out yields far larger than those of other teams. The central authorities later conceded the existence of the new form of farming, but required that it be restricted to poor agricultural regions, mainly to hilly or mountainous areas, and to poor collectives in which people had lost confidence in the collective system. However, this restriction was ignored in most regions. Production improved after a collective adopted the new system, regardless of its relative wealth or poverty.

Full official recognition of the household responsibility system as a nationally acceptable farming institution was eventually given in late 1981, exactly two years after the initial price increases. By that time, 45 percent of the collectives in China had already been dismantled and had instituted the household responsibility system. By the end of 1983, 98 percent of agricultural collectives in China had adopted the new system. When the household responsibility system first appeared, the land lease was only one to three years. However, the short lease reduced farmers' incentives for land-improvement investment. The lease contract was allowed to be extended up to 15 years in 1984. In 1993, the government allowed the lease contract to be extended for another 30 years after the expiration of the first contract.

Unlike the spontaneous nature of farming institution reform, the reform in the micro-management institution of the state enterprises was initiated by the government. Those reforms have undergone four stages. The first stage (1979–83) emphasized several important experimental initiatives that were intended to enlarge enterprise autonomy and expand the role of financial incentives within the traditional economic system. The measures included the introduction of profit retention and performance-related bonuses and permitted the state enterprises to produce outside the mandatory state plan. The enterprises involved in exports also were allowed to retain part of their foreign exchange earnings for use at their own discretion. In the second stage (1984–6) the emphasis shifted to a formalization of the financial obligations of the state enterprises to the government and exposed enterprises to market influences. From 1983, profit remittances to the government were replaced by a profit tax. In 1984, the government allowed state enterprises to sell output in excess of quotas at negotiated prices and to plan their output accordingly, thus establishing the dual track price system. During the third stage (1987–92), the contract responsibility system, which attempted to clarify the authority and responsibilities of enterprise managers, was formalized and widely adopted. The last stage (1993–present) attempted to introduce the modern corporate system to the state enterprises. In each stage of the reform, the government's intervention was reduced further and the state enterprises gained more autonomy.

The reform of the micro-management system has achieved its intended goal of improving technical efficiency. Empirical estimates show that almost half of the 42.2 percent growth of output in the cropping sector in the years 1978–84 was driven by productivity change brought about by the reforms. Furthermore, almost all of the productivity growth discussed was attributable to the changes resulting from the introduction of the household responsibility system (Fan 1991; Lin 1992; McMillan et al. 1989; Wen 1993). Estimates of the production function in several studies find that for industry the increase in enterprise autonomy increased productivity in the state enterprises (Chen et al. 1988; Gordon and Li 1991; Dollar 1990; Jefferson et al. 1992; Groves et al. 1994, 1995). Therefore, the reforms in the system of micro-management in both agriculture and industry have created a flow of new resources, an important feature of China's reforms.

The increase in enterprise autonomy under a distorted macropolicy environment, however, also invited managers' and workers' discretionary behavior.

Despite an improvement in productivity, the profitability of the state enterprises declined and the government's subsidies increased due to both a faster increase in wages, fringe benefits, and other unauthorized expenditures (Fan and Schaffer 1991) and the competition from the autonomous township and village enterprises (TVEs) (Jefferson and Rawski 1995). However, once the enterprises had tasted autonomy, it would have been politically too costly to revoke it. The decline in the profits of state enterprises and the competition from TVEs forced the government to try other measures that further increased the autonomy of state enterprises in the hope that the new measures would make the enterprises financially independent.

13.4 Resource allocation mechanism reform

The increase in enterprise autonomy put pressure on the planned distribution system. Because the state enterprises were allowed to produce outside the mandatory plans, the enterprises needed to obtain additional inputs and to sell the extra outputs outside the planned distribution system. Under pressure from the enterprises, material supplies were progressively delinked from the plan, and retail commerce was gradually deregulated. At the beginning, certain key inputs remained controlled. However, the controlled items were increasingly reduced. Centralized credit rationing was also delegated to local banks at the end of 1984.

An unexpected effect of the relaxation of the resources allocation system was the rapid growth of the nonstate enterprises, especially the TVEs.[21] Rural industry already existed under the traditional system as a result of the government's decision to mechanize agriculture and to develop rural processing industries to finance the mechanization in 1971. In 1978 the output of TVEs consisted of 7.2 percent of the total value of industrial output in China. Before the reforms, the growth of TVEs was severely constrained by access to credits, raw materials, and markets. The reforms created two favorable conditions for the rapid expansion of TVEs: (1) a new stream of surpluses brought out by the household responsibility reform provided a resource base for new investment activities, and (2) the relaxation of rigidity in the traditional planned allocation system provided access to key raw materials and markets. In the period 1981–91, the number of TVEs, employment, and the total output value grew at an average annual rate of 26.6 percent, 11.2 percent, and 29.6 percent, respectively. The annual growth of total output value for TVEs was three times that of the state firms in the same period. In 1993, TVEs accounted for 38.1 percent of the total industrial output in China. The share of industrial output from nonstate enterprises increased from 22 percent in 1978 to 56.9 percent in 1993 (State Statistical Bureau 1995: 73).

The rapid entry of TVEs and other types of nonstate enterprises produced two unexpected effects on the reforms. First, nonstate enterprises were the product of markets. Being outsiders to the traditional economic system, nonstate enterprises had to obtain energy and raw materials from competitive

Table 13.3 Growth rate of output and total factor productivity (average annual percentage change)

	1980–88	1980–84	1984–88
State Sector			
Output	8.49	6.77	10.22
TFP	2.40	1.80	3.01
Collective Sector			
Output	16.94	14.03	19.86
TFP	4.63	3.45	5.86

Source: World Bank (1992).

markets, and their products could be sold only to markets. They had budget constraints and would not survive if their management was poor. Their employees did not have an "iron rice bowl" and could be fired. As a result, the nonstate enterprises were more productive than the state enterprises, as the comparisons of output growth and total factor productivity growth between the state and collective sectors in Table 13.3 show. The dynamism of nonstate enterprises exerted pressure on the state enterprises and triggered the state's policy of transplanting the micro-management of the nonstate enterprises to the state enterprises and of delegating more autonomy to the state enterprises. Reform measures for improving the micromanagement institution of state enterprises-such as replacement of profit remittance by a profit tax, the establishment of the contract responsibility system, and the introduction of the modern corporate system to state enterprises-were responses to competitive pressure from TVEs and other nonstate enterprises (Jefferson and Rawski 1995).

Second, the development of nonstate enterprises significantly rectified the misallocation of resources. In most cases, nonstate enterprises had to pay market prices for their inputs, and their products were sold at market prices. The use of market prices induced most nonstate enterprises to adopt labor-intensive technology to concentrate on labor-intensive small industries.[22] Therefore, the technological structure of nonstate enterprises was more consistent with the comparative advantages of China's endowments. The entry of TVEs mitigated the structural imbalance caused by the HIODS.

13.5 Macropolicy environmental reform

Among the trinity of the traditional economic system, the distorted macropolicy environment was linked most closely to the development strategy, and its effects on allocative and technical efficiency were indirect. The reforms of the macropolicies were thus the most sluggish. We will argue later that most economic problems that appeared during the reforms-for example, the cyclic pattern of growth and the rampant rent seeking-can be attributed to the inconsistency between the distorted policy environment and the liberalized allocation and enterprise system. Therefore, the Chinese government constantly faced a dilemma: to make the macropolicy environment consistent with the liberalized micro-management institution and resource allocation mechanism or to redeprive the micro-management institution's autonomy and to recentralize resource allocation mechanism for maintaining the internal consistency of the traditional economic system. The deprivation of enterprise autonomy would definitely incur the resistance of employees of state enterprises. A return to the traditional economic system would also mean return to economic stagnation. Therefore, no matter how reluctant the government was, the only sustainable choice was to reform the macropolicy environment and make macropolicies consistent with the liberalized allocation and micro-management system.

Changes in the macropolicy environment started in the commodity price system. After the introduction of profit retention, the enterprises were allowed to produce outside the mandatory plan. The enterprises first used an informal barter system to obtain the outside-plan inputs and to sell the outside-plan products at premium prices. In 1984, the government introduced the dual-track price system, which allowed the state enterprises to sell their output in excess of quotas at market prices and to plan their output accordingly. The aim of the dual-track price system was to reduce the marginal price distortion in the state enterprises' production decisions while leaving the state a measure of control over material allocation. By 1988 only 30 percent of retail sales were made at plan prices, and the state enterprises obtained 60 percent of their inputs and sold 60 percent of their outputs at market prices (Zou 1992).

The second major change in the macroenvironment occurred in the foreign exchange rate policy. In the years 1979–80, the official exchange rate was roughly 1.5 yuan per US dollar. The rate could not cover the costs of exports, as the average cost of earning one US dollar was around 2.5 yuan. A dual rate system was adopted at the beginning of 1981. Commodity trade was settled at the internal rate of 2.8 yuan per dollar; the official rate of 1.53 yuan per dollar continued to apply to noncommodity transactions. After 1985, the yuan was gradually devalued. Moreover, the proportion of retained foreign exchange, which was introduced in 1979, was gradually raised, and enterprises were allowed to swap their foreign exchange entitlement with other enterprises through the Bank of China at rates higher than the official exchange rate. Restrictions on trading foreign exchanges were further relaxed with the establishment of a "foreign exchange adjustment center" in Shenzhen in 1985, in which enterprises could trade foreign exchanges at negotiated rates. By the late 1980s, such centers were established in most provinces in China and more than 80 percent of the foreign exchange earnings was swapped in such centers (Sung 1994). The climax of foreign exchange-rate policy reform was the establishment of a managed floating system and unification of the dual rate system on January 1, 1994.

Interest-rate policy is the least affected area of the traditional macropolicy environment. Under the HIODS, the interest rate was kept artificially low to facilitate the expansion of capital-intensive industries. After the reforms began in 1979, the government was forced to raise both the loan rates and the savings rates several times.[23] However, the rates were maintained at levels far below the market-clearing rates throughout the reform process. In late 1993, the government announced a plan to establish three development banks with the function of financing long-term projects, import/export, and agricultural infrastructure at subsidized rates and to turn the existing banks into commercial banks. The three development banks were established in 1994. The commercialization of the existing banks is expected to take at least another three to five years. Moreover, it is unclear whether after the reform the interest rate will be regulated or will be determined by markets. The mentality of the HIODS is deeply rooted in the mind of China's political leaders. To accelerate the development of capital-intensive industry in a capital-scarce economy, a distorted macropolicy environment-in the form of a low interest-rate policy is essential. It is likely that administrative interventions in the financial market will linger for an extended period.

Because reforms in macropolicies, especially those regarding the interest rate, lagged behind the reforms in the allocation system and micromanagement institutions, there were several economic consequences. The first one was the recurrence of a growth cycle. Maintaining the interest rate at an artificially low level gave enterprises an incentive to obtain more credits than the supply permitted. Before the reforms, the excess demands for credit were suppressed by restrictive central rationing. The delegation of credit approval authority to local banks in the autumn of 1984 resulted in a rapid expansion of credits and an investment thrust. As a result, the money supply increased 49.7 percent in 1984 compared with its level in 1983. The inflation rate jumped from less than 3 percent in the previous years to 8.8 percent in 1985 (see Figure 13.1). In 1988 the government's attempt to liberalize price controls caused a high inflation expectation. The interest rate for savings was not adjusted. Therefore, panic buying and a mini-bank run occurred. Loans, however, were maintained at the previously set level. As a consequence, the money supply increased by 47 percent in 1988. The inflation rate in 1988 reached 18 percent (see Figure 13.1). During the periods of high inflation, the economy overheated. A bottleneck in transportation, energy, and the supply of construction materials appeared. Because the government was reluctant to increase the interest rate as a way of checking the investment thrust, it had to resort to centralized rationing of credits and direct control of investment projects-a return to the planned system. The rationing and controls gave the state sectors a priority position. The pressure of inflation was reduced, but slower growth followed.

As mentioned earlier, although the reforms in the micro-management institution improved the productivity of the state sector, deficits increased due to a faster increase of wages and welfare as a result of the discretionary behavior of the managers and workers in the state enterprises. Therefore, fiscal income increasingly depended on the nonstate sectors. During the period of tightening state control, the growth rates of the nonstate sectors declined because access to credits and raw materials were restricted. Such a slowdown in the growth rate became fiscally unbearable. Therefore, the state was forced to liberalize the administrative controls to make room for the growth of the nonstate sectors. A period of faster growth followed. Nevertheless, conflicts arose again between the distorted macropolicy environment and the liberalized allocation mechanism and micro-management institution.

A second consequence of the inconsistency between the distorted policy environment and the liberalized allocation mechanism and micro-management institutions was rampant rent seeking. After the reforms, market prices existed, legally or illegally, along with planned prices for almost every kind of input and commodity that the state controlled. The difference between the market price and the planned price was an economic rent. It is estimated that the economic rent from the controlled commodity price, the interest rate, and the exchange rate was at least 200 billion yuan, about 21.5 percent of the national income in 1988. In 1992, the economic rent from bank loans alone reached 220 billion yuan (Hu 1994).[24] The nonstate enterprises as well as the autonomous state enterprises certainly had incentives to engage in rent-seeking activities through bribes and other measures to obtain the underpriced resources from the state allocation agencies. It is reported that under competitive pressure, the state enterprises in the heavy industries, which were given priorities in obtaining the state-controlled resources, also needed to give certain side payments to the banks and other allocation agencies to secure the earmarked loan and materials or to obtain them promptly.

Because of the rent-seeking activities of other types of enterprise, state enterprises often were unable to obtain the credits and materials indicated in the plans. The rent-seeking activities also caused widespread public resentment and became a source of social instability. To guarantee the survival of the state enterprises and to check social resentment, the government attempted to reinstitute tight controls on the allocation system in the austerity programs of 1986 and 1988. However, the controls were relaxed later to allow the growth of the nonstate sectors. Except for the interest rate, administrative controls on the prices of most materials and commodities have been removed.

13.6 The reform approaches: a comparison

There has been much discussion as to why China's reforms have been more successful than the reforms in Eastern Europe and the former Soviet Union (Chen et al. 1992; Qian and Xu 1993; Harrold 1992; McMillan and Naughton 1992; Gelb et al. 1993; McKinnon 1994). Except for the desirability of gradualism, the studies emphasized China's initial industrial structure (China has a large agricultural sector) or China's decentralized regional economic

structure. If China's success was mainly the result of her unique initial conditions, then that success does not have any implications for other economies,
where the initial conditions may be different. Nevertheless, the economic
problems in prereform China – namely, the structural imbalance and the
low incentives – are common to all socialist economies because they all
adopted a similar economic development strategy and because they all have a
similar macropolicy environment, planned allocation mechanism, and
puppet-like state enterprises. Empirical evidence shows that, as in prereform
China, Eastern European and Soviet economies were all over-industrialized
with oversized state enterprises; their service sectors and light industries were
underdeveloped; and employees' incentives were low (Newbery 1993; Brada
and King 1991; Sachs and Woo 1993).

For an economy with a given stock of resources, the efficient point in the
production plan is point E; however, under the HIODS, the actual production point is B, as illustrated in Figure 13.3. "Shock therapy" attempts to
reform the economic system so that the existing stock of resources can be
used more efficiently. Diagrammatically, the reforms attempt to move production from point B to point E. Stabilization, marketization, and privatization
are necessary conditions for achieving this goal. This is because, to induce
economic agents to move from B to E voluntarily, the agents should have a
stable expectation about the economy, correct relative-price signals, and the
incentives to respond to the price signals. The prescription of stabilization,
price liberalization, and privatization is internally consistent. The scheme is
equivalent to a replacement in a short sequence of the whole traditional
economic system, shown in Figure 13.2, which is endogenous to the HIODS.

If the transitional costs of reform were free, "shock therapy" would enable
the economy to jump from point B directly to point E, as the dotted line in
Figure 13.4a shows. However, some fixed equipment in heavy industries
cannot be used for production in light industries; for other equipment,

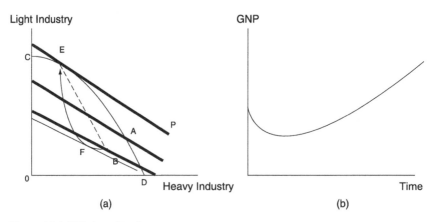

Figure 13.4 "Big bang" reform.

modifications are required for new uses (Brada and King 1991). Workers in heavy industry also need retraining before they can be assigned to new jobs. Moreover, the establishment of new market institutions takes time and resources (Murrel and Wang 1993, Lin 1989). During the initial stage of reforms, an increase in light industry would not be able to compensate for the decline in heavy industry. Therefore, instead of moving directly from point B to point E in Figure 13.4a, the economy moves first from B to F before reaching E. The resulting GNP path of growth is a "J-curve," as shown in Figure 13.4b. How large the decline in GNP would be and how long it would take before recovery would depend on how severe the initial distortion is and how quickly the necessary institutions can be established, something that can only be determined empirically. The experiences of Eastern Europe and the former Soviet Union suggest that a decline can be more than 50 percent of the GNP and that it may take several years before a turning point is reached. The government is certain to encounter a legitimacy crisis when the results of reforms are so dreadful (Dewatripont and Roland 1992). The leadership may not be able to hold a consensus on the course of further reforms, and political instability is likely to follow. Instead of a "J-curve," the result of "shock therapy" may be a big "L-curve."

When China began its reforms in the late 1970s, the political leadership did not question the feasibility or desirability of the traditional economic system. Its attempt was simply to improve incentives in the state enterprises and collective farms by giving agents in state enterprises and collective farms a degree of autonomy so that a closer link between personal rewards and individual efforts could be established; that is, the attempt was to move from point B to point A in Figure 13.5a. The empirical studies cited earlier show that the attempt was successful and a new stream of resources was created by the micro-management system reform.

The granting of partial microautonomy represented a small crack in the

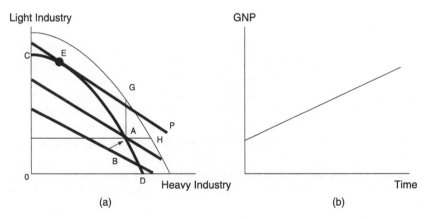

Figure 13.5 Gradual reform.

traditional economic system. However, partial autonomy also implies that entrepreneurs gain partial control over the allocation of the newly created stream of resources. The suppressed sectors in the traditional economy are the sectors that are consistent with the comparative advantages of the economy. The unexpected results of the micro-management reform are that, driven by profit motivation, the autonomous entrepreneurs allocated the new stream of resources under their control to the more profitable suppressed sectors. Because the planned allocation mechanism and distorted macropolicy environment were preserved, the state still had control over the old stream of resources and guaranteed that those resources would be allocated to the priority sectors. That is, the economy follows a dynamic path from point A to a point close to G, instead of to H, in Figure 13.5a. Therefore, throughout the reform process, the economy enjoys continuous growth as shown in Figure 13.5b. Moreover, as the economy grew, the proportion of resources that was allocated according to the planned prices became increasingly small. Therefore, by the time the price for a commodity was liberalized, the shock was much smaller than the gap between the market price and plan price would have suggested.[25]

If the above descriptions are a reasonable explanation of why China was able to enjoy continuous economic growth during the reform process, we can expect the following: first, the expansion of the suppressed sectors would not result in a decline in the priority sectors because the expansion of the suppressed sectors was supported by a new stream of resources; and, second, the economy should reach a higher rate of economic growth than the rate before the reforms because the new stream of resources was allocated to the more efficient sectors. Both assertions are confirmed by the empirical evidence. Table 13.4 shows the indexes and the growth rates of the major sectors in the national economy. It can be seen that no sector has declined since the reforms started and, except for the state enterprises, each sector's growth has accelerated.

13.7 Conclusion

Even though China's leaders did not have a blueprint in mind when reforms started, China's reforms have followed a path that can be explained by the theory of induced institutional innovation (Lin 1989, North 1990). The traditional economic system was itself a product of institutional innovation induced by the government's attempt to pursue a HIODS in a capital-scarce economy. The traditional system made the mobilization of resources for building up the strategy-determined priority sectors possible. However, its economic efficiency was low. Therefore, once the integrity of the traditional economic system was cracked by the introduction of microautonomy, institutional changes occurred in a way that was self-propelling toward the replacement of the traditional system with a more efficient market system. In the process, the efficiency of the state enterprises was improved through

Table 13.4 Index and growth rate of national income in selected sectors

| Year | Total | Industry | | | Construction | Transportation | Commerce |
		Agriculture	Total	State			
1952	100.0	100.0	100.0	100.0	100.0	100.0	100.0
1978	453.4	161.2	1,438.9	3,345.3	573.5	546.9	296.4
1993	1,695.7	346.2	8,546.7	10,385.8	2,764.3	2,037.7	783.6
Average Annual Growth Rate (percent)							
1952–78	6.0	1.9	10.8	14.5	6.9	6.8	4.3
1978–92	8.6	4.9	11.8	7.3	10.3	8.6	6.3

Source: State Statistical Bureau (1993: 34, 413: 1994: 34, 375).

greater autonomy and by meeting competition from the nonstate sectors. However, the dynamism of the economy came mainly from the swift entry of new, small, nonstate enterprises. The old planned allocation mechanism and distorted macropolicy environment gradually became unsustainable and were discarded. During the reform process, the state, the enterprises, and the people have had sufficient time to make adjustments to the new market system. The reforms benefit the majority of people as the economy has maintained strong growth throughout the whole process.

The "big bang" approach in Eastern Europe and the former Soviet Union also attempts to replace an inefficient economic system with a more efficient market system. The privately owned small firms emerged immediately after the lifting of the ban on private enterprises. However, the privatization of medium- and large-scale state enterprises was prolonged and proceeded slowly (Murrel and Wang 1993; Wang 1992). This resulting enterprise mix is in fact similar to what emerged in China. However, China's approach did not disrupt production in the state sectors. Therefore, China's gradual approach to reform achieved the same positive effects of the "big bang" approach but avoided its costs.[26] If transitional costs and the path-dependence of institutional changes are taken into account, China's gradual approach may be both theoretically and empirically preferable to the "big bang" approach (Wei 1993).

The overall performance of China's gradual approach to transition is remarkable, but China has paid a price. Because the reform of the macropolicy environment, especially interest-rate policy, has lagged behind reforms of the micro-management institution and resource allocation mechanism, institutional arrangements in the economic system have become internally inconsistent. As a result of the institutional incompatibility, rent-seeking, investment rush, and inflation have become internalized in the transition process. To mitigate those problems, the government often resorts to traditional administrative measures that cause the economy's dynamic growth to come to a halt and retard institutional development.

From the preceding analysis we find that it is imperative for China to complete the reform of the macropolicy environment so as to remove the institutional incompatibility and ensure a sustained, smooth growth path. Since the macropolicy environment is endogenous to the state's development strategy, the government must give up the anti-comparative advantage HIODS-or, in a modern version, the capital-intensive high-tech industry-oriented development strategy-and shift to a strategy based on China's comparative advantages. In addition, as the Chinese economy becomes a more mature market economy and is more integrated with the world economy, it is essential for the continuous growth of the Chinese economy to establish a transparent legal system that protects property rights so as to encourage innovations, technological progress, and domestic as well as foreign investments in China.

Thus far, most elements in China's reforms were induced rather than designed. However, the experience of China's transition may provide a useful lesson for designing reform policies in other economies where the heavy-industry-oriented strategy or other similar development strategies have been adopted under capital-scarce conditions.[27] Certainly, stages of development, endowment structures, political systems, and cultural heritage differ from one economy to another. To be effective, actual reform measures should take the economy's initial conditions into consideration and exploit all favorable internal and external factors.[28] Therefore, the specific design and sequence of reforms in an economy should be "induced" rather than "imposed." However, in addition to the general advice of maintaining economic and political stability and moving the reforms in a path-dependent manner, the following lessons may be useful for a government attempting reforms in an economic system similar to that of prereform China:

- Grant autonomy to the micro-management unit to improve the incentive structure and to create a new stream of resources by improving productivity.
- Allow the new stream of resources to be allocated by the autonomous enterprises outside the plan and at market prices to the suppressed sectors while maintaining the survival of the old priority sectors with the resources still under the state's plan control.
- Liberalize the distorted policy environment and planned allocation system to make them consistent with the autonomous micromanagement system when the new stream of resources allocated under the market outweighs the stream of resources allocated under the plan.

Acknowledgments

The authors gratefully acknowledge valuable comments by workshop participants at the Asian Development Bank, Australian National University Duke University, Hong Kong University of Science and Technology, Michigan State University, North Carolina State University Stanford University, the University, the University of California-San Diego, the University of Minnesota, the University of Wisconsin, and the World Bank.

Notes

1 Perkins and Yusuf (1984: 4) noted that a unique feature of China's economic development under socialism was the government's capacity to implement village-level programs nationwide through bureaucratic and Party channels. Therefore, the Chinese government was able to impose certain institutional arrangements in the economy, deemed important by ideology or by economic rationality, which may not be feasible in other economies (Perkins 1966).

2 The Five-Year Plan was disrupted from 1963–65, the period immediately after the agricultural crisis of 1959–62. The First to the Seventh Five-Year Plans covered, respectively, the periods from 1952 57, 1958–62, 1966–70, 1971–5, 1975–80, 1981–5, and 1986–90.

3 The construction of a light-industry project, such as a small textile factor; takes one or two years to complete. The construction of a large heavy-industry project, in general, takes a much longer time. For example, in China the average construction time for a metallurgy plant is seven years, for a chemical plant is five to six years, and for a machine-building plant is three to four years (Li and Zheng 1989: 170).

4 A real interest rate of 3 percent per month (36 percent per year) was normal in the informal financial markets that existed before the adoption of the development strategy.

5 Spontaneous development of heavy industry was impossible for several reasons. First, high interest rates would make any project that requires a long gestation unfeasible. For example, it takes on average seven years in China to complete the construction of a metallurgy plant. The market interest rate in the early 1950s in China was about 30 percent per year (2.5 percent per month). Suppose the funds for the project were borrowed at the market interest rate and repayment was made after the completion of the project. The principal and interest payment, calculated at a compound rate, for each dollar borrowed during the first year of the project would be $6.27. It is obvious that no project would be profitable enough to shoulder such a high interest burden. Second, because most equipment had to be imported from advanced countries, the limited supply of foreign exchange made the construction of heavy industry expensive under the market-determined exchange rate. Third, because the agricultural surplus was small and scattered, it was difficult to mobilize enough funds for any lump-sum project.

6 For example, the interest rate on bank loans was officially reduced from 30 percent per year to about 5 percent per year. For $1 borrowed at the beginning of a seven-year project, the principal and interest payment at the time the project was completed would be reduced from $6.27 to $1.41.

7 Although the real GNP per capita tripled between 1952 and 1978, the nominal wage was kept almost constant, increasing only 10.3 percent, during the same period (State Statistical Bureau 1987c: 151). For a more detailed discussion of the formation of low nominal-wage policy, see Cheng (1982: Chapter 8) and Wu (1965, Chapter 4). However, it is worth mentioning that, because of in-kind subsidies, the real wages to urban workers were not as low as the nominal wages suggested. Urban wage rates might have declined sharply if the restriction on the rural–urban migration had been removed (Rawski 1979, 67).

8 Even with all the above price distortions that facilitated heavy-industry development in China, the time required by a heavy-industry project to earn back the capital investment was, on average, about four to five times longer than the period required by a light-industry project (Li 1983, 37). Therefore, a profit-maximizing private owner would have a stronger incentive to invest in a light-industry project.

9 Under the New Democracy Policy, adopted by the Communist Party in the late 1940s, private enterprises were supposed to coexist with state-owned enterprises for an extended period after the revolution. However, the enterprises were nationalized soon after 1952 when the government adopted the HIODS. The attempt to secure profits for the heavy- industry projects was the motivation for the government's change in position toward private enterprises.

10 Theoretically, the Chinese government could use direct subsidies rather than macropolicy distortion, to facilitate the development of capital-intensive heavy industry in a capital scarce economy. It can be shown that the subsidy policy is more efficient economically than the policy of price control. However, with the subsidy policy, heavy industry would incur a huge explicit loss and the government would have to impose high taxes on other sectors to subsidize the loss. Under such a situation, the government would find it difficult to defend its position of

accelerating the development of heavy industry. Moreover, in an underdeveloped economy, government may not have the ability to collect huge taxes. This may explain why governments, not only in socialist economies but also in capitalist economies, use price controls instead of direct subsidies to facilitate the development of priority sectors.

11 In the literature in China and other socialist countries, many authors presumed that the distorted policy environment and the administrative controls were shaped by socialist doctrines. The socialist ideology might play a role in the formation of these policies; however, the existence of the policies and controls also have an economic rationale. They facilitate the implementation of a HIODS in a capital-scarce economy. This explains why nonsocialist developing economies such as India had a similar policy environment and administrative controls when they adopted the same development strategy under similar economic conditions.

12 An enterprise is bound to be loss-making if its outputs happen to be inputs to the other sectors, for example energy and transportation, because the prices of its outputs are suppressed. On the contrary, an enterprise is bound to be profit-making if its outputs are at the low end of the industrial chain, because the enterprise can enjoy low input prices and high output prices at the same time.

13 The state enterprises were granted some autonomy after the reforms in the late 1970s. As expected, one of the results of the reform was a rapid increase in wages, bonuses, and fringe benefits at the expense of the enterprise's profits.

14 When the reforms began in 1979, the government initially planned to increase agriculture's share in the state's fixed capital investment from 11 percent in 1978 to 18 percent in the following three to five years Because of the rapid agricultural growth brought about by the rural reforms, agriculture's share in the state fixed capital investment actually declined sharply to only about 3 percent in the late 1980s and early 1990s. However, the share of total fixed capital investment in agriculture in the nation as a whole did not decline as much as the figures suggest, because part of the decline in the state investment was compensated for by an increase in farmers' investment (Feder et al. 1992). Similarly, the share of heavy industry in the state's fixed capital investment did not decline after the reforms in 1979. However, the state's share in the total investment declined from 82 percent in 1980 to 66 percent in 1990. The nonstate sectors' investments are mostly in projects that are less capital-intensive. Therefore, the share of hear,' industry in the nation's fixed capital investment is less than the share in the state investment.

15 "Similarly, the development of a service sector was suppressed to facilitate the development of heavy industry. Agriculture, except for grain and cotton, was also suppressed.

16 The reason that grain and cotton were treated differently was because the government also pursued a grain self-sufficiency policy, and cotton was the basic raw material for industry. "The studies by Desai and Martin (1983) and by Whitesell and Barreto (1988) estimate the misallocation of capital and labor among the sectors of the Soviet economy, which also adopted the heavy-industry-oriented development strategy. Desai and Martin find losses from misallocation in the range of 3 to 10 percent-possibly up to 15 to 17 percent of the inputs employed in industry. Whitesell and Barreto find that in the early 1980s output gains equivalent to 4 to 6 percent could have been achieved by a reallocation of capital and labor among the sectors of Soviet industry.

17 The average annual rate of accumulation was raised from 24.2 percent of national income in the First Five-Year Plan to 33.0 percent and 33.2 percent in the Fourth and Fifth Five-Year Plans, respectively, whereas the average annual growth rate of national income dropped from 8.9 percent to 5.5 percent and 6.1 percent. As a result, wages for state employees were held almost constant between the years 1952 and 1978. As Deng Xiaoping admitted to visiting overseas Chinese in October

1974, wages were low the living standard was not high, and workers in China only had enough clothing and a full stomach (Cheng 1982, 248).

18 Brada (1991) estimates that overstaffing in Czechoslovak industry, was as high as 15 percent. The State Economic System Reform Commission in a recent report estimated that the total number of overstaffing in China's state enterprises was more than 30 million, about 30 percent of the total labor force in the state sectors (Zhonghua Zhoumo Bao 1995). A study by the World Bank (1985a) shows that, for the production of per unit gross domestic product, the consumption of energy, steel, and transportation in China were, respectively, 63.8 percent to 229.5 percent, 11.9 percent to 122.9 percent, and 85.6 percent to 559.6 percent greater than those of other developing countries. In the structure of total capital, the working capital accounted for the largest share in China and was 4.8 to 25.7 percentage points higher than that of other countries. This implied that inventories of inputs and outputs were larger and inventory, were kept longer in China than in other countries.

19 Lin (1992) estimates that losses due to low incentives in the agricultural collectives were as much as 20 percent of total factor productivity. For a theoretical model of the monitoring problems regarding incentives in a collective farm, see Lin (1989a).

20 The first attempt was made in 1958–60, the second in 1961–5, and the third in 1966–6 (Wu and Zhang 1993, 65–7).

21 The nonstate enterprises include the TVEs, the private enterprises, joint-venture enterprises, overseas Chinese enterprises, and foreign enterprises. Among them, the TVEs are the most important in terms of output share and number of enterprises. It is noteworthy that TVEs, although different in many aspects from state enterprises, are public enterprises that are funded, owned, and supervised by the township or village governments.

22 For example, in 1986 an average industrial enterprise in China had 179.9 workers, and the fixed investment per worker was 7,510 wan (State Statistical Bureau 1987a: 3); whereas an average TVE in the same year had 28.9 workers, and the fixed investment per worker was 1,709 yuan (State Statistical Bureau 1987c: 205).

23 To stop bank runs, the savings rates were indexed to inflation rates in October 1988. But the policy was revoked in 1991. In May 1993, the interest rate for a one-year time deposit was 9.18 percent, and for a one-to-three-year basic investment loan it was 10.80 percent (State Statistical Bureau 1993: 670–1). However, the market rate for a commercial loan was between 15 and 25 percent.

24 The total credit of the state banks was 2,161.6 billion yuan ($US 248.5 billion at the swap market exchange rate). The difference between the official interest rate and the market rate was about 10 percent. The rents from bank loans alone were as high as 216 billion yuan.

25 The official exchange rate was 5.7 yuan for one U.S. dollar and the swap market rate was 8.7 yuan for one US dollar when the exchange rate in China was unified to the swap market rate at the beginning of 1994. However, the shock was very small because before the unification about 80 percent of the foreign exchanges had already been traded in the swap markets.

26 The opportunity cost for the workers to move from the state sectors to the nonstate sectors might be higher in Eastern Europe and the former Soviet Union (EE/FSU) than in China because the subsidies to the workers were higher and the economies were more decentralized in EE/FSU than in China, as Sachs and Woo (1993) and Qian and Xu (1993) correctly emphasized. However, the higher opportunity cost is not a sufficient condition for nullifying the applicability of the Chinese approach. In China the differences between the state-regulated prices and the market prices in general were less than 30 percent and at most 100 percent before the reforms. However, the differences for many commodities in EE/FSU often reached factors of 10. Therefore, the expected returns for a worker to move

from the state sectors to the nonstate sectors were much higher in EE/FSU than in China. The existence of a large secondary economy in EE/FSU before the reforms suggests that resources would have flowed quickly into the suppressed sectors if the activities had been legalized. The rapid emergence of small private firms after lifting the ban on private enterprises confirms this proposition.

27 In essence, the HIODS is a forging-ahead strategy in which the government distorts the macropolicy environment to facilitate the development of some industries that exceed the stage of development dictated by the comparative advantages of the economy's endowment structure. The import-substitution strategy widely adopted in Latin America is another example of the forging-ahead development strategy.

28 The presence of overseas Chinese, the existence of a large stock of industrial resources in the rural sector before the start of reform, and the continuation of substantial marketing activity throughout the agricultural sector during the entire socialist period are among the important initial conditions that have contributed unequivocally to the success of China's reforms.

References

Brada, J. C. 1991. "The Economic Transition of Czechoslovakia from Plan to Market." *Journal of Economic Perspectives*, 5 (Fall): 171–7.

Brada, J. C. and A. E. King. 1991. "Sequencing Measures for the Transformation of Socialist Economies to Capitalism: Is There a J-Curve for Economic Reform?" Research Paper Series No. 13, Washington, DC: Socialist Economies Reform Unit, The World Bank.

Chen, K., H. Wang, Y. Zheng, G. Jefferson, and T. Rawski. 1988. "Productivity Change in Chinese Industry: 1953–1985," *Journal of Comparative Economics*, 12(4): 570–91 (December).

Chen, K., G. Jefferson, and I. J. Singh. 1992. "Lessons from China's Economic Reform," *Journal of Comparative Economics*, 16(2): 201–25, June.

Cheng, C.Y. 1982. *China's Economic Development: Growth and Structural Change.* Boulder, Colo.: Westview Press.

Desai, P. and R. Martin. 1983. "Efficiency Loss from Resource Misallocation in Soviet Industry," *Quarterly Journal of Economics*, 98(3): 117–29, August.

Dewatripont, M. and G. Roland. 1992. "The Virtues of Gradualism and Legitimacy in the Transition to a Market Economy," *Economic Journal*, 102(4): 291–300, March.

Dollar, D. 1990. "Economic Reform and Allocative Efficiency in China's State-Owned Industry," *Economic Development and Cultural Change*, 39(1): 89–105, October.

Fan, Q. M. and Schaffer, M. E. 1991. "Enterprise Reforms in Chinese and Polish State-Owned Industries," Research Paper Series No. 11. Washington, DC: Socialist Economies Reform Unit, The World Bank.

Fan, S. G. 1991. "Effects of Technological Change and Institutional Reform on Production Growth in Chinese Agriculture," *American Journal of Agricultural Economics*, 73(2): 265–75, May.

Feder, G., L. J. Lau, J. Y. Lin, and X. P. Luo. 1992. "The Determinants of Farm Investment and Residential Construction in Post-Reform China," *Economic Development and Cultural Change*, 41(1): 1–26, October.

Gelb, A., G. Jefferson, and I. Singh. 1993. "Can Communist Economies Transform

Incrementally?" in O. J. Blanchard and S. Fischer, eds, *NBER Macroeconomics Annual* 1993. Cambridge, Mass.: MIT Press.

Gordon, R. and Li, W. 1991. "Chinese Enterprise Behavior under the Reforms," *American Economic Review*, 81(2): 202–6, May.

Groves, T., Y. Hong, J. McMillan, and B. Naughton. 1994. "Autonomy and Incentives in Chinese State Enterprises," *Quarterly Journal of Economics*, 109(1): 183–209, February.

Groves, T., Y. Hong, J. McMillan, and B. Naughton. 1995. "China's Evolving Managerial Labor Market," *Journal of Political Economy*, 103(4): 873–92, May.

Harrold, P. 1992. "China's Reform Experience to Date," World Bank Discussion Paper No. 180, Washington, DC: The World Bank.

Hu, S. L. 1994. "1994: Reforms Have No Romantic Melody," Gaige (Refonn), 1, January.

Jefferson, G., and T. Rawski. 1995. "How Industrial Reform Worked in China: The Role of Innovation, Competition, and Property Rights," *Proceedings of the World Bank Annual Conference on Development Economics 1994* (Washington, DC: The World Bank): 129–56.

Jefferson, G., T. Rawski, and Y. Zheng. 1992. "Growth, Efficiency and Convergence in China's State and Collective Industry," *Economic Development and Cultural Change*, 40(2): 239–66, January.

Li, J. W. and Y. J. Zheng, eds. 1989. *Jishujinbu yu Chanye Jiegou Xuanze (Technological Progress and the Choice of Industrial Structure)*, Beijing: Kexue Chubanshe.

Li, Y. 1983. *Zhongguo Gongye Bumen Jiegou (The Structure of Chinese Industry)*, Beijing: China People's University Press.

Lin, J. Y. 1988. "The Household Responsibility System Reform in China's Agricultural Reform: A Theoretical and Empirical Study," *Economic Development and Cultural Change*, 36(3, supplement): S199–S224, April.

Lin, J. Y. 1989. "An Economic Theory of Institutional Change: Induced and Imposed Change," *Cato Journal*, 9(1): 1–33, Spring/Summer 1989.

Lin, J. Y. 1992. "Rural Reforms and Agricultural Growth in China," *American Economic Review*, 82(1): 34–51, March.

Lin, J. Y., F. Cai, and Z. Li. 1994. *The China Miracle: Development Strategy and Economic Development*. Chinese edn, Shanghai: People's Publishing House and Shanghai Sanlian Sudian (English edn, Hong Kong: Chinese University Press, 1996).

Lipton, D., and J. Sachs. 1990. "Privatization in Eastern Europe: The Case of Poland," *Brookings Papers on Economic Activities*, No. 2: 293–341.

Luo, H. X. 1985. *Economic Changes in Rural China*, Beijing: New World Press.

McKinnon, R. I. 1994. "Gradual versus Rapid Liberalization in Socialist Economies: Financial Policies and Macroeconomic Stability in China and Russia Compared." In Proceedings of the World Bank Annual Conference on Development Economics 1993: 63–94. Washington, D.C.: The World Bank.

McMillan, J. and B. Naughton. 1992. "How to Reform a Planned Economy: Lessons from China." Oxford Review of Economic Policy 8(1): 130–43, Spring.

McMillan, J., J. Whalley, and L. J. Zhu. 1989. "The Impact of China's Economic Reforms on Agricultural Productivity Growth," *Journal of Political Economy*, 97(4): 781–807, August.

Murphy, K., A. Schleifer, and R. Vishny. 1992. "The Transition to a Market Economy: Pitfall of Partial Reform," *Quarterly Journal of Economics*, 107(3): 889–906, August.

Murrel, P., and Y. J. Wang. 1993. "When Privatization Should Be Delayed: The Effect of Communist Legacies on Organizational and Institutional Reforms," *Journal of Comparative Economics*, 17(2): 385–406, June.

Newbery, D. M. 1993. "Transformation in Mature versus Emerging Economies: Why Has Hungary Been Less Successful than China?" Paper presented to the International Symposium on the Theoretical and Practical Issues of the Transition towards the Market Economy in China. Hainan, China: China Institute of Economic Reform and Development, July 1–3.

North, D. C. 1990. *Institutions, Institutional Change, and Economic Performance*, Cambridge, Mass.: Cambridge University Press.

Perkins, D. H. 1966. *Market Control and Planning in Communist China*, Cambridge, Mass.: Harvard University Press.

Perkins, D. H. 1988. "Reforming China's Economic System," *Journal of Economic Literature*, 26(2): 601–45, June.

Perkins, D. H. 1992. "China's 'Gradual' Approach to Market Reforms," paper presented at a conference on *Comparative Experiences of Economic Reform and Post-Socialist Transformation*, El Escorial, Spain, July 6–8.

Perkins, D. H. and S. Yusuf. 1984. *Rural Development in China*, Baltimore: The Johns Hopkins Press.

Qian, Y. Y. and C. G. Xu. 1993. "Why China's Economic Reforms Differ: The M-Form Hierarchy and Entry/Expansion of the Nonstate Sector," *The Economics of Transition*, 1(2): 135–70, June.

Rawski, T. G. 1979. *Economic Growth and Employment in China*, Oxford: Oxford University Press.

Sachs, J. D. and W. T. Woo. 1993. "Structural Factors in the Economic Reforms of China, Eastern Europe and the Former Soviet Union," paper presented at the Economic Policy Panel Meeting, Brussels, Belgium, October 22–3.

Singh, I. J. 1991. "China and Central and Eastern Europe: Is There a Professional Schizophrenia on Socialist Reform?" Research Paper Series, No. 17, Washington, DC: Socialist Economies Reform Unit, The World Bank.

State Statistical Bureau. 1987a. Zhongguo Gongye Jingyi 1987 (China Industrial Economy Statistical Material 1987). Beijing: Zhongguo Tongji Chubanshe.

State Statistical Bureau. 1987b. Zhongguo Gudingzichantouzi Tonggiziliao 1950–1985 (China Capital Construction Statistical Data 1950–1985). Beijing: Zhongguo Tongji Chubanshe.

State Statistical Bureau. 1987c. *Zhongguo Tongji Nianjian 1987 (China Statistical Yearbook 1987)*. Beijing: Zhongguo Tongji Chubanshe.

State Statistical Bureau. 1989. *Guanguo Geshenshi Zizhiqu Guominshouru Tongii Ziliao Huibian 1949–1989 (A Compilation of Provincial National Income Data 1949–1989)*. Beijing: Zhongguo Tongji Chubanshe.

State Statistical Bureau. 1993. *Zhongguo Tongzi Nianjian 1993 (China Statistical Yearbook 1993)*. Beijing: Zhongguo Tongji Chubanshe.

State Statistical Bureau. 1994. *Zhongguo Tongji Nianjian 1994 (China Statistical Yearbook 1994)*. Beijing: Zhongguo Tongji Chubanshe.

State Statistical Bureau. 1995. *Zhongguo Tongji Zaiyao 1995 (A Statistical Survey of China 1995)*. Beijing: Zhongguo Tongji Chubanshe.

Sung, Y. W. 1994. "An Appraisal of China's Foreign Trade Policy, 1950–1992," in T. N. Srinivasan (ed.), *The Comparative Experience of Agricultural and Trade Reforms in China and India: 109–53*, San Francisco: International ICS Press.

Wang, Y. J. 1992. "Communist Legacy, Pattern of Post Communism Organization, and the Problem of Transition," Mimeo. St Paul, Minn.: Industrial Relations Center, University of Minnesota.

Wei, S. J. 1993. "Gradualism Versus Big Bang: Speed and Sustainability of Reforms," Working Paper Series R93-2. Cambridge, Mass.: John F. Kennedy School of Government, Harvard University.

Wen, G. J. 1993. "Total Factor Productivity Change in China's Farming Sector: 1952–1989," *Economic Development and Cultural Change*, 42(1): 1–41, October.

Whitesell, R. and H. Barreto. 1988. "Estimation of Output Loss from Allocative Inefficiency: Comparisons of the Soviet Union and the U.S.," Research Memorandum RM-109. Williamstown, Mass.: Center for Development Economics, Williams College.

Woo, W. T. 1993. "The Art of Reforming Centrally-Planned Economies: Comparing China, Poland and Russia," paper presented at the Conference on the Tradition of Central Planned Economies in Pacific Asia. San Francisco: Asia Foundation in San Francisco, 7–8 May.

World Bank. 1985a. China: Economic Structure in International Perspective, Annex to China: Long Term Issues and Options. Washington, DC: The World Bank.

World Bank. 1985b. *China: Long-term Issues and Options*. Oxford: Oxford University Press.

World Bank. 1992. *Reform and Role of the Plan in the 1990s*, Washington DC: The World Bank.

Wu, J. L. and Z. Y. Zhang, eds. 1993. *Zhongguo Jingji Jianshe Baikequanshu (The Encyclopedia of China's Economic Construction)*. Beijing: Beijing Gongye Daxue Chubanshe.

Wu, Y. L. 1965. *The Economy of Communist China: An Introduction*, New York: Praeger.

Yusuf, S. 1993. "*The Rise of China's Nonstate Sector*," Mimeo. Washington DC: Department of China and Mongolia, The World Bank.

Zhonghua Zhoumo Bao (China Weekend Newspaper). 1995. "The OverStaffing in the State Enterprises Is over 30 Million," January 21.

Zou, G. 1992. "Enterprise Behavior under the Two-Tier Plan/Market System," Mimeo. Los Angeles: IBEAR/SBA, University of Southern California.

14 Regional decentralization and fiscal incentives: federalism, Chinese style

Hehui Jin, Yingyi Qian, and Barry R. Weingast[1]

Abstract

Aligning the interests of local governments with market development is an important issue for developing and transition economies. Using a panel data set from China, we investigate the relationship between provincial government's fiscal incentives and provincial market development. We report three empirical findings. First, we find that during the period of "fiscal contracting system" the discrepancy between *ex ante* contracts and *ex post* implementation was relatively small, suggesting that the fiscal contracts were credible. Second, we find a much higher correlation, about four times, between the provincial government's budgetary revenue and its expenditure during 1980s and 1990s as compared to 1970s, demonstrating that provincial governments faced much stronger *ex post* fiscal incentives after reform. Third, we find that stronger *ex ante* fiscal incentives, measured by the contractual marginal retention rate of the provincial government in its budgetary revenue, are associated with faster development of the non-state sector as well as more reforms in the state sector in the provincial economy. This holds even when we control for the conventional measure of fiscal decentralization. Finally, we compare federalism, Chinese style, to federalism, Russian style.

14.1 Introduction

Reforming the government is a crucial component of both the transition from a planned to a market economy and economic development. Creating thriving markets in these economies typically requires transforming a highly centralized and interventionist government into one that supports the market and fosters decentralized economic activities. Democracy, separation of powers, and the rule of law are among the important institutions that allow citizens to hold the government accountable for its economic actions and to secure markets from arbitrary state intrusion. By devolving power from the central to local levels, federalism is another institution that helps implement a limited yet effective government conducive to market development.

Economic theories of federalism have traditionally emphasized allocative benefits of decentralization in the provision of public goods and services, such as education and health care. There are two related ideas. First, Hayek (1939, 1945) discussed the use of knowledge in society, emphasizing that local governments have better access to local information, which allows them to provide public goods and services that better match local preferences than the national government. Second, Tiebout (1956) introduced the inter-jurisdictional competition dimension and argued that such a competition provides a sorting mechanism to better match public goods and services with consumers' preferences. Drawing on these ideas, Musgrave (1959) and Oates (1972) built a theory of fiscal federalism, stressing among other things the appropriate assignment of taxes and expenditures to the various levels of government to improve welfare.

Our main concern in this paper is the relationship between fiscal incentives facing local governments and local government promotion of market development in the local economy. Recent experiences of transition and developing economies have shown that a central barrier to economic development in these countries is from the governments, especially local governments, as their policies are often hostile to local business development. Local government policies, such as business regulation and levies, may have either favorable or adverse effects on the entry and expansion of local business enterprises. This leads to two types of government role that have been identified in the literature (Shleifer and Vishny 1998): The government either plays the role of the "grabbing hand" by restricting and preying on productive enterprises and protecting unproductive ones, or it plays the role of the "helping hand" by supporting productive enterprises and disciplining unproductive enterprises.

Our study of federalism centers around the question of how the central-local governmental relationship affects the local government's behavior toward business enterprises and market development. A crucial issue is what kind of federalism better aligns local government incentives with promoting markets and productive enterprises.[2] Inter-jurisdictional competition can serve as an important incentive device, as emphasized by Tiebout and Brennan and Buchanan (1980): competition rewards local governments friendly to markets as factors of production move to their regions, while it punishes heavily interventionist local governments as they lose valuable factors of production. But this mechanism is not perfect, competition may result in the phenomenon known as "race to the bottom."

Another mechanism, the focus of this paper, concerns the fiscal incentives of local government. This mechanism works when pro-business local government policy promotes local business development, which rewards local governments by increasing the local tax revenue base. A critical aspect of this incentive, however concerns whether the local government is able to keep a significant portion of the increased tax revenue that results from their policy decisions. If so, they have strong fiscal incentives to support market development. On the other hand, if a local government's fiscal reward is unrelated to, or even worse, negatively related to its policy effort, it has no fiscal incentives to support local business.

Studies on China's transition to markets have long noticed the general local government support for local business development, especially in the non-state sector (e.g. Montinola, Qian, and Weingast 1995). What are the reasons for the local governments in China to play the "helping hand" for local business development? Using a provincial panel data set, we conduct an empirical study on the Chinese style of federalism with a focus on provincial government's fiscal incentives.

We report three empirical findings. Our first two findings both concern the change in fiscal incentives facing provincial governments after the reform. First, in assessing the "fiscal contracting system" operating between the central and provincial governments from 1980–93, we find that the discrepancy between *ex ante* contracts and *ex post* implementation declined over time and was relatively small on average. These small differences imply that the fiscal contracts between center and province were credible. We also find that cases of extra subsidies were much more common than cases of extra revenue remittance. This suggests that, as far as the central-provincial relations in China, the "soft budget constraint" problem (Kornai 1996) was a greater problem than the "predation" problem.

Second, we find a strong correlation between the current provincial budgetary revenue and its expenditure for the period of 1982–91 when the "fiscal contracting system" was implemented, about four times as large in the magnitude as the before reform period of 1970–9, and such a strong correlation remained in the post-1994 period when the "fiscal contracting system" was replaced by the "separating tax system." The finding provides the evidence that provincial governments in China faced much stronger *ex post* fiscal incentives after the reform.

Our third finding concerns the effects of fiscal incentives on provincial economic development and reform. We use the *ex ante* marginal revenue retention rate of provincial governments, as specified in the fiscal contracts between the central and provincial governments in the period between 1982 and 1992, as the measure of fiscal incentives faced by provincial government.[3] We find that stronger fiscal incentives are associated with faster development of non-state enterprises in terms of the employment growth rates in rural enterprises and in all non-state enterprises, even controlling for the conventional measurement of fiscal decentralization. Similarly, stronger fiscal incentives are also associated with greater reform in state-owned enterprises, as measured by the increased shares of contract workers in the total state employment and bonuses in total employee wages.

With these results in mind, we compare federalism, Chinese style, with federalism, Russian style. Studies of Russia's transition stress the problematic role of the government in reform. Shleifer (1997) and Frye and Shleifer (1997), for example, provide evidence that local governments in Russia have been playing the role of "grabbing hands" that retard private business development. Zhuravskaya (2000) finds that the existing revenue sharing schemes between the Russian regional and local governments provide the latter with no fiscal incentives to increase their tax base: increases in local government revenues were almost entirely exacted by the regional government. The lack of fiscal incentives in part explains why local governments in Russia prey on private businesses.

This contrast in perspective suggests that the distorted incentives faced by local governments in part explains the different performances of the Chinese and Russian reforms. Interestingly, Russia has done more than China in terms of privatization of state-owned enterprises and liberalization of markets (Shleifer 1997; Frye and Shleifer 1997; de Figueiredo and Weingast 2001; Lavrov, Litwack, and Sutherland 2000; and OECD 2000). But apparently it has failed to provide local governments with appropriate fiscal incentives to pursue local prosperity. Liberalization and privatization without altering government fiscal incentives are insufficient to produce meaningful economic reform.

We emphasize the critical importance of government fiscal incentives for successful reform. In addition to fiscal incentives, political incentives facing local governments also matter in comparing the Chinese and Russian federalism (Blanchard and Shleifer 2000). A complementary approach studying the political incentives facing local governments in China has recently began. For example, Maskin, Qian and Xu (2000) documented an empirical correlation between the provincial economic performance and the provincial representation in the Party Central Committee. Li and Zhou (2004) found evidence that the central government uses personnel control over promotion and dismissal of provincial top leaders to induce provincial economic growth.

The remainder of the paper is organized as follows. Section 14.2 describes the changing fiscal system in China during the reform. Section 14.3 develops our theoretical perspective. Section 14.4 describes the data and the construction of variables. Section 14.5 assesses the credibility of the "fiscal contracting system" for the period of 1982–92. Section 14.6 examines the *ex post* link between provincial revenue collection and its expenditure before and after reform. Section 14.7 estimates the effects of fiscal incentives on provincial development and reform. Our conclusions follow.

14.2 Fiscal relations between the central and provincial governments in China

China's fiscal system has five hierarchical levels of government: (1) central; (2) provincial; (3) prefecture; (4) county; and (5) township.[4] In this paper, we will focus on the central-provincial fiscal relations. The central-provincial fiscal relations have evolved over time in three distinct phases: the pre-reform phase prior to 1979, the transitional phase of 1980–93, and the post-1994 phase.

Prior to the reform of 1979, the fiscal relations between the central and provincial governments are best described as the one of "unified revenue collection and unified spending" (*tongshou tongzhi*). Basically, the provincial governments collected most of revenue generated from within the province, on average over 80 percent, which included taxes and (mostly) profits from state-owned enterprises. Then the central government made a plan of spending for each province. This system earned a nickname "eating from one big pot" (*chi daguofan*), which captured its essence.

From 1980, the central-provincial fiscal relations altered in a dramatic way. Between 1980 and 1993, the institution governing the central and provincial fiscal relations is the so called "fiscal contracting system" (*caizheng chengbao zhi*), also known by its nickname "eating from separate kitchens" (*fenzao chifan*). Under the fiscal contracting system, provincial governments entered into relatively long-term fiscal contracts (typically five years) with the central government. Because of their experimental nature, the contractual arrangements varied across provinces and over time. The fiscal contracting system worked as follows (Wong 1997; Bahl 1999): First, "central fixed revenue" was defined to include custom's duties, direct tax or profit remittance from the central government supervised state-owned enterprises (SOEs), and some other taxes. All other revenue falls under the heading "local revenue." On average, the local revenue accounted for about 66 percent of total government budgetary revenue over these years. Second, the local revenue was then divided between the central and provincial governments according to pre-determined sharing schemes. For example, between 1980 and 1987, Guang-dong province agreed to remit a fixed amount per year, and between 1988 and 1993, it agreed to remit an amount that increased by a fixed 9 percent per year. Guizhou province agreed to receive subsidies that increased by a fixed 10 percent per year. On the other hand, Jiangsu province agreed to remit a fixed share of revenue to the central government. Over time, many provincial governments retained 100 percent of the total local revenue at the margin, which effectively made them residual claimants over the local revenue.

The actual (*ex post*) expenditure of local government did not necessarily match that from the sharing scheme for several reasons. After the division of local revenue according to the sharing scheme, some extra remittance and transfer payments took place between the central government and the provinces. For example, the central government sometimes "borrowed" funds from the provinces. On the other hand, the central government also made additional transfer payments (not specified in the sharing schemes) to provinces, which generally fell into two categories: earmarked subsidies (*zhuanxiang butie*), such as price subsidies for urban residents compensating them for food price increases, and matching grants (*peitao buokuan*), such as funds for highway building. Clearly, the larger this type of *ex post* redistribution, the less important the pre-determined revenue sharing schemes.

From 1994, the "fiscal contracting system" was replaced by "separating tax system." Under the new system, "local revenue" has been redefined as revenues from local taxes and the local portion of the shared taxes (Bahl 1999). The major local taxes are now the income taxes from all enterprises other than central government enterprises, business tax from the sales of services, and personal income tax. The most important shared tax is the value added tax (VAT), of which 25 percent belongs to the provincial government, uniform across provinces. The post-1994 phase has eliminated the variations of the revenue sharing rules from the 1980–93 phase.

In addition to the budgetary revenue, another category of revenue exists called "extra-budgetary revenue," which consists of tax surcharges and user fees levied by central and local government's agencies, as well as some earnings from SOEs. The extra-budgetary revenue emerged in the 1950s but only became institutionalized after the reform. Unlike the budgetary local revenues, the extra-budgetary local revenues are not subject to sharing with the central government. In 1978, total extra-budgetary revenue was about 10 percent of the GDP while total budgetary revenue was about 31 percent. In 1993, the extra-budgetary revenue was up to 16 percent of the GDP and the budgetary revenue was down to 16 percent of the GDP (*Statistical Yearbook of China, 1995*). While about three-quarters of the extra-budgetary funds are earnings retained by SOEs and by their supervisory government agencies at the central and local levels, about 30 percent of the extra-budgetary funds are used for government expenditures to supplement the budgetary funds (Fan 1996).

14.3 Fiscal incentives and economic development: a theoretical perspective

How do fiscal incentives of local government contribute to the local economic development? As Hayek stressed, decentralization of authority has the benefits of more efficient use of dispersed local knowledge possessed by the local government. In contrast, centralization of government authority is costly because information transmission from local to central government is often distorted and incomplete. But decentralization of authority is meaningless if the central government takes away all revenue generated in the local economy as a result of local government's action. This suggests a link between fiscal incentives of local government and local development which is a function of local government's policy.

Consider the following very simple model for the purpose of illustration. Let $Y(e)$ be the value created by the local business development, which is a function of local government's "effort" e. This effort is related to local government's policies concerning local productive enterprises, such as the non-state enterprises. These policies could reduce excessive regulation and controls over business entry, speed up of approval of projects and permits, eliminate of onerous fees imposed on firms, or fight against unfavorable ideology toward the development of non-state firms. This effort is also related to reform efforts in non-productive state enterprises in order to reduce their losses. Because effort here is interpreted as policies rather than public goods provisions such as those in education and health care, its effect on the local economy is immediate. Higher local government effort means more favorable local business environment and thus higher value of the local economy Y(e), which means a larger government revenue base.

We also assume that the revenue generated y is positively related to local economy Y. Then the relationship y(Y(e)) implies that total revenue generated y(e) is an increasing function of e. Note that in our interpretation e is not revenue collection effort by the local government, rather, it is the local government's policy effort in supporting productive business in its locality. On the other hand, effort e has a cost to local government C(e), which is also increasing in e. Such a cost could be the forgone bribes received by the local government officials, or more generally, the costs spent to facilitate local business development.

The first step in the fiscal contracting system is the designation of "central revenue" and "local revenue." For simplicity we assume that out of the total revenue generated y, vy is designated as "local revenue" and (1-v)y as "central revenue." The second step specifies the marginal provincial revenue retention rate which we denote as z; the province may also pay the center a fixed remittance (or subsidy) R. The provincial government's revenue retention is then given by zvy(e) − R. In the third step, the central government makes transfers T to local government. Therefore, the final local government's expenditure is determined by zvy(Y(e)) − R + T.

We assume that local government maximizes local expenditure net of cost of effort by choosing effort level e:

$$\max \{zvy(e) - R - c(e) + T\} \tag{1}$$

Under the usual assumptions of concavity of y(e) and convexity of c(e), the optimal effort level e*, as well as the local economy Y(e*), is an increasing function of revenue retention rate z:

$$de*/dz > 0,$$

and

$$dY(e*)/dz > 0, \tag{2}$$

assuming that v is constant. That is, the larger the marginal fraction of revenues a local government is allowed to keep, the stronger the local government's incentives to increase its revenue base, which in turn means better government policy to pursue local economic prosperity. This implies that strong links between local expenditures and local revenue help align the interests of local governments to local development.

In the above model, the central government delegates the tasks of supporting local business development to local governments because the latter have better local knowledge. The central government cannot dictate local effort level e because local effort is not easily observable or measurable. For example, even if the central government could announce a nationwide policy to support productive enterprises, it is still up to the local government to enforce such a policy. During enforcement, local circumstances play important role. Therefore, the above model already incorporates the assumption about the importance of local information. Hence the central government is limited to using the revenue retention rate, z, to motivate local governments by aligning the interests of local government with local prosperity.

This implication of the above simple model differs in an important way from the conventional perspective on revenue sharing between the central and local governments. While arguing for the benefits of decentralization of expenditure, the conventional fiscal federalism view does not consider a strong linkage between local governments' own revenue and their expenditures desirable. This view instead focuses on allocative distortions under decentralized revenue collection. It therefore recommends a centralized revenue collection together with decentralized expenditure system, allowing sizeable transfers from the central to local governments to fill the local revenue-expenditure gap. The traditional view therefore implies no necessary relationship between local expenditure and local revenue generated. In contrast, the above model stresses the importance of local governments' incentives in pursuing prosperity in the local economy which serves as the local revenue base. For that purpose, it is natural to emphasize the potential benefit of linking local governments' revenue with their expenditure.

Our model is especially relevant for transition and developing economies for several reasons. For transition economies, the pervasive revenue redistribution practice under central planning had long distorted local governments' incentives, and correcting this distortion has been an urgent need. Developing countries generally have excessive regulation over business development, and local governments in these countries also have more discretions affecting the well being of local business. Therefore, for these countries, aligning the fiscal incentives of local governments with local prosperity would have stronger effects on the local economy. In contrast, for developed countries, such a justification for local fiscal incentives may be weaker, because the formal legal environment is generally more hospitable to business.

Based on the above discussion, we conjecture that the higher the marginal proportion of revenue retained by the local governments, the faster development of the productive part of the local economy and more reform of the non-productive part of the local economy. Because onerous restrictions on enterprises reduce their revenue, lower governments facing stronger fiscal incentives are likely to impose fewer economic restrictions on and give more support for productive enterprises. However, local governments may fail to respond to fiscal incentives. Alternatively, these incentives may result in protecting the local economy rather than expanding it. Therefore, empirical testing is required to determine the validity of the hypothesis.

14.4 Data and variables

We use a panel data set of 29 provinces from 1970 to 1999, with a particular focus for the time period from 1982 to 1992.[5] We obtained our data from the official Chinese government publications at the national and subnational levels, including *China Statistical Yearbook* in various years published by the National Bureau of Statistics. Table 14.1 presents summary statistics of major variables for the period of 1982–92.

Measurement of provincial and central government expenditures is standard. However, we make one adjustment to the fiscal expenditure data because the original data has an inconsistency: price subsidies were netted out from revenue and expenditure before 1986 but added to both revenue and expenditure afterward. Most of the price subsidies are the central government's earmarked transfers to local governments (Wong 1997). To make the data consistent throughout the sample period, we exclude the price subsidies from the government expenditure data after 1986. Because explicit provincial data on their price subsidy expenditures are unavailable, we use the following method to estimate them. First, we apply the central and local shares of price subsidies nationwide (Hofman 1993) to calculate the total local expenditures of the price subsidies for each year. Because the price subsidies are exclusively

Table 14.1 Summary statistics of major variables (1982–92)

	Mean	Minimum	Maximum	Standard deviation
Ratio of local expenditure to central expenditure in a province	1.78	0.61	7.11	1.32
Provincial marginal revenue retention rate	0.84	0.11	1.00	0.23
Provincial marginal revenue retention rate (dummy)	0.57	0	1	0.50
Provincial budgetary revenue (100 million yuan)	53.56	1.30	222.64	42.01
Provincial budgetary expenditure (100 million yuan)	45.46	5.71	197.93	27.93
Provincial extra-budgetary revenue (100 million yuan)	44.21	0.46	160.47	33.89
Provincial extra-budgetary expenditure (100 million yuan)	42.20	0.49	161.40	32.96
Provincial growth of rural non-agricultural employment	0.06	−0.04	0.26	0.05
Provincial growth of non-state-non-agricultural employment	0.09	−0.11	0.56	0.11
Share of contract workers in total state employment in a province	0.09	0.00	0.33	0.06
Share of bonuses in total wage in state enterprises in a province	0.15	0.06	0.45	0.05

for urban residents and they are provided more or less uniformly across provinces, we then use the provincial share of urban residency in the country to allocate price subsidies to each province.

We investigate the marginal fiscal incentives facing local governments from both *ex post* and *ex ante* perspectives. To examine the *ex post* marginal fiscal incentives, we look at realized provincial *budgetary revenue* and *budgetary expenditure* separately. As explained in section 14.2, provincial budgetary revenue is the revenue generated in the province, excluding those revenues designated as the central government's fixed revenue. Provincial budgetary expenditure is the actual provincial government spending, after contractual obligations are fulfilled and renegotiation takes place. We also consider provincial *extra-budgetary revenue* and *extra-budgetary expenditure*. Although no sharing arrangements cover extra-budgetary revenue, the central government might extract a portion of these funds.[6]

We measure *ex ante* marginal fiscal incentives, defined as the contractual marginal retention rate of local revenue collection by provincial governments, as those determined by the fiscal contracts between the central and provincial governments during the period of 1980–93. In contrast to the ratio of local to central government expenditure, the fiscal incentive variable measures how local governments are rewarded (or punished) *at the margin* from an increase (or decrease) in local revenue collection. Therefore, it is the right variable that should be used to the study on the effects of fiscal incentives.[7]

The data on provincial marginal retention rates in the fiscal contracts are collected from several publications including Chen (1988), Oksenberg and Tong (1991), Bahl and Wallich (1992), and Bahl (1999), which are in turn obtained from the Ministry of Finance in China, the central government agency that formulates these contracts. In some cases the data shows more than one marginal retention rate in a contract for different revenue brackets. In those cases we use the rate for the highest revenue bracket because the data reveals that all the provinces in fact ended up with that bracket.

We exclude the data of 1993 because it is distortionary due to the anticipation of a major change in the fiscal system in 1994. For example, one provision of the 1994 reform, announced in the fourth quarter of 1993, compensated local governments based on their 1993 figures of local expenditure. This provision gave an incentive for local governments to inflate the local expenditure figures toward the year end. We also use the 1992 data with caution, because in that year four provinces were selected for the experiment of a new tax system to be implemented nationwide in 1994. Therefore, these provinces were not officially on the fiscal contracting system any more. Dropping off these four data points has little effect on our results.

The provincial marginal revenue retention rates involve one complication. Starting in 1986, several large cities became fiscally independent from their provinces, directly contracting with the central government (they are known as "separately plan listed cities"). We have tried to incorporate the information on these city contracts into the provincial contracts by constructing an average provincial marginal retention rate using city revenue and provincial revenue (excluding the relevant city) as weights.[8] Figure 14.1 plots the average of the provincial marginal revenue retention rates and the share of provinces with 100 percent marginal retention rates.

The non-state sector in urban and, especially, rural areas is widely regarded as the engine of China's growth. We use two variables to measure the development reflecting the entry and expansion of non-state enterprises: *growth of rural enterprise employment*, which covers all non-agricultural activities in the rural areas, and *growth of non-state non-agricultural employment*, which includes both urban and rural non-state industry and services.

We study the reform within the state sector by examining two variables: the changes in the *share of contract workers in total state employment* and in the *share of bonuses in total state employee wages*. Prior to 1992, China did not privatize any state enterprise. Nonetheless state-owned enterprises underwent modest reforms. For example, many changed their employment practices by hiring workers on a contractual basis rather than giving them permanent positions. They also increasingly used bonuses as a form of payment in addition to fixed salary. Both reforms were intended to improve workers' incentives. Groves et al. (1994) used the similar variables as their major measurements of state-owned enterprise reform in China, and their data came from the enterprise level survey in four provinces.

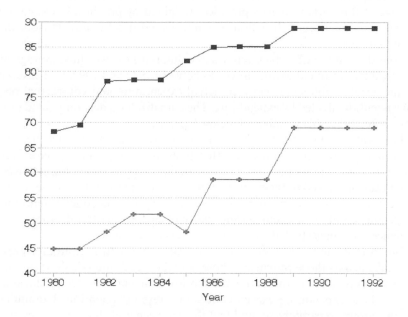

Figure 14.1 Provincial marginal revenue retention rates (1980–92)

Note: The upper line is the average of marginal retention rates and the lower line is the share of the provinces with 100% marginal retention rates.

14.5 How did fiscal incentives for provincial governments change: assessing the credibility of the fiscal contracting system

We assess the credibility of the fiscal contracting system for the period of 1982–92 by first comparing the actual provincial expenditure with the contractual revenue retention amount implied by the *ex ante* fiscal contracts (for example, the *ex ante* marginal retention rate times local revenue collection minus lump-sum remittance). This allows us to estimate the extent of *ex post* readjustment of revenue remittance and subsidies beyond the contracts. A small discrepancy between the *ex ante* contracts and *ex post* implementation implies that the fiscal contracts are credible, whereas a big discrepancy would emerge if the central government systematically sought greater than the contracted amounts from high-performing provinces.

Fiscal readjustment (*ex post*) measures the difference between actual provincial expenditure and contractual revenue retention as implied by the fiscal contracts.[9] A negative value of fiscal readjustment means that the province spends less than the contractual provision entailed. We interpret the first case to be the one in which the province *ex post* remitted extra revenue to the central government, for example, if it were forced to "lend" revenue to the central government. These cases represent the central government's "predation." A positive value of fiscal readjustment indicates that the province *ex post* received extra subsidies from the central government, a signal of the "soft budget constraint" (Kornai 1986).[10] For any given year, we use the average of this variable across provinces weighted by provincial expenditure to measure the average deviation of implemented fiscal contracts from the promised ones.

Consider Table 14.2, which reports in column (6) the weighted average of the fiscal readjustment across provinces between 1982 and 1992, as measured by the absolute difference between actual expenditure and contractual revenue retention divided by expenditure. The data display a declining trend over time. After 1986, this variable fell below 8 percent.

This evidence suggests that the extent of *ex post* readjustments has become more limited over time. Further, after 1986, these adjustments have been relatively limited in scope. On average, actual provincial expenditures correspond reasonably well to their contractual revenue retention. Of course, we do not expect an exact correspondence due to *ex post* adjustments reflecting exogenous events that occur during the year, such as natural disasters. The evidence thus suggests that the fiscal contracts are credible.

Next we divide the provinces into two categories: extra remittance provinces, defined as those provinces whose actual expenditure fall short of contractual revenue retention; and extra subsidy recipient provinces, defined as those whose expenditure exceed contractual revenue retention. Examining the two groups separately, we find that there are generally fewer extra revenue remitting provinces (see column (7), Panel A of Table 14.3) than extra subsidized provinces (see column (7), Panel B of Table 14.3). This indicates that the

Table 14.2 The discrepancy between the *ex ante* contracts and *ex post* implementation

	(1) Budgetary revenue	(2) Unadjusted budgetary expenditure	(3) Price subsidies	(4) Budgetary expenditure	(5) Contractual budgetary revenue retention	(6) Weighted average of fiscal readjustment (%)	(7) Number of provinces
All provinces							
1982	863.5	572.4	0	572.4	521.7	10.9	28
1983	881.6	645.3	0	645.3	546.7	15.3	28
1984	968.5	800.1	0	800.1	602.8	24.7	28
1985	1185.0	1038.2	0	1038.2	852.0	18.3	28
1986	1324.5	1366.5	256.0	1110.5	992.4	9.4	28
1987	1466.4	1411.5	292.9	1118.7	1124.6	6.0	28
1988	1597.6	1650.2	315.0	1335.2	1267.3	6.9	28
1989	1926.5	1937.2	370.3	1566.8	1624.6	7.4	29
1990	1967.7	2105.5	380.8	1724.7	1657.4	6.6	29
1991	2258.1	2402.5	373.8	2028.8	1917.2	6.8	29
1992	2430.7	2564.6	321.6	2243.0	2085.1	7.3	29

Note:
(1) Hainan became a separate province in 1989 so the total number of provinces increased from 28 to 29.

Table 14.3 Extra remittances vs. extra subsidies

	(1) Budgetary revenue	(2) Unadjusted budgetary expenditure	(3) Price subsidies	(4) Budgetary expenditure	(5) Contractual budgetary revenue retention	(6) Weighted average of fiscal readjustment (%)	(7) Number of provinces
Panel A: Provinces paying extra remittance (budgetary expenditure < contractual revenue retention)							
1982	193.4	110.1	0	110.1	116.0	-5.3	6
1983	0	0	0	0	0	N/A	0
1984	0	0	0	0	0	N/A	0
1985	184.2	46.1	0	46.1	47.9	-4.0	1
1986	79.8	82.9	16.3	66.6	72.0	-6.6	1
1987	611.5	702.8	150.9	551.9	597.2	-6.5	14
1988	418.2	392.6	79.1	313.4	336.6	-5.9	6
1989	1368.3	1313.7	259.4	1054.3	1155.1	-7.7	19
1990	873.7	827.3	149.8	677.6	713.5	-4.3	10
1991	694.4	742.2	107.8	634.4	660.2	-3.5	7
1992	591.7	596.4	60.0	536.4	550.8	-2.4	4
Panel B: Provinces receiving extra subsidies (budgetary expenditure > contractual revenue retention)							
1982	670.2	462.3	0	462.3	405.8	12.2	22
1983	881.6	645.3	0	645.3	546.7	15.3	28
1984	968.5	800.1	0	800.1	602.8	24.7	28
1985	1000.7	992.1	0	992.1	804.1	19.0	27
1986	1244.7	1283.6	239.7	1043.9	920.4	9.6	27
1987	855.0	708.8	142.0	555.8	527.4	5.6	14
1988	1179.4	1257.6	235.8	1021.8	930.7	7.3	22
1989	558.3	623.5	111.0	512.5	469.5	6.9	10
1990	1093.9	1278.2	231.0	1047.1	944.0	8.1	19
1991	1563.8	1660.4	266.0	1394.4	1256.9	8.3	22
1992	1839.0	1968.3	261.7	1706.6	1534.3	8.8	25

Note:
(1) Hainan became a separate province in 1989 so the total number of provinces increased from 28 to 29.

ex post extra transfers from the center to provinces (i.e., the problem of soft budget constraints) is quantitatively more significant than extra transfers from the provinces to the center.[11]

Because of the potential for central government predation, the phenomena of extra remitting provinces is of special interest. If the central government behaved in a predatory fashion – for example, if it consistently forced the more successful provinces to remit significant amount of additional revenue – the magnitude of this figure would be significant. The results in Panel A of Table 14.3 suggest that these additional remittances are small. After 1989, only one-third of the provinces remitted additional money, and the average amounted to a relatively small portion of their expenditure, under 4 percent.

Table 14.3 also reveals two aspects of a sudden increase in extra remittances from provinces to the central government in 1989. First, the average quantity of extra remittances increased to 7.7 percent of expenditures (see column (6), Panel A). Second, the number of provinces making the extra remittances jumped to 19 out of 28 (see column (7), Panel A). The table also shows a decrease in extra subsidies from the central to local governments as compared with other years, before and after (columns (6) and (7), Panel B).

The changes in 1989 are not surprising. In that year, conservatives in the government temporarily gained power after the Tiananmen Square incident, causing a temporary setback in reform. Importantly, Table 14.3 reveals two aspects of this setback. First, this change was relatively short lived: after 1989, the fiscal pattern returns to its previous trend. Second, the absolute amount was modest. Although many more provinces were subject to additional remittances in 1989, remittances averaged less than eight percent of expenditures. Indeed, these data support the common anecdotal evidence in the literature that the setback in reform after Tiananmen Square was temporary. By the early 1990s, the number of provinces with extra remittances were small, as was the average magnitude of the extra remittance.

14.6 How did fiscal incentives for provincial governments change: examining the *ex post* link between local revenue and expenditure

In this section, we provide evidence showing that reform has strengthened the fiscal incentives of provincial governments through a stronger link between (*ex post*) provincial marginal revenue collection and marginal expenditure. To that end, we look at the correlations between provincial *ex post* realized revenue and expenditure for both before and after reform. We run the following fixed effect model:

$$\text{(Local Expenditure)}_{it} = \alpha_i + \gamma_t + \beta \, \text{(Local Revenue)}_{it} + \mu_{it}, \tag{3}$$

where (Local Expenditure)$_{it}$ is province i's local expenditure in year t, (Local Revenue)$_{it}$ is province i's local revenue in year t, the α_is are provincial fixed effects, the γ_ts are the year dummies, and the μ_{it}s are the disturbance terms. These tests are designed to examine the link between local expenditures and local revenues, after controlling for provincial inherent characteristics and nationwide changes over time.

Panel B of Table 14.4 reports the results for data from 1982 to 1991, in which row (1) shows a coefficient of 0.752 on provincial budgetary revenue in its budgetary expenditure equation. It means that, on average, a one *yuan* increase in provincial budgetary revenue results in about three-quarters *yuan* of provincial budgetary expenditure. Considering the fact that during this period the local budgetary revenue is on average about two-thirds of the total budgetary revenue, the results demonstrate that, in terms of budgetary revenue and expenditure, the fiscal system in China's reform has produced a strong link between local expenditure and local revenue generation. Further, row (2) shows an even larger coefficient – 0.971 – for the extra-budgetary expenditure equation, that is, the relationship for extra-budgetary revenue and expenditure becomes almost one to one.[12] This provides additional fiscal incentives for local governments.

To put the above results in perspective, we run the similar regression for the pre-reform period. Using data from 1970 to 1979, row (1) of Table 14.4 in Panel A reveals a very small coefficient on provincial budgetary revenue in the budgetary expenditure equation, 0.172. This result shows that, prior to

Table 14.4 The correlations between local revenue and expenditure

	Panel A: 1970–9		Panel B: 1982–91		Panel C: 1995–9	
	β	R^2	β	R^2	β	R^2
Fixed effect						
(1) Budgetary expenditure on budgetary revenue	0.172*** (6.172)	0.930	0.752*** (19.73)	0.968	0.998*** (18.95)	0.986
(2) Extra-budgetary expenditure on extra-budgetary revenue			0.971*** (32.25)	0.991		
First difference						
(3) Budgetary expenditure on budgetary revenue	0.086*** (3.840)	0.448	0.481*** (8.767)	0.707	0.942*** (11.44)	0.481
(4) Extra-budgetary expenditure on extra-budgetary revenue			0.803*** (12.53)	0.674		

Notes:
(1) Each regression includes a full set of year dummies.
(2) Huber–White robust t-statistics are in parentheses.
(3) Asterisks indicate variables whose coefficients are significant at the 10% (*), 5% (**), and 1% (***) levels.

economic reform, the central government extracted revenue from high revenue provinces while subsidizing low revenue provinces. Indeed, a coefficient of 0.172 indicates that, prior to the reforms, the central government, on average, extracted over 80 percent of any increase in local revenue.

One has to be careful in attempting to compare the above numbers from the pre-reform and post-reform periods because the definition of "local revenue" changed somewhat between the two periods. Indeed, A comparison of our findings with similarafter the 1980 reform, some revenues previously designated as "local revenue" were later designated as "central revenue," mainly because some previously local government supervised state-owned enterprises were taken over by the central government and their revenues subsequently became central revenue. One way to think of this is to consider the value v in equation (3). Reclassification of some local revenue into central revenue after the 1980 reform reduces v, assuming that it reduces the local revenue proportionally to a fraction of the original revenue.[13] To the extent that this occurred in practice it implies that, when we regress "local expenditure" on "local revenue," the estimated coefficient would be larger simply because v becomes smaller.

Examining our data reveals that such an effect is not quantitatively significant. The average share of local budgetary revenue in total government budgetary revenue is 84 percent for the period of 1970–9 (with the maximum of 88 percent in a single year) as compared to 66 percent for the period of 1982–91 (with the minimum of 59 percent in a single year). These figures imply that, on average, the 1982–91 period local revenue share is about 0.79 times the share of the 1970–9 period. Therefore, due purely to the effect of reclassification of local revenues after the reform and not attributed to any improvement in incentives, the estimated correlation coefficient β after the reform could have been boosted by about 1/0.79 = 1.27 times (or by 1.48 times if the maximum and minimum values are used) on comparable basis. In other words, the comparable coefficient for the pre-reform period could be 0.218 instead of 0.172 (or 2.55 if the maximum and minimum values are used). Our estimated correlation during the reform, 0.752, is still 3.4 times that before the reform, instead of 4.4 times if reclassification of revenue is completely ignored. Therefore, the modest reclassification of revenues does not undermine our interpretation of the drastic improvement of local incentives after reform.

We also run the regression using the data from 1995 to 1999 to see how the fiscal incentives of local governments might have changed for the post 1994 period when "fiscal contracting system" was replaced by "separating tax system." Row (1) of Table 14.4 in Panel C shows a coefficient of 0.998 on provincial budgetary revenue in its budgetary expenditure equation. To make the results of the post-1994 period and the 1982–91 period comparable, we need to consider the change in the definition of "local revenue." Starting 1994, "local revenue" has been defined as revenues from local taxes and the local portion of the shared taxes (Bahl 1999). As a result of this change, the local revenue share as the total revenue shrank from 66 percent for 1982–91 to 50 percent for 1995–9, still a very high level. This implies that the average local revenue share for 1995–99 is about 0.76 times the share for the 1982–91 period. Because the marginal incentive of the local revenue for the 1995–9 period is approximately 1, when we take into consideration the effect of the reduced scope of local revenue for this period, the estimated correlation coefficient β is still be comparable to 0.752 as for the 1982–91 period.

We also examine the first difference version of model (5.1) by regressing the change of local expenditure over one year on the change of local revenue over one year, still including the year dummies. Row (3) of Table 14.4 shows a coefficient of 0.481 on provincial budgetary revenue in its budgetary expenditure equation for the data of 1982–91 in Panel B, a drop from 0.752 the fixed effect model estimation. This coefficient is 0.057 for the data of 1970–9 in Panel A, a even bigger proportional drop from 0.172 as in the fixed effect model estimation. It is 0.942 for the data of 1995–9 in Panel C, somewhat smaller than 0.998 as in the fixed effect model. However, the estimations from the first difference model may be biased toward zero since it may suffer from an error-in-variable or a misspecification problem.

We compare our findings on China with the related investigations of post-reform Russia. Zhuravskaya (2000) examined the fiscal incentives of local (i.e., city) governments in the region-local fiscal relationship in post-reform Russia, showing a striking pattern which she interpreted as predation. Using the data from 35 cities for the period 1992–1997 and regressing the change in the "shared revenue" between the regional and city governments on the change of the city's "own revenue," she finds that the coefficient is –0.90. She interprets this result as evidence that increases in a city's revenue are almost entirely offset by decreases in shared revenues from the region to the city. This implies that an increase in 1 ruble in city government's own revenue will result in only increase of 0.1 ruble in net revenue of the city government. Exaction of this magnitude destroys cities' incentives to increase their tax base.

Our above results suggest that, for the budgetary revenue and extra-budgetary revenue individually, the Chinese central government's post-reform treatment of provinces provides provincial governments with strong fiscal incentives.[14] Our data set from China does not allow us to perform the comparable investigations on province-city or prefecture-county fiscal relationships. However, studies on China's local fiscal reform document two aspects relevant for this discussion (Bahl and Wallich 1992; Wong 1997): first, throughout the 1980s, the fiscal contracting practice extended to all subnational levels of provinces, cities/prefectures, counties and townships; and second, the subnational fiscal contracting usually mimicked the center-province fiscal contracting applied to their province. To the extent that the subnational level inter-governmental fiscal relationships resemble that between the center and provinces, local government incentives within the provincial setting should parallel those we find at the central-provincial level.

Further research is needed to obtain subnational level results on China in order to make direct comparisons with the results on Russia.

14.7 How provincial governments responded to fiscal incentives: estimating the effects on development of non-state enterprises and reform in state enterprises

To investigate the effects of fiscal incentives on the local economy, we investigate the following model:

$$Y_{it} = \alpha_i + \gamma_t + \delta'Z_{it} + \sigma'W_{it-1} + u_{it}. \tag{4}$$

In equation (4), Y_{it} is a vector of variables measuring the development of the non-state sector and reform in the state sector in a province, and Z_{it} includes the variable of (*ex ante*) provincial marginal revenue retention rate which measures fiscal incentives as well as the variable of fiscal decentralization. The α_i's represent the provincial specific effects, which we assume are constant for each province, implying that our specification is a fixed effect model. The γ_t's are the year dummies, which are intended to capture the effects of nationwide macroeconomic fluctuation. As a common practice, we include W_{it-1}, the lagged per capita GDP, for the purpose of controlling for the level of development. The u_{it}'s are the disturbance terms. Our fixed effect model implies that any correlations between Y and Z cannot be attributed to inherent provincial characteristics.

Table 14.5 presents our results on the effects of fiscal decentralization and fiscal incentives on the development of non-state enterprises. The dependent variable in Panel A of Table 14.5 is the growth of rural enterprise employment, a narrower measure of non-state sector development; the dependent variable in Panel B is the growth of non-state-non-agricultural employment in both urban and rural areas, a broader measure.

The two panels give similar results. Column 1 of Table 14.5 reveals that fiscal decentralization has positive effects on the development of non-state enterprises.[15] Column 2 shows that fiscal incentives also have positive and significant effects on the development of non-state enterprises.[16] Is this possible that the fiscal incentives variable simply picks up the effect from fiscal decentralization? Column 3 shows that this is not the case: the effect of fiscal incentives remain significant even after controlling for fiscal decentralization. This implies that fiscal decentralization alone is insufficient to explain the growth of the non-state sector, fiscal incentives have additional explanatory power. Quantitatively, if the marginal revenue retention rate in a province increases by 10 percentage points, then the growth rate of non-state enterprises in that province would increase by 1.01 percentage points, when it is measured for rural enterprises only; and 0.97 percentage points, when measured for both rural and urban non-state enterprises. Because the average growth rate of employment in rural enterprises is 6 percent and that of all

Table 14.5 Fiscal incentives and the development of the non-state sector

Panel A. Dependent variable: growth of rural enterprise employment

Independent variable	(1)	(2)	(3)	(4)	(5)
Ratio of local expenditure to central expenditure in a province	0.051* (1.729)		0.038 (1.376)		0.047 (1.639)
Provincial marginal revenue retention rate		0.141** (2.145)	0.114* (1.837)		
Provincial marginal revenue retention rate (dummy)				0.056*** (2.677)	0.051** (2.493)
Per capita GDP$_{-1}$	0.004 (0.064)	0.043 (0.724)	0.023 (0.392)	0.040 (0.684)	0.020 (0.342)
Adjusted R^2	0.734	0.742	0.736	0.740	0.771

Panel B. Dependent variable: growth of non-state-non-agricultural employment

Independent variable	(1)	(2)	(3)	(4)	(5)
Ratio of local expenditure to central expenditure in a province	0.050** (2.265)		0.039* (1.829)		0.048** (2.179)
Provincial marginal revenue retention rate		0.131*** (2.714)	0.104** (2.309)		
Provincial marginal revenue retention rate (dummy)				0.042** (2.449)	0.038** (2.298)
Per capita GDP$_{-1}$	−0.024 (0.486)	0.023 (0.464)	−0.006 (0.122)	0.017 (0.349)	−0.012 (0.235)
Adjusted R^2	0.757	0.763	0.761	0.759	0.791

Notes:
(1) Each regression includes a full set of provincial dummies and year dummies.
(2) Huber–White robust t-statistics are in parentheses.
(3) Sample size is 319.
(4) Asterisks indicate variables whose coefficients are significant at the 10% (*), 5% (**), and 1% (***) levels.

non-state enterprises is 9 percent during this period, the estimated effects are economically quite significant.

One may worry about the reliability of our data on marginal revenue retention rates. To check the robustness of our estimations, we ran parallel regressions replacing the continuous marginal retention rate variable with a dummy variable. This is a kind of aggregation, intended to reduce the impacts of the possible error-in-variable problem in the measurement of the underlying variable. The dummy fiscal incentive variable takes value 1 if the marginal retention rate is 100 percent and 0 otherwise. The results of using the dummy fiscal incentive variable are reported in columns (4) and (5) of Table 14.5. In both regressions, the signs and significance of all our estimated coefficients of the dummy fiscal incentive variable remain the same.

The evidence demonstrates that the error-in-variable problem, if it exists, is not serious enough to distort our qualitative results.

We carry out a similar investigation for the reform of state-owned enterprises. Panel A of Table 14.6 reports our results on the change of the share of contract workers in total state employment and Panel B on the change in the share of bonuses in total employee wages. In contrast to permanent workers, who are under the traditional socialist labor conditions of "iron rice bowls," contract workers do not have tenure and are more likely subject to market conditions. More contract workers relative to permanent workers mean that enterprises are better restructured to market orientation. Bonuses, as compared to fixed wages, represent a compensation form that is

Table 14.6 Fiscal incentives and the reform of the state sector

Panel A. Dependent variable: change in the share of contract workers in total state employment

Independent variable	(1)	(2)	(3)	(4)	(5)
Ratio of local expenditure to central expenditure in a province	0.165 (0.257)		−0.366 (0.675)		0.048 (0.082)
Provincial marginal revenue retention rate		5.465* (1.714)	5.625* (1.914)		
Provincial marginal revenue retention rate (dummy)				1.549* (1.919)	1.545* (1.705)
Per capita GDP$_{-1}$	−0.540 (0.218)	0.165 (0.079)	0.343 (0.163)	0.078 (0.037)	0.563 (0.025)
Adjusted R^2	0.026	0.081	0.078	0.047	0.198

Panel B. Dependent variable: change in the share of bonuses in total employee wages

Independent variable	(1)	(2)	(3)	(4)	(5)
Ratio of local expenditure to central expenditure in a province	0.433 (0.772)		0.251 (0.665)		0.415 (0.796)
Provincial marginal revenue retention rate		1.877* (1.705)	1.700 (1.641)		
Provincial marginal revenue retention rate (dummy)				0.329 (0.473)	0.292 (0.319)
Per capita GDP$_{-1}$	−0.976 (0.667)	−0.580 (0.535)	−0.688 (0.629)	−0.733 (0.605)	−0.882 (0.687)
Adjusted R^2	0.445	0.450	0.449	0.443	0.518

Notes:
(1) Each regression includes a full set of provincial dummies and year dummies.
(2) Huber–White robust t-statistics are in parentheses.
(3) Sample size is 319.
(4) Asterisks indicate variables whose coefficients are significant at the 10% (*), 5% (**), and 1% (***) levels.

more closely linked to workers performance, a higher share of bonuses in total employee wages implies enterprise workers are better motivated.

We find that the degree of fiscal decentralization has no significant effects on both measures of reform (column 1). However, fiscal incentives have positive and significant effects in the specification for the change of the share of contract workers in total state employment (column 2, Panel A), such effects remain even after controlling for fiscal decentralization (column 3, Panel A). A 10 percentage point increase in the marginal revenue retention rate in a province is associated with a 0.50 percentage point increase in the share of contract workers. As for the change of the share of bonuses in total employee wages, incentives still have positive and significant effects (column 2, Panel B), except that the statistical significance is lost after controlling for fiscal decentralization (column 3, Panel B). Again, we replaced fiscal incentive variable with the corresponding dummy variable and reports the results in columns 4 and 5. Fiscal incentives still have positive and significant effects for the change of the share of contract workers in total state employment (column 4, Panel A), even after controlling for fiscal decentralization (column 5, Panel A), but not for the change of the share of bonuses in total employee wages (columns 4 and 5, Panel B).

We now turn to investigate the possibility of endogeneity problems. The marginal retention rates are treated as a predetermined variable in our model. The central government and the provinces renegotiate the fiscal contract rates every 3–5 years, and they remain rather stable within the intervals. The marginal retention rates either stay the same or are increased over time; none are adjusted downward, as Figure 14.1 demonstrates this feature in aggregate terms. This suggests some underlying momentum in the negotiation process. Indeed, the contractual arrangements started as an "experiment" and only expanded and strengthened over time. For one reason, both the central and provincial governments were not sure if they would work or how effectively they would work. For another reason, the experiment was also constrained by exogenous factors such as an ideology against high marginal retention rates (which was viewed as too capitalistic), and such a constraint was only relaxed over time.

One may worry that in the process of the experiment, the central government sets higher marginal retention rates for high growth and greater reform provinces. If this is the case, we cannot interpret the higher growth and greater reforms as a result of higher marginal retention rates. An unbiased estimation might be obtained by instrumenting the marginal retention rate variable. Lacking such an instrument, we go for the second best solution: instead of looking for unbiased estimations, we check to see if our estimations are biased upward, in such a case, our interpretation of the results would be problematic. To this end, we regress marginal retention rates on the lagged growth rates of the non-state sector and on the lagged reform variables in the state sector respectively. Table 14.7 reports the results with the marginal retention rate as the dependent variable, while Table 14.8 with the dummy

Table 14.7 The endogeneity problem: provincial marginal revenue retention rate

Panel A. Dependent variable: provincial marginal revenue retention rate

Independent variable	(1)	(2)	(3)	(4)
Growth of rural enterprise employment$_{-2}$	−0.017* (1.654)	−0.018* (1.738)		
Growth of non-state-non-agricultural employment$_{-2}$			−0.007 (0.903)	−0.008 (1.087)
Per capita GDP$_{-2}$	−0.208** (2.384)		−0.215** (2.432)	
Adjusted R^2	0.847	0.835	0.846	0.834

Panel B. Dependent variable: provincial marginal revenue retention rate

Independent variable	(1)	(2)	(3)	(4)
Change in the share of contract workers in state employment$_{-2}$	−0.086 (0.484)	−0.093 (0.503)		
Change in the share of bonuses in total employee wages$_{-2}$			−0.922** (2.169)	−1.043** (2.481)
Per capita GDP$_{-2}$	−0.140 (1.506)		−0.173** (2.021)	
Adjusted R^2	0.838	0.841	0.849	0.839

Notes:
(1) Each regression includes a full set of provincial dummies and year dummies.
(2) Huber–White robust t-statistics are in parentheses.
(3) Sample size is 307 (Panel A) and 298 (Panel B).
(4) Asterisks indicate variables whose coefficients are significant at the 10% (*), 5% (**), and 1% (***) levels.

fiscal incentive variable. In both tables, we found negative rather than positive coefficients, some of them are even statistically significant. That is to say, on average, high growth provinces are more likely to receive lower rather than higher marginal retention rates. Therefore, if our estimates are biased due to the endogeneity problem, it is more likely biased against our hypothesis, that is, we might have underestimated the claimed effect.

14.8 Conclusions

This paper studies the changing local government fiscal incentives and their impacts on market development. Many anecdotes suggest the importance of fiscal incentives in the previous studies on China's reforms. The econometric results in this paper provide some systematic evidence on the economic significance of fiscal incentives. We find that the reforms considerably strengthened the fiscal incentives of provincial governments, and they are generally conducive to provincial economic development and reform. These

Table 14.8 The endogeneity problem: provincial marginal revenue retention rate dummy

Panel A. Dependent variable: provincial marginal revenue retention rate dummy

Independent variable	(1)	(2)	(3)	(4)
Growth of rural enterprise employment$_{-2}$	−0.020 (0.475)	−0.021 (0.478)		
Growth of non-state-non-agricultural employment$_{-2}$			−0.067 (0.876)	−0.065 (0.763)
Per capita GDP$_{-2}$	−0.512*** (2.821)		−0.499*** (2.807)	
Adjusted R^2	0.843	0.815	0.845	0.817

Panel B. Dependent variable: provincial marginal revenue retention rate dummy

Independent variable	(1)	(2)	(3)	(4)
Change in the share of contract workers in state employment$_{-2}$	−0.144** (2.405)	−0.075 (1.233)		
Change in the share of bonuses in total employee wages$_{-2}$			−0.007 (0.219)	−0.044 (1.235)
Per capita GDP$_{-2}$	−0.636*** (3.119)		−0.524*** (2.954)	
Adjusted R^2	0.845	0.815	0.842	0.815

Notes:
(1) Each regression includes a full set of provincial dummies and year dummies.
(2) Huber–White robust t-statistics are in parentheses.
(3) Sample size is 307 (Panel A) and 298 (Panel B).
(4) Asterisks indicate variables whose coefficients are significant at the 10% (*), 5% (**), and 1% (***) levels.

results point to the important link between local government's fiscal incentives and local economic development.

Comparisons of local government's behavior toward local economic development between China and Russia are striking. Our study of federalism, Chinese style, and the other studies on federalism, Russian style (Zhuravskaya 2000; de Figueiredo and Weingast 2001), indicate that one crucial difference concerns the fiscal incentives provided for local governments to pursue market-supporting activities.

Our perspective yields an important insight about how federalism works in promoting economic development; namely, there exists a positive relationship between the strength of fiscal incentives faced by lower-level governments and local economic performance. Countries with strong fiscal incentives for local governments are expected to experience healthier local business development while those with low fiscal incentives are expected to experience the opposite. Instead of decentralization per se, we emphasize the importance of strong fiscal incentives. Whether this prediction holds empirically in other countries awaits further work.

Notes

1 We would like to thank Alberto Alesina, Bill Evans, Roger Gordon, John McMillan, Peter Murrell, Barry Naughton, Gerard Roland, Seth Sanders, Robert Schwab, Andrei Shleifer, Shang-Jin Wei, David Wildasin, Alwyn Young, Heng-fu Zou, and the participants at the Fifth Nobel Symposium in Economics held in Stockholm in 1999 for helpful comments and discussions and the Center for Research on Economic Development and Policy Reform at Stanford for financial support.

2 The recent theory of "market-preserving federalism" studies the general question of how federalism can be structured to promote market development (e.g. McKinnon 1997; Qian and Roland 1998; Qian and Weingast 1996; Weingast 1995; Wildasin 1997; and Zhuravskaya 2000).

3 The conventional, more readily available data of the *ex post* ratios of revenue retention over collection measures only the average realized revenue retention and is thus less suitable for the study of the effects of fiscal incentives on other economic variables.

4 Below the township level, the village is an informal level of government. A municipality can be one of the levels of a province, prefecture, or county; most municipalities are at the prefecture level.

5 The data excludes Tibet. Hainan obtained a provincial status only in 1989, and we treat Hainan as a separate province throughout the sample period.

6 All provincial budgetary and extra-budgetary data are consolidated figures within a province.

7 Akai and Sakata (2002) used an *ex post* measure of fiscal "autonomy" (defined as the ratio of local expenditure over local revenue) in their study of the US fiscal federalism. They found that this measure of fiscal autonomy contributes to economic growth at the state level in the US.

8 The incorporated information on "separately plan listed cities" include Wuhan (1986–92) in Hubei; Chongqing (1986–92) in Sichuan; Shenyang (1988–92) in Heilongjiang; Ningbo (1988–92) in Zhejiang; and Qingdao (1991–2) in Shandong. Information sources are the provincial and city statistical yearbooks.

9 Again, the data is adjusted for price subsidies after 1986: local portions of price subsidies are excluded from local expenditure. They were earmarked central government transfers and were determined solely by the number of urban residents anyway.

10 We make a few qualifications regarding the interpretation of the variable fiscal readjustment. First, we implicitly assume that each province has a balanced budget each year without carry-overs from the previous year or savings into the next year. This is basically true. Second, because our information about the fiscal contracts is limited to fixed subsidies/remittances and marginal retention rates, we have to omit other predefined transfers or transfers based on exogenous criteria such as natural disaster relief. However, such transfers are not significant. Third, because we look at net transfers (i.e. expenditure minus revenue retention), it is possible that two-way transfers are high but net transfers are low. Despite these limitations, this variable provides useful information on the significance of *ex post* readjustment of fiscal revenue retention.

11 This may also due to the fact that we were unable to account for some earmarked subsidies.

12 Using the three year data of 1983, 1987, and 1990 individually, Knight and Li

(1999) also found that the correlations between local extra-budgetary revenue and expenditure were generally higher than those between local budgetary revenue and expenditure, and the latter increased over time.

13 However, other possibilities of reclassification may not induce a bias as large as this. For example, if a reclassification decreases local revenue by a fixed amount (same for all provinces) but does not change v, then the estimated coefficients β for the two periods are comparable.

14 In a separate regression we also find that in China, increases in extra-budgetary revenue (roughly corresponds to "own revenue" in Russia) has little negative effect on the change of budgetary expenditure (roughly corresponds to "shared revenue" in Russia) as observed in Russia. The coefficient is actually positive, which in part reflects the fact that budgetary and extra-budgetary revenues have similar tax bases.

15 A previous study by Zhang and Zou (1998) reported a negative and significant effect of fiscal decentralization on provincial GDP growth during China's reform. We found that such negative effect would disappear and actually would turn into a positive effect if the set of annual time dummy variables is included in their regressions. This suggests that their findings perhaps resulted from the failure to filter out economy-wide cyclic effect.

16 Lin and Liu (2000) reported a positive effect of marginal retention rate on provincial GDP growth in the production-function-based growth regression. However, in their regressions they used the growth rate of investment instead of the growth rate of capital (or investment-output ratio) for capital input as standard in the literature, which makes their results hard to interpret. Furthermore, the t-value associated with the effect of marginal retention rate drops significantly, from 2.70 to 1.65, when the sample is restricted to the post reform period, suggesting the claimed effect might pick up the effects of other unmeasured reforms.

References

Akai, Nobuo, and Masayo Sakata. 2002. "Fiscal Decentralization Contributes to Economic Growth: Evidence from State-Level Cross-Section Data for the United States," *Journal of Urban Economics*, 52: 93–108.

Bahl, Roy. 1999. *Fiscal Policy in China: Taxation and Intergovernmental Fiscal Relations*, San Francisco: The 1990 Institute.

Bahl, Roy, and Christine Wallich. 1992. "Intergovernmental Fiscal Relations in China," Working Papers, Country Economics Department, The World Bank, WPS 863.

Blanchard, Olivier, and Andrei Shleifer. 2000. "Federalism with and without Political Centralization: China versus Russia." NBER Working Paper #7616.

Brennan, Geoffrey and James M. Buchanan. 1980. *The Power to Tax: Analytical Foundations of a Fiscal Constitution.* New York: Cambridge University Press.

Chen, Rulong (ed.). 1988. *The Fiscal System in Contemporary China* (*Dangdai Zhongguo Caizheng*), Beijing: China Social Science Press.

de Figueiredo, Rui J. P. Jr, and Barry R. Weingast. 2001. "Pathologies of Federalism, Russian Style: Political Institutions and Economic Transition," paper prepared for delivery at the Conference, "Fiscal Federalism in the Russian Federation: Problems and Prospects for Reform," Higher School of Economics, Moscow, Russia, January 29–20.

Fan, Gang. 1996. "New Norms in Public Revenue and Expenditure," in *Case Studies in China's Institutional Change*, Shuguang Zhang (ed.), Shanghai People's Publishing House.

Frye, Timothy, and Andrei Shleifer, 1997. "The Invisible Hand and the Grabbing Hand," *American Economic Review*, 87: 354–8, May.

Groves, Theodore, Yongmiao Hong, John McMillan, and Barry Naughton. 1994. "Autonomy and Incentives in Chinese State Enterprises," *Quarterly Journal of Economics*, 109(1): 183–209.

Hayek, Friedrich A. 1945. "The Use of Knowledge in Society," *American Economic Review*, 35: 519–30.

Hofman, Bert. 1993. "An Analysis of Chinese Fiscal Data over the Reform Period," *China Economic Review*, 4(2): 213–30.

Knight, John, and Shi Li. 1999. "Fiscal Decentralization: Incentives, Redistribution and Reform in China," *Oxford Development Studies*, 27(1): 5–32.

Kornai, Janos. 1986. "The Soft Budget Constraints," *KYKLOS*, 30(1), pp. 3–30.

Lavrov, Aleksei, John M. Litwack, and Douglas Sutherland. 2000. "Fiscal Federalist Relations in Russia: A Case for Subnational Autonomy," Working Paper, Organization of Economic Cooperation and Development (OECD), Paris, France.

Li, Hongbin, and Li-An Zhou. 2004. "Political Turnover and Economic Performance: The Incentive Role of Personnel Control in China," *Journal of Public Economics*, forthcoming.

Lin, Justin Yifu, and Zhiqiang Liu. 2000. "Fiscal Decentralization and Economic Growth in China," *Economic Development and Cultural Change*, 49(1): 1–21, October.

Maskin, Eric, Yingyi Qian, and Chenggang Xu. 2000. "Incentives, Information, and Organizational Form," *Review of Economic Studies*, 67(2): 359–78, April.

McKinnon, Ronald. 1997. "Market-Preserving Federalism in the American Monetary Union," in *Macroeconomic Dimensions of Public Finance: Essays in Honour of Vito Tanzi*, M. Blejer and T. Ter-Minassian, eds, London: Boutledge, pp. 73–93.

Montinola, Gabriella, Yingyi Qian, and Barry Weingast. 1995. "Federalism, Chinese Style: The Political Basis for Economic Success in China," *World Politics*, 48(1): 50–81, October.

Musgrave, Richard, *Theory of Public Finance: A Study in Public Economy*, New York: McGraw, 1959.

National Statistical Bureau. Various years. *China Statistical Yearbook*, Beijing: China Statistical Publishing House.

Oates, Wallace. 1972. *Fiscal Federalism*, New York: Harcourt Brace Jovanovich.

OECD. 2000. *OECD Economic Surveys: The Russian Federation*. Paris, France: Organization for Economic Co-operation and Development.

Oksenberg, Michel, and Tong, James. 1991. "The Evolution of Central-Provincial Fiscal Relations in China, 1971–1984: The Formal System," *China Quarterly*, March.

Qian, Yingyi, and Gerard Roland. 1998. "Federalism and the Soft Budget Constraint," *American Economic Review*, 88(5): 1143–62, December.

Qian, Yingyi, and Barry R. Weingast. 1996. "China's Transition to Markets: Market-Preserving Federalism, Chinese Style," *Journal of Policy Reform*, 1: 149–85.

Shleifer, Andrei. 1997. "Government in Transition," *European Economic Review*, 41: 385–410.

Shleifer, Andrei, and Robert W. Vishny. 1998. *The Grabbing Hand: Government Pathologies and Their Cures*, Cambridge, MA: Harvard University Press.

Tiebout, Charles. 1956. "A Pure Theory of Local Expenditures," *Journal of Political Economy*, 64: 416–24.

Weingast, Barry R. 1995. "The Economic Role of Political Institutions: Market-Preserving Federalism and Economic Growth," *Journal of Law, Economics, and Organization*, 11: 1–31, April.

Wildasin, David E. 1997. "Externalities and Bailouts: Hard and Soft Budget Constraints in Inter-Governmental Fiscal Relations," mimeo, Vanderbilt University.

Wong, Christine P. W. (ed.). 1997. *Financing Local Government in the People's Republic of China*. Hong Kong: Oxford University Press.

Zhang, Tao, and Heng-fu Zou. 1998. "Fiscal Decentralization, Public Spending, and Economic Growth in China." *Journal of Public Economics*, 67: 221–40.

Zhuravskaya, Ekaterina V. 2000. "Incentives to Provide Local Public Goods: Fiscal Federalism, Russian Style." *Journal of Public Economics*, 76(3): 337–68, June.

Index